Encyclopedic Dictionary
of the Sciences of Language

by Oswald Ducrot and Tzvetan Todorov

Translated by Catherine Porter

The Johns Hopkins University Press • Baltimore and London

Originally published in 1972 as *Dictionnaire
encyclopédique des sciences du langage*
© 1972, 1973, Éditions du Seuil

English translation © 1979 by The Johns Hopkins University Press
All rights reserved
Printed in the United States of America on acid-free paper

The Johns Hopkins University Press, 2715 North Charles Street,
Baltimore, Maryland 21218-4319

Originally published, 1979
Johns Hopkins Paperbacks edition, 1983
Softshell Books edition, 1994

Library of Congress Cataloging in Publication Data

Ducrot, Oswald.

    Encyclopedic dictionary of the sciences of
language.
    Translation of Dictionnaire encyclopédique
des sciences du langage.
    Includes bibliographical references.
    1. Linguistics—Dictionaries—French.
I. Todorov, Tsvetan, joint author. II. Title.
P29.D813   410´.3   78–23901
ISBN 0–8018–2857–0

A catalog record for this book is available from the British Library.

CONTENTS

DESCRIPTIVE CONCEPTS

Encyclopedic Dictionary
of the Sciences of Language

TRANSLATOR'S NOTE

This translation is based on the second French edition of the *Dictionnaire encyclopédique des sciences du langage* (Paris: Éditions du Seuil, 1973). It incorporates a number of revisions proposed by the authors; the articles on generative grammar and on time and modality in language in particular have been significantly altered and expanded. With the collaboration of the authors, the bibliographical material has been substantially updated. In addition, wherever possible, French titles have been replaced by English-language originals or translations. For the citation of sources within the body of the text, brief indications have been supplied in parentheses; full references are generally found in the adjacent bibliographical inserts.

I am indebted to Oswald Ducrot and Tzvetan Todorov for their patient and generous cooperation throughout the preparation of the manuscript. For their willingness to read substantial portions of the text and for their helpful suggestions, I should like to thank John Bowers (Cornell University), George Dillon (Indiana University and Purdue University), Philip Lewis (Cornell University), Hugh Olmsted (State University of New York, College at Cortland), and Linda Waugh (Cornell University). The completed manuscript owes much to the skillful and attentive editing of Joanne Allen; for its errors and deficiencies the responsibility is mine alone.

State University of New York,   CATHERINE PORTER
College at Cortland

INTRODUCTION

The title of this work entails two particularities that correspond to two fundamental options and should be explained here: the plural *sciences* and the singular *language*.

We have chosen to use the word *language* in the restricted—and banal—sense of natural language, not in the currently widespread sense of sign system. Thus we shall not be dealing here with documentary languages, with the various arts considered as languages, with science taken as a well- or ill-constructed language, with animal language, gestural language, and so on. There are several reasons for this restriction. First, were we to leave the domain of the verbal, we would be obliged to deal with an object whose limits are difficult to pinpoint and which, owing to its very indeterminacy, might well coincide with the object of all the social sciences, if not with that of all sciences in general. If everything in human behavior is a sign, the presence of a "language," in this broad sense, no longer allows us to delimit one object of knowledge among others. Moreover, social institutions, psychic structures, artistic forms, and the branches of science have been envisaged as sign systems only in recent times, and in order to discuss this development, we would be led much more often to create a science than to give an account of one, a task that would correspond neither with our aims nor with our capabilities. Finally, such an extension of the word *language* would imply the affirmation of a principial identity among the different sign systems; and we refused to grant this hypothesis the status of a postulate at the outset. The study of these systems may be the object of future works.

Although the word *language* is used here, then, in a restrictive sense, the plural *sciences* marks, on the other hand, our desire for openness. We have not wished at any point to separate the study of language from the study of its productions—by which we mean both the way it functions (hence the space allotted to enunciation, to linguistic acts, to language as it is actually used) and the resulting discursive sequences, whose organization is no longer directly controlled by the mechanism of language alone (hence the numerous articles devoted to literary questions, the discourse of literature having been more thoroughly studied than any other). Every attempt to isolate the study of language from the study of discourse turns out, sooner or later, to be detrimental to both. By bringing them together, moreover, we are simply reviving a long tradition, that of philology, which never conceived of the description of language without a description of texts. Thus beyond linguistics in the narrow sense we have represented in this volume poetics, rhetoric, stylistics, psycho-, socio-, and geo-linguistics, and even some research in semiotics and in the philosophy of language. We are subscribing thereby to the credo previously formulated by one of the masters of modern linguistics, Roman Jakobson: *Linguistica sum: linguistici nihil a me alienum puto.*

Although we are not casting ourselves here as adherents to any particular school, we have been led, more often than is customary in this type of work, to take a personal position and even to present, here and there, some original research, incomplete and provisional though we know it to be. Rather than a survey of opinions, which would reflect an illusory ideal of impartiality, we have sought to give a coherent overview of problems—an undertaking that always requires the choice of a point of view. Let us indicate ours briefly.

In order to study the problems of language, we have chosen to consider them in a perspective that is essentially semantic. The problems of meaning—of its levels, of its modes of manifestation—are central to this entire work. The importance attributed to meaning entails several consequences:

1. We have presented in detail the generative and transformational theory of Chomsky, who has contributed more than anyone else toward removing the suspicion with which semantic questions have been regarded by "scientific" linguistics for a long time. (This has led us moreover to point out certain difficulties that Chomsky's theory has encountered and that explain its recent evolution.)

2. Similarly, we have given an important place to the history of the sciences of language (locating its beginnings well before the nineteenth century), for this history is concerned with debates that, in the last analysis, also hinge upon the relationships between language and meaning: even the debate between Saussure and the historical linguistics of the nineteenth century, which crystallizes around specific technical questions, ultimately brings into play two different conceptions of the act of signification.

3. We have set forth, in connection with various problems—reference and modality, for example—the viewpoint of certain logicians. This viewpoint is today fairly commonly declared "linguistically irrelevant" (an expression that we do not find very appealing); it is alleged that logicians undertake, not to describe language, but only to propose rules

concerning its utilization. It seems to us, however, that research in logic can be quite revealing for the linguist, since the difficulties that the logician encounters in seeking to enunciate the laws of reasoning point up, by contrast, the specificity of natural languages.

4. "Purely literary" questions sometimes touch upon the examination of linguistic categories; thus the discussion of the character follows upon that of the parts of speech and of the syntactic functions. As a result, one finds an occasional unevenness in the level of rigor attained at one point or another, an unevenness that we hope will be temporary and that reflects the irregular rhythm of the development of the sciences. We have chosen this approach because we believe in the authenticity of the relationship that links linguistic and discursive categories and because we believe that studying these sciences concurrently will be to the advantage of both.

5. Conversely, we were obliged to treat less extensively the problems of phonic expression and the historical kinship of languages; however, we have tried to present in these areas the notions that have become the common stock and the constant reference points of linguists and that are indispensable to the understanding of current research on language.*

We admit to a certain temerity in presenting, in some four hundred pages, an overview of the sciences of language, given their extraordinary development, especially during the past fifty years, and the fact that they display at one and the same time a systematic cast (each notion must be understood in relation to a host of others) and a chaotic aspect (that is, they display neither fixed principles nor a stable terminology). In order to deal with these difficulties, we have proceeded in the following way.

The book is organized, not on the basis of a list of words, but according to a conceptual division of the domain under examination. The alternative solution (which was still possible at the time of J. Marouzeau's *Lexique de la terminologie linguistique*) would have entailed, at this point, either innumerable repetitions, taking up too much space, or a litany of cross references, requiring an unreasonable degree of patience from the reader. So we have written some fifty articles, each of which focuses on a well-defined topic, constitutes a whole, and allows for a sustained reading. Within these articles, about eight hundred terms are defined; an index at the end of the volume provides an alphabetical list of these terms, with a reference to the passage in the book where the

---

* For a detailed study of these problems, see the *Guide alphabétique de la linguistique*, produced under the direction of A. Martinet (Paris, 1969), a work that is more or less symmetrical to ours in the sense that it takes as central the problems that we deal with marginally—and vice versa.

definition can be found. In addition, the reader seeking information on a particular doctrine will find an index of authors, with references to the passages where they are discussed (we have omitted references to purely allusive or bibliographical remarks in which these authors may occasionally be mentioned).

Finally, wherever it has been necessary in the very development of an article to make use of terms or to allude to topics presented elsewhere, numbers in brackets indicate the page on which these terms or themes are explained.

The articles are arranged in an analytic order rather than an alphabetical one. Here is the principle followed.

The first section, "Schools," traces the major trends that constitute, in their evolution, the history of modern linguistics (general grammars, historical linguistics, glossematics, and so on).

The second, "Fields," describes the entire cluster of disciplines for which language is the object—the various branches of linguistics, poetics, stylistics, psycholinguistics, the philosophy of language, and so on.

The other two sections are devoted to describing the principal concepts we have used. Within the first, entitled "Methodological Concepts" —which includes the most general concepts, such as those of the sign, syntagma and paradigm, language (*langue*) and speech (*parole*), code and message—the order followed reflects our effort to proceed, insofar as possible and without envisaging a strict hierarchy, from basic to derived concepts. In the final section, entitled "Descriptive Concepts," more specific concepts are treated—for example, the phoneme, parts of speech, meaning and reference, style; their arrangement proceeds from the simple to the complex, starting with the distinctive phonic feature and concluding with complete linguistic acts.

Constructed in this manner, the volume seems to us to allow for a dual reading: it can be employed as a dictionary or as an encyclopedia. It is thus intended for specialists as well as for beginners in all the areas ranging from linguistics to literary studies.

The language in which the articles are written aims to be as non-technical as possible. Linguistics—and, to an even greater extent, each of the other disciplines represented here—lacks a unified terminology. Thus if we were to use a technical language, we would be forced either to combine diverse terminologies or to choose one from among them— which would amount to privileging, *a priori*, the doctrine that developed it. We have preferred to use the least specialized language possible and, with the help of this common language, to provide definitions of technical terms. For example, while we propose narrow and restrictive definitions for the terms "meaning" (*signification*), "language system" (*langue*), and "language" (*langage*), we use these terms throughout the work in the broader sense that they have in ordinary language. However, when we are obliged to use a technical expression, or to use an expression in a technical sense, we provide in our text a reference to the page where the expression is defined.

The bibliographies—provided within the articles, at the end of each development—are not intended to be exhaustive; they are only intended to indicate either some historically prominent texts or some works of incontestable relevance.

For certain articles we have sought the help of collaborators, namely, Mme Maria-Scania de Schonen, Mme Marie-Christine Hazaël-Massieux, and M. François Wahl. We should like to express our appreciation to them here.

OSWALD DUCROT
TZVETAN TODOROV

SCHOOLS

GENERAL GRAMMARS

After drawing up various grammars (Greek, Latin, and Spanish), Claude Lancelot, a professor at the Petites Ecoles of Port-Royal des Champs, wrote in 1660, in collaboration with Antoine Arnauld, a *Grammaire générale et raisonnée*, often called since then the *Grammaire de Port-Royal*. A **general grammar** aims at enunciating certain principles that govern all languages and provide the basic explanation of their uses. It thus represents an attempt to define the general phenomenon of language (*langage*), of which the individual languages are particular cases. The example of the Port-Royal grammarians was followed by a large number of eighteenth-century grammarians, especially in France; these scholars judged that the acquisition of particular **languages,** unless grounded in a general grammar, is reduced to a purely mechanical exercise involving only memory and habit.

If all languages have a common basis, it is because they all have the goal of allowing human beings to express themselves, to make their thoughts known to each other. Lancelot and Arnauld admit implicitly, and certain later grammarians (such as Beauzée) affirm explicitly, that the communication of thought through speech requires that the latter be a sort of "picture," an "imitation" of thought. When they say that the function of language is the **representation** of thought, this word must thus be taken in the strongest possible sense. It does not mean simply that speech is a sign, but that it is a mirror, that it sets up an internal analogy with the content it conveys. How does it happen, then, that these words that have "nothing in common with what happens in our minds" can nonetheless imitate "the various movements of our soul"?

It is not a question, for the authors of general grammars, of seeking in the materiality of the word an imitation of the thing or of the idea (although the belief in the imitative value of language sounds is found in all periods of linguistic reflection, even in the seventeenth century in certain texts of Leibnitz). For these authors, only the organization of words in the linguistic utterance (*énoncé*) has the power to represent. But how is it actually possible for a collection of separate words to represent a thought whose primary characteristic is "indivisibility" (the term is used by Beauzée)? Does not the fragmentation imposed by the

3

material nature of words contradict the essential unity of the mind? In order to answer this question (the same question that in the nineteenth century guided Humboldt's reflection on the linguistic expression of relationships), one must note that there exists an analysis of thought that respects its unity even while decomposing it—namely, the analysis undertaken by logicians. By distinguishing in a proposition a subject (that about which one affirms something) and a predicate (that which is affirmed about it), we do not shatter its unity, since each of these terms must be defined in relation to the other, since the subject is only a subject in relation to a possible predication, and since the predicate is not self-sufficient but includes a "confused idea" of the subject about which it is affirmed. As a result, the speech act can allow the indivisibility of the intellectual act to appear if the fragmentation into words reproduces the logical analysis of thought. It is on these terms that "the art of analyzing thought is the basis for the art of speaking, or, in other words, that a sound logic is the basis for the art of grammar" (Beauzée). We have moved, then, from the idea that language is simply representation to the idea that it is the representation of logical thought. By the same token, it was understood that there could be a general grammar; since hardly anyone doubted the universality of logic, it seemed natural that there should be principles, equally universal, that all languages must respect when attempting to render visible, through the constraints of written and oral communication, the structure of logical thought. It was understood as well that knowledge of these principles could be obtained in a "rational" (and not an inductive) fashion, starting from a reflection on the logical operations of the mind and on the necessities of communication. It became apparent, finally, that this general and rational grammar in turn made it possible to account for the practices observed in the various languages: it was a matter of "applying to the immutable and general principles of the spoken or written word the arbitrary and customary institutions" of particular languages.

Examples

The principal categories of words correspond to the fundamental moments of logical thought. Since judgment consists in attributing a property (predicate) to a thing, languages include words to designate things (substantives), properties (adjectives), and the act of attribution itself (the verb *to be*; the other verbs represent, according to the Port-Royal grammarians, an amalgam of the verb *to be* and an adjective: "the dog runs" equals "the dog is running"). Other categories, while linked to the exercise of logical thought, are determined in addition by the condition of communication. Thus the impossibility of having a name for each thing imposes recourse to common nouns, whose extension is then limited by articles or demonstratives. In the same way, by the combination of logical principles and the constraints of communication, certain rules—presented as universal—will be formulated. For example, the agreement between a noun and the adjective that determines it, an agreement necessary for clear communication (making it possible to know on which noun the adjective depends), must be an agreement of concord (identity of number, gender, and case), since according to their logical nature, the adjective and the noun refer to one and the same thing (the *Port-Royal Grammar* goes so far as to justify the agreement of the participle in French). Or again, there is a word order that is natural and universal (the one that places the noun before the attributive adjective, the subject before the verb), since in order to understand the attribution of a property to an object, one must first conceive of the object; only then is it possible to affirm something about it.

To the extent that counterexamples immediately spring to mind (Latin and German hardly respect this "natural order"), this last rule makes it clear that a theory of figures is indispensable to all general grammars. A rhetorical figure [273] is conceived of at this point in time as an artificial and improper way of speaking that, for reasons of elegance and expressivity, is voluntarily substituted for a natural way of speaking that must be reconstructed before the meaning can be understood. According to general grammars, such **figures** are found not only in literature but in language itself. They stem from the fact that language, destined at a primitive stage to represent logical thought, is eventually placed at the service of the passions. The latter impose, for example, abbreviations (elements that are logically necessary but convey no emotional content are left unexpressed) and, very frequently, a reversal of natural order (the most important word, not the logical subject, comes first). In all these cases, the implied words and the natural order were initially present in the mind of the speaker and must be reestablished by the hearer (the Roman who heard *Venit Petrus* was obliged, in order to understand, to reconstruct for himself *Petrus venit*). Thus Latin and German are called **transpositive** languages because they invert an initially recognized order. The existence of figures of speech, far from contradicting the general principles, confirms them. Figures do not replace the rules; rather they superimpose themselves on them.

● For the basic texts, see A. Arnauld and C. Lancelot, *Grammaire générale et raisonnée* (1660; reprint ed. with preface by M. Foucault, Paris, 1969), Eng. trans., *A General and Rational Grammar* (1753; facsimile reprint ed., Menston, England, 1968); N. Beauzée, *Grammaire générale* (1767; facsimile reprint ed., Stuttgart, 1974); and C. Chesneau du Marsais, *Logique et principes de grammaire* (Paris, 1769). For further information, see G. Harnois, *Les Théories du langage en France de 1660 à 1821* (Paris, 1929); G. Sahlin, *César Chesneau du Marsais et son rôle dans l'évolution de la grammaire générale* (Paris, 1928); N. Chomsky, *Cartesian Linguistics* (New York, 1966), a work discussed, for example, in H. M. Bracken, "Chomsky's Variations on a Theme by Descartes," *Journal of the History of Philosophy* (1970): 181–92; R. Donzé, *La Grammaire générale et raisonnée de Port-Royal* (Bern, 1967); J.-C. Chevalier, *Histoire de la syntaxe* (Geneva, 1968); P. Julliard, *Philosophies of Language in Eighteenth-Century France* (The Hague, 1970); and L. H. Hillman, *Vaugelas and the Port-Royal Grammar* (Ithaca, 1972).

What is the historical importance of general grammar? First, it marks, at least in intention, the end of the privilege accorded in preceding centuries to Latin grammar, which had tended to become the model for all grammar: general grammar is no more Latin than it is French or German; rather it transcends all language systems. It is understandable that it became a commonplace practice in the eighteenth century (repeated in many of the linguistic articles in the *Grande Encyclopédie*) to condemn grammarians who could only see one language through another (or, as O. Jespersen was to describe them in the twentieth century, those who speak of one language while peering at another). On the other hand, general grammarians avoided the dilemma, seemingly insurmountable until their time, of a purely philosophical and purely empirical grammar. The numerous treatises on modes of signifying (*De modis significandi*) in the Middle Ages were devoted to general reflection on the act of signification. From another standpoint, grammar as Vaugelas understood it was only a recording of practices, that is, of "good practices" (*bons usages*), the quality of the practice being judged primarily in terms of the quality of the language user in question. General grammar, for its part, attempted to explain particular practices by deducing and applying general rules. If these rules could claim such explanatory power, it was because, although grounded in logic, they were not content merely to repeat it: they expressed its possible transparency through the material conditions of human communication.

HISTORICAL LINGUISTICS IN THE NINETEENTH CENTURY

The Birth of Historical Linguistics

Although it is easy to observe (simply by comparing texts) that languages change with time, it was only toward the end of the eighteenth century that this transformation became the object of a particular discipline. Two ideas appear to be connected with this new approach.

a) *Change in language is not due simply to the conscious will of men* (the efforts of a group to make itself understood by outsiders, the decisions of grammarians who are "purifying" the language, the creation of new words to designate new ideas), *but to an internal necessity.* Language is not merely transformed; it transforms itself. (Turgot, in the article "Etymologie," in the *Grande Encyclopédie,* speaks of an "internal principle" of change.) This thesis became explicit when linguists began to distinguish two possible relationships between a word *a* of the period *A* and an analogous word *b* of the period *B*. There is **borrowing** if *b* has been consciously formed on the model of *a*, itself exhumed from a previous state of the language; thus the French *hôpital* was produced, in a given historical period, through imitation of the Latin *hospitale* (more precisely, first created was the word *hospital,* which later became *hôpital*). There is **inheritance,** on the other hand, when the passage from *a* to *b* is unconscious and when the difference between them, if there is one, stems from a progressive transformation of *a* (*hôtel* is the product of a series of successive modifications of the word *hospitale*). To say that through inheritance a word can come from a different word is to admit then that linguistic change can have natural causes. From this stems an important consequence: the filial relationship of two languages *A* and *B* does not imply their resemblance. *B* can be radically different from *A* and yet derive from *A*. Formerly, on the contrary, the search for filial linguistic relationships was one and the same as the search for resemblances, and, inversely, differences were used to combat the hypothesis of a filial relationship. The belief in natural change will lead instead to a search for proofs of kinship within the differences themselves.

b) *Linguistic change is regular and respects the internal organization of languages.* If the criterion of resemblance is rejected, how can kinship between two languages be proved? On what can one base a conclusion that the differences between them are the product of changes and not of substitutions? (N.B. This is the linguistic aspect of a very general problem encountered in any study of change; physics and chemistry resolve it, around the same time, by establishing as a criterion for change that through it, something is "conserved.") The solution towards which linguists were tending at the end of the eighteenth century and whose explicit acceptance was to constitute historical linguistics as a discipline consisted in considering a difference as a change only if it manifested a certain regularity within the language. As the belief in the conservation of matter occasioned the passage from alchemy to chemistry, the principle of the regularity of linguistic change marked the birth of linguistics on the foundation of what was then called **etymology.** The latter, even when it was presented as historical (which was not always the case [130]) and when it explained a word by finding, in a previous state, the word from which it derived, studied each word in isolation. This approach made it very difficult to find criteria, for it is frequently the case that different etymologies seem possible for a single word. In such a case, how does one choose? Historical linguistics, on the other hand, explains a word *b* by a preceding word *a* only if the passage from *a* to *b* is a particular case of a general rule that is valid for a number of other words and accounts for the fact that *a'* has become *b'*, *a''* has become *b''*, and so on. This regularity implies that the difference between *a* and *b* involves one or another of their constituents and that in all the other words in which this constituent appears, it is subject to the same change. From this, linguists can draw two consequences:

1) They may insist that the explanation of a word be based on a grammatical analysis of this word and that it explain separately the different signifying units (morphemes [200]) of which it is composed. That is why Turgot rejects, for example, the explanation of the Latin *britannica* ("Britannic") by the Hebrew *baratanac* ("tin country") with the argument that the Latin word is composed of two units (*britan* and the ending *ica*) that must be explained separately, whereas the alleged etymology explained the word in its totality (see p. 199 for another example, taken from Adelung). In order for linguistic change to possess this regularity, which is its only possible safeguard, it seems necessary that it respect the grammatical organization of the language and that it concern the word only in terms of its internal structure. (One can see how Turgot, in an article devoted to the search for etymological criteria, is led beyond etymology.)

2) They may go still further in the analysis of the word and look for regularity not only at the level of grammatical components but also at the level of phonetic components. It was in this area that historical linguistics achieved, in the nineteenth century, its greatest successes, culminating in the establishment of **phonetic laws.** To formulate a phonetic law concerning two languages (or two states of the same language)

A and *B* is to show that to every word of *A* that includes, in a fixed position, a certain basic sound *x*, there corresponds a word of *B* in which *x* is replaced by *x′*. Thus in the transition from Latin to French, Latin words containing a *c* followed by an *a* saw the *c* changed to *ch*: *campus* → *champ, calvus* → *chauve, casa* → *chez*, and so on. (N.B. [*a*] It is possible for *x′* to be zero; the change may be an elimination. [*b*] It would be difficult to clarify the term "corresponds" used above: in general, the word of *B* no longer has the same meaning as that of *A*, for meaning, too, evolves; and it differs materially from its predecessor in other respects ‿as well as by the substitution of *x′* for *x*, since other phonetic laws relate *A* and *B*. [*c*] Phonetic laws concern only the changes linked to inheritance and do not concern borrowings: the borrowed French *calvitie* was directly modeled on the Latin *calvities*.)

- On historical linguistics before comparative grammar, see J. F. Eros, "Diachronic Linguistics in Seventeenth-Century England with Special Attention to the Theories of Meric Casaubon" (Ph.D. diss., University of Wisconsin, 1972). For an amusing sample of a pre-linguistic history of languages, see "Discours historique sur l'origine de la langue française," *Le Mercure de France* (1757; facsimile reprint ed., Geneva, 1970).

Comparative Grammar

Notwithstanding certain of Turgot's intuitions or Adelung's, a work of the German F. Bopp is generally considered to mark the birth of historical linguistics: *Über das Conjugationssystem der Sanskrit-sprache in Vergleichung mit jenem der griechischen, lateinischen, persischen und germanischen Sprache* (Frankfort, 1816). The expression **comparative grammar** (or **comparativism**) is often used to designate the analogous research carried out, especially in Germany, in the first half of the nineteenth century, most notably by Bopp, the brothers A. W. and F. von Schlegel, J. L. K. Grimm, A. Schleicher, and the Dane R. Rask, whose work (often precursory) has been largely ignored. These studies have in common the following characteristics:

1. Instigated by the discovery at the end of the eighteenth century of the analogy existing between Sanskrit, the sacred language of ancient India, and most of the ancient and modern European languages, they are essentially devoted to this group of languages, called either Indo-European or Indo-Germanic.

2. They begin with the idea that there exist not only resemblances but **kinships** among these languages, which are thus presented as natural transformations (through inheritance) of a single mother tongue, **Indo-European.** This latter is known, not directly, but only through

reconstruction. (Schleicher even believed he could write fables in Indo-European.) (N.B. The first comparatists did not always reject the idea that Sanskrit *was* the mother tongue.)

3. Their method is comparative in the sense that they try first and foremost to establish correspondences between languages. To this end they compare them (irrespective of separation in time) and look for an element *x* in one that is equivalent to the element *x'* in another. But they have little interest in establishing, step by step, the details of the evolution that led from the mother tongue to the modern languages (Italic, Germanic, Slavic, and so on), which themselves were subsequently subdivided, giving rise to **families** (with still further subdivisions for most of the elements of these families).

4. The comparison of two languages is above all the comparison of their grammatical elements. Turgot had already proposed, as a necessary safeguard, that the etymologist should try to explain words, not taken as a whole, but rather in terms of their constitutive elements (see above, p. 8). Now which of these elements are the more interesting? Those that convey ideas (*aim* in the French *aimeront, troupe* in *attroupement*), often called **roots** or **lexical elements,** or the **grammatical elements** that surround the former and are supposed to indicate the relationships or viewpoints according to which the idea is considered? Discussion on this point began as early as the end of the eighteenth century. It was governed by the idea that all elements that may have been borrowed from one language by another (and therefore cannot be used to prove a natural evolution) must be eliminated from the comparison. Grammatical elements can hardly have been borrowed, since they constitute coherent systems (of tense, case, person, and so on) within a given language. Given the mutual solidarity of these elements, one cannot borrow an isolated grammatical element, but only an entire system, and the disruption that would result from such a borrowing renders it highly unlikely. This is why the comparison of languages was seen at the beginning of the nineteenth century essentially as the comparison of their grammatical elements.

The Thesis of the Decline of Languages

The goal of historical linguistics was linked to the idea of a double conservation in the process of change (see above, pp. 7ff.). The grammatical organization is conserved: it must be possible to subject words from state *A* and from an ulterior state *B* to the same decomposition into root and grammatical elements (otherwise whole-word comparisons would have to be made, and the uncertainty of this method was well known). The phonetic organization is conserved as well, so that phonetic laws can correlate the elementary sounds of *A* and *B* and show the variations in phonic form of the word components. But the facts made it difficult to maintain this double permanence, for the comparatists believed they had discovered that the phonetic laws destroy progressively, by a sort of erosion, the grammatical organization of the language that they govern. Thus they can bring about the confusion, in the state *B*, of grammatical elements that are distinct in *A*; they can even bring about the disappearance of certain elements (the disappearance of the Latin case system in French would stem from the phonetic evolution that led to the disappearance of the Latin word endings where case markers had appeared); finally the separation, within the word, between root and grammatical elements (a separation whose clarity in Sanskrit amazed the earliest comparatists) is often attenuated owing to phonetic changes.

Hence the pessimism of most of the comparatists (with the exception of Humboldt): the historian of languages finds nothing to trace but decline—a decline already underway in the classical languages—and Bopp often complains of working in a field of ruins. But this pessimism is useful: it allows grammarians to compare a modern word with an ancient one whose structure is apparently very different while insisting that comparison must respect grammatical organizations. It suffices to suppose —and Bopp does not hesitate to do so—that the two words have an analogous underlying structure and, more generally, to consider the former state to be the underlying grammatical structure of the new state. Is it not reasonable, after all, for the archaeologist who is mapping out a field of ruins to try to discover the outline of the former city? What comparatism could not allow, on the other hand, without abandoning its fundamental methodological principles, was the belief that languages, in transforming themselves, create new grammatical organizations.

How can this decline of languages during the course of history be explained? Most of the comparatists—Bopp and Schleicher in particular —attributed it to the attitude toward language of historical man, of the utilizer who treated language as a simple means, as an instrument of **communication** whose utilization must be made as convenient and economical as possible. The phonetic laws would in fact have as their cause this tendency toward the least effort, which sacrifices grammatical organization to the desire for communication at minimal cost.

If there has been a positive period in the history of languages, therefore, it must be sought in human prehistory, when language was not a means but an end: the human mind shaped it like a work of art, seeking therein to represent the mind itself. In this period, irretrievably lost to us, the history of languages was that of a creation. But it is only by deduction that we can picture its stages. Schleicher, for example, supposed that human languages must have taken, successively, the three major forms revealed by a classification of contemporary languages based on their internal structure (or typology). At first they were all **isolating,** that is, their words are unanalyzable units in which one cannot distinguish even a root and grammatical elements (Chinese was understood in this way in the nineteenth century). Then certain languages became **agglutinating,** that is, they included words with a root and grammatical markers but no precise rules governing the formation of words (the Amerindian languages would be a contemporary survival of this state). Finally, from among the agglutinating languages developed the **inflecting** languages, in which precise rules—those of morphology [51]—govern the internal organization of words (these are chiefly the Indo-European languages). Only in this latter case is the mind truly represented: the unity of the root and the grammatical markers in the word, cemented by the morphological rules, represents the unity of the empirical given and of the *a priori* forms in the act of thought. Unfortunately this state of perfection, generally attributed to the Indo-European mother tongue, was already destroyed at the classical period, when man, preoccupied with making history, no longer considered language as anything but an instrument of social life. Made subservient to communication, language has never since stopped destroying its own organization.

● Some major treatises of comparative grammar are the following: F. Bopp, *Vergleichende Grammatik des Sanskrit, Zend, Griechischen, Lateinischen, Lithauischen, Gothischen und Deutschen* (Berlin, 1833–52), Eng. trans., *A Comparative Grammar of the Sanskrit, Zend, Greek, Latin, Lithuanian, Gothic, German and Sclavonic Languages* (London, 1845–50); J. L. K. Grimm, *Deutsche Grammatik* (Göttingen, 1822–37); and A. Schleicher, *Compendium der vergleichenden Grammatik der indogermanischen Sprachen* (Weimar, 1866), Eng. trans., *A Compendium of the Comparative Grammar of the Indo-European, Greek and Latin Languages* (London, 1874–77). On language decline, see, for example, F. Bopp, *Vocalismus* (Berlin, 1836); and A. Schleicher, *Zur vergleichenden Sprachgeschichte* (Bonn, 1848). This decline is questioned by W. von Humboldt, for example, in "Über das Entstehen der grammatischen Formen und ihren Einfluss auf die Ideenentwicklung" (1821), in the *Gesammelte Schriften*, 17 vols. (Berlin, 1903–36), vol. 4 (1905), pp. 285–313. (For a commentary on Humboldt, see O. Ducrot, "Le Structuralisme en linguistique," in Ducrot et al., *Qu'est-ce que le structuralisme?* [Paris, 1968], pp. 13–95, esp. 23–29.) For an example of modern research in comparative grammar, see E. Benveniste, *Hittite et Indo-européen* (Paris, 1962). See also J. Arbuckle, "August Schleicher and the Linguistics/Philology Dichotomy: A Chapter in the History of Linguistics," *Word* 26 (1970–71): 17–31.

The Neogrammarians

In the second half of the nineteenth century a group of linguists, chiefly German, attempted to introduce into historical linguistics the positivist principles that were dominant in the contemporary sciences and philosophy. Their hope was to renew comparative grammar, and they called themselves **neogrammarians.** Their principal theses were the following:

1. Historical linguistics must be explanatory. It should not simply note and describe changes; it should also find their causes (a preoccupation that was of little concern to Bopp).

2. This explanation must be of the positivist type. Those vast philosophical explanations that appealed to Schleicher (a great reader of Hegel) are to be mistrusted. The only verifiable causes are to be sought in the activity of speaking subjects, who transform the language while utilizing it.

3. In order to carry out this search for causes, it is preferable to study those changes that extend over a limited period of time. Instead of comparing very distant language states, linguists will take as their object the passage from one state to the state that follows.

4. A first type of cause is of the articulatory order. The so-called phonetic laws lend themselves in fact to a physiological explanation. Thus their action is absolutely mechanical ("blind"): when a change takes place within a language state, no words—whatever their own semantic or grammatical situation might be—can escape it, and the exceptions (which Schleicher simply noted) are, for a neogrammarian, the indication of a law as yet unknown.

5. A second type of cause is psychological: the tendency to **analogy,** based on the association of ideas. Speakers tend (*a*) to group words and sentences in classes whose elements resemble each other in sound and in meaning and (*b*) to create new words or sentences capable of enriching these classes. Hence, for example, the creation of *modernize* and *actualize* on the model of *realize*, or of "I feel *badly*" by analogy with "I feel *well*."

6. Not only must the history of languages be explanatory, but there is no means of linguistic explanation other than the historical. Thus to speak of the fundamental meaning underlying the different senses of a word has explanatory value only if this meaning happens to be primary in chronological terms. Similarly, one has the right to speak of a **derivation** (to say that one word is drawn from another—for example, that *booklet* comes from *book*) only if one can show that the source word (*book*) existed prior to the derived word (*booklet*).

- The master recognized by most neogrammarians is G. Curtius (*Grund-züge der griechischen Etymologie* [Leipzig, 1858–68], Eng. trans., *Principles of Greek Etymology* [London, 1886]). Their principal theoretician is H. Paul (*Principien der Sprachgeschichte* [Halle, 1880], Eng. trans., from the second edition, by H. A. Strong: *Principles of the History of Language* [London and New York, 1891]). A particularly systematic search for phonetic laws appears in K. Brugmann, *Grundriss der vergleichenden Grammatik der indogermanischen Sprachen* (Strasbourg, 1886–1900), Eng. trans., *Elements of the Comparative Grammar of the Indo-Germanic Languages* (London, 1888–95). A collection of texts by comparatists and neogrammarians in English translation is found in W. P. Lehmann, *A Reader in Nineteenth-Century Historical Indo-European Linguistics* (Bloomington and London, 1967). An attempt to situate the neogrammarians in the history of linguistics is offered by K. R. Jankowsky in *The Neogrammarians: A Re-evaluation of Their Place in the Development of Linguistic Science* (The Hague, 1972). See also W. M. Norman, "The Neogrammarians and Comparative Linguistics" (Ph.D. diss., Princeton University, 1972).

SAUSSURIANISM

Having written, at age twenty-one, the *Mémoire sur le système primitif des voyelles indo-européennes* (Paris, 1878), a work that counts among the successes of the neogrammarian school [13], the Swiss linguist F. de Saussure almost completely abandoned research in historical linguistics. Finding its basis uncertain, he judged that this research should be suspended until a thorough recasting of the field had been achieved. He himself attempted such a recasting, and he presented the results of his work in three courses given in Geneva between 1906 and 1911. These were published three years after his death by some of his students, under the title *Cours de linguistique générale* (Paris, 1916).

- For a comparison of Saussure's manuscript notes, those taken by his students, and the published *Cours*, see R. Godel, *Les Sources manuscrites du "Cours de linguistique générale" de F. de Saussure* (Geneva and Paris, 1957). A critical edition of the *Cours* by R. Engler, has been in preparation since 1967 (Wiesbaden). The English translation, *Course in General Linguistics*, is by Wade Baskin (New York, 1959).

The theoretical foundation of comparative practice lay in a belief in the progressive disorganization of languages under the influence of phonetic laws, laws that were themselves linked to the activity of communication [11]. This thesis, which authorizes us to read the grammar of the previous state as a filigree within the present state, would allow us in fact to identify earlier grammatical elements with elements of the later state in order to compare them, even if the latter appear to have a very different grammatical status. But it is precisely this thesis that Saussure calls into question.

The first reason for this questioning is a general one that appears only implicitly in the *Course in General Linguistics*. Language, according to Saussure, is fundamentally (and not by accident or through depravation) an instrument of communication. One never finds in Saussure's writings the idea that language must represent a structure of thought that would exist independently of any linguistic formulation (whether this representation is conceived, in the comparatist fashion, as a fundamental function or, in the manner of the Port-Royal grammarians, as the necessary means of communication). The Saussurian viewpoint emerges most clearly from his theory of a fundamental linguistic arbitrariness [134] (to be distinguished from the arbitrariness of each isolated sign [131]): linguistic arbitrariness stems from the fact that thought, considered before language, is like an "amorphous mass," a "nebula" (*Course*, p. 112) that lends itself to all possible analyses without privileging one in relation to another, without requiring us to consider two given nuances of meaning as two aspects of a single notion and to separate certain others as deriving from two different notions. (For general grammars, on the contrary, there exists a logical analysis of thought that imposes itself in its own right and that language has to imitate as best it can; similarly, for the comparatists, the unity of the root and the grammatical elements in a word represents the unity of the intellectual act submitting experience to the *a priori* forms of the mind [200].) If, then, for Saussure each language, at each moment of its existence, presents a certain form of organization, this is certainly not the effect of a function that preexisted communication, for language can have no function other than communication.

This very general argument, based on the idea of function in language, is reinforced by a detailed examination of the actual role of linguistic activity in the evolution of languages. For it is not true, according to Saussure, that the functioning of language—its utilization by speaking subjects for the purpose of communication—is a cause of disorganization; it is not true that it leads to the grammatical leveling deplored by Bopp. Although Saussure, like the neogrammarians [13], maintains that the utilization of the linguistic code by speaking subjects—

that is, in the terminology of the *Course,* "speech" (*la parole*) [118ff.]
—is one of the essential causes of linguistic change, he denies that the
changes thus introduced can involve the very organization of language.
Analogic creation [13], for example, which is one of the most obvious
effects of speech, never does more than extend and enrich a category
whose existence it presupposes. The creation of *finalize* from *final* only
adds a supplementary couple to the series in which we already find
modern/modernize; *legal/legalize*; and so on. Thus analogy, according
to Saussure, is more likely to reinforce linguistic classifications than it
is to destroy them. Nor do the phonetic laws have the anarchic effect
that the comparatists attribute to them. A well-known example, given by
Saussure, is that of the expression of the plural in German. In a previous
state it was marked by the addition of an *i*: *Gast* ("guest")/*Gasti*
("guests"); *Hand* ("hand")/*Handi* ("hands"). Then various phonetic
changes transformed *Gasti* to *Gäste, Handi* to *Hände.* These changes,
although they have materially modified the mark of the plural, have
nevertheless left intact the grammatical phenomenon itself, the duality
in German of the singular and the plural; the duality has simply been
transposed, and it is manifested just as well in its new aspect as in the
old. A given grammatical organization, banished by the phonetic evolution of a certain phonic realization, can thus always reestablish itself
within another (for further details, see below, pp. 140ff.).

Thus, according to Saussure, neither language's function nor its effective utilization in this function is an anarchic factor that would endanger
its organized character. Proceeding now in a positive manner, Saussure
shows that language, at every moment of its existence, must present
itself as an organization. Saussure labels **system** what his successors often
call **structure:** this organization that is inherent in every language. The
particular nuance that the Saussurians introduce into these terms (which
is added to the general idea of order and regularity) stems from the very
approach through which they prove this organized character. They start
with the idea that knowledge of linguistic elements is not a given and
that there is no way to identify directly, on the basis of experience, the
elements put into play by a language (cf. *Course,* pt. 2, chap. 2, sec. 4).
The reason for this, according to Saussure, is that the operations necessary for the determination of a unit presuppose the situating of this
unit in relationship to the others and its reinsertion within an overall
organization. Here we see what the Saussurians mean when they speak
of a language system or structure: linguistic elements have no reality
independent of their relationship to the whole.

Saussure expresses the same idea when he says that the linguistic unit
is a **value.** By saying that an object—for example, a coin—is a value,
one is affirming in reality (*a*) that it can be exchanged against an object

of a different nature (merchandise) and especially (*b*) that its exchange capacity is conditioned by fixed relationships existing between itself and objects of the same nature (the exchange rate between the coin and the other monetary units of the same country and of other countries). The same principle applies to the linguistic element. This element, for Saussure, is the sign—the association of an acoustic image (signifier) and of a concept (signified). Thus the linguistic element satisfies condition (*a*): its exchange capacity allows it to designate a linguistic reality that is foreign to it, a reality that is reached through the intermediary of its signified but is not its signified (see below, pp. 247ff.). But the sign also satisfies condition (*b*), for the signifying power that constitutes it is strictly conditioned by the relationships uniting it with the other signs of the language, so that it cannot be grasped without being reinserted in a network of intra-linguistic relationships. (N.B. This notion of value rules out the insertion, in the comparatist manner, of the elements of the state *B* in the organization of the earlier state *A*, for either *B* no longer has its own organization, in which case it no longer has any elements, or else it has elements, but they are elements that must be situated in *B*'s own organization, the only one that gives them reality.)

More concretely, Saussure shows that the very activity that permits the linguist to specify the elements of language (signs) requires him to bring to light at the same time the system that confers value on these elements. This is because—appearances to the contrary—the specification of signs is a complicated and indirect operation that demands much more than intuition, or immediate feeling for language (*Course*, pt. 2, chap. 2, sec. 3). Even simply locating them is difficult to the extent that they do not always have a clearly delimited material manifestation. This is the case, for example, when the signifier of a sign is simply an **alternation** (that is, a modification of the root), not the addition to the root of a supplementary element (cf. the plural of the French *cheval* ("horse"), *chevaux*; cf. also the English irregular verbs, in which the mark of the past is constituted by a simple modification of the root vowel: *I bind/I bound*). Here there is "nothing positive" in the signifier; it is the simple difference between *bind* and *bound*, *cheval* and *chevaux*. In these cases, which for Saussure only illustrate a general situation, the sign *present* only has reality in relation to the sign *past*, the sign *singular* in relation to the sign *plural*, so that it is impossible to recognize a sign without at one and the same time classifying it among its competitors.

The same principle holds true for a second operation, the **delimitation** of units, that is, the **segmentation** of the chain, an operation that consists in discovering the minimal signs and, for example, in determining whether the verbs *discharge, disgust,* and *dispel* must be decomposed or taken as elementary signs. In this case, a fairly simple one, we "feel" that the correct solution is to break down only *dis-charge*. The justification of that solution cannot be simply intuitive, however, for the three verbs possess the same phonic element *dis*, and this element is always accompanied by a certain idea of negation, of suppression, which might suggest that we recognize the presence in these verbs of a sign *dis-*. Thus one is obliged to bring into play facts that are much more complex. We shall observe, for example, that the *dis* of *disgust* cannot be eliminated (there is no verb *gust*, whereas there is *charge*); nor can it be replaced by a different prefix (there is no *regust*, while there is *recharge*). *Disgust* then does not belong to a series of the type *charge/ discharge/recharge*. In order to justify not decomposing *dispel*—there is, after all, a pair *dispel/repel*—it is necessary to call upon a more complex classification and to note that the pair *discharge/recharge* belongs to a set of pairs (*displace/replace*; *disestablish/reestablish*; and so on) that manifest the same difference of meaning between the two terms, while such is not the case for *dispel/repel*. We shall retain from this example the fact that the simple segmentation *dis-charge* requires that we recognize in this verb a combinatorial schema that is generally applicable in English, or in other words, that we reinsert it in an overall classification of English verbs: recognizing the signs of which a verb is composed is equivalent to situating it within this classification.

Identification, the recognition of an element through its multiple uses (in different situations and contexts), is the final task indispensable to the determination of units. Why admit that there is the same unit *adopt* in "adopt a fashion" and "adopt a child"? And when an orator repeats, "Gentlemen, Gentlemen," with different nuances in pronunciation as well as in meaning, why do we say that he is using the same word twice (*Course*, p. 108)? The problem becomes more acute if we notice that the different nuances of meaning taken on by *Gentlemen* (or *adopt*) are often as distant from each other as are certain meanings of *my friends* (or *accept*). Then why do we decide to unite two given nuances of meaning by attributing them both to a single sign? Here again, the Saussurian response is that identification sends us back to the language as a whole. If a certain semantic acceptation must be attributed to the sign *adopt*, even if it is very far removed from the usual meaning of the word, this is necessary only insofar as none of the coexisting signs (*accept, take*, and so on) is found to be compatible with that nuance. The nuance belongs to *adopt* only because it does not belong to another sign. Thus Saussure declares that the "most precise characteristic [of signs] is in being what the others are not" (*Course*, p. 118). A weak form of this principle—a form easier to defend—consists in specifying that the unit is not *everything* that the others are not, but *nothing more* *than* what the others are not. In other words, the unit is defined only by its "differences" (hence its "differential" character); it is based upon nothing other than "its noncoincidence with the rest" (ibid.). Thus one arrives at the principle of **opposition,** according to which one must attribute to a sign only those elements (phonetic or semantic) through which it distinguishes itself from at least one other sign.

This conclusion is not precisely the one that was beginning to emerge when we were examining the operations of location and delimitation. At that point the unit appeared to be purely negative and relational, constituted only through its place in the network of relationships that make up the language. Now it appears to possess a positive reality, a reality reduced, to be sure, to that which differentiates it from others but one that nevertheless maintains its own consistency. This ambiguity governs the debate instituted among the successors of Saussure between the functionalists [24ff.] and the glossematicians [20ff.]. What all the Saussurians retain in common, however, is that the linguistic unit, through its phonic and semantic aspects, always refers back to all the other units and that it is impossible either to hear or to comprehend a sign without entering into the global play of the language.

● On Saussure's attitude toward historical linguistics, see below, p. 139. On the contrast between the purely relational and the oppositional concept of the sign, see R. S. Wells, "De Saussure's System of Linguistics," *Word* 3 (1947): 1–31. A presentation of Saussure's work is offered by G. Mounin in *Saussure ou le structuralisme sans le savoir* (Paris, 1968). On Saussure and his successor, with selected texts in French, prefatory matter in English, see R. Godel, *A Geneva School Reader in Linguistics* (Bloomington, 1969). See also a study by E. Benveniste, "Saussure After Half a Century," in *Problems in General Linguistics,* trans. M. E. Meek (Coral Gables, 1971), as well as the introduction and commentary accompanying T. De Mauro's Italian translation of the *Cours* (*Corso di linguistica generale* [Bari, 1968]). An attempt to situate the Saussurian contribution historically is found in E. F. K. Koerner, *Ferdinand de Saussure: Origin and Development of his Linguistic Theory in Western Studies of Language* (Brunswick, 1973). J. Culler offers a general study of Saussure's thought and its development in modern linguistics and semiotics in *Ferdinand de Saussure* (New York, 1977).

GLOSSEMATICS

The Danish linguist L. Hjelmslev, who developed the theory of **glossematics,** presented it as the elaboration of Saussure's fundamental intuitions. But this basic fidelity led Hjelmslev to abandon, on the one hand, those of Saussure's theses that he judged superficial and, on the other hand, the functionalist (predominantly phonological) interpretation of the Saussurian doctrine, an interpretation that he regarded as a travesty. From the *Course* Hjelmslev retained above all two affirmations: (1) language is not substance, but form; and (2) all language is at the same time both expression and content.

These two theses were united, for Saussure, in the theory of the sign. If each language must be characterized not only at the level of **expression** (by the sounds that it chooses for the transmission of meaning) but also at the level of **content** (by the way in which it presents meaning), it is because the signs of one language rarely have exact equivalents (synonyms) in another; for example, the German *schätzen*, usually translated by the English *value*, carries nuances that are foreign to the English word. It would thus be impossible to reduce a language to a set of labels serving to designate preexisting things or concepts. A language cannot be considered to be a **nomenclature;** it must also be described at the level of content.

A further reflection on the sign led Saussure to declare that language is above all **form,** and not **substance.** What in fact constitutes the difference between two languages from the semantic point of view? Certainly it is not in the meanings that they allow us to express, since these meanings can be translated: nothing prevents us from designating in English the nuance that is found in *schätzen* and not in *value*. The difference lies rather in the fact that certain nuances that are expressed by the same sign in the one language must be expressed by different signs in the other. Thus an original segmentation, one stemming directly from the system of signs, is introduced into the objective (substantial) semantic reality; this configuration is what Saussure sometimes called the form of the language (*Course*, pt. 2, chap. 6). It is evident then that the primacy given to this form derives directly from the principle of opposition [19]. To say in effect that a sign is characterized only by that which distinguishes it from others, by that which makes it different, is to say in particular that the frontiers of its meaning constitute a primary fact, unforeseeable and impossible to deduce from knowledge of nature or of thought; to say this is to take the form of the language as the object of an autonomous and irreducible science. (N.B. What has been demonstrated here with respect to the semantic aspect of the sign is equally applicable, according to Saussure, to its phonic aspect: that which constitutes the phonic value of a sign is what distinguishes it from other signs, so that the signs of a language also project, in the realm of sound, an original configuration that is dependent on the form of the language.)

Although Hjelmslev approved of the intention behind the Saussurian opposition of form and substance, he wanted to take this distinction much further. Unquestionably, linguistic units introduce into the world an original distribution of sound and meaning, but in order to do so, they must be something other than this distribution, something other than these regions of sound and meaning with which they coincide. In order to project themselves into reality, they must exist independently of that reality. But how is the linguist to define them if he refuses to take into account their realization, in the intellectual sphere as well as in the material sphere? Certainly not by taking recourse to the principle of opposition (which we shall call Saussure's concept 1), since this principle always leads to a positive characterization of the unit, requiring only that the unit be limited to that by which it differs from the others.

The Hjelmslevian solution is to develop to the extreme another Saussurian notion (concept 2) according to which the unit, purely negative and relational, can be defined, not in and of itself—what is important is the simple fact that it is different from the others—but only by the relationships that link it to the other units of the language. All that is required of the symbols of a formal system is that each be distinct from the others and that they be related to each other by explicit functional laws; thus both their meanings and their perceptible manifestations are excluded from consideration. If language then is form, not substance, this no longer stems from the fact that language introduces an original segmentation; rather it is because the units of a language must be defined by the rules that allow their combination, by the interplay that they authorize. Hence the idea that a language can remain essentially unchanged when both the meanings it expresses and the material means it deploys are modified (for example, when a spoken language is transformed into a language that is written, gestural, or pictorial or into a system of flag signals, and so on).

Although this thesis depends on certain passages in Saussure (*Course*, pt. 2, chap. 4, sec. 4), Hjelmslev considered himself the first to make it explicit and in particular the first to pursue its elaboration (see below, pp. 109ff., for Hjelmslev's definition of the constitutive relations of all languages). Hjelmslev's thesis distinguishes three levels where Saussure saw only two. What Saussure called substance—that is, semantic or phonic reality considered independently of any linguistic utilization—Hjelmslev calls **matter,** or purport. Form, in Saussure's concept 1—

understood now as segmentation, configuration—is called **substance** by Hjelmslev, and he reserves the term **form** for the relational network that defines units (form in Saussure's concept 2). In order to relate the three levels, glossematics utilizes the notion of **manifestation:** substance is the manifestation of form in matter.

This reinterpretation of the Saussurian principle according to which "language is form and not substance" leads Hjelmslev at the same time to reinterpret the affirmation that languages are to be characterized simultaneously at the level of expression and at the level of content. This affirmation indicates, for Saussure, that the way in which the signs of a language apportion signification among themselves introduces into meaning a segmentation that is as original as the one introduced within the phonic realm. But let us suppose now that these segmentations (considered as phenomena of substance) are to be disregarded, so that only the combinatorial relations among units—the authentic form, according to Hjelmslev—remain under consideration. It is then necessary to abandon the distinction between expression and content, since their form is identical: the combinatorial relationships that link the signs link their meanings as well as their phonic realizations. In order to preserve the distinction between expression and content, Hjelmslev must thus give up the idea that the fundamental linguistic unit is the sign. This task is made easier for him by virtue of the fact that phonologists, using commutation [25], have brought to light linguistic units smaller than signs: the phonemes [171] (the sign *calf* is made up of the three phonemes /k/, /æ/, and /f/). The same method applied to content allows the distinction, in this same sign, of at least three semantic elements, sometimes called distinctive semantic features, or semes [265]: /bovine/, /male/, /young/. Now it is clear that the semantic and phonic units thus located can be distinguished from the formal point of view: the combinatorial laws concerning the phonemes of a language and those applying to the semes cannot be shown to correspond to each other; this is what Hjelmslev is affirming in stating that the two levels are not conformal. (N.B. This lack of conformity does not rule out **isomorphism** between the levels; in other words, the same type of combinatorial relations may be found on both sides.) Matter, substance, and form are thus realized differently according to whether expression or content is in question; thus, finally, six fundamental linguistic levels are produced. We should note in particular that Hjelmslev speaks of a form of content. His formalism, unlike that of the distributionalists [31ff.], therefore implies, not a refusal to consider meaning, but rather the intention to give a formal description of the elements of signification. (A. Culioli calls this undertaking formal semantics.) (N.B. If Hjelmslev utilizes the phonological method of commutation to combat the primacy of the

sign, he subjects it nonetheless to the same criticism to which he subjected the principle of opposition—which, moreover, is the very principle from which commutation is derived. Commutation serves, in
Hjelmslev's view, only to locate the linguistic elements that are lesser
than the sign; it does not allow him to say what these elements are. While
the phonologist defines each phoneme by that which distinguishes it from
the others, Hjelmslev defines the elements only by their combinatorial
relations [see p. 125 below, for his distinction between the schema and
the norm]. To underline this difference from phonology, Hjelmslev created a special terminology: the linguistic element brought to light by
commutation but defined formally he called a **glosseme.** The glossemes
of expression are called **prosodemes** and **cenemes** [corresponding, respectively, to the prosodic features and to the phonemes]; those of content
are called **morphemes** [201] and **pleremes** [corresponding, respectively,
to the signifieds of the grammatical and lexical elements]. [The notion
of **taxeme,** utilized only in sporadic fashion, supplies a formal analogue
to the distinctive feature 173.])

To the extent that glossematics gives a central role to form purged of
all semantic or phonic reality, it necessarily relegates function—in particular the role of language in communication (since this role is tied to
substance)—to the background. This exclusion at the same time allows
natural languages to be brought together with a host of languages that
are functionally and materially very different. When carried out in a
sufficiently abstract fashion, then, the study of natural languages can
lead, as Saussure hoped, to a general study of languages (semiology).
Hjelmslev thus proposes a global typology of languages based on their
formal properties. If a language is defined by the existence of two levels,
we shall describe as a **conformal language** one in which the two levels
have exactly the same formal organization and differ only in substance.
(This would be the case for the natural languages if their fundamental
units were signs. It is the case for the formal systems of mathematicians,
according to Hjelmslev's image of them; for him, their elements and
their relations are always in a biunivocal correspondence with those of
their semantic interpretations.) Among the nonconformal languages, we
shall call **denotative languages** those in which neither of the two levels
is in itself a language (an example would be the natural languages, in
their customary usage). If the level of content is a language in its own
right, we shall be dealing with a **metalanguage** (for example, the technical
language used for the description of natural languages). Finally, if it
is the level of expression that is a language in its own right, we are confronting a **connotative language.** Connotation is found in fact, in Hjelmslev's view, when the signifying element is the actual utilization of a
given language. When Stendhal uses an Italian word, the signifier is

not simply the term employed, but the fact that in order to express a certain idea, the author decided to take recourse to Italian, which recourse has as its signified a certain idea of passion and of liberty that is linked, for Stendhal, to Italy. The natural languages, in their literary usage, provide a ready example of connotative language, since in this usage the signifier is less the word chosen than the fact of having chosen it. The counterpart of Hjelmslev's efforts toward abstraction is thus a considerable enlargement of the linguistic field, from which enlargement all of modern semiology has profited.

● Hjelmslev's principal works are *Prolegomena to a Theory of Language*, trans. F. J. Whitfield, rev. ed. (Madison, 1961); *Language: An Introduction*, trans. F. J. Whitfield (Madison, 1970); *Essais linguistiques*, a collection of articles written in French (Copenhagen, 1959). An essay in applied glossematics, somewhat blended with distributionalism, is offered in K. Togeby, *Structure immanente de la langue française*, 2d ed. (Paris, 1965). Important commentaries are found in A. Martinet, "Au sujet des fondements de la théorie linguistique de L. Hjelmslev," *Bulletin de la société de linguistique* 43 (1946): 19–42; Siertsema, *A Study of Glossematics* (The Hague, 1953); and a review of the English translation of the *Prolegomena* by P. L. Garvin, in *Language* 30 (1954): 69–96. *Langages* 6 (1967), ed. K. Togeby, is devoted to Hjelmslev's heritage in Denmark. The opposition of form and substance was at the center of numerous linguistic discussions until 1960; among the most interesting texts is C. E. Bazell, *Linguistic Form* (Istanbul, 1953). For Culioli's approach to formal semantics, see "La Formalisation en linguistique," in *Les Cahiers pour l'analyse* 9 (July 1968).

FUNCTIONALISM

One innovation of Saussurian linguistics was to declare essential to language its role as an instrument of communication, a role that the comparatists had considered, on the contrary, a cause of degeneration. Taking this declaration as their point of departure, certain of Saussure's successors—often called **functionalists**—regard the study of a language as the pursuit of the functions fulfilled by the elements, classes, and mechanisms that enter into it. (N.B. The consideration of function leads to the idea that to study a language state independently of all historical considerations may have an explanatory value and not merely a descriptive one.)

This functionalist tendency appears in particular in the method of investigating phonic phenomena that was first defined, under the name of phonology, by N. S. Trubetzkoy and developed principally by A. Martinet, R. Jakobson, and what is known as the Prague school. (On the differences between Martinet and Jakobson, see below, pp. 173ff.) What is the essential function in communication of the elementary sounds whose combination constitutes the spoken chain? The sounds in themselves do not bear meaning (the sound [a] of the French *bas* ["low"] has no meaning when it is isolated), although they are capable of taking on meaning (cf. the [a] of the preposition *à* ["to"]). Thus their function is above all to allow the distinction of units that in themselves are meaningful: the [a] of *bas* permits us to distinguish this word from *bu* ("drunk"), *beau* ("beautiful"), *boue* ("mud"), and so on, and it has been selected only in order to make these distinctions possible. This remark, however elementary, has important consequences. It provides the linguist with a principle of abstraction: the physical characteristics that appear in a given instance when the sound [a] is pronounced do not all have this distinctive value; that is, their choice is not always guided by an intention to communicate. For example, whether [a] is pronounced short or long, in the front or in the rear of the buccal cavity (anterior [a] or posterior [a]), it so happens that in contemporary French the identity of the word in which this [a] appears is unchanged. (This has not always been the case: there used to be a recognized distinction between *bas* and *bât* ("pack") according to the pronunciation of the [a].) On the other hand, the proximity of [b] imposes upon the [a] certain features that occur also in the [u] of *bu* and that, since they are obligatory (in French at least), do not correspond to an intention to communicate. Functionalism leads then to the isolation of those phonetic features physically present in a given pronunciation that have a distinctive value, that is, of those that are chosen to permit the communication of information. These alone are regarded as phonologically pertinent.

In order to specify these features, phonologists have elaborated the method known as **commutation.** Taking as an example the study of the French [a], we begin with a particular pronunciation of a word that contains this [a] (a pronunciation of *bas*, for example). Then we vary, in all possible phonetic directions, the sound pronounced in this word. Certain sounds substituted here for the initial pronunciation do not lead to confusion with another word; that is, they do not commute with it (nor, in consequence, among themselves). Conversely, certain sounds lead to the perception of the signs *beau, bu,* and so on; these sounds commute with the initial pronunciation. We repeat the operation on the other signs containing the sound [a] (such as *table* and *car*), and we make the observation—which was unforeseeable and constitutes an empirical justification of the method—that there is a whole set of pronunciations that do not commute in any sign. The set is called the phoneme /a/, its elements are labeled variants of /a/, and the features that differentiate them are regarded as *nondistinctive*; the nondistinctive features that are imposed by context (imposed by the proximity of the sound [b], for example) we call **redundant,** and the others are known as *free variants* [172] (for example, the pronunciations of /a/ that differ only in length). The phonic characteristics existing in all the variants of /a/, which therefore distinguish any pronunciation of /a/ from a pronunciation of /o/, /u/, /p/, and so on, are all retained as *distinctive.* (For further details on these notions, see below, pp. 171ff.)

Starting from the Saussurian principle that the elements of language must be studied according to their function in communication, phonologists thus arrive at the point of applying a second Saussurian principle, that of opposition [19], according to which any given linguistic entity is constituted only by that which distinguishes it from another. Concerning this trend of thought, the following observations are pertinent:

a) It is absent from the work of the Polish writer J. N. Baudouin de Courtenay, a body of work often regarded as the precursor of phonology. In studying the elementary language sounds in terms of their function in communication, Baudoin de Courtenay concluded that one must examine above all the way in which they are perceived (rather than their physical reality). Now this abstraction is not equivalent to the phonological abstraction; it has even been possible to show that the characteristics that are perceived can be distinguished from the differential characteristics of these elementary sounds (the former contain features lacking in the latter, and vice versa).

b) The units studied by phonologists are in fact distinctive units (units that serve to distinguish meaning-bearing units—words, for example—from each other); thus it is not surprising that the functional aspect should be the one in which these units differ among themselves. The passage from the functional principle to the oppositional may well be less self-evident if we study units that are themselves meaning-bearing (that is, signs) and even less so if we study strictly semantic units.

c) Even the purely phonic elements of language can have other than distinctive functions. This is the case for redundant features, which can facilitate the correct identification of the message in the case of faulty transmission (in the terminology of information theory, they provide protection against **noise**). This is also the case for numerous prosodic phenomena [176ff.], and thus it is inevitable that the nondistinctive phonic features have a nonetheless indispensable function in communication.

● On the phonological method, see the bibliography on p. 172. On its theoretical foundations, see K. Bühler, "Phonetik und Phonologie," *Travaux du Cercle Linguistique de Prague* 4 (1931): 22–53; and L. Prieto, "La Découverte du Phonème," *La Pensée* 148 (1969): 35–53. Prieto's interpretation of the phonological discovery is taken up again in chapter 5 of his *Pertinence et pratique* (Paris, 1975).

G. Gougenheim has attempted to apply to grammatical description the principles of phonological functionalism. His basic idea is that in order to define the function of a given grammatical element (person, tense, mood, conjunction, preposition, and so on), it is necessary to compare it with the other grammatical elements of the language, since the speaker chooses it in relation to them and since this choice alone plays a role in communication. Gougenheim calls all coupled grammatical elements oppositions, and among these he distinguishes three types, according to the phonological trichotomy (see above, p. 26). In certain cases the choice of one of the two elements is imposed (in French, the indicative is imposed after *Je sais que*, the subjunctive after *Je veux que*; hence there is **grammatical constraint** (cf. phonological redundancy [26]). In other cases both elements are possible, and a choice of one over the other introduces no differences in meaning (in contemporary spoken French, for "If you come and I'm here," one has the option of saying "Si tu viens et que je sois [subjunctive] là" or "Si tu viens et que je suis [indicative] là"); this is **stylistic variation** (cf. what phonologists call free variation [26]). Finally, the choice may introduce a difference of meaning (cf. "Je cherche un livre qui a été écrit [indicative] au XVIᵉ siècle" ["I am looking for a book—a particular book—that was written in the sixteenth century; I know that this book exists, but I do not know where to find it" and "Je cherche un livre qui ait été écrit [subjunctive] au XVIᵉ siècle" ["I am looking for a book—any book at all—that was written in the sixteenth century, but I am not certain that such a book can be found"]): here we have **opposition of meaning** (cf. distinctive differences [26]). According to Gougenheim, only these latter oppositions allow us to define the meaning of the morphemes studied (just as the distinctive features alone define the phonemes).

On the basis of these examples, it is easy to see the difficulty that arises when one attempts to extend to the significative units the concepts elaborated by phonologists with reference to the distinctive units. One can readily accept the radical distinction between the features of the [a] of *bas* that depend on the proximity of [b] and those that are phonologically distinctive. But can one admit the same separation between the constraint that imposes the subjunctive after "Je veux que" and the free choice of this mood in "Je cherche un livre qui ait été écrit au XVIᵉ siècle"? Here dependency and free choice seem to have the same basis (the notion of uncertainty linked to the subjunctive), and one cannot explain the function of the "free" subjunctive without also indicating the situations in which it is required. It should be noted that E. Benveniste, studying the middle voice in ancient Greek, drew his conclusions by and large from the verbs in which that voice is necessary (that is, in which there is neither an active nor a passive voice). Thus in grammatical description the functionalist concern does not lead to the principle of opposition and differential value as directly as it did in phonology.

Similarly, when a phonologist such as A. Martinet undertakes to construct a functional syntax, he introduces analytical principles that have no counterpart in phonology. He recognizes, for example, that every utterance has as its function the communication of an experience (by analyzing and schematizing it) and that as a result, it is constituted by a predicate (designating the process that the speaker posits as central in this experience), which may be accompanied by a series of complements (including the subject) each type of which has as its function the contribution of a particular type of information concerning the process [210]. Now these functions usually cannot be established by commutation. For example, most of the expressions that can fulfill the role of temporal complement cannot fulfill that of spatial complement; there is thus no point in asking whether these two functions commute or not. (The same holds true of course for the subject-function and the predicate-function.) Thus functionalism in grammar does not lead readily to the rediscovery of the Saussurian axiom that "in a language, there are only differences."

- On Martinet's functional grammar, see below, pp. 213ff. G. Gougenheim's principal text in his *Système grammatical de la langue française* (Paris, 1938); it is discussed in G. Barnicaud et al., "Le Problème de la négation dans diverses grammaires françaises," *Langages* 7 (1967): 58–73. E. Benveniste's study of the middle voice is found in *Problems in General Linguistics*, trans. M. E. Meek (Coral Gables, 1971), chap. 14, esp. p. 147. On the research of the Prague school, in which the methods of phonology are applied m other areas, see J. Vachek, ed., *A Prague School Reader in Linguistics* (Bloomington and London, 1964; and idem, the very useful *Dictionnaire de linguistique de l'école de Prague* (Antwerp and Utrecht, 1966).

The same thing can be said of semantics. Certain linguists have tried to introduce into semantics the methods of phonology almost unchanged. Thus Prieto thought that commutation could be applied to the meaning as well as to the phonic aspect of a language (Hjelmslev had had this same idea). Let us call **message** the total information communicated by an utterance in given circumstances. Thus in some circumstances the utterance "Give it back to me" serves to communicate the message "You are ordered to give back the speaker's pencil." The linguist must then ask himself what role the utterance itself (considered independently of the circumstances) played in the communication of this message. It is in such a case as this that Prieto takes recourse to commutation, but instead of varying the phonic manifestation, as one would do in phonology, he varies the message and notes the modifications that would require a material change in the utterance. The substitution of the idea of a notepad or a book for that of the pencil would not require such a change. *Pencil* is thus a nondistinctive linguistic element of the message. On the other hand, the idea that a single object has been requested is distinctive, since its replacement by the idea of plurality would require that the *it* be replaced by *them*. The distinctive features— and these alone, according to Prieto—are attached to the utterance itself, not directly, by the messages it is capable of transmitting, but by the difference between these messages and those of other utterances. It should be noted that the application of the commutational method leads Prieto to represent each utterance as a "bundle" of distinctive characteristics that, like the distinctive features of the phonemes, are independent of each other. Now it is clear that the function of an utterance depends on the way in which its semantic elements are interrelated. In attempting to define this semantic organization, however, Prieto must fall back on notions that are no longer based on commutation; thus in addition to distinctive features, he identifies **contrastive features,** which express the point of view according to which the distinctive feature is envisaged. In the utterance of "Give it back to me," he will posit a unit *singular* (*object*), in which the expression in parentheses is a contrastive feature indicating that the characteristic *singular* pertains to the object of the verb. Now it is difficult to see what commutation would bring that element to light. Here again, functionalism and the principle of opposition converge only momentarily.

● L. Prieto, *Principes de noologie* (The Hague, 1964). The same ideas are presented in simplified fashion in his *Messages et signaux* (Paris, 1966). They are integrated into a general theory of ideology in his *Pertinence et pratique* (Paris, 1975).

Their separation appears even more sharply in the "functional linguistics" defined by H. Frei, one of Saussure's students. Frei seeks to describe not language itself so much as the functioning of language, that is, the way it is utilized in reality at a given historical moment. For this reason he studies not only the language that is considered correct but also "everything which is out of harmony with the traditional language: errors, innovations, popular language, slang, unusual or disputable cases, grammatical perplexities, etc." In fact he is especially interested in these deviations, to the extent that they reveal what the speaking subject expects from the language and fails to find there; thus deviations serve as indicators pointing to the needs that govern the exercise of speech. The principal linguistic needs tend to be the following:

a) Assimilation. The need for assimilation leads speakers to standardize both the system of signs (which produces analogical creation [13ff.]) and the elements that are related sequentially in discourse (for example, the phenomenon of grammatical agreement).

b) Differentiation. In order to ensure clarity, speakers tend to distinguish phonically the signs that have different meanings, to distinguish semantically the signs that have different phonic realities, and to introduce separations in the spoken chain.

c) Brevity. The need for brevity is the cause of ellipses, innuendos, and the creation of compound words (which avoid syntactic liaisons).

d) Invariability. The need for invariability leads speakers to give the same form, insofar as possible, to a given sign, whatever the grammatical function of that sign may be.

e) Expressivity. The speaker seeks to stamp his discourse with his own personality, notwithstanding the objectivity of the code. This gives rise to a perpetual invention of figures [273] and a constant distortion of signs and locutions, by which means the speaking subject convinces himself that he is repossessing the common language.

All of these (often incompatible) functions, which according to Frei explain not only the errors but also numerous aspects of "correct usage" (constituted by the errors of an earlier period), lead linguistics much farther away from the framework proposed by Saussure than did Martinet's grammar or Prieto's semantics. They even thrust into the background the systematic character of language that Saussure considered essential. This is doubtless due to the difficulty linguists experience in distinguishing, once they have begun to enumerate the functions of language, between those functions that are exercised *on the occasion* of the communicative act and those that are linked to it of necessity (see below, pp. 339ff.).

● H. Frei's principal work is *La Grammaire des fautes* (Bellegarde, 1929). He draws upon ideas already formulated by another of Saussure's students, C. Bally, in *Le Langage et la vie* (Paris, 1926).

DISTRIBUTIONALISM

At the same time that the work of Saussure was beginning to be known in Europe, the American L. Bloomfield (initially a specialist in the Indo-European languages) proposed his own general theory of language. Developed and systematized by his students under the name **distributionalism,** Bloomfield's theory dominated American linguistics up to 1950. This theory manifests not only some flagrant differences from Saussure's but also a number of similarities, especially with the formalist, glossematic interpretation of Saussurianism [21ff.].

Antimentalism

Bloomfieldian linguistics took as its point of departure the behaviorist psychology that had been dominant in the United States since 1920. A speech act is only an instance of behavior of a particular type—according to Bloomfield's apologue, language is the possibility that Jill, seeing an apple, may ask Jack to pick it instead of doing it herself. Now, behaviorism maintains that human conduct is totally explicable (that is, predictable) on the basis of the situations in which it occurs, independently of all "internal" factors. Bloomfield concludes from this that speech must also be explained by the external conditions surrounding its production. He calls this thesis **mechanism,** and he opposes it to **mentalism,** according to which speech must be explained as an effect of the thoughts (intentions, beliefs, feelings) of the speaking subject; this latter view is inadmissible in Bloomfield's eyes. As a preliminary to his mechanistic explanation of speech—an explanation that cannot be immediately achieved—Bloomfield requests that linguists content themselves for the time being with describing speech acts (hence a descriptivism that is opposed both to the historicism of the neogrammarians [13] and to functionalism [24]). So that the description of speech acts will not be influenced by prejudices that would render eventual explanation impossible, Bloomfield asks that it be undertaken apart from any mentalist considerations and in particular that it avoid alluding to the meaning of the spoken words.

● In addition to numerous technical articles, Bloomfield's works include three essential theoretical works: *Introduction to the Study of Language* (London, 1914), written when he was still under the influence of classical psychology; *Language* (New York, 1933), in which he presents his most original theses; and *Linguistic Aspects of Science* (Chicago, 1939), in which he makes a linguistic contribution to neopositivism.

Distributional Analysis

To study a language, then, is more than anything else to gather as varied as possible a set of utterances produced by users of the language at a given historical period (this set is known as the **corpus**). Then without inquiring into the meaning of the utterances, one attempts to bring to light certain regularities in the corpus, so that the product will be an orderly and systematic description, not simply an inventory. Since recourse to function and meaning are ruled out, the only notion on which this search for regularities can be based is that of linear context, or **environment**. To indicate the environment of a unit a_1 in an utterance U is to indicate the series of units $a_1, a_2, \ldots, a_{i-1}$, which precedes it in E, and the series $a_{i+1}, a_{i+2}, \ldots, a_n$, which follows it. The notion of **expansion** is defined on this basis. Let b be a segment (unit or a series of units) of the utterance U. We will say that b is an expansion of c if: (1) c is a segment of another utterance U' of the corpus, (2) c is not more complex than b (that is, c is composed of as many or of fewer units), (3) the substitution of c for b in U produces another utterance U'' belonging to the corpus (b and c thus have a common environment). The environment also serves to define the **distribution** of a unit, that is, the set of environments in which the unit is encountered in the corpus. (The fundamental role of this notion led linguists associated with Bloomfield, particularly Wells and Harris at the beginning of their work, to call themselves distributionalists.)

From the preceding notions, the distributionalist draws, first, a method for decomposing the utterances of the corpus, or in the conventional terminology, for breaking them down into their **immediate constituents** (abbreviated IC). This analysis, which leads the distributionalist to attribute a hierarchical construction to the sentence, consists in first decomposing the utterance into a few rather large segments, called its IC, then in subdividing each of the latter into subsegments, known as the IC of the IC, and so on until the minimal units are reached.

Take for example the analysis of the utterance U "The President of the United States has opened the World Series."

a) We note that there also exists in the corpus the utterance "George gossips," whose analysis is evident (since there are only two units). We seek then to determine which segments of U are expansions of *George* and of *gossips*. These are, respectively, *The President of the United States* and *has opened the World Series,* since we also find in the corpus "George has opened the World Series" and "The President of the United States gossips." Thus we obtain a first segmentation into two IC: "The President of the United States / has opened the World Series."

b) Next we decompose the first IC by comparing it, for example, with the segment *my neighbor*, whose elements are evident. We see then that *the* is an expansion of *my*, and *neighbor* of *President of the United States*. From this we obtain a new breakdown: "The / President of the United States."

c) The comparison of *President of the United States* with *representative-elect* leads to a new segmentation: "President / of the United States," and so on.

The final analysis can be represented by the following schema, in which each box represents an IC and can itself contain other boxes:

A second task for distributionalists preoccupied with ordering the corpus is to arrive at a classification of the IC. To this end, they attempt to regroup all the IC with identical distributions, in order to obtain **distributional classes;** but this task is complicated by the fact that two segments with exactly the same distribution are rarely found in a corpus, so that the linguist must decide which distributional differences to neglect and which to retain. In traditional. linguistics this decision is based on functional or semantic criteria. These criteria, which the distributionalist cannot use, would allow us to deem it important that after *has opened* we find *the World Series, the door,* or *the road,* and not *easy* or *beautiful*; and less important that where we find *the door,* we rarely find *the chair, the stick, the song.* In order to establish distributional classes, we must thus proceed in stages. For a first, very broad series of classes, we will require only that they be related by rules of the following type: for every element of the class *A*, we find at least one element of the class *B* such that their juxtaposition constitutes an IC in the corpus— and vice versa (with the stipulation that the IC obtained must all be of the same nature distributionally). In other words, we constitute classes such that there are regularities in their mutual combination, but not necessarily in the combination of their elements (i.e., for every element of class *A* there is an element of class *B* such that their combination produces an element of class *C*, and conversely, but all elements of *A* are not necessarily combinable with all elements of *B*). In a second stage, we shall subdivide, according to the same principle, the main classes that we have previously obtained. Let us look again at the preceding classes *A* and *B*. We shall subdivide them, respectively, into A_1 and A_2, B_1 and B_2, in such a way as to allow every element of A_1 to be associated with at least one element of B_1, and vice versa; we shall do the same for A_2 and B_2. Then we shall begin the operation again with A_1, A_2, B_1, B_2, and so on. (N.B. The actual procedure is much more complicated, particularly when the distributional properties of the IC obtained by joining the elements of *A* and of *B* are taken into account.)

Certain distributionalists believe that by rendering this procedure rigorously explicit, one would be able to make it automatic and thus to define a **discovery procedure** that would mechanically produce a grammatical description based on a corpus. The postulate of this method is that when one pursues, stage by stage, the process of subdivision, one arrives at classes that are increasingly homogeneous from the distributional viewpoint. In other words, the elements of the classes obtained at a given stage resemble each other more, in terms of their distribution, than they resemble the elements of the classes obtained at the preceding stage, so that the whole process leads, with a constantly improved approximation, toward the rigorous specification of distributional classes. For Harris, to admit this postulate is to attribute to language a **distributional structure.** In order to refute the existence of such a structure, one would thus have to observe that from a given stage onward no new subdivision can improve the approximation and that an improvement would require the abolition of subdivisions made at a preceding stage and would thus necessitate the regrouping of previously separated elements.

- On the distributionalist principles, see Z. S. Harris, "Distributional Structure," *Word* 10 (1954): 146–162; and W. P. Lehmann, *Descriptive Linguistics: An Introduction* (New York, 1972). On the method, see Z. S. Harris, *Methods in Structural Linguistics* (1951; reprint ed., *Structural Linguistics* [Chicago, 1960]). On IC analysis, see R. S. Well, "Immediate Constituents," *Language* 23 (1947): 81–117; cf. also H. A. Gleason, *An Introduction to Descriptive Linguistics*, rev. ed. (New York, 1961). The most important texts of the distributionalist school are found in M. Joos ed., *Readings in Linguistics I: The Development of Descriptive Linguistics in America, 1925–1956,* 4th ed. (Chicago, 1966).

Distributionalism and Saussurianism

From the viewpoint of Saussurian linguistics, distributionalism raises certain difficulties, of which the most frequently observed concerns the specification of units. For Saussure, the elements are never given, and their discovery is one with the discovery of the system [16ff.]. A distributional study, on the other hand, seems to imply by definition a prior knowledge of the elements: in order to establish the distribution of a unit, it is necessary to have identified this unit (that is, to have delimited it [17] in the spoken chain and to be capable of recognizing it [18] throughout its diverse occurrences) and to have specified as well the units that constitute its environment. Part of the difficulty disappears, to be sure, if the search for distributional classes is preceded by a breakdown into IC, for such an analysis, which depends upon elementary distributional criteria (the study of certain particular environments), allows for the demarcation of the segments, whose distribution can then be studied more closely. The following observations must be made, however:

a) The technique of IC analysis is not well-suited to the demarcation of units smaller than the word. And if one attempts, by means of minor alterations in the analysis, to adapt it to the problem of the segmentation of words, one runs the risk of imposing segmentations that a Saussurian would reject because of their semantically debatable character. Thus, once the customary segmentation *dis-charge* is allowed, an analysis into IC seems to impose the segmentation *re-pel*. (It is easy to find an utterance in which *repel* may be replaced by *discharge*, and one can then say that *re* is an expansion [32] of *dis*, since there exists *dispel*, and that *pel* is an expansion of *charge*, since there exists *recharge*.) And we would arrive at the same analysis of *dispute, distort*, and *dissent*.

b) Analysis into IC does not help in the identification of the occurrences of a given unit. To be sure, in order to make up for this deficiency, linguists have elaborated distributional methods allowing for the identification of: (1) the variants of a single phoneme (in French, the /a/ of *bas* and that of *la*); and (2) the various manifestations of a single significant element (the *in* of *indistinct* and the *i* of *immobile* [see below, allophones, p. 172, and allomorphs, p. 201]). But these methods, difficult to utilize, can hardly do more than justify the decisions made on the basis of other criteria. Moreover, they do not apply very well to the case in which a single phonic realization seems, for semantic reasons, to belong to different units (will it be shown that there is the same or a different *re-* in *repose* and *report*?).

Furthermore, these difficulties pertaining to the specification of units fail to eliminate—indeed, they actually reinforce—the analogy between distributionalism and certain aspects of Saussurian linguistics, glossematics in particular. For Hjelmslev, as for the distributionalists, what characterizes a language is a set of combinatorial regularities, the acceptance of certain associations and the rejection of others; one can even find fairly specific resemblances between the combinatorial glossematic relationships [109] and those that govern IC analysis or the constitution of distributional classes. Two major differences remain nonetheless:

a) Hjelmslevian formalism is concerned both with the level of expression and with the level of content [20]. Distributional formalism, however, is concerned only with the former; it is thus formal, not only in the mathematical sense, but also in the trivial sense that it is concerned only with the perceptible form of language.

b) Contrary to the distributional combinatorial, Hjelmslev's, since it must be applied also in the semantic realm, is not linear; it is not concerned with the way in which the units are juxtaposed in space or in time, but with the possibility that they may coexist within units of a higher level.

It is significant that among Saussure's disciples, the opposition between the glossematicians and the functionalists has its correlative in the American school, namely, in the opposition between Pike's theory of **tagmemics** and strict distributionalism. According to Pike, a description of a human event can be approached from either of two points of view. The **etic** consists in refusing all hypotheses concerning the function of the events being reported and in characterizing them only by means of spatio-temporal criteria. The **emic,** on the contrary, consists in interpreting events according to their particular function in the particular cultural world to which they belong. (N.B. The adjectives *etic* and *emic* were created from the suffixes of the adjectives *phonetic* and *phonemic*.) According to Pike, distributionalism is an example of an etic, or exterior, point of view on language; for this reason, it can provide no more than a point of departure for description. In order to choose among the multiple rules and classifications that are equally acceptable from the distributionalist viewpoint, it is necessary to superimpose on it an emic study, which would characterize the units by the function that the speaking subject gives them. A detailed study would uncover in the opposition between Pike and Harris most of the arguments invoked in the controversy between phonology and glossematics.

● K. L. Pike's early theoretical works include *Phonetics* (Ann Arbor, 1943) and *Phonemics* (Ann Arbor, 1947); a more recent work is *Language in Relation to a Unified Theory of Human Behavior*, 2d ed., rev. (The Hague, 1967). Pike's work has been applied to French by E. Roulet in *Syntaxe de la proposition nucléaire en français parlé* (Brussels, 1969). Pike has prepared an annotated bibliography of tagmemic studies, "A Guide to Publications Related to Tagmemic Theory," in *Current Trends in Linguistics*, ed. T. A. *Sebeok*, 14 vols. (The Hague, 1963–76), vol. 3, *Theoretical Foundations* (1966), pp. 365–94. Pike's most important articles have been reissued in R. M. Brend, ed., *Kenneth L. Pike: Selected Writings* (The Hague, 1972). For a general study of tagmemics, see V. G.

Waterhause, *The History and Development of Tagmemics* (The Hague, 1975). On the problem of segmentation, from the distributional point of view, see Z. S. Harris, "From Phoneme to Morpheme," *Language* 31 (1955): 190–220. For a Saussurian critique of Harris, see H. Frei, "Critères de délimitation," *Word* 10 (1954): 136–45.

GENERATIVE LINGUISTICS

Generative Linguistics and Distributionalism

At the outset a student of Z. S. Harris, the linguist who pushed distributionalism [31ff.] to its most extreme consequences, the American N. Chomsky was himself for a time interested in the formalization (in the logico-mathematical sense of the term) of the fundamental distributionalist notions. He has since proposed a new conception of linguistics that he calls **generative;** this conception contradicts the distributionalist dogmas and has rapidly replaced them as the basis for American linguistic research.

Chomsky seeks to retain distributionalism's explicit character. Distributionalism is **explicit** in the sense that the descriptions of languages to which it leads do not allow any notion whose comprehension implies prior knowledge either of the language being described or of language in general to serve as an elementary (that is, undefined) concept. The basic concept of distributionalism—the notion of environment, in which a given unit, in a given utterance, is surrounded by certain other units— is comprehensible even for someone who, to take an absurd hypothesis, might have no personal experience of speech. Herein lies, for Chomsky, the superiority of distributionalism over the traditional grammars and over the linguistics known as functionalism [24], all of which take recourse to notions such as dependence (according to which a certain word refers to a certain other word), the subject-function (according to which a given word represents that about which we are speaking), and so on, notions whose comprehension is an integral part of the linguistic faculty and which therefore cannot be utilized, without a vicious circle, to describe that faculty.

But Chomsky accuses distributionalism of achieving its explicit character at the price of totally unacceptable exclusions. First, it excessively limits the empirical domain that is its object. A language, after all, is not the same as a corpus [32].

a) Whereas a corpus is by definition a finite set of utterances, all languages make possible an infinite number of utterances: since there is no limit to the number of clauses that one can introduce into an English sentence, one can create from any utterance in English (by adding, for example, a relative clause) another whose construction is just as regular. Distributionalism is condemned by its method to ignore this infinitizing power included in every language.

b) Even more important is the fact that a language is not simply a set of utterances (finite or infinite) but a whole body of knowledge concerning these utterances. It will not be said of someone that he knows a language if he is incapable of distinguishing ambiguous utterances from those admitting of only one interpretation, if he does not recognize that certain utterances have similar syntactic constructions and others have very different constructions, and so on. The distributionalists deliberately exclude from their descriptive field this knowledge on the part of speaking subjects concerning their own language, and they content themselves with describing the way in which units are combined in utterances (see, below, Chomsky's notion of competence, pp. 120ff.).

Even if we were to accept this reduction of the domain to be described (we cannot presume to describe everything), there is a second limitation for which Chomsky reproaches the distributionalists, namely, their satisfaction with description, their refusal to explain. In this respect Bloomfield's successors would be faithful to an empirical conception according to which science has only to describe phenomena, while seeking to introduce a bit of order into their apparent disorder; the essential task of the researcher would then be classification, or **taxonomy.** We have here in fact the sole objective of the distributionalists, for whom a grammar is simply a classification of the segments (phonemes, morphemes, words, word groups) that appear in the utterances of the corpus. To the extent that the principle of this classification is the regrouping of elements with identical (or similar) distribution [32], it can be regarded, in Harris's words, as a "compact description" of the corpus; thus once one is in possession of this classification, one should in fact be able to reconstitute all the utterances of the corpus with no difficulty. According to Chomsky, on the contrary, every developing science eventually establishes a more ambitious goal than description and classification. The same must hold true for linguistics, which can presume to present hypotheses with explanatory value concerning the faculty that is at the origin of linguistic activity. It does not suffice to point out—

even "compactly"—which utterances are possible and which impossible, which ones are ambiguous, which are syntactically related to each other, and so on, but it is necessary to be able to relate all these details to an overall conception of language. It was in order to reconcile the concern for being explicit with that of being explanatory that Chomsky was led to propose a new definition of the nature of grammar and of linguistic theory.

Generative Grammar

What does the syntactic description (or **generative grammar**) of a particular language comprise, according to Chomsky? It comprises a set of rules—of instructions—whose mechanical application produces the acceptable (that is, grammatical) utterances of that language, and those utterances alone. (On the notion of acceptable utterances, see below, pp. 127ff.; for the rules in detail, see pp. 226ff.) The automatic character of the grammar ensures that it will be explicit. In order to understand a grammar, which is a kind of formal system (in the logician's sense), nothing more is needed than a knowledge of how to carry out the (entirely elementary) manipulations prescribed by the rules (they consist essentially in replacing one symbol with another). It is precisely because the grammar does not presuppose on the part of its user any linguistic knowledge whatsoever that it can be considered a total description of the language.

In order for a grammar, understood in this sense, to be **adequate,** two requirements must be met:

a) The grammar must generate all the utterances of the language and those alone, without exception. When this requirement is met, we have **observational adequacy.** According to Chomsky, this is weak adequacy, since for a given language a multitude of different grammars can achieve it. What makes it even weaker is that numerous utterances are neither clearly acceptable nor clearly unacceptable, and thus we have to allow, at this level, both the grammars that generate them and those that exclude them.

b) It must be possible to represent, in this grammar, the intuitive knowledge that speaking subjects possess concerning the utterances of their language; in other words, it must be possible to express this knowledge in terms of generative mechanisms. Thus in the process of derivation a formal device is needed to indicate the ambiguity of an utterance (Chomsky requires, for example, that each ambiguous utterance be derived in as many different ways as it has meanings). To take another example, if two utterances are felt to be syntactically close to each other, this ought to be visible in a simple comparison of the way in which they are derived (Chomsky requires, for example, that the processes that generate them be identical up to a certain point). A grammar answering this requirement will be termed **descriptively adequate** (the term "strong adequacy" is also used).

N.B. (*a*) To require this strong adequacy was, for Chomsky, to abandon the distributionalist ambition of establishing mechanizable procedures for the discovery of grammars [34], procedures that would construct grammars on the basis of corpuses. It is clear in fact that the type of data governing strong adequacy—data concerning the intuition of the speaking subjects—is not directly discernible by a machine; the grammar thus can only be discovered by the actual work of the grammarian, which does not make it impossible that, once discovered, the grammar might consist in an automatic procedure of sentence production. (*b*) Although a generative grammar is an (abstract) machine producing sentences, Chomsky does not assume that the speaking subject produces a sentence according to the procedure by which a sentence is generated in generative grammar. Generative grammar is not a production model for the sentences of everyday discourse (in which, undoubtedly, many other factors intervene). Generative grammar simply provides—and Chomsky insists on this point—a mathematical characterization of a competence possessed by the users of a given language (and not a psychological model of their activity). However, in requiring that the rules that produce sentences and those that represent ambiguity be the same and furthermore that this representation be fairly "natural" (like the one that gives an ambiguous sentence as many derivations as it has meanings), Chomsky was opening the door to the psychological interpretation that assimilates the generative processes defined in the grammar to the cerebral mechanisms involved in the production of sentences. If in fact this interpretation is being abandoned, why not choose the most arbitrary modes of representation?

Linguistic Theory

Even strong adequacy leaves the possibility of several grammars for a single language; and thus there is the problem of choice. This is a problem that linguistic theory must help to resolve. One can in fact classify grammars according to the mechanisms they use to generate sentences, or more precisely, according to the form of the rules that they include (on this classification, see below, pp. 226ff.). Chomsky calls each of the principal types of grammars a **linguistic theory.** A linguistic theory is thus a sort of mold that serves to fabricate grammars. It goes without saying that if we had reasons to choose one theory over another, we could make a rigorous selection among the grammars possible for a given language, since these are often very different in form. What then are the major requirements that an **adequate** theory must satisfy?

1. For each language, it must be possible to construct, on the model of this theory, a grammar that is both descriptively and observationally adequate. This condition is not sufficient, however, for a universal theory may authorize several different grammars for a given language. We shall therefore add another requirement:

2. One must be able to associate to the theory a mechanizable procedure allowing, for each language, an evaluation of the different grammars that conform to the theory; this would aid in choosing among them. It is furthermore essential that this evaluation not be arbitrary. Thus we arrive at the following criterion:

3. Let G_1 and G_2 be two grammars of a language L, in conformity with the theory T, both possessing observational adequacy. It is necessary that the evaluation procedure associated with T give precedence (based on the simple examination of G_1 and G_2 and thus *independently of all considerations of descriptive adequacy*) to the one that shows itself to be, in other respects, more descriptively adequate; this must hold true for all the grammars of type T and for all languages. Thus the theory must be capable, so to speak, of "guessing" the grammar that best represents the intuitions of the speaking subject. Let us suppose that a theory T satisfies this third criterion (since to date too few languages have been described in generative terms for verification to be possible at present, the criterion simply provides a long-term perspective for the elaboration of linguistic theory); one would then attribute to T the adequacy termed **explanatory.**

Let us attempt to specify, departing perhaps from Chomsky's text (he is not entirely explicit on this point), why one can label "explanatory" the theory that satisfies the preceding criterion (for the purpose of simplification, we will suppose that such a theory exists, and we shall designate it by the symbol TT). TT allows us to understand certain characteristics of particular languages; once TT has been discovered, these characteristics in fact appear to be necessary consequences of a universal linguistic faculty, innate in all human beings. In order to demonstrate this, it is necessary to bring to light two points: (1) that one can deduce on the basis of TT certain characteristics of the particular languages; and (2) that TT represents a linguistic faculty inscribed (before any actual social communication) in human nature.

Let us begin with the second point. The child who learns his mother tongue proceeds, according to Chomsky, with the construction of a generative grammar: he creates a set of rules that generates the grammatical sentences of this language, and these alone. In order to do this, the child takes as his point of departure the sentences that he hears spoken around him (at least those that the adults present to him as acceptable). In other words, he accomplishes the same task that the linguist will undertake later; to do so, he bases his work on the material that is offered to the observation of the linguist (taking "observation" in the sense defined above, that is, as opposed to "description": we are thus to exclude feelings and linguistic intuition from the observable material).

In this work, as Chomsky conceives of it, the child has an advantage over the linguist in that he possesses a linguistic theory that is innate, an element of human nature, so that he knows *a priori* what general form he will have to give to his grammar; the linguist, for his part, has to establish a linguistic theory at the same time that he is constructing grammars. But the linguist also has an advantage: to the extent that he already speaks the language he is studying, he possesses with respect to it a whole set of intuitive knowledge, precisely the information that constitutes the object material of "description" (information that can be acquired by the child only little by little as he fabricates the grammar). A diagram will sum up these two situations:

	Child	*Linguist*
Point of departure	Set of grammatical sentences (object of observation)	Set of grammatical sentences (object of observation)
	Linguistic theory	Intuitive knowledge (object of description)
Destination	Generative grammar	Generative grammar
	Intuitive knowledge	Linguistic theory

For the child, intuitive knowledge of linguistic phenomena is constituted as a by-product of generative grammar. The child spontaneously uses a linguistic theory that, in order to generate the set of observed sentences, necessitates the construction of a certain generative grammar, and the latter is then found to provide, in return, certain information about the ambiguity of the sentences, their syntactic proximity, and so on. For the linguist, on the contrary, intuitive knowledge is a point of departure. Let us suppose now that although his objective is observational adequacy alone, the linguist manages to elaborate his generative grammars according to a theory that produces descriptive adequacy as well (in the sense that the grammars constructed account for the intuitions of the speaking subjects). In this case one can say that the theory chosen by the linguist has the same properties as the one spontaneously put into practice by the child. It therefore has, to say the least, a good chance of being in conformity with the universal faculty by means of which children develop the grammar of their own language.

The second phase of the demonstration will be much briefer. Once we have recognized that *TT* represents a real constituent of human nature, we can easily see that it has explanatory value with respect to the particular languages. In fact, in order for a linguistic theory, whatever it may be, to supply a grammar for a given language, this language must possess certain characteristics. (Thus a linguistic theory lacking in recursive symbols [230] is incapable of generating a language in which the number of grammatical sentences would be infinite.) Let us suppose then the possibility of demonstrating that a theory is based on human nature (Chomsky, as we have seen, believes that this demonstration can be made). In that case, if the natural languages possess characteristics that can be deduced from this theory, such characteristics may be regarded as explained; they appear henceforth as necessary consequences of the linguistic faculty, itself an integral part of human nature.

N.B. *a*) Certain of Chomsky's adversaries reproach him for taking recourse, in order to decide between the various possible grammars, to the old criterion of simplicity, a criterion that is hardly satisfactory, since there are numerous types of simplicity (a small number of symbols in the grammar, a small number of rules, internal simplicity of each rule). This reproach rests on a misunderstanding. The criterion of evaluation, according to Chomsky, is in fact an element of linguistic theory and must be constructed in such a way as to render this theory adequate; it therefore has nothing to do with an *a priori* requirement of simplicity.

b) It remains true that the construction of this criterion (still programmatic at present) is of vital importance for all of Chomskyan linguistics. It alone can justify the project—which is very ambitious and does not rest on any evidence—of describing phenomena such as ambiguity, syntactic proximity, and so on, in terms of generative processes.

c) In this article we have not used the word *transformation*. This is because transformationalism is but one of the possible generative theories (the one which Chomsky believes to be correct).

d) For a formal definition of the notion of transformation, see below, pp. 231ff. On the linguistic use of this notion and on the overall organization of a transformational grammar, see below, pp. 242ff., especially the diagrams on p. 245.

● There is an extensive body of literature on generative linguistics. In particular, three important works by Chomsky must be noted: *Syntactic Structures* (The Hague, 1957); *Aspects of the Theory of Syntax* (Cambridge, Mass., 1965); and *Current Issues in Linguistic Theory* (The Hague, 1964), the second chapter of which is concerned with the different types of adequacy discussed above. J. Lyons offers a rather elementary introduction in *Chomsky* (London, 1970). For a study in greater depth, see N. Ruwet, *An Introduction to Generative Grammar*, trans. N. S. H. Smith (Amsterdam, 1973), and *Langages* 14 (1969); *Tendances nouvelles en syntaxe générative*, ed. N. Ruwet; see also A. Akmajian and F. Heny, *An Introduction to the Principles of Transformational Syntax* (Cambridge, Mass., 1975). On the type of argumentation used in generative linguistics, see J. C. Milner, *Arguments linguistiques* (Paris, 1973). For applications to French, see J. Dubois, *Grammaire structurale du français*, 3 vols. (Paris, 1965–69), vols. 2, *Le Verbe* (1967), and 3, *La Phrase et les transformations* (1969); and M. Gross, *Grammaire transformationnelle du français: Syntaxe du verbe* (Paris, 1968), previously published as *Transformational Analysis of French Verbal Construction*, University of Pennsylvania Transformations and Discourse Analysis Papers, no. 64 (1968). An application to English is offered in R. P. Stockwell et al., *Major Syntactic Structures of English* (New York, 1973). A more critical viewpoint can be found in O. Ducrot, "Logique et langage," *Langages* 2 (1966): 21–28; B. Grunig, "Les théories transformationnelles," *La Linguistique* 2 (1965) and 1 (1966); B. Pottier, "La grammaire générative et la linguistique," *Travaux de linguistique et de littérature* 6, no. 1 (1968): 7–26; F. M. Uhlenbeck, *Critical Comments on Transformational-Generative Grammar* (The Hague, 1972); and G. Sampson, *The Form of Language* (London, 1975).

APPENDIX: ANCIENT AND MEDIEVAL LINGUISTICS

In the preceding section we have dealt only with recent schools. This is not because "serious" linguistics begins, in our eyes, with Port-Royal. On the contrary, we would judge in fact, that the work of linguists in every period consists above all in integrating previous discoveries into a new conceptual system. However, we did not consider it possible to present in a few pages a theoretical synthesis of Hindu, Greek, Latin, and medieval linguistic research, and we have chosen to refer to these efforts with respect to particular problems treated in the following sections. We will thus content ourselves here with indicating some general orientations and providing some bibliographical information.

Reflection on language is contemporaneous with human history; one finds traces of it among the earliest documents we possess. It could hardly be otherwise, since writing, which has preserved these texts for us, rests necessarily upon a preliminary analysis of language. Most of the time, however, this reflection announces linguistics only indirectly; we find instead meditations on the origin, the form, and the power of words. Research into the origin of language, in particular, is sustained in the period in which the first grammars appear and is pursued throughout Occidental history up to the first half of the nineteenth century.

● A. Borst, *Der Turmbau von Babel,* 4 bks. in 6 vols. (Stuttgart, 1957–63), retraces the history of theories concerning the origin of languages and their diversity. The best overview of the history of linguistics is by R. H. Robins, in *A Short History of Linguistics,* 2d ed. (London, 1969); in French, see J. Joyaux, *Le Langage, cet inconnu* (Paris, 1969). The collection edited by H. Parret (*History of Linguistic Thought and Contemporary Linguistics* [Berlin and New York, 1976]) contains studies of the major currents of linguistic thought.

The first text on linguistics available to us is the Sanskrit grammar of Pānini (circa the fourth century B.C.). As irony would have it, this book, perhaps the first scientific work in Western history, remains without equal in its field even today. Pāṇini's treatise deals essentially with the processes of derivation and of morphological composition, which he described by means of ordered rules. The brevity of his formulations is striking, and it has given rise to abundant commentary, the earliest and most important being that of Patañjali.

Sanskrit linguistics is not limited to morphology. At the level of general linguistic theory, we have retained in particular the notion of *sphota,* an abstract linguistic entity, in opposition to *dhvani,* the individual realization of that entity; the *sphoṭa* can be situated at the level of the sentence, the word, or the sound. One of the great philosophical grammarians, Bhartrhari, even distinguished three levels of abstraction in language instead of two. In phonetics the philosophical grammarians achieved an exhaustive description of the Sanskrit language on the basis of an articulatory analysis. In semantics they raised the problem of the relationships between diverse meanings of a word, that of the interaction of individual words in the formation of the meaning of a sentence, and so on.

● Pānini, *The Ashtādhyāyi,* ed. and trans. S. C. Vasu (Delhi, 1962); L. Renou, trans., *La Grammaire de Pānini,* 2d ed., 2 vols. (Paris, 1966); P. C. Chakravarti, *The Linguistic Speculations of the Hindus* (Calcutta, 1933); J. Brough, "Theories of General Linguistics in the Sanscrit Grammarians," *Transactions of the Philological Society* (London, 1951), pp. 27–46; D. S. Ruegg, *Contributions à l'histoire de la philosophie linguis-*

tique indienne (Paris, 1959); W. S. Allen, *Phonetics in Ancient India* (London, 1953); K. K. Raja, *Indian Theories of Meaning* (Madras, 1963); and J. F. Staal, ed., *A Reader on the Sanskrit Grammarians* (Cambridge, Mass., 1972).

In Greece the study of language is inseparable from the philosophy of language (among the pre-Socratics, Plato, Aristotle, and the Stoics) or from commentary on literary texts (the Alexandrian school). Research was undertaken in three major areas: etymology, phonetics, and morphology. In etymology there was a celebrated controversy over the natural or conventional origin of words, and the etymologies of individual words were subsequently shown to have no historical value. The systematic use of the phonetic alphabet implies some rudiments of phonological analysis, but the most highly developed aspect of linguistic studies is the theory of the parts of speech. Inaugurated by Plato and Aristotle and pursued by the Stoics, this theory was to be presented systematically by the author of the first grammatical treatise in Greek, Dionysius of Thrace; he distinguishes eight parts of speech, as well as some secondary categories (gender, number, case). The problems of syntax would be raised three centuries later, in the second century A.D., by Apollonius Dyscolus.

The Roman grammarians continued and extended the works of the Greeks. Varro (second century A.D.), the author of a voluminous description of the Latin language, bears witness to the fertile influence of Greek grammatical schools; Donatus and Priscian (fifth century) would codify the Latin language for posterity, determining already in large part the form of our textbooks. In a parallel development (dating back to remotest antiquity), one finds a rhetorical theory whose influence will likewise be perpetuated up until the nineteenth century.

● L. Lersch, *Die Sprachphilosophie der Alten* (Bonn, 1838–41); H. Steinthal, *Geschichte der Sprachwissenschraft bei den Griechen und Römern,* 2d ed. (Berlin, 1890); R. H. Robins, *Ancient and Medieval Grammatical Theory in Europe* (London, 1951); M. Pohlenz, "Die Begründung der abendländischen Sprachlehre durch die Stoa," *Nachrichten von der Gesellschaft der Wissenschraft zu Göttingen, Philologisch-historische Klasse, Fachgruppe I: Altertumswissenschaft,* n.s. 3–6 (1939); E. Egger, *Apollonius Dyscole; Essai sur l'histoire des théories grammaticales dans l'Antiquité* (Paris, 1854); J. Collart, *Varron: Grammairien latin* (Paris, 1954); and L. Romeo and G. E. Tiberio, "The History of Linguistics and Rome's Scholarship," *Language Sciences* 17 (1971): 23–44.

The specific character of medieval linguistic research is obscured by the fact that it is usually presented as a commentary on the Latin grammarians, Priscian in particular. But this constant reference to authority (which in the Middle Ages forms an almost integral part of scientific rhetoric) did not in any way prevent the medieval grammarians—or the logicians and the philosophers—from developing a highly original train of thought.

This originality began to become apparent as early as the tenth century. Two themes of the new grammar are particularly significant: First, the will to constitute a general theory of language that was independent of any given language in particular, and most notably of Latin (Priscian took explicitly as his objective the description of the Latin language), and second, the bringing together of grammar and logic; the latter discipline, having been rediscovered in the same period, tended more and more to present itself as the universal instrument of all thought. Among the most celebrated grammarians between the tenth and the twelfth century were Gerbert d'Aurillac, Saint Anselm, Abelard, and Pierre Hélie.

The second and most remarkable period of medieval linguistics began in the thirteenth century and was dominated by the so-called modist school. Although the **modists,** too, set as their objective the constitution of a general theory of language, they believed in the absolute autonomy of grammar in relation to logic. (When the grammarians of Port-Royal, four centuries later, subordinated grammar to logic, they were returning in fact to a point of view that the modists had sought to leave behind.) The independence of the linguistic approach manifests itself fundamentally in the concept, introduced at the time, of **mode of signifying** (*modus significandi*). A grammatical element (for example, a part of speech [203]) must be defined not by its signified but by the way in which this signified is indicated, by the type of relationship instituted between words and things. Grammatical theory is thus above all a detailed inventory and a classification of these possible modes of access to things (thus the difference between the adjective and the substantive resides less in their object than in the point of view according to which they present that object). Among the principal modists we must mention Siger de Courtrai, Johannes Aurifaber, and Thomas of Hereford.

- Only a very few grammatical texts of the Middle Ages have been published, among them the treatises of Siger de Courtrai (ed. G. Wallerand [Louvain, 1913]), Thomas of Hereford (in the works of Duns Scotus [Paris, 1890]), and Jean le Dace (ed. A. Otto [Copenhagen, 1955]). The most important studies on medieval grammar are doubtless C. Thurot, *Notices et extraits pour servir à l'histoire des doctrines grammaticales du Moyen Age* (Paris, 1868); M. Heidegger, *Die Kategorien und Bedeutungslehre des Duns Scotus* (Tübingen, 1916), dealing largely with Thomas of Hereford; H. Ross, *Die Modi significandi des Martinus de Dacia* (Münster and Copenhagen, 1952); J. Pinborg, *Die Entwicklung der Sprachtheorie im Mittelalter* (Münster and Copenhagen, 1967); and G. L. Bursill-Hall, *Speculative Grammar of the Middle Ages* (The Hague, 1971). There is interesting information in J.-C. Chevalier, *Histoire de la syntaxe* (Geneva, 1968), pt. 1, chap. 1, and in G. L. Bursill-Hall, "Medieval Grammatical Theories," *Canadian Journal of Linguistics* 9 (1963): 40–53.

FIELDS

COMPONENTS OF LINGUISTIC DESCRIPTION

What are the principal tasks to be accomplished in describing a language, considered at a given moment in its history? Occidental tradition distributes the work under three major categorial headings, moving from the most external features to those that touch most closely upon meaning:

1. The material means of expression (pronunciation and writing).

2. **Grammar,** which is subdivided into two parts: morphology and syntax.

a) **Morphology** deals with words independently of their relationships in the sentence. Words are arranged in different classes labeled "parts of speech" (noun, verb, and so on); and all the variations that a single word may undergo are indicated, along with the rules for the formation of gender and number, for declension, and for conjugation.

b) **Syntax** treats the combination of words in sentences. Syntax comprises word order; the phenomena of **concord** (government, or **agreement**), that is, the way in which certain words impose on others certain variations in case, number, gender; and finally, especially since the eighteenth century, the principal functions of words in sentences [209ff.].

3. The **dictionary,** or lexicon, indicates the meaning(s) that words possess. For this reason it is the semantic component of description *par excellence* (the dictionary also provides—but only as a convenience—information on the morphological variations peculiar to each word).

The development of linguistics in the twentieth century has led to several (sometimes mutually incompatible) criticism of this categorization: .

a) It is based on the notion of *word*; yet now the word is rarely regarded as the fundamental unit of meaning [199ff.].

b) It puts on the same level the *constraints* that the language imposes on the speaker and the *options* that the language allows. Thus the rules of agreement, which consist in pure subordination (the agreement of the verb with the subject is obligatory, for example, in French), coexist in syntax with the inventory of the functions, which represent, on the contrary, a range of possibilities. This coexistence was not particularly shocking in a period when the primary object of language seemed to be to "represent" thought [3]. The Port-Royal grammarians, for example

—and later W. von Humboldt—attach particular importance to the phenomena of agreement, for they regard this action of one word on another as the perceptible image of the linking of concepts in the mind. But if the primary function of language is "communication," it is hard to grant that a mechanism such as agreement—which, being obligatory, cannot be used to convey information to the listener—is equally as important as a system of options that allow the speaker to make his intentions known.

c) The relegation of semantics to the dictionary suggests that semantic description is limited essentially to the sequential characterization of the significant units utilized by the language. One of Saussure's least-disputed teachings, however, holds that the most fruitful study of all is the study of the relationships between elements, both paradigmatic relationships (contemporary semantics takes as its object not so much words or morphemes as the categories of words or morphemes pertaining to a single area [semantic fields]) and syntagmatic relationships (a problem that appears essential today is that of determining how the meanings of the elements of a sentence combine to constitute its total meaning—something that certainly does not occur through simple addition).

The priority given to words in the traditional scheme of things is particularly unacceptable, from the viewpoint of glossematics [20ff.], for two reasons. First, the intrinsic units of the language are either pleremes (units of content) or cenemes (units of expression), and each plereme is defined by its relations with the other pleremes, each ceneme by its relations with the other cenemes. Words, on the contrary, are defined only by the union of elements belonging to distinct levels. This association of a signifier and a signified thus produces only extrinsic units, which depend not on the language itself but on its conditions of use. Nothing guarantees, for example, that the signifieds of words constitute elementary content units or even complex units; perhaps an authentic description of linguistic content would never encounter the lexical signifieds. Second, the word can only be defined "substantially": it is made up of a concept and a phonetic sequence. Linguistic description is first of all "formal," and it characterizes units only by their possible combinations in language. In applying these principles, description will have to be divided along two distinct lines. We shall begin by distinguishing two principal components that are independent of each other and are devoted, respectively, to content and to expression. For each component, we shall then conduct, first, a study of the formal relationships existing between the units and, second, a study, subordinated to the first, of the material realizations of these units. Only as a supplement can we add the purely utilitarian description of the relationships between the two levels, that is, of the traditional object of the dictionary and of morphology.

● See especially L. Hjelmslev, "La Stratification du langage," *Word* 10 (1954): 163–88.

If A. Martinet also rejects the classical distribution, it is to the extent that he attaches a fundamental importance to the notion of choice that governs in particular the theory of **double articulation.** To describe a language is to describe the set of choices available to the speaker of that language and recognizable by a listener who understands that language. These choices are of two types:

a) First-articulation choices, which have signifying value; that is, they concern meaningful units. In the utterance "John began after you," compare the choice of *you* with that of *me, him, two, the war*, and so on. To say that these choices constitute an articulation is to make a double hypothesis: on the one hand, that there exist minimal choices (among elementary units of meaning, or monemes [201]—for example, *you*); on the other hand, that the larger choices (like the choice of *after you*) can be understood on the basis of the choice of monemes (we thus have the very strong hypothesis that the difference between *began after you* and *began after the war* is explained by the difference between *you* and *the war*.

b) Second-articulation choices, which involve units that are merely distinctive, the phonemes [171], whose unique function is to allow for the distinction of monemes. Thus the choice of the *y* (/j/) of *you* stems from a desire to signify, but only indirectly, to the extent that it is necessitated by the choice of the moneme *you*, which it distinguishes from *two*, for example. Here again, Martinet hypothesizes that there is articulation, that is, that there are minimal choices (among phonemes such as /j/) that form the basis for the choice of higher segments.

Linguistic description will thus have two essential components: (1) phonology—concerned with the second articulation—which establishes the list of phonemes, determines their distinctive features [173], classifies them according to these features, and indicates the rules that govern their combination; and (2) **syntax**—devoted to the first articulation—which establishes the list of monemes, indicates the possible functions of each one in the utterance, and categorizes them according to function. To these two components, which describe the choices offered by the language, are attached two types of (almost indispensable although theoretically marginal) study, which indicate the conditions imposed by the language for the manifestation of these choices. A phonetic study identifies the nondistinctive features that accompany the distinctive ones in the phonemes; a **morphological** study indicates how the monemes are realized phonologically according to the contexts in which they appear. Here we find, simultaneously, a portion of traditional morphology (to give the conjugation of the French verb *aller* ["to go"] is to assert that the single moneme *aller* is realized as *i* when it is accompanied by the moneme *future*, as *all* when it is accompanied by the moneme *imperfect*, and so on), as well as the portion of traditional syntax devoted to the phenomena of agreement (to say that in French the article agrees in number with the noun, and the verb with its subject, is to assert that the single moneme *plural* in *les chevaux boivent* ["the horses drink"] is realized by a succession of three discontinuous marks [in French, the *es* of *les*, the *aux* of *chevaux*, the *vent* of *boivent*; in English, the *s* of *horses* and the absence of *s* in *drink*].

● Cf. A. Martinet, *La Linguistique synchronique* (Paris, 1965), chap. 1.

The same concern for separating linguistic latitudes and dependencies that led Martinet to oppose traditional grammar is also at the origin of an internal evolution of the generative school. For Chomsky, the **grammar** of a language is the totality of its description. It includes three principal components. **Syntax** (which is the generative part of the grammar, "generative grammar" in the literal sense) is assigned the task of generating, according to purely formal mechanisms [226ff.], all the strings of morphemes regarded as grammatical, and these alone. (Syntax itself has two subcomponents: the base, which gives the deep structures of sentences, and the transformations, which give the surface structures [242ff.].) In the strings generated by the syntax, morphemes are aligned side by side (the participles *eaten* and *drunk* would be represented as *eat en* and *drink en*). Moreover, the phenomena of agreement are for the most part not taken into account ("the horses are drinking" would be represented as *the horse plural present be ing drink*). Finally, the representation of morphemes is purely conventional and does not in any way constitute a phonetic representation. Once generated by the syntax, these strings must be treated by two other components that have only interpretative (and not generative) power: the **semantic component** translates the strings into a semantic metalanguage in such a way as to give a representation of the meaning of the sentences, and the **phonological component,** by means of the translation that it operates, accounts for the pronunciation of the strings. Chomsky's phonological component must thus assume all the tasks that Martinet assigned to phonetics, phonology, and morphology. Chomsky does not even distinguish these disciplines as subdivisions of the phonological component; that is why this component is sometimes called **morphophonological.**

N.B. Trubetzkoy gave the term "morphophonology," or **morphonology,** to the area of linguistic description concerned with the ways in which the sounds (more precisely the phonemes [171] are utilized for the expression of grammatical notions or categories. Morphonology would study, for example, the phenomenon of alteration, that is, the modifications that such expression can entail—particularly in the Indo-European languages—*inside* the root itself [10]: in order to make, from the German noun *Tag* ("day") the adjective *täglich* ("daily"), the *a* of the root of *Tag* (pronounced like the English *a* in *father*) is changed to *ä* (pronounced like the English *e* in *beg*).

This lack of distinction, which amounts to a denial of a purely phonological language structure (in the traditional sense of phonology), is based essentially on economy: construction of the phonetic representation of a sentence on the basis of its representation as a string of morphemes would be gratuitously complicated by prior phonological representation retaining the distinctive features, and those alone. Given, in particular, the phenomena of **juncture** (the occurrence of phonic modifications within a word at the point of juncture between two morphemes), it would be possible to formulate simpler, more general laws if we were to deduce directly, on the basis of a word's morphemic organization, the sequence of sounds that constitute it physically rather than first to construct the sequence of phonemes that manifest it and only then to construct the physical sounds on the basis of the phonemes.

- N. S. Trubetzkoy introduced the term "morphonology" in a notice published in the first volume of the *Travaux du Cercle Linguistique de Prague* (1929, pp. 85–88; it was reprinted in *A Prague School Reader in Linguistics*, ed. J. Vachek [Bloomington and London, 1964], pp. 183–86). The association of phonology and morphology is proposed by E. Sapir in *Language: An Introduction to the Study of Speech* (1921: reprint ed., New York, 1955), chap. 4. An historical presentation of the question is found in J. Kilbury, "The Emergence of Morphophonemics: A Survey of Theory and Practice from 1876 to 1939," *Lingua* 33 (1973): 235–52. On the Chomskyan conception of phonology, see N. Chomsky, *Current Issues in Linguistic Theory* (The Hague, 1964), chap. 4, and M. Halle, "Phonology in Generative Grammar," *Word* 18 (1962): 54–72; see also F. Dell, *Les Règles et les sons* (Paris, 1973), and S. A. Schane, *Generative Phonology* (Englewood Cliffs, 1973). A. Martinet proposes a critique of the idea of morphonology in "La morphonologie," *La Linguistique* 1 (1965): 15–30.

If the grammar of a language were to be regarded as a hypothesis about the way speaking subjects produce sentences (an interpretation that was rejected by Chomsky but reappears often in the work of his students), the regrouping of morphology, phonology, and phonetics in collective opposition to syntax could have a second justification: the generation of a sentence within the syntax would represent the series of choices made by the speaker. As for the morphophonological component, it would represent the automatic process through which these choices are converted into a series of sounds. (To be sure, one may speak, with

Martinet, of a choice of phonemes, but this means placing oneself in the position of the listener, who only discovers the speaker's intentions by deciphering the phonemes as they appear in succession and who therefore lacks the means to foresee these phonemes. The speaker, for his part, does not choose the phonemes; they are imposed on him by the prior choice of monemes.) Nevertheless, once caught up in this interpretation of generative grammar, one is led to a fairly thoroughgoing reorganization of the Chomskyan system. Since about 1965 generativists have in fact been working with the hypothesis that the transformational aspect of syntax has no effect on sentences' semantic interpretation proper; this has led to the elimination of most of the transformations formerly regarded as optional (negation and interrogation, for example). They admit that at best these transformations can determine nuances of a stylistic nature (such as emphasis on a given aspect of the idea expressed) [on this evolution, see below, pp. 244ff.]. Let us suppose that this latter function, quite difficult to distinguish from a semantic effect proper, were to be withdrawn: one could then regard the set of transformations as a sort of machinery that automatically converts deep structures into surface structures. It would seem reasonable then to relate them to the morphophonological mechanisms (U. Weinreich, "Explorations in Semantic Theory," p. 445). Given, moreover, the fact that all of the syntactic constructions existing in deep structure are supposed to have a potential semantic interpretation, each one corresponding, for example, to a type of semantic combination [269], and that the choice of syntactic construction depends upon the semantic interpretation, it may appear legitimate to regroup the base of the syntax and the semantic component. We arrive then at the idea, maintained for example, by J. R. Ross and G. Lakoff, of a **generative semantics.** A generative component would generate, in a process analogous to that of deep syntax in orthodox Chomskyanism, all the possible semantic structures, and transformations and morphonological laws would then give them a phonic dress. In this perspective one can easily conceive of the first component as universal; languages would then be differentiated only by the second.

● Weinreich is regarded as a precursor of generative semantics: see his "Explorations in Semantic Theory," in *Current Trends in Linguistics*, ed. T. A. Sebeok, 14 vols. (The Hague, 1973–76), vol. 3, *Theoretical Foundations* (1966), pp. 395–478. For the contributions of Ross and Lakoff, see G. Lakoff and J. R. Ross, "Is Deep Structure Necessary?" mimeographed (Cambridge, Mass., 1967); cf. G. Lakoff, "On Generative Semantics," in *Semantics: An Interdisciplinary Reader*, ed. L. A. Jakobovits and D. D. Steinberg (Cambridge, 1971). On other recent developments in this area, cf. E. Bach and R. Harms, eds., *Universals in Linguistic Theory* (New York, 1968), esp. J. D. McCawley, "The Role of Semantics in Grammar." Cf. also G. Lakoff, "Linguistics and Natural Logic," in *Semantics of Natural Language*, ed. D. Davidson and G. Harman (Dordrecht, 1972), pp. 545–665. For a critique of generative semantics, see N. Chomsky, *Deep Structure, Surface Structure and Semantic Interpretation* (Cambridge, Mass., 1968), reprinted in idem, *Studies on Semantics in Generative Grammar* (The Hague, 1972); see also J. J. Katz, "Interpretative Semantics vs. Generative Semantics," *Foundations of Language* 6 (May 1970): 220–59, and R. S. Jackendoff, *Semantic Interpretation in Generative Grammar* (Cambridge, Mass., 1972).

GEOLINGUISTICS

To speak of *the* French language, *the* German language, and so on, is to produce a considerable (and often unconscious) abstraction and generalization, for there are as many different ways of speaking as there are different collectivities using a language, as many even, if we are to be rigorous, as there are individuals using it (nor do we rule out the possibility that there may be several individuals in each person, linguistically speaking). We can call **geolinguistics** the study of all the variations linked to the social and geographical roots of language users.

The principal concepts utilized in such a study are the following:

Idiolect. The term "idiolect" designates those aspects of an individual's speech pattern that cannot be attributed to the influence of the groups to which the individual belongs. Certain linguists deny that the ordinary methods of linguistics can be used to study idiolects; they even deny that an idiolect is a language. In fact, if we regard a language as an instrument of communication, as a code, it is absurd to speak of individual language. We can say, in phonological terms, that the peculiarities of each idiolect are free variants [172]—by definition lacking all distinctiveness, at best they allow each individual to mark his originality with respect to others (a function of marginal interest to linguists). On the other hand, if we see in language an attempt to imitate thought [3], we cannot rule out the possibility that idiolectal creation may stem from the same human attitude that is at the origin of language (another example might be the "willful" mistakes that certain writers, in fidelity to their object, deem necessary).

- The notion of idiolect has not been the object of much study; see, however, C. F. Hockett, *A Course in Modern Linguistics* (New York, 1958), chap. 38. More information can be gleaned from novelists (Proust, for example) and literary critics.

Dialect. By "dialect" (or **patois**) is meant a regional speech pattern (Alsatian, Cajun, and so on) within a nation in which another pattern dominates officially (as determined by the government, the schools, and so on). N.B. (*a*) Each dialect is itself made up of a multitude of local speech patterns that are not always mutually intelligible. (*b*) We use "patois" to describe only those speech patterns that are historically (and fairly directly) related to an "official" language. If Alsatian, which is related to German, and Provençal, which is related to French, are examples of patois, then Breton and, to an even greater extent, Basque are viewed as independent languages; in many cases, however, the frontier is indistinct. (*c*) Although there exists an historical relationship between the various patois and the official language, this relationship is not necessarily genealogical. In most cases, the official language is simply a regional dialect that has been extended by authoritarian means to the whole of a nation. (Thus modern German is a Germanic dialect that was imposed upon all of Germany; its extension was facilitated particularly by the fact that it was the language Luther used for his translation of the Bible.) (*d*) Since the official languages and their related dialects often have a common origin, it is easy to understand why linguists have been interested in patois. The neogrammarians [13] in particular insisted on the usefulness of dialect study; they saw it as a necessity if linguistic evolution was to be reconstituted *in detail* (whereas the comparatists [9] established correspondences between language states that were often far apart in time). This study, called **dialectology,** led to the constitution of **linguistic atlases** (initiated in France by J. Gilliéron). To establish the atlas of a region, first a standardized questionnaire is developed that usually includes three main types of questions: how a given notion is expressed; how a given word is pronounced; how a given sentence is translated. Then investigators are sent into certain localities in the region (the choice of localities raises some difficult problems), where they attempt, by questioning and observation, to answer all the questions for each of the chosen areas. (This dialectal study, recommended by the neogrammarians, led Gilliéron to question certain of their theses, in particular the belief in the blindness of the phonetic laws of a language to the synchronic organization of that language [13].)

- On dialectology, see especially: J. Gilliéron and M. Roques, *Etudes de géographie linguistique* (Paris, 1912); W. von Wartburg, *Bibliographie des dictionnaires patois* (Paris, 1934); S. Popp, *La Dialectologie* (Louvain, 1950); U. Weinreich, "Is a Structural Dialectology Possible?" *Word*

10 (1954): 388–400; E. Sapir, "Dialect," in *Encyclopedia of Social Sciences*, ed. E. R. A. Seligman, 15 vols. (New York, 1930–35), vol. 5; and W. G. Moulton, "Geographical Linguistics," in *Current Trends in Linguistics*, ed. T. A. Sebeok, 14 vols. (The Hague, 1963–76), vol. 9, *Linguistics in Western Europe* (1972), pp. 196–222.

National language. The term "national language" refers to the official language within a state (there may of course be more than one, as in Belgium or Switzerland). Generally established rather late in the life of a state, often simply a local dialect that has achieved supremacy, the official language is imposed by the government (it is to be used in dealings with the state) and by cultural life (it is taught in the schools, and often it is the only language to have given rise to a literature—certain dialects are even difficult to write because they lack orthographical conventions). It is not unusual for the official language to be used by the power structure as a political instrument. (The struggle against dialects is part of the politics of centralization. Nationalism is often accompanied by attempts to "purify" the language of foreign contamination, like the efforts of the Nazis to eliminate borrowed words [7] from German.)

Jargon. By "jargon" is meant the modifications that a socioprofessional group brings to the national language (especially in vocabulary and pronunciation); sometimes it is not possible to distinguish whether the modifications are linked (1) to the particular nature of what is said; (2) to a desire not to be understood; or (3) to the desire of the group to mark its own originality. (Unlike the dialect, jargon thus appears as a divergence from the national language.) Linguists, notaries, mountain climbers, and so on, each have their jargon. **Slang** (*argot*) may be regarded as a particular case of jargon: it is a jargon that presents itself as the sign of a social situation—not just a private one—but a marginal one (in Hjelmslevian terms, recourse to slang entails an asocial connotation [23]). (N.B. The use of the term "slang" to designate the speech of a social class judged to be inferior must be distinguished from the use we are making of it here.)

● On slang in French, see P. Guiraud, *L'Argot* (Paris, 1966).

Language blends. The existence of regular relations between two communities speaking different languages often leads to the creation of a **mixed language** that permits direct communication without recourse to translation. The resulting language is known as a **lingua franca** (not without pejorative nuances) (1) when it is used only for episodic relations with limited objectives (especially for commerce); and (2) when it does not have a well-defined grammatical structure and allows in particular the juxtaposition of words. We speak, on the contrary, of **pidgin** when the result is a grammatically coherent language that satisfies, in the same way that the natural languages and the dialects do, the overall communicative needs of its users (including the possibility of giving rise to a literature). When this language becomes the major (or only) language of a community, we call it **Creole** (the Creole of the Antilles has given its name to the entire category). (N.B. It has been observed that even when a mixed language has not been constituted, the geographical proximity of several linguistic communities often leads to certain common features, called **affinities**, in their respective dialects; this allows for the grouping of these dialects in **linguistic associations.** These common features may have a structural character, that is, they may consist in an overall modification of the languages under consideration. [There may be modifications not only in the phonetic materiality of the language but also in the phonological system (171).] The common features are observable furthermore even when the languages spoken by the collectivities are not historically related.)

● A theoretical study of the problem of language blends is in L. Hjelmslev's "Les Relations de parenté des langues créoles," *Revue des études indo-européennes* 2 (1938): 271–86. For concrete descriptions, see several articles from the acts of the *Symposium on Multilingualism (Brazzaville, 1962)* (London, 1964); and D. Hymes, *Pidginization and Creolization* (Cambridge, 1971). On linguistic alliances, see N. S. Trubetzkoy, *Principles of Phonology*, trans. C. A. M. Baltaxe (Berkeley, 1969), appendices 3 and 4, by N. S. Trubetzkoy and R. Jakobson, respectively. For a general bibliography, see J. E. Reinecke et al., *Bibliography of Pidgin and Creole Languages* (Honolulu, 1975).

Multilingualism. An individual is said to be multilingual if he possesses knowledge of several languages, all learned as mother tongues. (There are degrees of multilingualism, since the difference between the "natural" and the "learned" acquisition of a language by a child is not always clear.) The most interesting theoretical problem for the linguist here is to discover whether—and to what extent—the plurilinguistic situation influences the knowledge of each of the languages involved. This situation is interesting especially because such influence, when it exists, is not always apparent (the **bilingual** individual may speak the two languages "perfectly") and may operate at a relatively abstract level: at the level of the phonological system (as opposed to that of the phonetic realizations [171]), at the level of the applied grammatical rules (without visible influence on the sentences produced), at the level of the categories of thought (if it is true that each language implies a particular categorization of meaning).

● Literature on bilingualism is particularly abundant in the United States. The classic work of U. Weinreich, *Languages in Contact* (New York, 1953), is informative. See also the *Symposium on Multilingualism* cited in the preceding bibliography. For more specific studies, see R. W. Metraux, "A Situation of Bilingualism Among Children of U.S.-French Parents," *The French Review* 38 (1965): 650–66; P. F. Kinzel, "A Description of Lexical and Grammatical Interference in the Speech of a Bilingual Child" (Ph.D. diss., University of Washington, 1964); and H. W. Contreras, "The Phonological System of a Bilingual Child" (Ph.D. diss., Indiana University, 1961).

SOCIOLINGUISTICS

The relationship between language, on the one hand, and society or culture or behavior, on the other, has never been denied, but up to now no agreement has been reached among researchers as to the nature of this relationship. That is why we find ourselves dealing here, not with a single discipline, but with a set of propositions and studies whose inconsistency is reflected even in the nomenclature: sociology of language, sociolinguistics, ethnolinguistics, linguistic anthropology, anthropological linguistics, and so on.

Most often researchers postulate the existence of two separate entities, language and society (or culture or behavior), and then study the one through the other. One of the entities is regarded as cause, the other as effect, and the effect is studied with a view to gaining knowledge of the cause, or vice versa, according to whether the one or the other lends itself better to rigorous analysis. Most of the time, society or one of its surrogates is the object of knowledge, and language is taken as the easy-to-handle intermediary that leads to the goal.

According to the most traditional viewpoint, it is society that determines language; consequently, the study of linguistic variants will allow for the precise circumscription of the sociological (cultural, behavioral) variants that produced them. Thus in French one can address someone by using *tu* or *vous*, by calling him Pierre, Dupont, Monsieur Pierre, Monsieur Dupont, and so on. An analysis of these different possibilities (one such has been inaugurated in the work of R. Brown) will allow us to discern certain categories that are pertinent for the description of the act of communication in a given society. Another work with the same perspective has permitted the identification of a certain number of phonological variants in the speech of New Yorkers; these variants are correlated with social differences (profession, education, income). According to W. Labov, author of this study, language here is "a sensitive index of many other social processes"; it is a relatively easily studied matter that allows us to draw conclusions about the structure of society. The term **sociolinguistics** might be reserved for this resolutely sociological perspective.

With the work of W. von Humboldt, in the nineteenth century, an inverse perspective was introduced: language was no longer the reflection of social, cultural, or psychic structures; it became their cause. Humboldt granted to language a much greater importance than did his predecessors: for him, it did not serve to designate a preexisting reality; rather it was language that organized the surrounding world. These ideas, which remained for Humboldt a philosophical stance, gave rise in the twentieth century to several types of empirical studies.

The works of the "neo-Humboldtian" group in Germany (Weisgerber, Trier, Porzig) must be cited first. According to them, language is linked to a world vision, and since there exists one language per nation, the study of each language will allow us to know the spirit of the nation— German as opposed to French, for example. This study is based on the analysis of semantic fields [135]—differently organized in each language —which are observable in the realm of nature, as well as in the domain of material or spiritual culture (see, for example, Trier's classic work on the concept of reason and related concepts in German, *Der deutsche Wortschatz*).

A parallel development took place in the United States in the thirties and forties, namely, the so-called Sapir-Whorf hypothesis. Basing his work on some of Sapir's affirmations, B. L. Whorf sought to show that the most fundamental categories of thought—those of time, space, subject and object, and so on—are not the same in English and, for example, in a non-Indo-European language such as that of the Hopi Indians. Unlike the Germans, Whorf was much more interested in grammatical categories than in lexical structures.

A third tendency—related to the first two, although it is less Humboldtian in derivation—may be seen in the work of American ethnologists, who are fond of describing the "popular taxonomies" in indigenous languages. Their project is thus similar to Trier's, but their work, which deals with kinship or with colors, plants and animals, illnesses and trades (in short, what has lately come to be called **ethnoscience**), does not aim at knowledge of a hypothetical national spirit.

Two tendencies can be observed in all the works described. On the one hand there is a semantic project in the narrow sense; the studies of semantic fields and the componential analysis of the American ethnologists are at the basis of modern semantics [265]. On the other hand, the extrapolation of a linguistic configuration as a property of the national spirit runs the risk of being tautological: either our knowledge of this "spirit" is so general as to make its relationship to language trivial or else the "spirit" is to all intents and purposes coextensive with the language, which is the only means by which it can be known. Whatever the case, the explicit goal of this research (except for American ethnologists) is once again the knowledge of some other element (spirit, culture) through the intermediary of language. The term **ethnolinguistics** might be reserved for this type of research.

One encounters much less often the inverse attitude, which consists in illuminating certain properties of language by means of one's knowledge of society: either because one finds, in this case, only a rather loose determinism or because the sociological categories are too imprecise to serve as linguistic criteria. Here one could cite distinctions such as "bureaucratic" or "scientific" style, which obviously come from the social categories.

It is appropriate to recall, finally, that on the methodological level, linguistics, which has recently been thrust into the vanguard, has exerted a certain influence on the social sciences. Ethnology and sociology have borrowed certain concepts and procedures from linguistics in order to utilize them in their own fields. The work of C. Lévi-Strauss demonstrates how fruitful such borrowing may be, although Lévi-Strauss's object is not the same as that of sociolinguistics.

● Several collections of representative articles have been published recently: D. Hymes, ed., *Language in Culture and Society* (New York, 1964); W. Bright, ed., *Sociolinguistics* (The Hague, 1968); J. A. Fishman, ed., *Readings in the Sociology of Language* (The Hague, 1968), a particularly interesting selection; A. K. Romney and R. G. d'Andrade, eds., *American Anthropologist* 66, no. 3 (1964), pt. 2: *Transcultural Studies in Cognition*; P. P. Giglioli, ed., *Language and Social Context* (Harmondsworth, 1972); and B. G. Blount, ed., *Language, Culture and Society* (Cambridge, Mass., 1974). For recent work in French, see *Langages*, vols. 11 (1968): *Sociolinguistique* and 18 (1970): *Ethnolinguistique*.
Examples of sociolinguistic studies (in the narrow sense) are found in R. Brown and M. Ford, "Address in American English," in Hymes, *Language*, pp. 234–44; R. Brown and A. Gilman, "The Pronouns of Power and Solidarity," in Fishman, *Readings*, pp. 252–76; W. Labov, *Sociolinguistic Patterns* (Philadelphia, 1972); and J. J. Gumperz, *Language in Social Groups* (Stanford, 1971).
Examples of ethnolinguistic studies (in the narrow sense) are L. Weisgerber, *Von den Kräften der deutschen Sprache*, 4 vols. (Düsseldorf, 1949–51); J. Trier, *Der deutsche Wortschatz im Sinnbezirk des Verstandes* (Heidelberg, 1931); W. Porzig, *Das Wunder der Sprache* (Bern, 1950);

B. L. Whorf, *Language, Thought and Reality*, ed. by J. B. Carroll (Cambridge, Mass., 1956); H. Hoijer, ed., *Language in Culture* (Chicago, 1954); H. C. Conklin, "Lexicographical Treatment of Folk Taxonomies," and C. O. Frake, "The Ethnographic Study of Cognitive Systems," both in Fishman, *Readings*, pp. 414–33 and 434–46, respectively; W. C. Sturtevant, "Studies in Ethnoscience," in *Transcultural Studies*, ed. Romney and D'Andrade, pp. 49–131.

Surveys include J. A. Fishman, *Sociolinguistics: A Brief Introduction* (Rowley, Mass, 1970); J.-B. Marcellesi and B. Gardin, *Introduction à la sociolinguistique* (Paris, 1974); P. Trudgill, *Sociolinguistics: An Introduction* (Harmondsworth, 1974). For a bibliography, see G. Simon, *Bibliographie zur Soziolinguistik* (Tübingen, 1974). On linguistics and ethnology, see C. Lévi-Strauss, *Structural Anthropology*, trans. C. Jacobson and B. G. Schoepf (New York, 1963).

There exists yet another, entirely different possibility for studying the language-society relationship: it is possible to suspend the opposition of the two and to study the language *as* a social phenomenon, as a type of behavior. Here we are no longer bringing together two separate entities; rather we are constituting a new theoretical object. We could christen **linguistic anthropology** the studies that are situated in this new perspective.

The idea that language can be considered a mode of action is certainly not new; nevertheless, not until the work of the English ethnologist B. Malinowski did it acquire the status of a scientific hypothesis. Moreover, it is fairly difficult to accept all the propositions that, for Malinowski, accompany the birth of this idea. He distinguishes several types of linguistic utterances according to their function: those common in our "Western" languages serve essentially to express thought; those common in the "primitive" languages serve to accomplish an action. It is only when the meaning of the utterance is totally lacking in importance that Malinowski regards the utterance as illustrating language's "mode of action" (for example, sentences about the weather that have no function other than to establish contact). One might object that to express or to inform is like any other action and that in this sense all utterances of all languages possess this specific mode; the examples cited by Malinowski (polite expressions, remarks about the weather, questions about the state of one's health) are only the most evident. But this objection in no way diminishes Malinowski's merit.

Malinowski's ideas will be taken up again by the English linguist J. R. Firth and his disciples. Firth admits this actional dimension in all utterances but tends to confuse it with the meaning of a sentence. Now even if the meaning may be pertinent for the description of this dimension, nonetheless the actional dimension may be situated elsewhere. ("I am coming tomorrow" may be either a promise or a warning, even while the meaning remains unchanged.) The recognition of this dimension leads Firth to postulate the importance of the situational context (here again he is following Malinowski) and to suggest the possibility of carrying out his study at two levels: that of a typology of situations (appellations; salutations; indications of relationships, such as "at church," "in the judge's home," and so on) and that of a typology of functions (for example, to be or not to be in agreement, to encourage, to condemn, to take responsibility; or to wish, curse, bless, boast, defy, invoke, annoy, injure, declare one's hostility, praise, blame, and so on). But Firth does not go beyond this list, which obviously belongs to the realm of enumeration rather than to that of the operative hypothesis.

At about the same time, and in a completely independent fashion, similar work was being undertaken within the Linguistic Circle of Prague. The approach of the Prague linguists [25] is resolutely functional; as a result, they are attentive not only to the principal functions of language, in the spirit of Bühler [340ff.], but also to those functions—far more numerous—that a particular utterance can assume. B. Havránek postulates that it is the response of the addressee that determines the function of the utterance, and he proposes the following classification: (1) factual communication, information; (2) exhortation, persuasion; (3) general explanation; (4) technical explanation; and (5) codifying formulation. Havránek does not always distinguish this functional description from a stylistic description founded on the presence or the absence of certain linguistic features, although he formulates the difference very clearly: it "consists in the fact that the *functional style* is determined by the specific purpose of the given verbal response; it is a function of the verbal response (of the act of speech, 'parole'), whereas the *functional dialect* . . . is a function of the linguistic pattern ('langue')" ("The Functional Differentiation of the Standard Language," pp. 15–16). More recently, M. Joos has attempted to describe the articulation of all languages according to five functional styles that he calls intimate, informal, consultative, formal, and frozen. These styles correspond to five degrees of elaboration and can be observed, according to Joos, at all the linguistic levels—phonological, syntactic, lexical. For example, the careful pronunciation of all the sounds of which a verbal sequence is composed or the elision of certain sounds will allow us to identify formal or informal style. We have thus come back to the interrelationship of two independent units, language and society, the one reflecting the other.

French ethnologists (Durkheim, Mauss, Granet) have always been sensitive to the facts of language; and French linguists (Saussure, Meillet, Vendryes) have tried to ground their conception of language in a theory of social facts. Nevertheless, not until the work of a student of Meillet,

M. Cohen, was there a systematic presentation of the field. In place of the *function* referred to by Malinowski, Firth, and Havránek, Cohen speaks of the *powers* of language, which he groups in the following manner:

1. Speech and extra-human forces (totemic ceremonies, conciliation of the spirits: magic, sorcery, divination; religion; names of beings; names of places).

2. Formulas that are efficacious in human relationships (meeting and separation; request and thanks; enthronement and exclusion; congratulation, wish, blame, condolence, dedication; pledges, oaths, hostility, and pacification; codified prescriptions).

3. Persuasion and instruction (oratorical contests; pleadings; discourse in deliberative assemblies; edification and exhaltation; religious and political propaganda; advertisement; teaching; inquiry and suggestion; formal reasoning and terminological analysis).

4. Diversion (literature; theatre; radio and television; word games). Once again we confront a list that is chaotic but at least bears witness to the wealth of the field of study.

An unexpected contribution to linguistic anthropology has come from the English philosophers, specialists in "ordinary language." Wittgenstein and especially Austin have sought to describe the different uses of language; this has led Austin to elaborate the notion of illocutionary force (in which one recognizes Malinowski's *function* and Cohen's *power*) [343ff.]. His illocutionary force is a dimension of every utterance, linked to its meaning but not identical with it. Seeking to itemize these forces, Austin tests the complete list of English verbs that signify a verbal action (such as *assert, declare, suggest, appraise, characterize, define; order, advise, beg; name, recommend, propose; promise, guarantee, pledge; thank, pardon, excuse,* and so on); he thus produces a "popular taxonomy" whose scientific pertinence is not guaranteed (do all of the illocutionary forces possess distinct names?). Nevertheless, this concrete point of departure allows him to describe the facts much more precisely than his predecessors and to demonstrate the variety of forces in question. Austin's work does not seek to be anthropological, and its classifications are purely formal; it constitutes nonetheless one of the most interesting contributions to this controversial field.

Since the sixties, in the United States, under the combined influence of linguists, ethnologists, and psychologists, a linguistic anthropology has begun to constitute itself as an autonomous discipline. The advantage of studies such as those of D. Hymes and S. Ervin-Tripp is that they take into account the preceding traditions and do not limit themselves to pure descriptivism. Hymes, who designates this activity as "the ethnography of speaking," bases his work on the analysis of the communicative act, carried out by Jakobson, into six factors and six functions [341]. Ervin-Tripp also distinguishes the setting, the participants, the topic, the functions of the interaction, and the formal features of communication. The functions, for example, are categorized in the following groups: (1) requests for goods, services, or information; (2) requests for social responses; (3) offering information or interpretation; (4) expressive monologues; (5) routines (greetings, thanks, apologies, and so on); and (6) avoidance conversations (in which the goal is to speak in order to avoid participating in another, less pleasant activity). Ervin-Tripp's criterion of classification, like Havránek's, is, the hearer's response.

The future of linguistic anthropology is promising, but it obviously depends on further progress in the study of enunciation [323] and in semantics [54].

● See B. Malinowski, "The Problem of Meaning in Primitive Languages," in *The Meaning of Meaning*, ed. C. K. Ogden and I. A. Richards (London, 1923); idem., *The Language of Magic and Gardening* (London, 1935); J. R. Firth, *Papers in Linguistics 1934–1951* (London and New York, 1957); B. Havránek, "The Functional Differentiation of the Standard Language," in *A Prague School Reader on Esthetics, Literary Structure and Style*, ed. P. L. Garvin (Washington, D.C., 1964), pp. 3–16; M. Joos, *The Five Clocks* (Bloomington, 1962); M. Cohen, *Pour une sociologie du langage* (Paris, 1956); L. Wittgenstein, *The Blue and Brown Books* (New York, 1965); J. L. Austin, *How To Do Things With Words* (Cambridge, Mass., 1962); D. Hymes, "The Ethnography of Speaking," S. M. Ervin-Tripp, "An Analysis of the Interaction of Language, Topic and Listener," and L. Marshall, "Sharing, Talking and Giving: Relief of Social Tensions Among 'Kung Bushmen"—all in *Readings in the Sociology of Language* (The Hague, 1968), ed. J. A. Fishman, pp. 99–138, 192–211, and 179–84, respectively; G. Calame-Griaule, *Ethnologie et langage: La Parole chez les dogons* (Paris, 1965); J. J. Gumperz and D. Hymes, eds., *The Ethnography of Communication, American Anthropologist* 6 (1964), pt. 2; idem. eds., *Directions in Sociolinguistics* (New York, 1972); R. Bauman and J. F. Sherzer, eds., *Explorations in the Ethnography of Speaking* (Cambridge, 1974); and D. Hymes, *Foundations in Sociolinguistics: An Ethnographic Approach* (Philadelphia, 1974). See also the journal *Language in Society*, published in London and edited by D. Hymes since 1972.

PSYCHOLINGUISTICS

The importance attached to the psychological processes of language production and language comprehension is not new, and one might well be surprised that psycholinguistics has emerged only recently. It has been necessary, paradoxically, to wait for linguistics to rid itself of psychological considerations and to constitute itself as the autonomous study of linguistic systems. But we have also had to wait until psychology developed descriptive and explanatory concepts of behavior that were compatible with as complex an activity as that of language; for a long time what the psychologist called language did not have very much to do with linguistic considerations.

Language and Behaviorism:
The Stimulus-Response Schema (S-R)

In 1924, J. B. Watson, founder of **behaviorism** (a theory establishing experimental psychology as a study of observable behavior in which observability is defined in opposition to mentalist notions on the one hand and to introspectionist methods on the other), entitled a chapter as follows: "*Talking and Thinking*, which, when rightly understood, go far in breaking down the fiction that there is any such thing as 'mental' life" (*Behaviorism*, chap. 10). "What the psychologists have hitherto called thought," he concluded, "is in short nothing but talking to ourselves" (ibid., p. 238). And talking, if it is not precisely laryngeal movement (since one can whisper without a larynx), is nevertheless simply a motor activity. Psychological studies can only be made of observable responses (reactions). This position, as such, was not upheld very long, but it underlies a dominant current of thought that renders impossible all problematics on language. Psychology attempts to account for all human behavior in terms of the formation of habits (verbal habits, among others) whose underlying schema is the conditioned reflex. In a stimulus situation a response (reaction) is produced. If the latter is reinforced (by a reward, for example), then the **association** between the stimulus and the response is itself reinforced; this means that the response will very probably be triggered by every reappearance of the stimulus. I. Pavlov, conscious of the problem posed by the peculiar system of signals that is language, invented the vague notion of a **second signaling system** to designate the possibility of substituting the linguistic mode of signaling for a more elementary system. C. Hull (1930) attempted to describe the diversity of behavior in a given situation by proposing a more complex schema: he introduced the notion of hierarchy of habits, that is, of patterns of response that have a greater or lesser probability of occurring. In other words, language remains reduced to its secondary aspects: a set of **verbal responses** to situations. We find this confusion today between verbal responses and language (for example, in B. F. Skinner's *Verbal Behavior*); it persists implicitly in certain pedagogical methods for learning a second language. Moreover, in 1969 and 1970 experiments attempting to teach a language to chimpanzees by conditioning techniques gave new life to this theoretical perspective. Since the chimpanzee lacks the capacity to modulate sounds, researchers have used either the sign language of deaf-mutes (R. A. Gardner et al.) or tokens of varying forms, and the animal arranges them in order (D. Premack). Chimpanzees learn in fact to manipulate properties of the predicate type [269], in which there are no syntactic marks other than the order in which the terms appear. This language is of the same type as that of children about eighteen months old. (It corresponds, in a general way, according to what was already known about the chimpanzee's intelligence, to the developmental state of an eighteen-month-old child's sensory-motor intelligence.) The possibility of teaching a language by conditioning techniques does not mean that the learning thus acquired has been produced by associations between stimulus and response. The results obtained are interesting inasmuch as they make it possible to study the limits of the means of communication taught to chimpanzees as compared with those of human language and to relate these limits to the problematic nature of the **semiotic function** that they presuppose in the animal; however, this possibility of learning does not by any means justify the stimulus-response theory of language.

● Representative texts are J. B. Watson, *Behaviorism* (New York, 1924), and B. F. Skinner, *Verbal Behavior* (New York, 1957); for a critique of the latter, see N. Chomsky, "A Review of B. F. Skinner's *Verbal Behavior*," *Language* 35 (1959): 26–58. On the chimpanzee, see R. A. Gardner and B. T. Gardner, "Teaching Sign Language to Chimpanzees," *Science* 165 (1969): 664–72.

Language, Mediationist S-R Schema, and Schemas of Communication

In this period of struggle by psychology to acquire the status of a natural science, a positive element emerges: since the conditioning schema does not suffice to account for all the types of learning, the notion of intermediary processes—not directly observable and susceptible to interference on the basis of controlled modifications of the stimuli and the responses—has become necessary. At the moment when these intermediary processes become clearly the principal object of study, research on language is about to begin, and theories of **mediation** arise. The notion of mediation appears in order to account, on the one hand, for the possibility of establishing relations between stimuli that are not actually linked by an objective resemblance (a word and the object it designates, for example) and, on the other hand, for the possibility of choosing among responses for a single stimulus. For example: (1) a word (sound pattern) is learned in association with an object that it designates; (2) the subject has, in addition, a certain global reaction to the sight of that object; (3) the presentation of the word-object couple will result in the transference to the word of a (not directly observable) part of the reaction to the object. We see in this example an attempt to utilize the notion of mediation to account for the acquisition of the signification of a word. But if the notion of mediation is important, its direct application in a stimulus-response schema corresponds to a conception of language as a set of verbal responses, in which the production of meaning is reduced to the labeling of objects.

The **gestaltist theory** had been developed earlier to counter the notion of association as the basis of the constitution of behavior patterns. The gestaltists insisted on the necessity of considering thought, perception, and language as structured and structuring activities. In 1933, in his analysis of aphasic disorders [161ff.], the gestaltist K. Goldstein treated language as a global activity, although he found it necessary to distinguish between the problem of the organization of the verbal means by which thought may be represented (word order, inflection, and so on) and the problem of categorial conceptualization. By and large, the gestaltists were relatively unconcerned with the genesis of the organization they described—except to deny it.

At about the same time, J. Piaget was elaborating his own theory of this **genesis.** The results of his research clearly ran counter to a conception of development based on an accumulation of habits progressing with age; they also contradicted the conception according to which the structure of the organizing activity was innate. He demonstrated at the same time the relative independence of the intellectual development of the child, in the earliest stages, with respect to the development of language: the symbolic (or semiotic) function, of which language is one element, appears before language develops. The notion of structuring activity, of productive behavior—a notion essential to this theory and similar to those that N. Chomsky develops later concerning language—had little immediate impact. Critics labeled "mentalist" the notion of the subject's structuring activity; they did not see that the theory provided a way to describe how the system, formed by the subject-environment pair, could progressively transform itself. This notion has found wider acceptance in biology than in psychology.

This perspective on intellectual development, which later would allow the problem of language acquisition to be reformulated, was not reconsidered in the United States until the early sixties, when Chomsky's work offered a serious challenge, from a linguistic point of view, to the behaviorist perspective on language acquisition.

At the time when mediationist behaviorism was beginning to develop, C. E. Shannon's *The Mathematical Theory of Communication* appeared (1949). This theory first led to the consideration of language as communication behavior (J. Janet had already insisted on this point in 1920) and to the study of the processes of encoding and decoding verbal messages in different situations. Defining this program in 1954, C. E. Osgood and T. A. Sebeok labeled it **psycholinguistics.** More precisely, the probabilist mathematical model used in communication theory came to be used to describe the hierarchy of responses: the system of transitional probabilities between successive units (Markov chains) is directly related to the system of habit forces. The syntagmatic liaisons [106] in particular were studied in this framework. It was shown, for example, that a satisfactory approach could be made to the factors that account for the facilitation of learning—formerly described as "meaning" or "structure"—through the Markovian structure of dependency among letters or words (the role of redundancy). But in fact this model can only describe the statistical manifestations of the regularities of language; it cannot provide a description of the way in which these regularities function. The correspondence set up between systems of habit forces and Markovian language structure was thus an illusory one.

It is entirely possible that mastery of language has a bearing on, among other things, the transitional probabilities among phonemes, monemes, and so on, and that the speaker's implicit knowledge of these probabilities plays a role in error avoidance as he encodes and decodes messages. But the basic criticism addressed to the notion of an associative force of variable intensity among successive elements bears upon the following points: (1) The processes of encoding and decoding have to function upon messages that are always new (the sentences and sets of sentences produced and understood are always new). (2) The production of an utterance, like its comprehension, does not take place sequentially, unit by unit (whatever the level of the units considered). The neurophysiologist K. Lashley had already pointed out in 1951 that the order of production of the sounds of a word, of the words of a sentence, and so on, cannot correspond to the order of preparation for production; he used the term "syntactic" to describe the organization underlying most apparently **sequential behavior.** (3) Under these conditions, it is difficult to see (*a*) how the forces of association between stimulus and response can be at the root of the encoding and decoding processes and (*b*) how the child could learn to speak and to understand by constituting habits of this type for himself [157ff.].

- Representative texts are S. Saporta, ed., *Psycholinguistics: A Book of Readings* (New York, 1961); and J. de Ajuriaguerra et al., eds., *Problèmes de psycholinguistique* (Paris, 1963). An overview (as of 1964) is offered by F. Bresson, "Language and Communication," in *Experimental Psychology: Its Scope and Method,* ed. P. Fraisse and J. Piaget, 9 vols. (New York, 1968–70), vol. 8 (1969), chap. 26. See also T. G. Bever, "The Interaction of Perception and Linguistic Structures: A Preliminary Investigation of Neo-Functionalism," in *Current Trends in Linguistics,* ed. T. A. Sebeok, 14 vols. (The Hague, 1963–76), vol. 12, *Linguistics and Adjacent Arts and Sciences* (1974), pt. 6, pp. 1159–1233; and T. G. Bever, J. J. Katz, and D. T. Langendoen, *An Integrated Theory of Linguistic Ability* (New York, 1976). Some recent introductory texts are H. H. Clark and E. V. Clark, *Psychology and Language* (New York, 1977); and D. J. Foss and D. T. Hakes, *Psycholinguistics* (New York, 1978).

Psycholinguistics and Generative Grammars

In 1956 N. Chomsky insisted that the Markovian probabilist models of learning, models of finite automata [229] are not compatible with a "context-free" language [227]. In a general way, Chomsky's work permitted a renewed emphasis on the productive aspects of linguistic conduct. In Europe these considerations found the ground already prepared for them in the framework of Piaget's theory of the genesis of intellectual development. In the United States, on the other hand, a renewed questioning of the behaviorist schema took its point of departure in Chomsky's work.

A whole current of psycholinguistics has thus been devoted to the study of the mode of passage from deep structure to surface structure [244] and to the effort to bring to light the psychological reality of transformations (by techniques that relate, for example, to the time it takes to produce or to understand sentences; the time differentials depend on the transformations imposed). But these techniques have raised the problem of justifying the transformations: to the extent that the idea of purely voluntary transformations has been abandoned, generative linguists have been led to reconsider semantic problems, as well as the problems of the enunciative process [323ff.] (for example, the problem of understanding ambiguous sentences, in which for a single surface structure two or more different deep structures must be decoded; the problem of transformations applied to different classes of verbs, and so on). By reintroducing semantics, linguists have expanded the study of the production and the comprehension of language to include the **cognitive processes.** The investigation of language acquisition in particular has demonstrated that the cognitive processes must be introduced as an integral part of the problematics [156ff.]. The new perspective provided by generative grammars have also revealed the limitations of experimental techniques based solely on isolated sentences.

● Representative texts are J. A. Fodor et al., "Psycholinguistics and Communication Theory," in *Human Communication Theory*, ed. F. E. Dance (New York, 1967); J. Mehler, ed., *Langages*, vol. 16 (1969), which contains French translations of articles that appeared between 1959 and 1967; G. A. Miller and N. Chomsky, "Finitary Models of Language Users," in *Handbook of Mathematical Psychology*, ed. D. R. Luce et al., 3 vols. (New York, 1963–65), vol. 2; G. A. Miller, "Linguistic Aspects of Cognition: Predication and Meaning," in *Cognitive Psychology Handbook*, ed. J. Mehler (Englewood Cliffs, 1970). For an overview and bibliography covering the years 1958–65, see S. M. Ervin-Tripp and D. I. Slobin, "Psycholinguistics," *Annual Review of Psychology* 17 (1966): 435–74; cf. also the references provided on pp. 160 and 167 below.

RHETORIC AND STYLISTICS

The birth of **rhetoric** as a specific discipline is the first indication in the Western tradition of a reflection on language. It is first attested in Sicily in the fifth century B.C. A legend relates that Hieron, at that time tyrannical ruler of Syracuse, had forbidden his subjects to speak. Thus made conscious of the importance of speech, the Sicilians (Corax, Tisias) created rhetoric. They began to study language, not as a tongue (the way one learns to speak a foreign language), but as discourse.

In the democracies of the period, eloquence became a necessary weapon; the idea of "teaching speech" probably arose from this need. At the outset rhetoric was above all a technique intended to allow its possessor to achieve, within a discursive situation, the desired goal. Thus it had a pragmatic character: to convince the interlocutor of the rightness of a cause. But in order to make a more effective use of discourse, one must be well acquainted with its properties. Aristotle and his contemporaries already had available to them a body of knowledge—categories and rules—that only partly overlaps with what we call linguistics. One rhetoric of the period, slightly later than Aristotle's, included the following components: (1) *inventio*: subjects, arguments, places, techniques of persuasion and amplification; (2) *dispositio*: arrangement of the major parts of the discourse (exordium, narration, discussion, peroration); (3) *elocutio*: choice and disposition of words in sentences, detailed organization; (4) *pronuntiatio*: enunciation of the discourse; and (5) *memoria*: memorization. Parts (1), (4), and (5) appear to us today as preceding or following the discourse itself. Ancient rhetoric proposed to study only three types of discourse, defined by the circumstances in which they were produced: (1) *deliberative*, corresponding approximately to our political discourse, customarily addressed to an assembly and through which one advises or dissuades; (2) *judiciary*, in which one accuses others or defends oneself; and (3) *epidictic*, in which one praises or blames. The Greek and Roman authors (Cicero, Quintilian, Dionysius of Halicarnassus) emphasize one part or another of the rhetoric but maintain the overall scheme in its essential outline.

During the twenty subsequent centuries, rhetoric has undergone several essential modifications. First, it has lost its immediate pragmatic aim: it no longer teaches persuasion, but rather production of "beautiful" discourse. Thus it has been increasingly disinterested in the deliberative and judiciary genres, for example, and has shown a predilection for taking literature as its object. It has also increasingly cut back its field. *Pronuntiatio* and *memoria* disappeared first, then *inventio*, and finally *dispositio*; in other words, rhetoric now finds itself reduced to *elocutio*, or the art of style. The later rhetorics (in the eighteenth and nineteenth centuries) often, though not always, present only a simple enumeration of figures [273ff.].

The beginning of the nineteenth century saw the last of the great rhetorics (Fontanier's is one of the best examples). Several reasons for this disappearance can be proposed: the advent of the romantic spirit, with its conception of poetry as the irrational and unknowable activity of a solitary genius, proclaiming the uselessness of all rules; the predominance of the historicist mentality in contemporary studies of language (discovery of Indo-European), rhetoric being above all synchronic; the classifying tendency of the rhetoricians, who were more devoted to labeling than to analyzing and discovering the underlying linguistic categories. Whatever the reasons may be, rhetoric disappeared from education as an obligatory discipline, and its categories and subdivisions began to be forgotten.

In our day a certain renewal of interest can be observed in regard to the definition of figures. This renewal originates, however, more in contemporary linguistics than in the old rhetoric. Today stylistics, discourse analysis, and linguistics itself are reconsidering, in a different perspective, the problems that formerly constituted the object of rhetoric.

● Histories of rhetoric include O. Navarre, *Essai sur la rhétorique grecque avant Aristote* (Paris, 1900); A.-E. Chaignet, *La Rhétorique et son histoire* (Paris, 1888); C. S. Baldwin, *Ancient Rhetoric and Poetic* (1924; reprint ed., Gloucester, 1959); idem, *Medieval Rhetoric and Poetic* (1928; reprint ed., Gloucester, 1959); idem, *Renaissance Literary Theory and Practice* (New York, 1939); G. Kennedy, *The Art of Persuasion in Greece* (Princeton, 1963); idem, *The Art of Rhetoric in the Roman World* (Princeton, 1972); J. Murphy, *Rhetoric in the Middle Ages* (Berkeley, 1974); E. R. Curtius, *European Literature and the Latin Middle Ages*, trans. W. R. Trask (1953; reprint ed., Princeton, 1967); and A. Kibedi Varga, *Rhétorique et littérature* (Paris, 1970).

Representative rhetorical treatises, recently reprinted, include D. Bailay, ed., *Essays on Rhetoric* (New York, 1965), comprising excerpts from Aristotle, H. Blair, Campbell, Cicero, Joos, Plato, Quintilian, and H. Spencer; C. C. Dumarsais, *Les Tropes*, followed by P. Fontanier's *Commentaire raisonné* (1818; facsimile ed., Geneva, 1967); P. Fontanier, *Les Figures du discours* (Paris, 1968); and H. Lausberg, *Handbuch der literarischen Rhetorik* (Munich, 1960), a summation of the classical rhetorics.

Recent research includes J. Cohen, *Structure du langage poétique* (Paris, 1966), and J. Dubois et al., *Rhétorique générale* (Paris, 1970); and *Communications* 16 (1970): *Recherches rhétoriques.*

Stylistics is rhetoric's most direct heir, and it is certainly not by chance that it was elaborated at the end of the nineteenth century and the beginning of the twentieth. But if the idea of stylistics is new, the notion of style is not, and the immediate origin of stylistics must be sought in meditations on this latter concept [300ff.]. Two approaches in particular are of interest to us here. First, as early as the eighteenth century the critique of style, or the art of writing, was pursued in collections of practical indications on the ways of writing well, indications often supported by examples drawn from classical works; such treatises, normative and didactic, continue to exist today. At the same time, a certain conception was being developed that we find summarized in Buffon's celebrated formula, "The style is the man himself" (this has a different meaning in context), the conception of the author expressing himself in his work, marking it with his inimitable stamp, his individual specificity.

C. Bally's *Stylistique* (1905), the first work of its type, stood in direct opposition to the approaches presented above. In the first place, it was descriptive, not normative; in the second place, it was not concerned with writers nor even with literature in general. Bally sought to develop a stylistics of the language, not of literary works. Starting from the idea that language expresses thought *and* feelings, he concluded that the expression of feelings constituted the proper object of stylistics. This amounts to saying that stylistics is concerned, not with the utterance itself, but with the introduction into the utterance of the process of enunciation. Bally distinguished two types of relationships, which he called natural effects and evocation effects: by the former we are informed about the feelings experienced by the speaker; by the latter we are informed about his linguistic milieu. These effects are achieved, according to Bally, by a judicious choice in the lexicon and, to a lesser degree, in the syntax; the two types of effects possess forms that are identical with respect to the expression of thought but have different affective expressivity.

A few years later, in the same spirit, J. Marouzeau and Cressot systematically described all the sounds, parts of speech, and syntactic constructions of the French language, as well as the lexicon, focusing in each case on features exterior to the notional content. At the same time, stylisticians were moving beyond Bally's deductive system in efforts to extract the affective common denominator from each category on the basis of a few examples—always drawn from classical literature. (Other researchers have often judged such efforts futile.)

Some ten years after Bally, the work of L. Spitzer, the other great initiator of modern stylistics, was inaugurated. Early in his work Spitzer sought to establish a correlation between the stylistic properties of a text and the psyche of the author. Once again we hear that "the style is the man himself," although Spitzer was more interested in the world view of the writer than in the details of his biography. In a second phase of his work, Spitzer abandoned the idea of an author exterior to the text and described exclusively the system of stylistic devices present in the text. The notion of stylistic fact is broader for Spitzer than for Bally; it can refer to thought as well as to feelings. What distinguishes the stylistic fact is its mode of existence in the text: it strikes the reader (the critic) because it is too frequent or because it is unjustified in its context or because it is excessively accentuated, and so on. In the course of these two phases Spitzer remained attached to the analysis of works and never sought to establish the stylistic system of a language. This attitude (sometimes called new stylistics) has had many adherents since Spitzer's day.

Critique

These two attitudes, Bally's and Spitzer's, prefigure very accurately the ambiguity of today's stylistic research. Under different labels these two orientations continue to compete for first place: linguistic stylistics versus literary stylistics, stylistics of the code versus stylistics of the message, stylistics of expression versus genetic stylistics, and so on. However, the opposition is perhaps more apparent than real, or at least it can perhaps be reduced to that of a theory and its application. When the interaction of certain categories is shown to create the stylistic specificity of a text, these categories are borrowed from a (linguistic or rhetoric or stylistic) theory. Conversely, when the stylistic properties of a language are studied, it is no less necessary to base the study on concrete texts that illustrate these properties. This relationship is homologous with that of poetics to reading [80]. It is true that the stylistic analysis of texts (like reading) is characterized by certain techniques that remain its own. Thus Jakobson has indicated directions for studying the paradigmatic relationships among the constitutive elements of a text, as Riffaterre has done for the study of syntagmatic relationships; but in isolation these techniques do not constitute a type of knowledge that theory alone can elaborate. It is easy to conceive of a stylistics that would have a theoretical scope larger than Bally's (that is, one that would not be limited to the "expression of affectivity" in language) and that would provide the means for analyzing individual texts or—another version of the same thing—an analysis of stylistic facts modeled on Spitzer's but attempting to systematize its theoretical implications in a coherent doctrine bearing on the properties of language.

Ultimately, it is essential to specify the proper object of stylistics. For a long time the stylistician's role was that of an explorer who annexes new territories but does not exploit them seriously before the arrival of the well-equipped technician, in this case the linguist. The job, accomplished by Bally, of comparing and distinguishing synonyms by rights belongs to semantics today, for the postulate that the difference between two synonyms is only stylistic leaves no place, between the stylistic and the referential, for meaning—an inconceivable approach. A stylistics limited to the role Bally assigned to it would thus have a merely preliminary and provisional function. But we can envisage quite a different domain as the province of stylistics if we postulate that in every linguistic utterance there are a certain number of relations, laws, or constraints that can be explained, not by the mechanism of language, but only by that of discourse. A new science of discourse analysis, replacing the earlier rhetoric as a general science of discourse, would have vertical subdivisions, such as poetics (which is concerned with a single type of discourse, the literary), and horizontal subdivisions, such as stylistics (whose object would be constituted not by all the problems related to one type of discourse but rather by one type of problem concerning all discourse). This new science would cover much the same ground as the old *elocutio*: with the exception of the problems raised by the thematic aspect of discourse or of its syntactic organization, it would include all and only that which we have defined elsewhere [294] as the verbal aspect of the text. Discourse analysis so construed would thus constitute the study of styles [300ff.]. A large number of current projects are heading in this direction.

• Bibliographies include H. A. Hatzfeld, *A Critical Bibliography of the New Stylistics*, 2 vols. (Chapel Hill, 1953–1966), *I. 1900–1952* and *II. 1953–1965*; L. T. Milic, *Style and Stylistics: An Analytical Bibliography* (New York, 1967); and R. Bailey and D. Burton, *English Stylistics: A Bibliography* (Cambridge, Mass., 1968).
Overviews are A. Juilland, *"L'Epoque réaliste; première partie: Fin du romantisme et Parnasse. Par Charles Bruneau. Histoire de la langue française.* Reviewed by A. G. Juilland," in *Language* 30 (1954): 313–38; G. Antoine, "La Stylistique française, sa définition, ses buts, ses méthodes," *Revue de l'enseignement supérieur*, January 1959; H. Mitterand, "La Stylistique," *Le Français dans le monde* 6, no. 42 (1966): 13–18; P. Guiraud, *La Stylistique* (Paris, 1970); and T. Todorov, "Les Études du style," *Poétique* 1 (1970): 224–32.
Representative texts are C. Bally, *Traité de stylistique française*, 3d ed. (Geneva, 1951); L. Spitzer, *Linguistics and Literary History: Essays in Stylistics* (Princeton, 1967); J. Marouzeau, *Précis de stylistique française* (Paris, 1946); M. Cressot, *Le Style et ses techniques* (Paris, 1947); S. Chatman and S. Levin, eds., *Essays in the Language of Literature* (Boston, 1967); P. Guiraud and P. Kuentz, eds., *La Stylistique: Lectures* (Paris, 1970); P. Guiraud, *Essais de stylistique* (Paris, 1970); and M. Riffaterre, *Essais de stylistique structurale* (Paris, 1971).

POETICS

The term "poetics," as transmitted to us by tradition, designates, firstly, any internal theory of literature. Secondly, it applies to the choice made by an author among all the literary possibilities (on the order of thematics, composition, style, and so on): a critic may speak of "Hugo's poetics" in this sense. Thirdly, it refers to the normative codes con-structed by a literary school, a set of practical rules whose use is obliga-tory. Only the first use of the term will concern us here.

Poetics thus understood proposes to elaborate categories that allow us to grasp simultaneously the unity and the variety of literary works. The individual work will illustrate these categories; its status will be that of example, not of ultimate end. For example, poetics will be called upon to elaborate a theory of description that will bring to light not only what all descriptions have in common but also what permits them to remain different; but it will not be asked to account for particular de-scriptions in a given text. Poetics will then be capable of defining a con-junction of categories of which we know of no instance *at the moment*. In this sense, the object of poetics is constituted more by potential works than by existing ones.

This primary option defines the scientific ambition of poetics: the object of a science is not the particular fact but the laws that allow us to account for it. Unlike the known attempts to establish what is (in such cases) improperly called a science of literature, poetics does not pro-pose as its task the "correct" interpretation of the works of the past; rather it proposes the elaboration of instruments permitting the analysis of these works. Its object is not the set of existing literary works, but literary discourse itself as the generative principle of an infinite number of texts. Poetics is thus a theoretical discipline nourished and fertilized by empirical research but not constituted by it.

Among its major tasks poetics must first supply an answer to the question, What is literature? In other words, it must try to reduce this sociological phenomenon that has been called literature to an internal and theoretical entity (or else demonstrate the lack of such an entity); or, to take another approach, it must define literary discourse with respect to other types of discourse and thus give itself an object of knowledge that is the product of a theoretical undertaking and, con-sequently, at a certain distance from observable facts. The answer to this first question will be at once a starting point and a final goal; every-thing in the work of the poetician must contribute to this elucidation, which by definition can never be complete.

Second, poetics must supply instruments for the description of a literary text; that is, it must be able to distinguish levels of meaning, to identify the units that constitute them, and to describe the relationships in which the units participate. With the assistance of these primary cate-gories, we can begin to study certain more or less stable configurations. We can undertake, in other words, the study of types, or genres [149ff.]; we can also study the laws of succession, that is, of literary history [144ff.].

The goals and objects of poetics must be distinguished from those of neighboring disciplines: (1) **Reading** assigns itself the task of describing the system of a particular text. It uses the instruments elaborated by poetics, but it is more than the simple application of these instruments; its goal—which is different from that of poetics—is to bring to light the meaning of a particular text, insofar as the meaning cannot be exhausted by the categories of poetics. (2) The object of linguistics is the language itself, the object of poetics, a discourse; nevertheless, both often depend on the same concepts. Each is inscribed within the framework of semiotics [84ff.], whose object is all signifying systems. (3) The acquisitions of poetics may provide a contribution to anthropological or psychological research. The problems of esthetic value in particular, intimately linked as they are to the whole of cultural evolution, arise in the anthropological framework.

● See Barthes, *Critique et vérité* (Paris, 1966); and T. Todorov, *Poétique* (Paris, 1973).

Historical Background

Although poetics has been constituted as a theoretical discipline only recently, it has a long prehistory. Theoretical reflection on literature seems inseparable from literature itself; this could be explained by the tendency of the literary text to take itself as its own object. In the West we are in the habit of locating the beginning of poetics in Greek antiquity; however, a similar body of thought was constituted at the same time, or even earlier, in China and in India.

Aristotle's *Poetics* was the first systematic treatise, and no other text compares to it in historical importance. In a certain light, the entire history of poetics is nothing but the reinterpretation of the Aristotelian text. It is not so much a book as notes in view of a course, notes that contain both lacunae and unintelligible passages; but Aristotle aims explicitly at the constitution of a general theory of literature, which he develops only with respect to two genres, tragedy and the epic.

Aristotle's influence is not immediate. His treatise is not mentioned in the principal writings of the succeeding centuries—the anonymous treatise *On the Sublime*, Horace's *Ars Poetica*, and so on. The Middle Ages follow Horace more than Aristotle; innumerable texts codify the rules of the poetic art at that time.

With the Renaissance, reference to Aristotle becomes obligatory. Italy is the center of the renewal (Scaliger, Castelvetro). During subsequent periods this center moves to Germany (Lessing and Herder), especially with the beginning of romanticism (the Schlegel brothers, Novalis, Hölderlin), and to England (Coleridge). With what is sometimes called symbolism, a doctrine whose principles are first formulated by Edgar Allen Poe, we pass to France (Mallarmé, Valéry).

Theoretical reflection on literature was never again to find the autonomy it had for Aristotle. As early as Latin antiquity the description of the poetic fact was swallowed up by rhetoric [741], and there was no more concern for the specificity of literary discourse. The poets themselves had a tendency to set up their own practice as a norm rather than to seek a coherent description of the facts. Beginning with the eighteenth century, poetics became a subdivision of philosophical esthetics (most particularly in Germany); and all interest in the concrete working of the text disappeared.

M. H. Abrams has recently proposed a **typology** of poetic theories, which accounts for their historical situation as well. He bases his typology on what he calls the four constitutive elements of the literary process— author, reader, work, universe—and on the greater or lesser emphasis placed by each theory on one or the other of these elements. The earliest theories were essentially concerned with the relationships between the work and the universe; these are **mimetic theories.** In the seventeenth and eighteenth centuries certain doctrines arose that were more concerned with the relationship between the work and the **reader;** these are **pragmatic theories.** Romanticism placed the emphasis on the personal genius of the author; here we can speak of **expressive theories.** Finally, with symbolism was inaugurated the era of **objective theories,** which describe the work itself. This division, of course, remains schematic and corresponds only rather imperfectly to the actual evolution of poetics; thus Aristotle's theory would be at once mimetic and objective.

● For the history of poetics, see the following:

a) General: G. Saintsbury, *History of Criticism and Literary Taste in Europe*, 3 vols. (London, 1900–1904); W. K. Wimsatt and C. Brooks, *Literary Criticism: A Short History* (New York, 1957).

b) By periods: On the Middle Ages, see E. Faral, *Les Arts poétiques du XIIᵉ et du XIIIᵉ siècle* (Paris, 1924); E. de Bruyne, *The Esthetics of the Middle Ages*, trans. E. B. Hennessy (New York, 1969); and E. R. Curtius, *European Literature and the Latin Middle Ages*, trans. W. R. Trask (1953; reprint ed., Princeton, 1967). On the Renaissance, J. E. Spingarn, *A History of Literary Criticism in the Renaissance* (New York, 1899). On Romanticism, M. H. Abrams, *The Mirror and the Lamp: Romantic Theory and the Critical Tradition* (New York, 1953). And on the modern period, R. Wellek, *A History of Modern Criticism 1750–1950*, 4 vols. to date (New Haven, 1955–); and J. Culler, *Structuralist Poetics* (Ithaca and London, 1975).

c) By country: For India, see S. K. De, *History of Sanscrit Poetics*, 2 vols. (Calcutta, 1960). For Greece and Rome, J. W. H. Atkins, *Literary Criticism in Antiquity*, 2 vols. (Cambridge, 1934); and G. M. A. Grube,

The Greek and Roman Critics (London, 1965). On Italy, B. Weinberg, *A History of Literary Criticism in the Italian Renaissance,* 2 vols. (Chicago, 1961). For Germany, Z. von Lempicki, *Geschichte der deutschen Literaturwissenschaft* (Göttingen, 1920); and B. Markwardt, *Geschichte der deutschen Poetik,* 3 vols. (Berlin, 1936–58). For England, J. W. H. Atkins, *English Literary Criticism,* 2 vols. (London, 1947–51). For Spain, M. Menendez y Pelayo, *Historia de las ideas estéticas en España,* 5 vols. (Madrid, 1883–89). Finally, for France, F. Brunetière, *L'Evolution de la critique depuis la Renaissance jusqu'à nos jours* (Paris, 1890); and R. Fayolle, *La Critique littéraire* (Paris, 1964).

Since the beginning of the twentieth century the evolution of criticism in several countries has heralded the advent of poetics as an autonomous theoretical discipline. This evolution can be observed through the example of formalism (in Russia), the morphological school (in Germany), new criticism (in the United States and in England), and structural analysis (in France).

Russian formalism links together a handful of researchers in Leningrad and Moscow between 1915 and 1930. It is organized around a refusal to regard literature as the transposition of any other series, whatever the nature of the latter might be (the author's biography, contemporary society, philosophical or religious theories); the formalists insist on whatever is specifically literary in the work (its "literarity"). It is Jakobson who formulates, as early as 1919, the point of departure for all poetics: "If literary studies wish to become a science, they must recognize the literary device as the unique character under investigation" (translated from "La nouvelle poésie russe," in *Questions de poétique* [Paris, 1973], p. 15). The formalists' research thus bears, not upon the individual work, but upon narrative structures (Shklovskii, Tomashevskii, Propp), stylistic structures (Eikhenbaum, Tynianov, Vinogradov, Bakhtin, Voloshinov), rhythmic structures (Brik, Tomashevskii), sound patterns (Brik, Jakobson), without leaving out literary evolution (Shklovskii, Tynianov), the relationship between literature and society (Tynianov, Voloshinov), and so on.

The activity of the **morphological school** can be located in Germany between 1925 and 1955. This school takes up, on the one hand, Goethe's heritage, his writings on the natural sciences as well as those on literature; on the other hand, under the influence of Croce and Vossler, it rejects historicism. Historically distinct from the stylistic studies of Spitzer [76ff.] or, later, of Staiger and Auerbach, the morphological school focuses on the genres and the forms of literary discourse rather than on the style of a writer. Here we should mention the work of André Jolles on the elementary genres (morality, enigma, proverb, legend, and so on) [155ff.]; that of O. Walzel on the registers of speech (objective narration, free indirect style) [303]; that of G. Müller on temporality [320ff.]; and that of E. Lämmert on narrative composition [322ff.]. The work of Wolfgang Kayser synthesizes this research but displaces the emphasis (toward an immanent reading of *each* work of art). He pays particular attention to the verbal matter of the literary text.

The correct use of the term **new criticism** is much more restricted than its current popularity might have us suppose. Without entering into terminological detail, we must not forget that a large part of Anglo-Saxon criticism (including new criticism) is openly hostile to all theories, and thus to poetics, considering as its exclusive task the interpretation of texts. It is nonetheless true that since the twenties, Anglo-Saxon critics have proposed hypotheses on the functioning of meaning in literature (I. A. Richards, W. Empson) [276], as well as on the problem of the narrator in fiction (P. Lubbock) [329ff.]. More recently, the problems of the poetic image, linked to categories such as those of ambiguity, irony, and paradox (Brooks, Wimsatt), have become central. The *Theory of Literature* of Wellek and Warren stems from a double influence: indirectly, that of Russian formalism, and directly, that of new criticism.

In France the domination of the historicist mentality on the one hand and of journalistic impressionism on the other for a long time prevented any development of poetics (in spite of the project announced by Valéry). Only since 1960, under the double influence of structuralism in ethnology and linguistics (Lévi-Strauss, Jakobson, Benveniste) and of a certain philosophico-literary undertaking (incarnated for example by M. Blanchot), have the first attempts at **structural analysis** emerged. They have taken the form of a renewed interest in rhetorical figures and versification and an exploration of narrative or textual structures; this work has been constantly linked to the name of R. Barthes.

● Texts of the Russian formalists in translation are L. T. Lemon and M. J. Reis, ed., *Russian Formalist Criticism: Four Essays* (Lincoln, 1965); T. Todorov, ed., *Théorie de la littérature* (Paris, 1965); L. Matejka and K. Pomorska, eds., *Readings in Russian Poetics* (Cambridge, Mass., 1971); J. Striedter and W. Kosny, eds., *Texte der russichen Formalisten*, 2 vols. (Munich, 1969–72) (bilingual edition); M. Bakhtin, *Problems of Dostoevsky's Poetics*, trans. R. W. Rotsel (Ann Arbor, 1973); V. Propp, *Morphology of the Folktale*, trans. L. Scott (Bloomington, 1958); J. Tynianov, *Le Problème de la langue du vers* (Paris, 1977); and V. Shklovskii, *Sur la théorie de la prose* (Lausanne, 1973).
On the morphological school, see O. Walzel, *Das Wortkunstwerk: Mittel seiner Erforschung* (Leipzig, 1926); A. Jolles, *Einfache Formen* (Halle

[Saale], 1956); G. Müller, *Morphologische Poetik* (Darmstadt, 1965); H. Oppel, *Morphologische Literaturwissenschaft* (Mainz, 1947); E. Lämmert, *Bauformen des Erzählens* (Stuttgart, 1955); and W. Kayser, *Das sprachliche Kunstwerk* (Bern, 1948).

On new criticism and related work, see I. A. Richards, *The Philosophy of Rhetoric* (New York, 1936); W. Empson, *Seven Types of Ambiguity* (London, 1930); idem, *Some Versions of Pastoral* (London, 1935); idem., *The Structure of Complex Words* (London, 1951); P. Lubbock, *The Craft of Fiction* (New York, 1921); R. B. West, ed., *Essays in Modern Literary Criticism* (New York, 1952); C. Brooks, *The Well Wrought Urn* (London, 1949); W. K. Wimsatt, *The Verbal Icon* (Lexington, 1954); R. Wellek and A. Warren, *Theory of Literature*, 3d ed., rev. (London, 1966); N. Frye, *Anatomy of Criticism* (Princeton, 1957); and S. Crane, ed., *Critics and Criticism* (Chicago, 1952). For a bibliography and overview, see K. Cohen, "Le New Criticism aux Etats-Unis," *Poétique* 10 (1972): 217–43.

On structural analysis, see R. Barthes, *Critical Essays*, trans. R. Howard (Evanston, 1972); idem, *Critique et vérité* (Paris, 1966); idem, *S/Z*, trans. R. Miller (New York, 1974); A. Kibedi Varga, *Les Constantes du poème* (The Hague, 1963); J. Cohen, *Structure du langage poétique* (Paris, 1966); G. Genette, *Figures* (Paris, 1966); idem, *Figures II* (Paris, 1969); idem, *Figures III* (Paris, 1972); T. Todorov, *Littérature et signification* (Paris, 1967); idem, *The Fantastic: A Structural Approach to a Literary Genre*, trans. R. Howard (Ithaca, 1975); idem, *The Poetics of Prose*, trans. R. Howard (Ithaca, 1977); R. Scholes, *Structuralism in Literature* (New Haven, 1975); and J. Culler, *Structuralist Poetics* (Ithaca and London, 1975).

SEMIOTICS

Historical Background

Semiotics (or semiology) is the science of signs [99ff.]. Since the verbal signs have always been in the limelight, reflection on signs was for a long time inseparable from reflection on language. There is an implicit semiotic theory in the linguistic speculations bequeathed to us by antiquity, in China as well as in India, Greece, and Rome. The modists of the Middle Ages also formulated some ideas on language that have semiotic implications. But the term "semiotics" itself did not appear until Locke. During the whole of this period, semiotics was not distinguished from the general theory—or philosophy—of language.

Semiotics became an independent discipline with the work of the American philosopher C. S. Peirce (1839–1914). For him it was a frame of reference that encompassed all other studies: "It has never been in my power to study anything—mathematics, ethics, metaphysics, gravitation, thermodynamics, optics, chemistry, comparative anatomy, astronomy, psychology, phonetics, economic [*sic*], history of science, whist, men and women, winè, metrology—except as a study of semiotic . . ." (*Letters to Lady Welby,* p. 32). It follows that Peirce's semiotic writings are as varied as the objects he enumerates. He failed to leave a coherent single work that would summarize the major principles of his doctrine. This has resulted in a certain ignorance of his thought that persists even today; his doctrines are all the more difficult to grasp in that they changed from year to year.

The initial originality of the Peircian system consists in his very definition of the sign. One of its formulations follows: "A *Sign,* or *Representamen,* is a First which stands in such a genuine triadic relation to a Second, called its Object, as to be capable of determining a Third, called its Interpretant, to assume the same triadic relation to its Object in which it stands itself to the same Object" (*Collected Papers,* vol. 2, *Elements of Logic,* p. 156). In order to understand this definition, it must be recalled that for Peirce, *all* human experience is organized at three levels that he calls firstness, secondness, and thirdness; these correspond roughly to the felt qualities, to the experience of effort, and to the signs. The sign is in turn a triadic relation, its three terms being (1) that which sets off the process of linkage; (2) its object; and (3) the effect that the sign produces (the interpretant). In a broad sense, the **interpretant** is thus the meaning of the sign; in a narrower sense, it is the paradigmatic relation between one sign and another. The interpretant is thus always also a sign, which will have its interpretant, and so on (this relation of sign to interpretant continues ad infinitum in the case of the "perfect" signs).

This conversion process between sign and interpretant could be illustrated by the relationships that a word maintains with the terms in the dictionary that define it—synonyms or paraphrases, all terms whose definitions (which will never be composed of anything but words) can be sought in turn. As Peirce used to remark, any sign may itself be translated into another sign in which it is more fully developed. Finally, it must be noted that this conception is alien to all psychologism: the conversion of sign to interpretant(s) occurs within the sign system, not in the minds of the users (consequently we are obliged not to take into account certain of Peirce's formulae, according to his own suggestion: "My insertion of 'upon a person' is a sop to Cerberus, because I despair of making my own broader conception understood" [*Letters to Lady Welby*, p. 29]).

A second remarkable aspect of Peirce's semiotic activity is his classification of the varieties of signs. We have already noticed that the number *3* plays a fundamental role (as the number *2* does for Saussure); the total number of varieties distinguished by Peirce is sixty-six. Certain of these distinctions have become quite commonplace, such as that of type and token, or legisign and sinsign [105].

Another recognized (but usually misinterpreted) distinction is that between **icon, index,** and **symbol.** These three levels of the sign correspond once again to the gradation firstness, secondness, thirdness and are defined in the following manner: "I define an Icon as a sign which is determined by its dynamic object by virtue of its own internal nature. . . . I define an Index as a sign determined by its Dynamic object by virtue of being in a real relation to it. . . . I define a Symbol as a sign which is determined by its dynamic object only in the sense that it will be so interpreted" (ibid., p. 12). The symbol refers to something through the force of a law; this is the case, for example, for the words of a language. The index is a sign that is placed in contiguity with the denoted object—for example, a symptom of illness; the lowering of the barometer; the weathervane, which shows the direction of the wind; the gesture of pointing. In language everything that relates to *deixis* [252] is an index: words such as *I, you, here, now*, and so on, are thus called indexical symbols. Finally, the icon is that which exhibits the same quality, or the same configuration of qualities, that the denoted object exhibits—for example a black spot for the color black; onomatopoeias; diagrams that reproduce relations among properties. Peirce further subdivided the icon into images, diagrams, and metaphors. It is readily apparent, however, that the iconic relationship can in no case be assimilated (as it often is, mistakenly) to that of resemblance between two signifieds (in rhetorical terms, the icon is a synecdoche rather than a metaphor: one can hardly say that the black spot *resembles* the color black); still less can one assimilate the indexical relationship to that of contiguity between two signs (contiguity in the index obtains between sign and referent, not between two entities of the same nature). Peirce expressly warns, moreover, against such an identification.

More or less simultaneously, but entirely independently, semiology is announced by F. de Saussure. Saussure functions as a linguist, not as a philosopher, and he needs semiology in order to inscribe linguistics within it. "Language [*la langue*] is a system of signs that express ideas, and is therefore comparable to a system of writing, the alphabet of deaf-mutes, symbolic rites, polite formulas, military signals, etc. But it is the most important of all these systems. *A science that studies the life of signs within society* is conceivable; it would be a part of social psychology and consequently of general psychology; I shall call it *semiology* (from Greek *sēmeîon*, 'sign'). Semiology would show what constitutes signs, what laws govern them. Since the science does not yet exist, no one can say what it would be; but it has a right to existence, a place staked out in advance" (*Course*, trans. W. Baskin [New York, 1959], chap. 3, sec. 3, of intro., p. 16). Saussure's direct contribution to non-linguistic semiology is more or less limited to these sentences, but they have played a major role; at the same time, his definitions of sign, signifier (*signans*), and signified (*signatum*), although formulated in function of verbal language, have gained the attention of all semioticians.

A third source of modern semiotics is the work of the German E. Cassirer. In his monumental work *The Philosophy of Symbolic Forms*, he poses the following principles clearly: (1) The role of language is more than instrumental; language serves not to denominate a preexisting reality but to articulate it, to conceptualize it. In this role, the symbolic—understood here in the broad sense of everything that has meaning (compare, to the contrary, the definition of *symbol*, below [102])—distinguishes man from the animals, who possess only systems of reception and of action (of firstness and secondness, Peirce would have said), and earns for man the name of *animal symbolicum*. (2) Verbal language is not the only system to enjoy this privilege; it is shared with a series of other systems that constitute together the sphere of the "human": myth, religion, art, science, history. Each one of these symbolic forms informs the world rather than imitating it. Cassirer's merit is that he wondered about the specific laws that govern symbolic systems and about their difference from the rules of logic. Multiple meanings here replace general concepts; representative figures replace classes; the reinforcement of ideas (through repetition, variation, and so on) replaces proof. Cassirer's work remains, however, a philosophic project much more than a scientific contribution.

A fourth source of modern semiotics is logic. Peirce himself had been a logician; but his ideas in this area had little immediate influence. We have to follow instead another line of succession that starts with Frege (whose distinction between *Sinn* and *Bedeutung* [249] is crucial for semiotics) and passes through Russell and Carnap; the latter constructed an ideal language that quickly came to serve as a model for semiotics. It was the American logician and philosopher C. W. Morris who introduced it, in the 1930s. Morris formulated a series of clear distinctions, for example, between *designatum* and *denotatum:* "A *designatum* is not a thing but a kind of object or class of objects—and a class may have many members or one member or no members. The *denotata* are the members of the class" (*Writings*, pp. 20–21). He distinguishes similarly between the semantic, syntactic, and pragmatic dimensions of a sign: the relation between signs and designata or denotata is semantic; that between signs themselves is syntactic; that between signs and their users, pragmatic. Morris's other suggestions have not enjoyed the same popularity.

We must note another effort at semiotic construction in E. Buyssens's *Les Langages et le discours* (1943), which takes its starting point in the Saussurian categories. Grounding his work on the one hand in verbal language, on the other in various other semiological systems (road signs, for example), the author establishes a certain number of notions and distinctions (seme and semic act, intrinsic and extrinsic semies, direct and surrogate semies) that will not be discussed here because they have not been taken up in subsequent work. Buyssens's inspiration is resolutely functionalist: a system is organized by its own syntax. In the same period, the writings of all the principal representatives of what is called structural linguistics (Sapir, Trubetzkoy, Jakobson, Hjelmslev, Benveniste) take the semiological perspective into account and try to specify the place of language among the other sign systems.

The arts and literature in particular attracted the attention of the early semioticians. In an essay entitled "Art as a Semiotic Fact," J. Mukařovský, one of the members of the Linguistic Circle of Prague [25], postulates that the study of the arts must become part of semiotics and tries to define the specificity of the esthetic sign: it is an autonomous sign, one that acquires importance not only as a mediator of meaning but in and of itself. Alongside this esthetic function, common to all the arts, those arts dealing with a "subject" (literature, painting, sculpture) have a function that is identified with verbal language, the communicative function. "Every work of art is an autonomous sign. . . . The arts with a 'subject' . . . have yet a second semiotic function, which is *communicative*" ("Art As a Semiotic Fact," in *Structure, Sign, and Function*, p. 88). C. W. Morris defines the artistic sign on the basis of an opposition founded in the icon: there exist "two main classes of sign vehicles: those which are like (i.e., have properties in common with) what they denote, and those which are not like what they denote. These may be called *iconic signs* and *non-iconic signs*" ("Esthetics and the Theory of Signs," in *Writings*, p. 420). Esthetic signs are usually iconic signs. An American philosopher, S. Langer, follows a parallel path, taking her inspiration from Cassirer. Insisting on the difference between a linguistic system and a system of the arts (although they are both symbolic forms), she sees it simultaneously in their formal properties ("Music is not a language because it has no vocabulary") and in the nature of the signified ("Music is 'significant form' . . . which by virtue of its dramatic structure, can express the forms of vital experience which language is peculiarly unfit to convey. Feeling, life, motion and emotion constitute its import") (*Feeling and Form*, p. 32).

After the Second World War, efforts were made to bring together and to coordinate these different traditions, especially in the United States, the Soviet Union, and France. In the United States the description of symbolic systems other than language (gestures, zoosemiotics) has generally followed the procedures of descriptive linguistics [31ff.]. In the Soviet Union an intense semiotic activity has been developing since the sixties under the influence of cybernetics and of information theory; Soviet studies of "secondary systems" (founded on language but not identical to it) are particularly original.

In France, under the influence of C. Lévi-Strauss, R. Barthes, and A.-J. Greimas, semiology has turned in particular toward the study of social forms that function in the manner of a language (kinship systems, myths, fashion, and so on) and toward the study of literary language. On the other hand, a certain critique of the most basic notions of semiotics has been developed, a critique of the sign and of the presuppositions implied by that notion, as we shall see [361ff.].

The journal *Semiotica*, the organ of the International Association of Semiotics, has been appearing since 1969.

- The sources of modern semiotics include C. S. Peirce, *Collected Papers*, ed. C. Hartshorne and P. Weiss, 6 vols. (1932; reprint ed., Cambridge, Mass., 1960); *Charles S. Peirce's Letters to Lady Welby*, ed. I. C. Lieb (New Haven, 1953); P. Weiss and A. W. Burks, "Peirce's Sixty-Six Signs," *Journal of Philosophy* 42 (1945): 383–88; A. W. Burks, "Icon, Index, Symbol," *Philosophy and Phenomenological Research* 9 (1949): 673–89; J. Dewey, "Peirce's Theory of Linguistic Signs, Thought and Meaning," *Journal of Philosophy* 43 (1946): 85–95; F. de Saussure, *Course in General Linguistics*, trans. W. Baskin (New York, 1959); R. Godel, *Les Sources manuscrites du "Cours de linguistique générale," de F. de Saussure* (Geneva and Paris, 1957); E. Cassirer, *The Philosophy of Symbolic Forms*, trans. R. Manheim, 3 vols. (New Haven, 1953–57); idem, *An Essay on Man* (New Haven, 1944); idem, "Le Langage et la construction du monde des objets," in *Essais sur le langage* (Paris, 1969); C. Ogden and I. A. Richards, *The Meaning of Meaning* (London, 1923); R. Carnap, *Logical Syntax of Language*, trans. A. Smeaton, 2d ed. (London, 1949); C. W. Morris, *Writings on the General Theory of Signs* (The

Hague, 1971); E. Buyssens, *Les Langages et le discours* (Brussels, 1943). A partial history is found in T. Todorov, *Théories du symbole* (Paris, 1977).

On semiotics and art, see J. Mukařovský, *The Word and Verbal Art*, trans. J. Burbank and P. Steiner (New Haven and London, 1977); idem, *Structure, Sign, and Function*, trans. J. Burbank and P. Steiner (New Haven and London, 1978); and S. Langer, *Feeling and Form* (London, 1953).

On semiotics in the Soviet Union, see *Simpozium po strukturnomu izucheniiu znakovyky sistem* (Moscow, 1962); *Trudy po znakovym sistemam* 2 (1965), 3 (1967), 4 (1969), 5 (1971), 6 (1973), 7 (1975), 8 (1977). On the history of semiotics (on Eisenstein and Bakhtin in particular), see V. V. Ivanov, *Ocherki po istorii semiotiki v SSSR* (Moscow, 1976).

On semiotics in the United States, see T. A. Sebeok et al., eds., *Approaches to Semiotics* (The Hague, 1964); T. A. Sebeok, "Animal Communication," *Science* 147 (1965): 1006–14; idem, *Contributions to the Doctrine of Signs* (Bloomington, 1976); and R. L. Birdwhistell, *Introduction to Kinesics* (Washington, D.C., 1952).

On semiotics in France, see R. Barthes, *Mythologies*, trans. A. Lavers (London, 1972); idem, *Elements of Semiology*, trans. A. Lavers and C. Smith (New York, 1968); idem, *Système de la mode* (Paris, 1967); *Langages* 10 (1968): *Pratiques et langages gestuels*, ed. A.-J. Greimas; A.-J. Greimas, *Du sens* (Paris, 1970); L. Prieto, *Messages et signaux* (Paris, 1966); and J. Kristeva, *Semeiotikè* (Paris, 1969). For a philosophical critique, see F. Wahl, "La Philosophie entre l'avant et l'après du structuralisme," in O. Ducrot et al., *Qu'est-ce que le structuralisme?* (Paris, 1968).

An anthropological critique is proposed by D. Sperber, in *Rethinking Symbolism* (Cambridge, 1975).

Critique

Despite the existence of these works and of nearly a century of history (and twenty centuries of prehistory), semiotics remains more a project than an established science, and Saussure's prophetic sentences retain their wishful character. This is due not only to the necessarily slow rhythm of a science at its inception but also to a certain uncertainty as to its basic principles and concepts, in particular the concept of the sign, linguistic and nonlinguistic [99ff.]. Either we start with the nonlinguistic signs in order to locate the place of language among them (this was Peirce's approach)—however, these signs do not lend themselves well to precise identification, or when they do, they prove themselves to be of minor importance, completely unable to illuminate the status of language (for example, the highway code)—or we start with language in order to study the other sign systems (Saussure's approach), in which case we risk imposing the linguistic model on phenomena that differ from language and thus reducing semiotic activity to denomination (or renomination). To call well-known social phenomena signifiers or signifieds, syntagmas or paradigms, in no way advances our knowledge.

The causes of this difficulty are questionable. They seem fundamentally linked to the particular place language occupies within semiotics and to the very nature of the sign [99ff.]. One can speak, with Benveniste, of a "principle of non-redundance" between semiotic systems: "Two semiotic systems of different type cannot be mutually convertible. . . . Man does not dispose of several distinct systems for the *same* relationship of signification" (translated from "Sémiologie de la langue," in *Problèmes de linguistique générale II*, p. 53). The signified cannot exist outside its relationship with its signifier, and the signified of one system is not that of another. On the other hand, verbal language is the only system that possesses the quality of secondness [104]. As Cassirer had already remarked, language is the only semiotic system by means of which we can speak of other systems, and of language itself. According to Benveniste, "One thing at least is certain: no semiology of sound, of color, of image will be formulated in sounds, in colors, in images. Every semiology of a non-linguistic system must borrow the device of language" (ibid., p. 160). If these two principles are accepted, it is impossible for semiotics to exist as it has customarily been conceived to exist until now.

The difficulty does not come from the absence of nonlinguistic meaning—for it certainly exists—but from the impossibility of speaking of it except in linguistic terms, which are, however, incapable of grasping the specificity of the nonlinguistic meaning. A semiotics erected on the basis of language (and we know no other semiotics, for the moment) must give up the project of studying the central problem of any semiotic system, that is, the problem of signification: it will never deal with anything but linguistic signification, substituting it surreptitiously for its true object. The semiotics of the nonlinguistic is short-circuited, not at the level of its object (which certainly exists), but at the level of its discourse, which contaminates the results of its own work by verbalizing them.

This is why a little-noticed displacement has occurred in recent semiotic studies: rather than speak, misleadingly, of the relationship of signification, semioticians focus on the relationship of symbolization [102], that is, on that second relationship that links homogeneous entities, not in a necessary way (inexpressible outside of itself), as does the sign, but in a way that is motivated—and thereby revelatory of the mechanisms at work in a society. The domain of the symbolic, usually reserved to ethnology, the history of religion, psychology, or psychoanalysis, would thus be the object of semiotics. As for the usefulness of linguistics (at least in its present state), it appears problematic here: the two disciplines deal with different objects, and even when they encounter each other through a common subject matter (for example, language), they envisage it in different perspectives. Language is rich in symbolic devices, but these do not stem from the linguistic mechanism as such.

The assimilation of nonsymbolic codes [104] to the object of semiotics seems still less justified; for example, in music the relationship of symbolization (and, on a third side, that of signification) is sufficiently specific to necessitate its own field of study.

It is evident that semiotics—if one sets aside the problem of writing [193ff.]—remains for the moment more a set of propositions than a body of established knowledge.

- See R. Barthes, *Elements of Semiology*, trans. A. Lavers and C. Smith (New York, 1968); G. Klaus, *Semiotik und Erkenntnistheorie* (Berlin, 1963); M. Bense, *Semiotik* (Baden-Baden, 1967); A. A. Vetrov, *Semiotika i ee osnovnye problemy* (Moscow, 1968); E. Benveniste, *Problèmes de linguistique générale II* (Paris, 1974); J. Kristeva, "La Sémiologie comme science des idéologies," *Semiotica* 1 (1969): 196–204; R. Jakobson, "Language in Relation to Other Communication Systems," *Selected Writings II* (The Hague, 1971), pp. 697–708; and U. Eco, *A Theory of Semiotics* (Bloomington, 1976). A collection representing current trends is offered by T. A. Sebeok, ed., *The Tell-Tale Sign: A Survey of Semiotics* (Lisse, 1975).

PHILOSOPHY OF LANGUAGE

At least two meanings are possible for the expression **philosophy of language.** We may be dealing, first of all, with a philosophy about language, that is, an external study that considers language as an already known object and seeks out its relationships with other objects that are supposed, at least at the beginning of the inquiry, to be distinct from language. Questions will be raised, for example, about the relationship between language and thought. (Does one have priority over the other? What are their interactions?) A whole idealist current in French philosophy at the beginning of the twentieth century thus attempts to show that the crystallization of meaning into congealed words is one of the causes of the substantialist illusion—of belief in things as given and in stable states.

● This thought congealed by words is liberated, according to L. Brunschwicg (*Les Ages de l'intelligence* [Paris, 1947]), by the science of mathematics; according to H. Bergson, by psychological or biological intuition (*Time and Free Will: An Essay on the Immediate Data of Consciousness*, trans. F. L. Pogson [London and New York, 1971]; *Creative Evolution*, trans. A. Mitchell [New York, 1911]).

Another question, much debated in nineteenth-century German philosophy, is that of the role of language in human history. Following the comparatists [9], who believed they could observe a degradation in language throughout history, philosophers such as Hegel and Hegelian linguists like A. Schleicher attempted to explain this supposed fact by postulating that historical man tends to adopt an attitude of user vis-à-vis language; language supplies him with the double possibility of acting on others and of perpetuating the memory of that action, a possibility that is at the very basis of history. Only in the pre-history of humanity can man have been interested in language for its own sake and thus been able to bring it to its intrinsic perfection.

● Schleicher presents his philosophy of language, linking it to Hegelian philosophy, in *Zur vergleichenden Sprachgeschichte* (Bonn, 1848).

Another approach is possible for the philosopher who is interested in language; this is to submit language to an "internal" study, to consider language itself as an object of investigation. From its inception philosophy has been drawn to this type of research insofar as it has presented itself as a reflection. If in fact the philosophical approach to a problem is first of all to elucidate the notions implied in the formulation of the problem, notions that are generally represented by words from everyday language, then the philosopher is led to undertake an analysis—which might be called linguistic—of the meaning of words. The beginning of Plato's *Laches* dialogue is significant. Two interlocutors are quarreling over whether or not fencing makes one brave. The intervention of Socrates, while giving the problem its philosophical dimension, transforms it at the same time into a problem of language: "What is the meaning of the word *courage*?" asks Socrates. And he proceeds to seek a general signification from which could be deduced all the particular uses of the word. In the Platonic dialogues, however, linguistic inquiry always ends in failure, in aporia, and serves only to prepare the ground for a direct, intuitive grasp of the notion (a grasp that only occurs, moreover, in a certain number of dialogues, the most "finished" ones).

- On the role of linguistic inquiry in Plato, see V. Goldschmidt, *Les Dialogues de Platon* (Paris, 1947).

Present to a certain extent in any philosophy that attempts to examine its own premises, linguistic analysis was practiced in a systematic fashion —and often was considered to be the only legitimate philosophical research—by most of the English philosophers of the first half of the twentieth century, who call themselves philosophers of language and their research, **analytic philosophy.** Developing certain ideas of the neopositivist logicians like R. Carnap, and influenced especially by the work of G. E. Moore, B. Russell, and L. Wittgenstein, they maintain that most of what has been written in philosophy is not false but meaningless and only draws its apparent profundity from a misuse of ordinary language. The so-called philosophical problems will thus disappear as soon as the terms in which they are raised have been subjected to analysis. Thus the debates of moral philosophy will appear to be without object as soon as the meanings, in ordinary language, of words such as *good, bad, duty, value,* and so on, have been clarified.

Although this approach to language is their common starting point, the members of the analytic school do not all agree as to the value of language. For some, the philosophers' error is due to an inconsistency that is a property of language and has been transferred uncritically into philosophical research because ordinary language is not well made, a fact that philosophers have failed to notice. Just as Lewis Carroll's king takes *nobody* to be the name of a particular individual for the simple reason that *nobody*, in English grammar, is a word of the same nature and function as *somebody*, philosophers have repeatedly concluded that two expressions resemble each other semantically on the basis of grammatical resemblance. Thus they have believed that goodness is a quality of objects or of actions, on the pretext that one says "This book is good" just as one says "This book is red." Or, to take an example from Russell, they have failed to see that the statement "The king of France is bald" expresses an existential judgment ("There is someone who is king of France and who is bald"), misled as they have been by the grammatical form of this statement, which relates it to subject-predicate propositions such as "This is blue." (N.B. The Stoic Chrysippus had made remarks that were analogous in spirit; he noted, in his treatise *On Anomaly*, that fundamentally positive qualities are often designated by grammatically negative expressions ["immortality"], the inverse being just as frequent ["poverty"].) Accusing language of having corrupted philosophy, these authors thus conceive of the analysis of language as being first of all a critique, and they sometimes conclude that a logical reconstruction of language is necessary.

● These tendencies come to light in R. Carnap, *Logical Syntax of Language*, trans. A. Smeaton, 2d ed. (London, 1949); and in Wittgenstein's first major work, the *Tractatus logico-philosophicus* of 1922 (trans. D. F. Pears and B. F. McGuinness, rev. ed. [London and New York, 1974]). They are shared by the philosophers who claim direct descendancy from R. Carnap's neopositivism; cf. Y. Bar-Hillel, "Analysis of 'Correct' Language," *Mind* 55 (1946): 328–40. See also the collection edited by P. A. Schilpp, *The Philosophy of Rudolf Carnap* (La Salle, Ill., and London, 1963).

The dominant tendency in the analytic school is, however, the inverse. It is the one represented by the **Oxford school,** whose participants call themselves **ordinary language** philosophers. They question not language itself but the way in which philosophers use it. Philosophical problems arise, in this view, from the fact that ordinary words are employed inappropriately. (There is a sort of linguistic Kantianism here: for Kant, the philosophical antinomies come from the fact that the categories of thought are applied outside of the conditions that alone give them an objective meaning.) The central thesis of the Oxford philosophers is expressed by the slogan "Meaning is use": to describe the meaning of a word is to give its manner of use, to indicate the language acts that it allows us to accomplish (thus the basic value of the adjective *good* would be that it makes possible a particular language act, that of recommending. To say "This is good" is to say "I recommend this to you"). And the error of traditional philosophy is precisely to have assigned to words certain functions that they were not destined to have in ordinary language (for example, to use "This is good" as a description of an object). Consequently, one must not say that language is illogical; it has a particular logic—which philosophers have not discerned—which is closer to the logic of action than to that of mathematics. We will find, then, in the work of the Oxford school, on the one hand a detailed classification of the various possible language uses and on the other hand the indication of the types of usage that are appropriate to the particular expressions of a given language.

● This second tendency of analytic philosophy is linked to Wittgenstein's *Philosophical Investigations* (trans. G. E. M. Anscombe [Oxford, 1967]). Among its best-known representatives are J. L. Austin (see for example *Philosophical Papers* [Oxford, 1961]), and P. F. Strawson (*Logico-linguistic Papers* [London, 1971]). This tendency is dominant in the journal *Analysis* (Oxford) and in four important collections of articles: A. Flew, ed., *Essays on Logic and Language*, 2 series (Oxford, 1951 and 1953); *La Philosophie analytique* (Paris, 1962); C. E. Caton, ed., *Philosophy and Ordinary Language* (Urbana, 1963); and J. R. Searle, ed., *The Philosophy of Language* (Oxford, 1971).

Most philosophers of the analytic school insist on distinguishing their approach from a linguistic study proper. Conversely, most linguists, until quite recently, did not concern themselves with research that had the irremediable defect of declaring itself philosophical. For this gap there are two principal reasons (which are tending to lose their importance, given the current evolution of linguistics):

a) Those analytic philosophers who are most directly tied to neo-positivism have the feeling that their research leads to a critique of language, a critique that would inevitably be incompatible with the descriptive attitude of the linguists. This feeling stems from their tendency to assimilate the grammatical reality of a sentence to the visible ordering of words and to speak of illogicality as soon as the same ordering covers different semantic organizations (thus *somebody* and *nobody* would have the same grammatical nature because they may both be either subject or object; grammar would then invite the sophistry that consists in taking them both to be designations of existing things). Now the development of the notion of linguistic transformation [242ff.] authorizes a much more abstract conception of grammatical reality. For many generativists, for example, the deep structures of sentences containing *nobody* and *somebody* are certainly very different, in spite of the similarity of their visible organization. From this point of view, language seen in depth is perhaps less illogical than it seems. More important still, in this perspective the search for apparent illogicalities may be integrated into linguistic investigation; it would supply indices, or at least hypotheses, concerning the deep structures.

b) Those analytic philosophers who devote themselves to the study of language acts often consider this research to be alien to linguistics, under the pretext that the latter studies the language (or the code) and not its use in speech. In reality, certain linguists, basing their work on that of E. Benveniste, try to reintegrate into language the intersubjective relationships that are realized in an instance of speech. One could not describe language, according to them, without taking into account at least certain of the effects of its use. The linguist would then have much to learn from the contemporary "philosophy of language."

● E. Benveniste was one of the first linguists to be interested in the research of analytic philosophy (cf. *Problems in General Linguistics*, trans. M. E. Meek [Coral Gables, 1971], pt. 5). For a philosophy of language closely related to its linguistic utilization, see J. R. Searle, *Speech Acts* (London, 1969). On the relationships between speech (*parole*), in the Saussurian sense, and use, in the terms of analytic philosophy, see O. Ducrot, "De Saussure à la philosophie du langage," preface to the French translation of the preceding work (Paris, 1972).

METHODOLOGICAL CONCEPTS

SIGN

Definition

The sign is the basic notion of every science of language, but owing to its very importance, it is one of the most difficult notions to define. The difficulty increases with the fact that modern sign theory attempts to take into account not only linguistic entities but nonverbal signs as well.

The classical definitions of the sign often prove, under careful examination, to be either tautological or else incapable of grasping the concept in its specificity. It is supposed that all signs refer necessarily to a relation between two relata; but simply to identify signification with relation ignores the distinction between two levels that are, however, very different: on the one hand, the sign *mother* is necessarily linked to the sign *child*; on the other hand, what *mother* designates is "mother" and not "child." As Saint Augustine suggested in one of the earliest sign theories: "A sign is a thing which causes us to think of something beyond the impression the thing itself makes upon the senses" (quoted by B. D. Jackson, "The Theory of Signs in St. Augustine's *De Doctrina Christiana*," in *Augustine*, ed. R. Markus [Garden City, N.Y., 1972], pp. 92–147). But causing us to think (or evoking) is at once too narrow and too broad a category; it presupposes, on the one hand, that meaning exists outside the sign (so that it can be summoned in) and, on the other hand, that the evocation of one thing by another is always situated on the same plane. The siren may *signify* the beginning of a bombardment and *evoke* war, the anguish of the inhabitants, and so on. Are we saying that the sign is something that is *substituted* for something else, or replaces it? It would be a very peculiar substitution, not possible in fact in either direction: neither the meaning nor the referent in itself can be inserted within a sentence in place of the word. Swift understood this well. Supposing that we take with us the things about which we wish to speak (since words are only substitutes for them), he was forced to arrive at the following conclusion: "If a Man's Business be very great, and of various Kinds, he must be obliged in Proportion to carry a greater Bundle of Things upon his Back"—at the risk of being crushed under their weight (*Gulliver's Travels*, ed. R. A. Greenberg [New York, 1961], p. 158).

We will define **sign** prudently, then, as an entity that (1) can become perceptible and (2) for a particular group of users, marks a lack in itself. Since Saussure, the aspect of the sign that can become perceptible has been called the **signifier**; the absent aspect, the **signified**; and the relationship between them, that of **signification.** Let us make explicit, one by one, the terms of this definition.

A sign may exist, certainly, without being perceived. All the words of the English language taken together, at a specific point in time, have no perceptible existence; nevertheless, this perception is always possible. A K. Burke would propose to invert the order of signification, that is, to regard things as signs of words (ideas); but this para-Platonic conception still supposes that the signifier can become perceptible. Nor is this property contradicted by the existence of the phoneme "behind" sounds or the grapheme "beyond" letters.

The sign is always institutional; in this sense it exists only for a well-defined group of users. This group may be reduced to a single person (for example, when I tie a string around my finger as a reminder to myself). But outside of a society, however limited it may be, signs do not exist. It is incorrect to say that smoke is the natural sign of fire; it is rather the consequence, or one of the aspects, of fire. Only a community of users can institute it as a sign.

The most debatable point of the theory concerns the nature of the signified. It has been defined here as a lack, an absence in the perceptible object, which thus becomes a signifier. This absence is therefore equivalent to the imperceptible aspect of the sign—whoever speaks of a sign must accept the existence of a radical difference between signifier and signified, between perceptible and imperceptible, between presence and absence. The signified, let us say tautologically, does not exist outside of its relation with the signifier—before, after, or elsewhere. The same gesture creates both the signifier and the signified, concepts that are inconceivable apart from each other: a signifier without a signified is simply an object; it *is*, but it does not *signify*. A signified without a signifier is the inexpressible, the unthinkable, the nonexistent itself. The relationship of signification is, in a certain sense, the opposite of identity with self; the sign is at once mark and lack, originally double.

Two complementary aspects of every signified must be considered. The first, in a sense vertical, is revealed to us in the necessary relationship that the signified maintains with the signifier; this relationship marks the place of the signified but does not allow us to identify it positively. It is that which the signifier lacks. The second, which might be depicted as horizontal, is the relationship of this signified with all other signifieds, within a system of signs [16]. This determination is equally negative (as Saussure says, it makes the signified "what the others are not"; it would be more precise to call it relational), but it is made within a continuum constituted by the set of signifieds forming a system (the nature of this continuum is not explained by designations such as thought, concepts, essence, and so on, although numerous philosophers and psychologists have not failed to propose such "explanations"). In either case, access to the signified is only possible through the sign; therein lies the major difficulty of all discourse on the sign. Meaning cannot be examined independently of the signs wherein it is apprehended; it exists only through the relationships in which it participates.

In the Vicinity of the Sign

This narrow definition of the sign obliges us to introduce other concepts in order to describe relationships that are similar and nonetheless different, customarily undifferentiated under the name "signification" or "sign." Thus we will make a careful distinction (as almost all sign theorists have done) between signification and the referential function (sometimes called denotation) [247]. Denotation takes place not between a signifier and a signified but between the sign and the **referent,** that is, in the case that is the easiest to imagine, the real object: It is no longer the phonic or graphic sequence *apple* that is linked to the meaning "apple"; rather the word (that is, the sign itself) *apple* is linked to real apples. It must be added that the relation of denotation concerns tokens, not types (see below, p. 105); however, this relation is much less frequent than one might think: we speak of things in their absence more often than in their presence. At the same time, it is difficult to imagine what would be the referent of most signs. Peirce and Saussure both insisted on the marginal role of denotation in the definition of the sign.

We must also distinguish signification from **representation,** which is the appearance of an image in the sign-user's mind. This mental image depends on the degree of abstraction of the different vocabulary levels. In the context of the parts of speech, this gradation goes from proper nouns to particles, conjunctions, and pronouns. From a semantic perspective, one can also observe varying degrees of abstraction. Fiction [260] makes much use of the representative properties of words. For a long time one of its goals has been the highest possible degree of evocation; hence the habit of speaking of literature in terms of atmosphere, action, events, and so on.

These oppositions were already noted by the Stoics, who distinguished three relationships of the perceptible part of the sign: with the real thing (denotation); with the psychic image (representation); and with the expressible (signification). In reality, denotation and representation are particular cases of a more general use of the sign that we shall call **symbolization,** in which the sign is opposed to the **symbol** (Hjelmslev deals with related phenomena under the name "connotation," but this latter term is usually taken in a narrower sense). Symbolization is a more or less stable association between two units of the same level (that is, two signifiers or two signifieds). The word *flame* signifies flame, but it also symbolizes love in certain literary works; the expression "you're my pal" signifies "you're my pal," but it also symbolizes familiarity; and so on. The relationships established in these latter cases are specific enough to warrant special names [256, 275ff.].

The practical test that allows us to distinguish between a sign and a symbol is the examination of the two related elements. In the sign, these elements are necessarily different in nature; in the symbol, as we have just seen, they must be homogeneous. This opposition sheds light on the problem of the arbitrary aspect of the sign, a problem brought back into focus in linguistics by Saussure. The relation between a signifier and a signified is necessarily unmotivated; the two are different in nature, and it is unthinkable that a graphic or phonic sequence should resemble a meaning. At the same time, this relation is *necessary* in that the signified cannot exist without the signifier, and vice versa. On the other hand, in the symbol, the relation between symbolizer and symbolized is unnecessary (or arbitrary), since the symbolizer and the symbolized (the signifieds *flame* and *love*) sometimes exist independently of each other; for this reason, the relation cannot be other than motivated, since if it were not motivated, nothing would compel its establishment. These motivations are customarily classified in two major groups drawn from the psychological classification of associations: resemblance and contiguity. (Sometimes the terms "icon" and "index" are used as well, but with a different meaning from the one given them by C. S. Peirce [86]. Let us add that just like the relation between the symbolizer and the symbolized, the one established between sign and referent, between sign and representation, can be motivated. There is a resemblance between the sounds of the word *cuckoo* and the song of the bird (the referent or auditory representation), just as there is a resemblance between the meanings of *flame* and *love*. But there cannot be any motivation between the sound and the meaning of *cuckoo*, between the word *flame* and its meaning. The learning of meanings is thus not based on associations of resemblance, participation, and so on; relations of this nature could not exist between signifiers and signifieds. It must be noted that verbal communication consists in the use of symbols at least as much as, if not more than, in the use of signs.

Finally, we must distinguish the sign from some more distant neighbors. American linguists of the Bloomfieldian school have tended to reduce the sign to a **signal.** The signal provokes a certain reaction but does not carry any relationship of signification. Animal communication is usually reduced to signals; in human language the imperative form can function as a signal. But it is possible to understand the command "Close the door!" without accomplishing the action indicated—in which case the sign has functioned, not the signal.

One distinction whose usefulness may appear problematical is that between sign and **symptom,** or natural sign. The symptom is in fact a sign that is a component of the referent; for example, fever is a symptom of illness. In reality, the relationship described here is not of the type signifier-signified (illness, as a real phenomenon, is not meaning, properly speaking) but of the type sign-referent (or representation). Moreover, it seems that even these "natural" (and thus universal) signs are much less natural and universal than we might think. The French people do not cough in the same way as the people of New Zealand. The sign is always conventional.

- See C. S. Peirce, *Collected Papers*, ed. C. Hartshorne and P. Weiss, 6 vols. (Cambridge, Mass., 1932), vol. 2, *Elements of Logic*; F. de Saussure, *Course in General Linguistics*, trans. W. Baskin (New York, 1959); E. Benveniste, *Problems in General Linguistics*, trans. M. E. Meek (Coral Gables, 1971); W. Borgeaud, W. Bröcker, and J. Lohmann, "De la nature du signe," *Acta linguistica* 3 (1942–43): 24–30; J. Piaget, *Play, Dreams and Imitation in Childhood*, trans. C. Gattegno and F. M. Hodgson (New York, 1962); H. Sprang-Hanssen, *Recent Theories on the Nature of the Language Sign* (Copenhagen, 1954); R. Engler, *Théorie et critique d'un principe saussurien: L'Arbitraire du signe* (Geneva, 1962); E. F. K. Koerner, *Contribution au débat post-saussurien sur le signe linguistique* (The Hague, 1972); E. Ortigues, *Le Discours et le symbole* (Paris, 1962); K. Burke, "What Are the Signs of What?" *Anthropological Linguistics* 6 (1962): 1–23; F. Edeline, "Le Symbole et l'image selon la théorie des codes," *Cahiers internationaux du symbolisme* 2 (1963): 19–33; G. Durand, *L'Imagination symbolique* (Paris, 1964); R. Barthes, *Elements of Semiology*, trans. A. Lavers and C. Smith (New York, 1968); J. Derrida, *Positions* (Paris, 1972); and T. Todorov, *Théories du symbole* (Paris, 1977).

Verbal and Nonverbal Signs

Thus defined, the sign is not necessarily linguistic: the flag, the swastika, certain gestures, and highway markers are also signs. The specificity of **verbal language** must be sought elsewhere.

In the first place, language—language in general—is characterized by its systematic aspect. We cannot speak of language if we are dealing with only a single isolated sign. It is true that the very existence of an isolated sign is more than problematic. Firstly, the sign is necessarily opposed to its own absence. Furthermore, it is always set in relation (even if not in such a way as to constitute a system) to other analogous signs: the swastika with the star, one flag with another, and so on. In any case, we customarily take the term "language" to mean a complex system.

Secondly, verbal language presupposes the existence of signification in the narrow sense defined above. It is thus a fairly loose analogy that allows us to speak of language in speaking of a different symbolic system.

Thirdly, verbal language is the only language that includes certain specific properties: (*a*) we can use it to speak of the words that constitute it and, more appropriately still, of other systems of signs; (*b*) we can produce sentences that disallow not only denotation but representation as well—for examples, lies, periphrases, repetition of previous sentences; (*c*) we can use words in a sense previously unknown to the linguistic community and make ourselves understood by means of the context (for example, in using original metaphors). If we call **secondness** that which allows verbal language to assume all these functions, we will say that secondness is a constitutive trait of language.

Secondness seems to be a qualitative element that separates human verbal language from all the other, analogous systems. When a system is characterized by only the first two of the above properties, we may speak of it as a **sign system,** not as language. When only the first is present, we will speak of **code** (even though the system in question is analogous to that of language); the word *code* signifies here a system of constraints. Thus music is a code: all the elements of a composition (pitches, intensities, tones) are interrelated, but they do not signify, nor do they possess the quality of secondness. The majority of the signifying systems that surround us are mixed. They are at once codes, sign systems, and symbolic systems, but none of them possesses all three of the properties of language. Literature illustrates the imposition of a second code on a language (for example, the formal constraints of poetry or the narrative); at the same time, words are used, particularly in the tropes, as symbols rather than as signs.

By virtue of belonging to a system, the sign acquires dimensions that are not discernible when it is considered in isolation. The sign enters into paradigmatic relationships [108ff.] with other signs. We can observe that two signs are identical or different, that one includes or excludes the other, that one implies or presupposes the other, and so on, which amounts to saying that the vocabulary of a language is organized, and that the signs of a language are defined, with respect to each other. Peirce described this property of the verbal signs by the term "interpretant," or "collateral knowledge"; these paradigmatic relations allowing for interpretation are part of what Saussure called value, and Hjelmslev, form of content. Following Benveniste, we shall call this aspect of the sign **interpretative capacity.**

For a long time it has been observed that there is an important difference between the sign itself and the particular use to which it may be put: Peirce thus opposed the **type** and the **token** (*legisign* and *sinsign*; in French, *signe-type* and *signe-occurrence*). The total number of words in a text-gives us the number of tokens; the total number of different words gives the number of types.

Finally, entering into a sentence, the token undergoes internal modifications: it can combine with certain signs and not with others; furthermore, these combinations are different in nature. We can call **signifying capacity** this aspect of the sign that allows it to enter into discourse and to combine with other signs.

Benveniste has remarked that verbal language is the only language that possesses interpretative capacity and signifying capacity simultaneously. The constitutive elements of the other codes, for example, are endowed with (simulated) signifying capacity; thus the musical tones combine according to certain precise rules, but they do not form paradigms. On the contrary, the constitutive elements of sign systems other than verbal language enter into a relation of interpretative capacity but not of signifying capacity. The red and green lights of a traffic signal alternate without ever really combining. Here again we find a feature specific to human verbal language.

- See C. S. Peirce, *Collected Papers*, ed. C. Hartshorne and P. Weiss, 6 vols. (Cambridge, Mass., 1960), vol. 2, *Elements of Logic*; E. Benveniste, *Problems in General Linguistics,* trans. M. E. Meek (Coral Gables, 1971); idem, *Problèmes de linguistique générale II* (Paris, 1974); V. V. Ivanov, "Iazyk v sopostavlenii s drugimi sredstvami peredachi i khraneniia informatsii," in *Prikladnaia lingvistika i mashinnyi perevod* (Kiev, 1962); J. H. Greenberg, ed., *Universals of Language*, 2d ed. (Cambridge, Mass., 1966); U. Weinreich, "Semantics and Semiotics," in *International Encyclopedia of Social Sciences*, ed. D. L. Sills, 17 vols. (New York, 1968), vol. 14.

SYNTAGMA AND PARADIGM

Syntagma. There is hardly any utterance in a language that does not present itself as the association of several (successive or simultaneous) units that are capable of appearing in other utterances as well. In the broad sense of the term "syntagma," the utterance U contains the syntagma uv if u and v are two units, not necessarily minimal, that both appear in U. We can say furthermore that there is a **syntagmatic relationship** between u and v (or between the classes of units X and Y) if we can formulate a general rule determining the conditions of appearance, in the utterances of the language, of the syntagmas uv (or of syntagmas constituted by an element of X and an element of Y). Hence arises a second, narrower meaning for the term "syntagma" (the one most frequently adopted and the one that will be used here): u and v form a syntagma in U if they are co-present in U and if at the same time there is known or believed to be a syntagmatic relationship conditioning this co-presence. Saussure in particular insisted on the dependence of the syntagma with respect to the syntagmatic relationship. For him, the only reason why the French verb *défaire* ("to undo") can be described as a syntagma containing the two elements *dé* and *faire,* is that there exists in French a latent "syntagmatic type" manifested also by the verbs *dé-coller* ("to unstick"), *dé-voiler* ("to unveil"), *dé-baptiser* ("to unchristen") (cf. the English *disarm, disjoin, dismount*). Otherwise there would be no reason at all to analyze *défaire* as two units (*Course*, pt. 2, chap. 6, sec. 2). The Saussurian "syntagmatic type" is what we've just called a "syntagmatic relationship" defined by means of a rule such that: "the morpheme dé- can be prefixed to verbs expressing a perfective process, i.e. an action with a result." This restriction, moreover, entails another. Given that syntagmatic relationships usually involve units of the same level, u and v will form a syntagma only if they are of the same level. Thus, in the statement "The vase is cracked," the article *the* and the noun *vase* form a syntagma, as do the sounds *v* and *a* of *vase,* and the semantic traits *container* and *household object* inherent in the word *vase,* but not the article *the* and the sound *v,* nor the article *the* and the semantic trait *container* (N.B. In order to simplify the discussion, we have dealt only with associations of two units; however, most linguists recognize syntagmas with more than two elements.).

Syntagma and syntagmatic relationship. The preceding definitions are such that different linguistic theories, depending on the type of syntagmatic relationships they accentuate, can lead us to grant or deny syntagmatic status to a given segment. Thus Saussure saw in several distinct sequences the realization of a single syntagmatic type only if each sequence manifested the same relationship between the meaning of itself as a whole and that of its component parts (*dé-faire* is to *faire*, in terms of meaning, what *dé-coller* is to *coller*, *dé-voiler* to *voiler*; cf. the English *dis-arm* and *arm*, *dis-join* and *join*, *dis-mount* and *mount*). Therefore he would not have recognized the preceding syntagmatic type in *déterminer* ("determine") nor in *dévider* ("unwind") (cf. the English *discern, discuss, dismiss, dismay*), and unable to define another type, he would doubtless not have considered these verbs as syntagmas combining the prefix *dé-* and a simple verb—although this would be possible in a less semantic conception of the syntagmatic relationship. It is even less possible for a strict Saussurian to speak of syntagmas when the elements combined are not signs—units endowed with both signifier and signified—but simply sounds (Saussure makes an exception to this rule, however, in one text that is in fact controversial [cf. ibid., pp. 130–31]). On the other hand, phonologists [171] do not hesitate to present a group of phonemes as a syntagma, for they consider it important to discover regularities in the way in which the phonemes of a language combine with each other.

Another important divergence regarding the nature of syntagmatic relationships and, by correlation, of syntagmas concerns **linearity.** Speech unfolds in time. Time can be represented as a one-dimensional space, like a line, in which to every instant corresponds a point, to the order of appearance of instants corresponds the order of juxtaposition of points. This suggests the possibility that the order of appearance of the elements of discourse (which is the object of syntagmatic studies) can itself be represented by a line (or, given the discontinuous character of discourse, by a dotted line). Saussure sets forth as a principle (*Course*, pt. 1, chap. 1, sec. 3) that not only is this representation possible (at least insofar as the signifiers are concerned), but it must be a basis for linguistic description. This principle has two consequences:

a) The linguist recognizes no order except that of succession. The elements that would be simultaneous (the various phonetic constituents of a single phoneme or the semantic features of a word) are squeezed into a single point of the linear representation. No one will be interested, then, in seeking regularities in their occurrence (that is, in the conditions under which a given feature combines with another), and consequently the coexistence of two simultaneous features will not be regarded as constituting a syntagma. (Thus Martinet rejects a syntagmatic study of the distinctive features [173] of the phonemes; Jakobson, however, has advocated such a study.)

b) To describe the way in which different elements combine with each other is to say inter alia what respective positions they may take in the linear chain of discourse. Thus for a distributionalist [31ff.], the syntagmatic study of an element is the indication of the different environments in which it may occur, that is, of the elements that may precede and follow it. As a result, to describe a syntagma is to say which units constitute it, in what order of succession and, if they are not contiguous, how far apart they are. For the glossematician [20ff.], on the other hand, who sees in linear order only a substantial and contingent manifestation, independent of the linguistic form itself [22], syntagmatics would be much more abstract: it would only be concerned with the conditions of coexistence of the units—independent of their linear arrangement. This view requires a new formulation of the syntagmatic relationship. Since almost any unit can coexist with any other within an utterance, it will be necessary to spell out in a more precise way the framework of the coexistence and to formulate rules such as the following: u may (or may not) coexist with v in a larger unit of the type X. It follows that in order to describe a particular syntagma, it will be necessary to specify not only which units constitute it but also within which unit it occurs.

Paradigm. In the broad sense, we may call every class of linguistic elements a paradigm, whatever the principle that leads us to group them together. In this sense we will regard as paradigms the **associative groups** of which Saussure spoke (ibid, pt. 2, chap. 5, sec. 5), whose elements are hardly linked by anything except association of ideas. Jakobson, too, sometimes seems to base the paradigmatic relationship on simple similarity, on that association by resemblance referred to by associationist psychology (which, like Jakobson, included association by contrast in this category). Faced with the multitude of divergent criteria on which such paradigms could be based, many modern linguists have sought to define a principle of classification that would be linked uniquely to the role of the units within a language. Given that the syntagmatic relationships seem to be in large measure specific to individual languages, linguists have come to base the linguistic paradigms on them. In this narrow sense, two units u and u' belong to the same paradigm if, and only if, they are capable of replacing each other in the same syntagma; that is, if there exist two syntagmas vuw and $vu'w$. This argument leads to the now classic image of two secant strips, the horizontal representing the syntagmatic order of the units, the vertical representing the paradigm of u, that is, the set of units that could have appeared in its place.

● The essential texts are in F. de Saussure's *Course in General Linguistics*, trans. W. Baskin (New York, 1959), especially chapters 5 and 6. (N.B. Saussure did not use the term "paradigm"; he spoke of relationships and of "associative groups.") For Jakobson's approach, see "Two Aspects of Language and Two Types of Aphasic Disturbances," in *Selected Writings II* (The Hague, 1971), pp. 239–59.

Syntagmatic and paradigmatic relationships. Although there is a big consensus in favor of subordinating paradigmatic study to syntagmatic study in practice, linguists diverge on the meaning that subordination should have. According to the distributionalists [31ff.], discovery of syntagmatic relationships constitutes the fundamental object of linguistic investigation, for language is above all a combinatorial system. The establishment of paradigms must therefore be understood only as a convenience to aid in the compact formulation of syntagmatic relationships. Instead of spelling out each unit's possibilities of combination with all the others, it is more economical to constitute classes of units having approximately the same combinatorial possibilities, even if one must then establish subclasses, whose units would have stronger combinatory analogies among themselves, and so on, each new subdivision corresponding to a refinement of the approximation.

Most European linguists, on the other hand, have made an effort to give the paradigmatic organization of language an intrinsic justification. It is remarkable (and paradoxical) that this tendency appears even among the glossematicians, for whom, however, as for the distributionalists, the fundamental reality of language—its form—is purely combinatorial in nature [38]. Hjelmslev, for example, constructs two distinct combinatorials, one syntagmatic and the other paradigmatic. The three primary relationships that are the basis for syntagmatics link classes first and foremost. The class A **presupposes** (or **selects**) the class B with respect to the class C if in every element of C one cannot find an element of A without an element of B and if the inverse is not true (the adjective presupposes the noun in the subject-group in French). A and B are in **solidarity** with respect to C if one cannot find in an element of C an element of A without an element of B, and vice versa. We have thus a sort of reciprocal presupposition (there is solidarity, with respect to the class of verbs, of the class of tenses and that of moods: in a verb, one cannot find, a tense without a mood, and vice versa). Finally, A and B are in **combination** with respect to C if one finds in the elements of C sometimes an element of A accompanied by an element of B, sometimes an element of A without a representative of B, sometimes finally an element of B without a representative element of A (there is combination between the noun and the adjective in the attribute group in French). To these syntagmatic relationships, which are based on coexistence in the text and which allow for the characterization of classes by their reciprocal relationships, Hjelmslev adds certain paradigmatic relationships—which he calls **correlations**—that seem intended to characterize individual elements. Their basis is the coexistence of terms within the previously defined classes. There are three major correlations, parallel to the syntagmatic relationships: (1) a **specifies** b if every class containing a contains also b and if the inverse is not true; (2) a and b

are **complementary** if every class containing the one contains the other (we have here a sort of reciprocal specification); and (3) *a* and *b* are **autonomous** if each of them belongs to certain classes from which the other is absent and if they happen also to belong to the same class. Thus, even though the discovery of the syntagmatic relationships necessarily precedes that of the paradigmatic relationships, paradigmatics is not content to reproduce syntagmatics, but adds to it new information. We are dealing with two different combinatorials.

● On the glossematic combinatorial, see L. Hjelmslev, *Prolegomena to a Theory of Language*, trans. F. J. Whitfield, rev. ed. (Madison, 1961), chaps. 9 and 11. For an attempted formalization, see L. Hjelmslev and H. J. Uldall, *Outline of Glossematics* (Copenhagen, 1957).

The importance of the paradigmatic relationships will be even more clearly brought to light in a theory of functional linguistics [24]. According to Martinet, the only linguistic reality is the one that serves the communication of thought in discourse; in other words, the choices that the language allows the speaking subject. Whether he is describing a distinctive unit (phoneme [171]) or a unit of meaning (moneme [201]), the linguist must retain only that which, in the unit, can be the object of a choice. In order to know what is chosen when a unit *A* is used at a given moment in discourse, it is indispensable to know what other units would have been possible in its place. What is chosen in *A* is only that through which *A* distinguishes itself from these other units. Thus, in order to understand the value of the adjective *good*, used in diplomatic language to qualify the "atmosphere" of a negotiation, it is necessary (1) for syntagmatics to draw up a list of all the adjectives that could appear in this position and (2) for paradigmatics to show that of the words on this list *good* is the least euphoric adjective. The syntagmatic study thus does not interest Martinet except insofar as it determines, at each moment of discourse, the inventory of the possible choices. Then paradigmatics, comparing the possibilities with each other, reveals what is chosen when any one of them is chosen. A spectacular confirmation of this approach has been encountered in the study of the phonetic evolution of languages: often a change involves neither an isolated phoneme nor even the general organization of the phonemes, but a paradigm of phonemes (Martinet speaks then of a **system**), that is, the set of phonemes appearing in a particular syntagmatic context, and the change takes place only in this context. Facts of this nature prove that the paradigms possess a sort of autonomy.

● For a paradigmatics based on the notion of choice, see the writings of A. Martinet, in particular *Economie des changements phonétiques* (Bern, 1955), esp. pt. 2, chap. 3.

Whereas Martinet's functionalism makes syntagmatics a means, a simple preliminary to paradigmatics, Jakobson's functionalism attributes independent value to these two types of relationship (similarly, but in the opposite direction, the glossematic combinatorial reestablishes between them an equilibrium denied by the distributionalist combinatorial). For Jakobson, the interpretation of any linguistic entity brings into play at every instant two independent intellectual mechanisms: comparison with similar units (units that could thus be substituted for it) and establishment of a relationship with coexisting units (units that belong to the same syntagma). Thus the meaning of a word is determined both by the influence of those that surround it in discourse and by the memory of those that could have taken its place. It is in speech disorders that Jakobson finds proof that the two mechanisms are independent; these disorders could be divided into two categories: the impossibility of linking the elements to each other, of constituting syntagmas (the utterance is a discontinuous sequence), and the impossibility of linking the elements used to the other elements in their paradigm (the utterances no longer refer to a code). This duality, for Jakobson, has a very broad application. It would serve as the basis for the rhetorical figures most commonly employed in "literary language": metaphor (an object is designated by the name of a similar object) and metonymy (an object is designated by the name of an object associated with it in experience) would stem, respectively, from the paradigmatic and the syntagmatic interpretation, so that Jakobson sometimes uses as synonyms *syntagmatic* and **metonymic,** *paradigmatic* and **metaphoric.**

● See especially Jakobson's "Two Aspects of Language and Two Types of Aphasic Disturbances," in *Selected Writings II* (The Hague, 1971), pp. 239–59. The difficulty of this text has to do with the fact that the constitutive relationship of the paradigm appears sometimes as the relationship of selection (here the term "paradigm" is used in the narrow sense it has in linguistics), sometimes as the relationship of similarity (in this case a paradigm may be simply a category, in an extremely broad sense).

LINGUISTIC CATEGORIES

A **linguistic category** (paradigm [108]) is generally much more than a collection of elements (or "set," in the mathematical sense). It usually involves an internal organization and institutes particular relationships among its elements. Linguists have determined, by comparing these diverse organizations, that they have certain properties in common, in many cases at least.

Neutralization. Phonologists have often noted that many phonemic oppositions [171], while possible in certain contexts, are no longer possible in certain others. The opposition is then said to be neutralized. Let us compare the vowel of the French *fée* ("fairy"), written phonetically as *e*, and that of the French *fait* ("fact"), written ε. These vowels contrast in final position, since by substituting one for the other, we pass from the pronunciation *fe* (with the meaning *"fée"*) to the pronunciation *fε* (with the meaning *"fait"*). But there are contexts in which the opposition is neutralized. Sometimes there is neutralization because the substitution does not introduce a difference in meaning. Such is the case when *e* and ε are found in open syllables (those not terminated by a consonant) within a word: the pronunciations *pε-i* and *pe-i* both give us the meaning *"pays"* ("country"). The two sounds are thus in free variation [172]. Sometimes there is neutralization because of the impossibility of finding either of the two sounds in a certain context; for example, we never find in French, except in proper names, either *e* or ε after the sound *a*. Finally, there may be neutralization if only one of the two elements is possible: in a syllable ending with the sound *r*, we can find ε but not *e*; for example, there is *fεr* (*"fer"* ["iron"]), but not *fer*.

Markedness. It is this latter type of neutralization that has given rise to the notion of markedness. The element that appears in a context in which only one of the two may appear is said to be **unmarked.** We sometimes also call it **extensive** (the other one, more limited in use, is called **intensive,** or **marked**). In the contexts in which only the unmarked element is possible, this element is said to represent the entire opposition, or the **archiphoneme,** that is, that which is common to the two phonemes of the opposition. Thus Trubetzkoy only consented to speak of markedness in the case of a **privative,** wherein one of the two terms, the marked one, possesses distinctive features [173] that the other one lacks.

Discovered in phonology, the notion of markedness has also been applied to the significative units [199ff.]. In this area, however, the criterion of neutralization is less useful. In fact, one rarely finds contexts in which only one of two opposed morphemes is possible. We can cite expressions such as "How old is he?" in which the use of *young* in the place of *old* presents problems; the parallel with phonology can be pursued fairly far here, since one can say that in this usage *old* has the same value as the opposition *old/young* taken in its totality and that it is an **archimorpheme** representing the category of age. However, there are few cases as clear as this one. We could look at a French context such as *Ce livre est peu . . .* ("This book is not very . . ."), in which we find for example *intéressant* ("interesting") but not *ennuyeux* ("boring"). The phenomenon is more complicated than this, however, for the situation reverses itself with *un peu* ("a little bit"); we find *Ce livre est un peu ennuyeux* but not *Ce livre est un peu intéressant.* K. Togeby has proposed (*Structure immanente,* pp. 102–3) the use of the phenomenon of deficiency in order to distinguish extensive and intensive morphemes. Let us suppose that no element of a class *A* can occur without being combined with an element of a class *B* (in a French verb one cannot have a mood unless it is accompanied by a tense). There is **deficiency** if certain elements of *A* cannot be combined with certain elements of *B*: the subjunctive cannot be combined, in French, with the future. From the fact that the indicative alone is possible with the future, Togeby concludes that the indicative is the extensive term of the opposition indicative / subjunctive. We will note, however, that the parallel with phonology here is a bit forced: it would oblige us to say that in the form *Je viendrai* ("I shall come") the mood is an archimorpheme representing that which is common to the indicative and the subjunctive.

If instead of considering the significative units, we look at the semantic units themselves (that is, the constitutive elements of signification), we find an incontestable application for the notion of markedness, since it allows us to describe an asymmetry very frequently encountered in the semantic categories. Take the two semantic units *man* (meaning here "human male"; cf. the Latin *vir*) and *woman*, which together constitute the semantic category *human.* The element *man* will be said to be unmarked in English, since there exists a signifier, the word *man*, which sometimes designates man, sometimes human. In the semantic category *interesting–boring*, the pole *interesting* will be called unmarked, since the same adjective *interesting* that is capable of representing it ("this book is interesting") can also represent the entire category. This is what happens for example in a comparison: by saying that *A* is more interesting than *B* we do not imply that *A* and *B* deserve to be called interesting, in the strong sense of the word (on the contrary, the expression "*A* is more boring than *B*" suggests that *A* and *B* are both boring). The distinction of marked and unmarked semantic elements is also useful in understanding the mechanism of negation. Certain expressions (like the French *ne . . . pas*, the English *not*) have a special effect when they are applied to the word representing the unmarked term of a category: the expression obtained has a tendency to represent the opposite (marked) pole. On the other hand, the same negation, when applied to the word designating the marked pole, does not lead back to the unmarked pole, but to an intermediary region in the category. An example follows (the arrows represent the effect of negation):

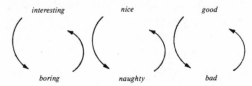

- On the notions of neutralization and markedness, see N. S. Trubetzkoy, "Diacritics," *Principles of Phonology*, trans. C. A. M. Baltaxe (Berkeley, 1969), secs. 3 and 5; R. Jakobson, "Zur Struktur des russischen Verbums," in *Selected Writings II* (The Hague, 1971), pp. 3–15; C. E. Bazell, "On the Neutralisation of Syntactic Oppositions," *Travaux du cercle linguistique de Copenhague*, 1949; K. Togeby, *Structure immanente de la langue française*, 2d ed. (Paris, 1965); and R. Vion, "Les Notions de neutralisation et d'archiphonème en phonologie," *La Linguistique* 10, no. 1 (1974): 33–52. On the semantic aspects of the problem, see M. Van Overbeke, "Antonymie et gradation," *La Linguistique* 11, no. 1 (1975): 135–53.

Participation. Hjelmslev and Brøndal interpreted the asymmetry of the linguistic categories that is revealed by the phenomenon of markedness as a particular case of the principle of participation, which according to L. Lévy-Bruhl characterized primitive mentality. This principle would allow us to distinguish the logic of language (which Hjelmslev called **sublogic**) from the logic of logicians. In fact, if instead of saying that the word *man* designates sometimes the semantic unit *human male*, sometimes the category *humanity*, we recognize a single semantic unit corresponding to the set of meanings of *man*, we will have to say that the word includes the semantic unit *woman*. There will be, then, a partial overlap (participation) between the two units that seem incompatible with the logic of noncontradiction, according to which A and not-A are exactly disjunctive.

Hjelmslev and Brøndal even believed it possible to define, through an *a priori* calculation, the different possible types of linguistic categories according to the mode of participation of their units. Brøndal, for example, began by determining what would be the maximal category. It would include (a) a term B_1 (positive) and a term B_2 (negative), which are disjunctive and which thus present two qualities as incompatible—for example, "imperative" (idea of order) and "subjunctive" (idea of desire); (b) a **neutral** term A, which indicates the absence of both of these qualities, the nonapplication of the category—for example, "indicative"; (c) a **complex** term C, which includes both B_1 and B_2 and indicates only the application of the category—for example, the blend of order and desire that in certain languages would be the "optative"; and (d) two terms at once complex and polar opposites, D_1 and

D_2, which are equivalent to C but have an insistence either on the part B_1 or on the part B_2 of C. These are called **complex-positive** and **complex-negative**. It is difficult to find semantic units in English illustrating D_1 and D_2 that are expressed by simple morphemes. However, we might consider the meanings of the compound words *half-full* and *half-empty*. By withdrawing one term or another from this maximal category, one can envisage, according to Brøndal, fourteen other categories (a large number of mathematically possible combinations of the six basic elements are linguistically inadmissible, since it would be unacceptable to have a positive without a negative or a complex-positive without a negative, and vice versa).

● See L. Hjelmslev, "La Catégorie des cas," *Acta Jutlandica*, vol. 7 (1935), pt. 1, pp. i–xii, 1–84, and vol. 9 (1937), pt. 2, pp. i–vii, 1–77; and V. Brøndal, *Essais de linguistique générale* (Copenhagen, 1943), chap. 3. Documentation on other, analogous systems is found in K. Togeby, *Structure Immanente*, pp. 104–5.

Logical hexagon. The notion of participation is conceived by Hjelmslev and Brøndal as pre-logical. It is all the more remarkable that the philosopher and logician R. Blanché has managed to define, for the categories of "natural" thought, a rather similar type of organization, but on the basis of the most traditional logical relationships (A.-J. Greimas, pointing out the similarities between Blanché and Brøndal, argues that the existence of "elementary structures of signification" accounts for this convergence). For Blanché:

a) The logical relationships constituting the Aristotelian square do not simply unite the four traditional propositional forms *A, E, I,* and *O*; that is, they are not based solely on quantity and on the positive or negative character of judgment. It is also possible to find them in quaternary groups of the type $P(a)$, $Q(a)$, $R(a)$, $S(a)$, where *a* is the name of an object and *P, Q, R,* and *S* are predicates belonging to the same category of thought. If *P, Q, R,* and *S* are the predicates *miserly, prodigal, thrifty,* and *generous*, we have the following square:

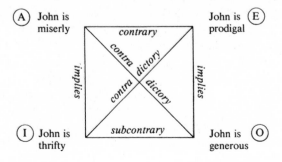

Similarly, in the category of heat, one could place *hot* at *A, cold* at *E, warm* at *I,* and *cool* at *O.*

b) A second possible extension of the Aristotelian theory would be to transform the square into a hexagon, by adjoining two supplementary positions, *Y* (defined as "either *A* or *E*"), and *U* (defined as "both *I* and *O*"). One would then have the complete schema (in order to simplify we will indicate, for each position, only the predicate):

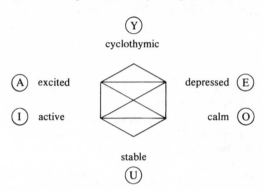

The relationship between Brøndal's neutral term and Blanché's *U* will be noted, as will that between the complex term and the *Y.* There remains, however, this essential difference: unlike the complex, *Y* includes no contradiction, nor even any participation; it signifies that one of the two contrary terms has to apply but does not specify which one, whereas the complex unites in itself the two opposites.

● See R. Blanché, *Les Structures intellectuelles* (Paris, 1966).

Gradation. A large number of categories are **oriented** (or **graduated**). We mean by this that there exists among their terms a linear order, a logical structure much simpler than the relationships studied by Blanché. This order can be defined by various convergent criteria. In order to orient a category of adjectives, for example, the most convenient criteria consist in applying to its terms quantitative modifiers such as *less than, almost, only, more than.* Each of these modifiers in reality has meaning only with respect to the orientation of the category of the modified term. They signify, respectively, "below," "very little below," "not above," and "above." Thus, since we know through direct observation that *only warm* is used to deny of a thing that it is hot and we know in addition that *only* equals "not above," we can conclude that there is a category in which *hot* is "above" *warm.* And since *only cool* is used to deny of a thing that it is cold, *cold* must be found "above" *cool.* These conclusions —which can be confirmed through the use of other modifiers—imply the existence of two oriented categories:

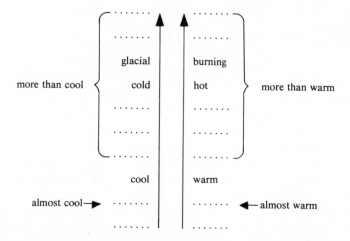

Another criterion, which converges with the preceding ones, can be drawn from the application of the rhetorical figure known as the litotes [278] to the terms of these categories. Used in a litotes, a word has a stronger meaning than usual. But the idea of stronger or weaker meaning implies the existence of a gradation: *stronger* equals "above, in the orientation of the category." Knowing moreover that the expression "it is cool," when used as a litotes, signifies "it is cold" and that "it is warm" signifies "it is hot," we have confirmation that *cold* is "above" *cool* and that *hot* is "above" *warm*.

● On this little-studied problem, see especially E. Sapir, "Grading: A Study in Semantics," *Philosophy of Science II* (1944): 93–116; and R. Valin, "Esquisse d'une théorie des degrés de comparaison," *Cahiers de linguistique structurale*, no. 2 (Quebec, 1952), in which the problem of gradation is treated in a Guillaumian perspective. On the relationships between litotes and orientation, see O. Ducrot, "Présupposés et sous-entendus," *Langue française* 4 (1969): 41–42. Two recent attempts to construct a theory of linguistic gradation are made by O. Ducrot, "Les Échelles argumentatives," in *La Preuve et le dire* (Paris, 1973), chap. 13; and G. Fauconnier, "Pragmatic Scales and Logical Structure," *Linguistic Inquiry* 6 (1975): 353–75.

LANGUAGE AND SPEECH

Empirical research only becomes science, according to certain phi-losophers, when it decides to "construct" its object; instead of welcoming pell-mell all the observable phenomena in a certain field of investigation, it elaborates for itself the concepts with the aid of which it will inter-rogate experience. Saussure was doubtless one of the first to render explicit, for linguistics, the necessity of accomplishing what Kant calls a Copernican revolution. He distinguished in effect the **subject matter** of linguistics, the linguist's field of investigation—which includes the whole set of phenomena closely or distantly related to language use—from its **object,** that is, the sector or the aspect of these phenomena that will in-terest the linguist. Why introduce such a separation? Saussure assigned it a double function. First, the object must constitute a "whole in itself," that is, a closed system with its own intrinsic intelligibility. Second, the object must be a "principle of classification": it must be the basis for a better comprehension of the subject matter (for Saussure saw com-prehension as classification), it must make the empirical data intelligible. The role of general linguistics, preparatory for specialized linguistic studies, is to define certain concepts that allow us to discern, in the empirical investigation of any particular language, the object within the subject matter. Saussure called the object **language (la langue)** and the subject matter, **speech (la parole)**. Although most modern linguists agree on the methodological necessity of such a distinction, they diverge on the question of which criteria allow us to recognize language and speech.

Saussure himself indicated a series of rather diverse criteria:

1. Language is defined as a code; thus there is an established corre-spondence between "auditory images" and "concepts." Speech is the utilization, the deployment, of this code by speaking subjects.

2. Language is pure passivity. Its possession brings into play only the receptive faculties of the mind, memory above all. All activities linked to human language (*langage*) belong to speech. Added to the preceding characterization, this latter has two consequences:

a) The linguistic code consists only of a multitude of isolated signs (words, morphemes), each of which associates a particular sound with a particular meaning; thus Saussure spoke of language as a treasure house where the signs would be stored (he recognized, at the most, that a coordinating faculty would be needed to sort out these signs). As for the organization of the signs in sentences and the combination of their meanings to constitute the global meaning of a sentence, it would be necessary—to the extent that they imply an intellectual activity—to attribute them to speech, to language use. Thus Saussure suggested that the sentence lies within the domain of speech (*Course in General Linguistics*, trans. W. Baskin [New York, 1959], pt. 2, chap. 5, sec. 2).

b) In the linguistic code, signifiers and signifieds are purely static. The act of enunciation itself [323], of using a given expression in a given circumstance, thus will not be regarded as a signifier of the language; and, moreover, the practical effect produced by the use of these expressions, the way in which they transform the respective situations of the interlocutors, can never be introduced into the code with the status of signifieds. (N.B. Of these two consequences, [*a*] is incompatible with generative grammar [39], [*b*] with analytic philosophy [94].)

3. Language is a social phenomenon, whereas speech is an individual one. In order to make this third criterion compatible with the first, we have to concede that the linguistic code of individuals is constituted in its entirety by society. This obliges us to believe, for example, either that the mechanisms for interpreting sentences are identical for all members of a linguistic community or that they lie outside the sphere of language. Given that in reality individuals offer a very wide range of interpretations for a sentence that is the slightest bit complex, this third criterion may well give us cause to question the legitimacy of the place of semantics within linguistics. On the other hand, if we bring together the characterization of speech as an individual phenomenon and its definition as activity (criterion 2), we are led to deny that linguistic activity has social norms, that the conditions of language use and its effect on the interlocutors' situation can be governed not only by habits but also by conventions. This thesis can be challenged empirically; it is contested in particular by socio- and ethnolinguistics [61ff.].

Although almost all the major linguistic doctrines include criteria for separating the subject matter from the object of research, most such criteria are incompatible with Saussure's, even when they are formulated as clarification of the language-speech opposition. Trubetzkoy, for example, opposed **phonetics** and **phonology** as studies of "speech sounds" and "language sounds," respectively. The phonetician describes *all* of the acoustic phenomena linked with language use and does not allow himself to privilege certain ones with respect to others; thus he studies the speech sounds. The phonologist, on the other hand, extracts from these phenomena only the elements that play a role in communication, that serve in one way or another in the transmission of information. These alone pertain to language; these alone are, in the customary terminology, "linguistically relevant" [171]. Take the task of describing the way in which a given speaker of English pronounces the sound /l/. The phonologist will retain only the informative features that allow this /l/ to be distinguished from other English phonemes. He will thus pay no attention to the fact that /l/ may or may not be voiced (that is, accompanied by vibrations of the vocal cords), for this feature is automatically determined by the context in the case of the English /l/ (the /l/ is unvoiced when it is surrounded by voiceless consonants, voiced when it is not). (N.B. This conception of the language-speech opposition, although in harmony with Saussure's criterion 1, is hardly compatible with his criterion 3: the influence of the context on the pronunciation of the /l/ is an eminently social phenomenon, characteristic of certain linguistic communities, so criterion 3 would lead to reintroducing it into language. It is this difficulty that has led Coseriu to situate the contextual variants [171] in an intermediary zone between what he calls "schema" and "speech," namely, the "norm" [126ff.].)

● The relationship between phonology and the notion of language is presented by N. S. Trubetzkoy in the introduction to his *Principles of Phonology*, trans. C. A. M. Baltaxe (Berkeley, 1969).

Chomsky and his exegetes have often assimilated their opposition of linguistic **competence** and linguistic **performance** to the distinction between language and speech. The competence of a speaker of English (which must be represented in the generative grammar [39] of English) is the set of possibilities given the subject owing to the fact—and to this fact alone—that he has mastered the English language. These possibilities include constructing and recognizing the infinite number of grammatically correct sentences; interpreting each of these that is endowed with meaning (also an infinite number); noting the ambiguous ones; feeling that certain sentences that may sound very different nevertheless have a strong grammatical resemblance and that other phonetically similar ones are very dissimilar grammatically. These possibilities—which constitute, for Chomsky, *the* competence common to all speakers of English and represent, by the same token, the "English language"—are distinguishable through (*a*) excesses and (*b*) deficiencies in the speech acts that the speaking subjects are in fact capable of performing:

a) The grammatical sentences of English are infinite in number, since no upper limit can be placed on their length (if a sentence X is correct, then one has only to add to it a relative clause in order to obtain a sentence Y that is longer than X and is also correct). Of course the finite capacity of memory makes it impossible to construct or to interpret a sentence that surpasses a certain length (so the number of sentences that can actually be realized is finite). This finitude of practical performance does not, however, prevent us from speaking of a theoretically infinite competence (in the sense in which mathematicians say that a function is theoretically calculable, even if the machine that could perform the calculation would have to have more electrons than the solar system contains and is thus impossible in practical terms).

b) Many of the performances of speaking subjects (foreseeing the effect of a sentence in a given context, abridging a sentence while trusting that the discursive situation will make the result intelligible, and so on) do not fall within the realm of linguistic competence, for they put into play a knowledge of the world and of others, as well as a certain experience of human relations, that may seem independent of linguistic activity.

It should be noted that the Chomskyan opposition has exactly the same role as Saussure's: just as we are supposed to be able to study language independently of speech, but not the reverse, we are supposed to be able to study competence in advance of performance, and at the same time competence is supposed to be the necessary foundation for the study of performance (this is expressed in the statement that the constitution of a generative grammar is preliminary to any psychology of language). Furthermore, the Chomskyan opposition coincides more or less with Saussure's first criterion, since the competencies, taken together, do no more than manifest the possibility of giving a semantic interpretation to phonic sequences. On the other hand, it is incompatible with the second criterion—since a sentence without a combinatorial activity is inconceivable—and also with the third—since linguistic competence includes, beyond the knowledge that is peculiar to each language, a universal linguistic faculty [31] that cannot be regarded as social.

Finally, for certain linguists oppositions exist that cannot be clearly linked to any of Saussure's three criteria, even though they play the same epistemological role as Saussure's and are explicitly assimilated to his. Thus glossematics [201ff.] distinguishes schema and usage in every language. The schema has a purely formal, algebraic nature; it is the set of relations (paradigmatic and syntagmatic [108ff.]) existing among the elements of a language independently of the way in which these elements are manifested, that is, independently of their meaning and their phonic realization. The functioning of language as code, which supposes that the linguistic units have been semantically and phonically defined, is thus not inscribed in the linguistic schema, but only in what Hjelmslev called usage. It is usage, in fact, that determines the mode of manifestation of the units. In describing usage, then, we will indicate both the manifest features that are distinctive [171] (they constitute what Hjelmslev called norm [125]) and those that are not and the features imposed by social conventions, as well as those that are improvised by the individual. It becomes evident that the Saussurian language-speech opposition—if we limit ourselves to Saussure's own explicit criteria—operates within what Hjelmslev calls usage. What links this opposition to the glossematic distinction between schema and usage is in particular the methodological function common to both.

- Hjelmslev presents his schema-usage opposition by declaring it essentially analogous to the language-speech distinction, in "Langue et parole," *Cahiers Ferdinand de Saussure* 2 (1942): 29–44; the article is reprinted in Hjelmslev's *Essais linguistiques* (Copenhagen, 1959).

The same can be said of Guillaume's use of the notions of language and speech. These notions serve especially to distinguish what he calls **meaning** and **meaning effect.** To each word, or more precisely, to each minimal significative unit, there corresponds, in language, one and only one meaning; this is true in spite of the infinite number of significations (or meaning effects) that it may have in discourse, each of which would represent a partial viewpoint, a particular approach to meaning. The meaning of a word, in fact, cannot be directly lodged in discourse, for it must be described as a movement of thought, as the progressive development of a notion (this is why language is called a **psychomechanics**). Thus the meaning of the French article *un* ("a") is the intellectual movement of particularization, which goes from the general to the particular, and the meaning of the article *le* ("the") is the inverse movement of generalization. When articles are used in discourse, the effect of the context is that of stopping these movements, or, to put it another way, of taking sightings or snapshots of them, thereby preserving a single instant. It is understandable, then, that in spite of the diversity of their meanings, the two articles might give rise to very similar meaning effects. This will be the case, for example, of sightings taken at the origin of the movement of generalization and at the end of the movement of particularization—we then obtain (*a*) *L'homme que tu as connu* ("The man you have known") and (*b*) *Un ami est venu* ("A friend has come") —and also of sightings taken at the end of generalization and at the beginning of particularization—cf. (*c*) *L'homme est faillible* ("Man is fallible") and (*d*) *Un homme est faillible* ("A man is fallible").

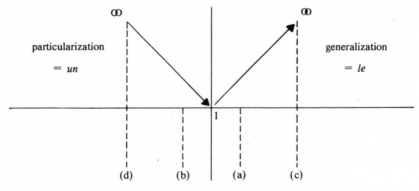

The left-hand arrow represents the meaning of *un*, the right-hand arrow, the meaning of *le*; and the dotted lines show the viewpoints corresponding to the meaning effects (a), (b), (c), and (d).

Once again, what Guillaume and Saussure have in common is not so much the content of the opposition utilized as it is the existence of the opposition, conceived as the basis for all linguistic research (prior knowledge of meaning alone allows one to understand meaning effects).

● See G. Guillaume, *Langage et science du langage* (Paris and Quebec, 1964), especially the chapters entitled "Observation et explication" and "Particularisation et généralisation."

Given that Saussure's successors have retained from the language-speech opposition less its content than its methodological function, it is essential, in order to justify any given form of such an opposition, to ask whether it fulfills this function in reality. The construction of an abstract linguistic object, in consequence, can only be legitimized at the completion of a study by the specific intelligibility manifested in the abstract object and by that which is conferred on the observable data. Justifiable by its results alone, a particular presentation of the opposition can thus never be regarded as being intrinsically self-evident and therefore as a possible basis for a polemic: a linguist who would reproach another for taking as language [*langue*] that which "in reality" is speech [*parole*], would be presupposing the definitive accomplishment of the task of linguistics.

● For a general examination of the language-speech distinction, see K. Heger, "La Sémantique et la dichotomie de langue et de parole," *Travaux de linguistique et de littérature* 7 (1969), pt. 1, pp. 47–111, esp. sec. 1. There is considerable information dispersed throughout the collection of Guillaume's texts published by R. Valin under the title *Principes de linguistique théorique de Gustave Guillaume* (Paris, 1973). For a synthetic overview of the theory, consult R. Martin, *Theories of Language and Methods in Syntax* (Paris, 1975), pp. 30–38. For a comparison with generative grammar, see S. Clarke and R. Sheen, "Comments on Guillaume's langue-discours in the Light of Chomsky's Competence-Performance Dichotomy," in *Grammaire générative transformationnelle et psychomécanique du language*, a collection edited at the University of Lille III (Paris, 1973).

NORM

Among the motivations that have led people to describe languages, we often encounter the desire to establish with precision a correct usage, a linguistic **norm**—which would retain only some of the speech patterns actually in use and would reject the others as careless, incorrect, impure, vulgar (this norm may concern pronunciation [in which case we call it orthoepy], word choice, morphology, or syntax). It is significant that the first known linguistic description, that of classical Sanskrit, appeared just at the moment when the cultivated Sanskrit language (*bhasha*), threatened by the invasion of popular dialects (*prakrits*), needed to be stabilized—if only to ensure the literal preservation of the sacred texts and the precise pronunciation of the prayer formulas. In Occidental societies the distinction of good and bad language is no less important, since the possession of good language is one of the marks of the dominant social classes (in his *Remarques sur la langue française*, published in 1647, Vaugelas defined correct usage as being "composed of the elite among voices. It is the manner of speaking of the healthiest part of the Court"). It is thus not surprising that Occidental linguistic tradition has given the grammarian a double role: he not only presumes to say what the language is, but at the same time he privileges certain usages and says what the language should be. This tradition survives in French pedagogical practice, which connects the study of grammar to the learning of correct grammatical usage (whereas recent Anglo-Saxon pedagogy has tended to dispense with the teaching of grammar). The conjunction of the descriptive and normative is justified by various arguments. Among several possible expressions, the correct one would be the one that (*a*) coincides best with the habitual practices of the language (it is governed by analogy), or (*b*) is susceptible to a "logical" justification, or (*c*) has the deepest roots in the history of the language. These three reasons converge in fact to produce the conclusion that the correct usage is the one whose description is the most interesting, for that is the one that manifests the greatest order or rationality.

● These three types of considerations will be found in the Girault-Duvivier *Grammaire des grammaires* (Paris, 1812), the basic text for teaching French in the nineteenth century; a detailed commentary on this work is by J. Levitt, *The "Grammaire des grammaires" of Girault-Duvivier* (The Hague, 1968), esp. chap. 7.

The development of linguistic research in the nineteenth century led to an increasing separation between scientific knowledge of a language and the determination of its norm. For one thing, historical linguistics, when it began to study linguistic transformations in detail, showed that the evolution of a language often has its origin in popular, slang, or dialectal speech, so the correct usage of one period often simply consecrates the incorrect usages of the preceding period.

● Numerous examples and bibliographical references can be found in W. von Wartburg, *Problems and Methods in Linguistics*, trans. M. H. Reid, rev. ed. (Oxford, 1969), chap. 2.

Moreover, it became apparent that the fundamental linguistic processes are just as much at work in so-called incorrect speech (that of children, the uneducated, and so on) as in speech that conforms to the official norm—and often more so. The child who conjugates "bring— I brang" on the model of "sing—I sang" is guided by that tendency to **analogy,** by that search for proportions (in the mathematical sense) in which H. Paul and F. de Saussure saw one of the most fundamental wellsprings of linguistics. Thus Saussure (*Course*, pt. 2, chap. 4, sec. 2) criticized the turn-of-the-century linguists who saw in analogy an "irregularity, an infraction of an ideal norm," since analogy constitutes in fact the device by means of which languages "pass from one state of organization to another." In a still more systematic fashion, H. Frei tried to show that so-called mistakes in language use are produced by the same psychological mechanisms that permit so-called correct language to carry out its functions [29ff.].

● On analogy, see H. Paul, *Principles of the History of Language*, trans. from the second edition by H. A. Strong (London and New York, 1891), chap. 5; and F. de Saussure, *Course in General Linguistics*, trans. W. Baskin (New York, 1959), pt. 2, chap. 4. For a functional analysis of errors, see H. Frei, *La Grammaire des fautes* (Bellegarde, 1929). On the general problems raised by the normative viewpoint in linguistics, see *Langue française* 16 (1972), ed. R. Lagane and J. Pinchon.

In the first part of the twentieth century, the rejection of the normative point of view in linguistics seemed so definite that certain linguists believed it possible to recuperate the word *norm* and to use it in a new sense in which it would no longer serve to distinguish a particular language usage. For Hjelmslev, the **system** of a language (its **schema**) is a purely formal reality; it is the set of abstract relations existing among its elements independently of any phonetic or semantic characterization of these elements (the French *r* is defined, in the system, by the way in which it enters into combination, in the syllable, with the other phonemes). The **norm,** on the other hand, is the set of distinctive features [173] that allow us, in the concrete manifestation of this system, to tell the elements apart. (From the viewpoint of the norm, the *r* is defined as a vibrant consonant; that suffices to distinguish it from all other French phonemes.) **Usage** now refers to the semantico-phonetic phenomena by means of which the system manifests itself in reality (*r* is characterized then by the whole set of features, including the nondistinctive ones, that constitute its pronunciation: it is sometimes a voiced, rolled, alveolar vibrant, sometimes a voiced, uvular constrictive). The norm thus represents a sort of abstraction produced with respect to usage.

E. Coseriu presents the same terminological hierarchy, but dislocated to the extent that the system, according to Coseriu, does not have the formal character that it did for Hjelmslev. Coseriu's **system** is close to Hjelmslev's norm: it is the functional aspect of language. Thus the systematic definition of a phoneme will indicate in essence its distinctive features. The **norm,** for Coseriu, corresponds to part of what Hjelmslev includes under the heading "usage." It involves all that is socially obligatory in the use of the linguistic code. The normative aspect of the phoneme is then the set of constraints imposed, in a given society, on its actual realization (including the nondistinctive features and, for example, the contextual variables [171]). At a third level, that of **speech** (*parole*), we must situate all the variations (free variants [172]) that the speaking subject may embroider onto the social canvas. The notion of norm, for Hjelmslev and Coseriu, thus defines a certain level of abstraction in the analysis of the data, in the study of actual use—and not, as was formerly the case, that of a certain type of use. The following chart summarizes the terminological differences between Hjelmslev and Coseriu:

	Coseriu	*Hjelmslev*
Abstract formal relations		System Schema
Concrete distinctive features	System	Norm
Concrete nondistinctive but obligatory features	Norm	Usage
Concrete nondistinctive and nonobligatory features	Usage	

● L. Hjelmslev presented the idea of norm in "Langue et parole," *Cahiers Ferdinand de Saussure* 2 (1942): 29–44; the article is reprinted in his *Essais linguistiques* (Copenhagen, 1959). E. Coseriu uses this notion particularly in *Systema, norma y habla* (Montevideo, 1952); N. C. W. Spence summarizes Coseriu's principal theses in "Towards a New Synthesis in Linguistics," *Archivum linguisticum* 12 (1960): 1–34.

The recent evolution of linguistics has led nevertheless to a certain rehabilitation of the idea that in the mass of empirical linguistic data, not everything is of equal value, that the linguist cannot put on the same plane all the usages he observes in a given speech community. Generative linguists [37ff.] admit, for example, that among the utterances actually used by speaking subjects, certain ones are **grammatical** and others are **ungrammatical.** The distinction is so important that a necessary condition of adequacy for a generative grammar is that it generate the former and not the latter. Given that the traditional grammars also propose to make their readers capable of constructing correct sentences and of avoiding incorrect ones, Chomsky has often been reproached with resurrecting the old notion of normativity, pure and simple. Certain clarifications are necessary in order to demonstrate the injustice of this reproach:

1. *Grammaticality and ungrammaticality are categories pertaining to judgment and not to use.* What assures the linguist of the grammatical character of an utterance is not, for Chomsky, the social category of those people who tend to use it, nor the circumstances in which it is principally used. It is an intuitive judgment that all the members of a given linguistic community pass on it (every speaker of English recognizes "it is hot" as grammatical and "it are hot" as ungrammatical). The ability to make this judgment, according to Chomsky, is part of the linguistic competence [120ff.] of speaking subjects.

2. *In speaking of grammaticality, the linguist intends to formulate, not an evaluation, but an observation.* According to the preceding argument, in fact, the grammarian does not base his judgments on the usage of a particular social class ("cultivated" people), but on a feeling that is common to a whole community. If in certain cases there is disagreement—if, for example, certain speakers of English find "Who do you like?" to be grammatical, and others reject it—it is not appropriate to regard one of these judgments as the right one; rather one must recognize that he is confronted with two different varieties of English each of which must be described by a particular generative grammar or by a particular variant of the grammar that describes English in general.

3. *Impossible utterances may be grammatical.* To the extent that grammaticality has as its criterion not a use but a judgment, it is possible to question the grammaticality of utterances that are never used in reality. Thus no one would hesitate to deem grammatical the statement "This locomotive weighs one ounce," even if reasons of credibility make its use highly unlikely. Or let us imagine a sentence that includes several overlapping relative clauses, for example: "The mouse which the cat which the neighbor who came bought has eaten was poisoned." No one will say this; doubtless it would even be impossible to understand. However, if someone recognizes as grammatical "The cat which my neighbor bought has eaten a mouse," it is possible to make him understand that the same constructions are involved in the two cases and that the grammaticality of the second statement implies that of the

first (it will be recalled that Descartes used a similar argument to prove that everyone possesses all of mathematics: whoever can recognize that two plus two equals four can be led to understand the most complicated theorems, for the latter do not bring into play any mathematical relationships of a different order). This possibility of judging as grammatical certain utterances that it is in fact impossible to use thus prevents us from seeing in the complexity of an utterance a cause of ungrammaticality. This is an indispensable notion if we are to understand the Chomskyan assertion that the set of grammatical sentences is infinite.

4. *The judgment of grammaticality is based on rules.* If the speaking subject can make a judgment of grammaticality (or can be brought to make such a judgment) on an infinite set of sentences, even if he has never heard them before, it is because this evaluation is based not on memory and experience but on a system of general rules that have been internalized in the course of language learning. Thus, by constructing a generative grammar that produces only grammatical sentences, the linguist is formulating a hypothesis on the mechanisms utilized unconsciously by the speaking subject. To each type of ungrammaticality there corresponds, then, a component of the grammar [54ff.]. The rules of the syntactic component are the ones that will thus prohibit the syntactically ungrammatical utterance "it are hot"; those of the phonological component will eliminate phonological anomalies that result from pronunciations that are impossible in the language described (that of an utterance, for example, that would include in a single syllable the consonant sequence *pfl*, impossible in English). The semantic component, finally, will rule out semantic anomalies such as "Steel weighs six pounds."

● On this latter theme, see J. J. Katz and J. A. Fodor, "The Structure of a Semantic Theory," *Language* 39 (1963): 170–210.

5. *The search for and the explanation of anomalies becomes an essential linguistic method.* If every judgment of ungrammaticality is founded on a grammatical rule that is most often unconscious, the linguist will have to seek to construct a systematic inventory of ungrammatical utterances. Thus numerous generative studies will have as their starting point such questions as, "Why is this utterance troublesome?"

● A study of the **semantic anomalies** spotted in a corpus of surrealist poetry, anomalies that represent deliberate choices on the part of their authors, thus allows T. Todorov to establish by contrast certain laws of the semantic combinatorial of French ("Les Anomalies sémantiques," *Langages* 1 [March 1966]: 100–123).

The generatist conception of ungrammaticality has nonetheless given rise to a certain number of criticisms:

a) Does it not imply a hidden and shameful return to the normative conception of grammar? Perhaps the judgments of ungrammaticality passed by speaking subjects are only the effect of rules learned in school, rules themselves based on a clearly normative grammar. In a general way, certain psycho- and sociolinguists wonder whether the "observations" leading the grammarian to judgments of grammaticality are not skewed and largely determined by the very situation of the grammarian.

● On this topic, see, for example, N. J. Spencer, "Differences Between Linguists and Non-Linguists in Intuitions of Grammaticality-Acceptability," *Journal of Psycholinguistic Research* 2 (1973): 83–98.

b) Are the speaking subjects themselves the ones who determine the three types of ungrammaticality, or is not this determination rather a simple reflection of the division of generative grammar into three components?

c) Is there not, between grammatical and ungrammatical sentences, a vast no man's land à propos of which no one can pass judgment with assurance? How can this phenomenon then be explained in the framework of a generative grammar that recognizes only two possibilities for an utterance (to be or not to be generated by the grammar)? The Chomskyans respond that the dualistic character of the grammar does not make it impossible to distinguish degrees of ungrammaticality: the least ungrammatical sentences will be prohibited by the most marginal rules of the grammar. But these notions of degree of ungrammaticality and marginality of rules remain very vague for the moment.

d) Does a feeling of peculiarity or strangeness experienced in the face of an utterance always have its origin in the fact that this utterance violates rules? Might not the explanation be on the contrary that the utterance systematically pushes the use of the rules beyond the usual limits? In that case, what the Chomskyans call ungrammaticality would no more bear witness to a deviation with respect to the rules than would the mistakes in which H. Frei sees the most obvious manifestation of true grammar. The semantic anomaly "and the axe cursed the men" (line 642 of "Ce que dit la bouche d'ombre," in V. Hugo, *Les Contemplations,* 2 vols. (Paris, 1964), vol. 2, p. 620) can in fact be described in two opposing ways. Either there is a violation of the rule according to which *to curse* requires a human subject or there is an exploitation of this rule that leads to the humanization of the subject *axe* (the latter is certainly Hugo's intention).

● This second possibility is developed by U. Weinreich in "Explorations in Semantic Theory," in *Current Trends in Linguistics,* ed. T. A. Sebeok, 14 vols. (The Hague, 1963–76), vol. 3, *Theoretical Foundations* (1966), pp.

429–32. In his critique of Katz and Fodor, Weinreich speaks of **transfer features.** In our example, the feature *human* would have been transferred from *curse* to *axe*. For divergences at the level of style, see, below, pp. 273ff.

ARBITRARINESS

From the outset, reflection on language has sought to discover whether a given language is an original reality, unforeseeable and irreducible to any extra-linguistic reality, or whether, on the contrary, it can be partially or totally explained, even justified, by the natural order of things or of thought. The first thesis is that of **linguistic arbitrariness;** the second, that of **motivation.** The alternative can be presented on at least four levels that are largely independent of one another.

Sound and Meaning

The Sophists posed the problem of the relationship between sound and meaning with respect to the attribution of names to things. According to Plato's *Cratylus*, there were two schools of thought. One, represented by Cratylus and linked more or less explicitly to Heraclitus, maintained that there is a natural relationship ($\varphi\upsilon\sigma\epsilon\iota$) between names and the things they designate and that without this relationship, no name is authentic. The name, imitation of the thing, has the particular virtue of instruction. "Whoever knows names also knows things" (435*d*). In order to show the wisdom hidden in vocabulary, one begins by taking recourse to **etymologies:** by adding, suppressing, or modifying certain letters of an apparently arbitrary word, one can produce in its place another name or sequence of names that correctly describes the thing designated by the initial name; it is thus a question not of historical research but of an effort to discover the "truth" ($\dot{\epsilon}\tau\upsilon\mu\omicron\nu$) of words. Concerning the **primitive names,** that is, those on which etymology can no longer operate, one seeks a direct relationship between their meaning and their sound, on the assumption that the elementary sounds of the language have natural representational value (*i* expresses lightness, *d* and *t* a stop, and so on). The idea that speech is an obscure revelation of the true enters into conflict, as early as the *Cratylus*, with the thesis—inspired by Democritus and linked to a relativist current of thought ("Man is the measure of all things")—according to which the attribution of names falls within the sphere of the arbitrary: naming is a matter of law (νομοι), of institution (θησει), of convention (κατα συνθηκην). As for Plato, although he recognized the arbitrariness that reigned in the existing languages (his etymologies are intentionally fanciful), he refused to see in this a lesson in relativism and a justification of rhetoric. He concluded on the contrary that truth is to be sought outside of language, in the intuition of essences [93]. Only the grasp of essences would allow us to create an ideal language; moreover, even in this language, names would not be images, but only the diacritical signs of essences (388*b*).

● See V. Goldschmidt, *Essai sur le Cratyle* (Paris, 1940); also G. Genette, "L'Eponymie du nom," *Critique* 28 (1972): 1019–44.

In the modern period, the thesis of the arbitrariness of linguistic denominations was affirmed by Saussure in the *Course in General Linguistics* (pt. 1, chap. 1). This thesis is moreover implicit in all the works that show, for the phonic aspect of language, a causality independent of that which governs its semantic aspect—the phonetic laws of diachronic linguistics [8]; the opposition, for Martinet, of the two articulations of language [53]; and the cleavage established by the generative grammarians between the phonological component, which works on the surface structure of utterances, and the semantic component, which exploits their deep structure [244]. The thesis is furthermore linked, in the history of linguistics, to the idea that language forms a system, that it possesses an internal organization. If each sign were in fact an imitation of its object, it could be explained by itself, independently of the others, and would not have any necessary relationship with the rest of the language. This is why, from classical times onward, the grammarians who were seeking regularity—called **analogy**—within language took the side of arbitrariness (conversely, most etymologists wished to see in language only irregularity and disorder, or, to use the established term, **anomaly;** to do so removed all hindrance to etymological speculation). We find in Saussure a rather similar undertaking (*Course*, pt. 2, chap. 6). It is because each sign, taken alone, is **absolutely arbitrary** that human need for motivation leads to the creation of classes of signs in which only a **relative arbitrariness** reigns (the adjective *blueish* receives a kind of secondary motivation from the fact that there exists a class <green-ish, red-dish, purpl-ish>, in which the same type of derivation is accompanied by an analogous semantic content). The organization of language into categories of signs is connected with the arbitrariness of the isolated sign: the latter is counterbalanced by the former.

Etymological research and the idea of a sort of natural truth of sound remain present, however, in all periods of philosophical and linguistic reflection. The Stoics were great seekers of etymologies (and militant anomalists). Leibniz himself believed etymology to be capable of bringing man closer to primitive language, a language that would have exploited better than ours the expressive value of sounds. Certain linguists are still seeking today to find motivations for the phonic form of words, while giving this research the scientific guarantees it has often lacked. In order to do this, they attempt to ground etymology on historically verifiable derivations, and at the same time they base their study of the expressive value of sounds on detailed psychological and acoustic observations.

- On classical etymological research, see Varro, *On the Latin Language*, trans. R. G. Kent (Cambridge, Mass., 1951), bks. 5–7; and J. Collart, *Varron: Grammairien latin* (Paris, 1954). On the Stoics in particular, see K. Barwick, *Probleme der stoïschen Sprachlehre und Rhetorik* (Berlin, 1957). An example of modern research is found in P. Guiraud, *Structures étymologiques du lexique français* (Paris, 1967); see also Y. Malkiel, "Etymology and Modern Linguistics," *Lingua* 36 (1975): 101–20. On the expressive value of sounds in language and discourse, see R. Jakobson, "Quest for the Essence of Language," *Selected Writings II* (The Hague, 1971) pp. 345–59.

Signifier and Signified

Saussure taught linguists to distinguish rigorously between the sign's referent (that is, the set of things to which the sign refers) and its signified (the concept evoked in the mind by its signifier). Post-Saussurian linguistics has found itself confronted with the question of the relationships between the signifier and the signified, a problem very different from the first one, since what is in question here is a relationship within the sign [100]. On this point most linguists, except for a few of Saussure's students, maintain that one must no longer speak of arbitrariness and that in a given language, the signified of a sign cannot be conceived independently of its signifier. Their principal argument is that the signifieds of the language have no logical or psychological basis: they correspond neither to objective essences nor to subjective intentions that would have motivations outside of language. Constituted at the same time as the language, contemporaneous with the attribution made to them of a phonic signifier, they have no unity except for this common signifier, and they dissolve as soon as one seeks to separate them (there is no general idea to which the word *courage* would eventually apply; it is the use of this word that collects and unifies a multitude of different moral attitudes, attitudes that doubtless have no business being subsumed under a single label, so it is an artifact of linguistic reflection that makes us imagine an intellectual unity corresponding to the word *courage*). We should note that an argument of this sort, although it proves well enough the necessity of the signifier-signified link within language, does not however bear witness to a motivation. Moreover, such an argument rests in· fact on the intuition of a fundamental linguistic arbitrariness; it is based on the belief in an irreducible originality of the order created by language with respect to that of the world or of thought.

- C. Bally, one of Saussure's own students, has tried to defend the arbitrariness of the signifier-signified relationship ("L'Arbitraire du signe, valeur et signification," *Le Français moderne* 8 [1940]: 193–206). The opposite point of view is presented by P. Naert ("Arbitraire et nécessaire en linguistique," *Studia linguistica* 1 [1947]: 5–10) and by E. Benveniste ("Nature du signe linguistique," *Acta linguistica* 1 [1939]: 23–29). For a theoretical overview, see R. Engler, *Théorie et critique d'un principe saussurien: L'Arbitraire du signe* (Geneva, 1962). For a historical viewpoint, see R. Hiersche, "Zur Entstehung von F. de Saussures Konzeption vom arbitraire du signe linguistique," *Archiv für das Studium der Neueren Sprachen* 211 (1974): 1–17.

Syntactic Organization

The problem of linguistic arbitrariness goes well beyond the framework of the isolated sign, and one can attempt to determine whether the categories and the syntactic rules put into operation by a language tend to express the very structure of thought or whether they constitute an original creation. Most of the general grammars of the seventeenth and eighteenth centuries [3ff.] maintain that there are two aspects to the grammar of a language. The first is a set of categories and rules that are common to all languages, for they are imposed by the necessary and universal exigencies of the expression of logical thought. This would be the case for the distinction of the principal parts of speech (adjective, substantive, verb), for the rule that prescribes the presence of a verb in every proposition, for the rule that holds that, in sentences, the word that is determined precedes the one that determines it. The second specific aspect of each language is due to a series of habits peculiar to it that either complete the universal rules (by fixing the lexical form of words, the details of declension, certain mechanisms of agreement) or oppose them after the fact (when they authorize or prescribe "inversions" in the natural order of words, when they permit the verb to be "understood," when they give rise to illogical idioms). To the extent that the logical aspect of grammar is regarded as its deepest level and that the idiomatic specificities only graft themselves onto it secondarily, language, from the perspective of the general grammars, may be regarded as fundamentally motivated and only accidentally arbitrary. A formula from the *Port-Royal Grammar* draws the following conclusions from this thesis: "The knowledge of what passes in the mind is necessary, in order to comprehend the foundation of grammar" (A. Arnauld and C. Lancelot, *A General and Rational Grammar* (1753; facsimile reprint, ed., Menston, England, 1968), pt. 2, chap. 1, p. 21).

● C. Serrus presented a systematic critique of the Port-Royal logicism in *Le Parallélisme logico-grammatical* (Paris, 1933).

The thesis of the motivation of syntax has reappeared in our day— but with notable differences—in generative linguistics [37ff.].

● N. Chomsky has shown the connections between general grammars and generative grammar in *Cartesian Linguistics* (New York, 1966).

The transformationalists believe in fact that the basic constituent of syntax must be identical for all languages (its rules constitute **formal universals**) and that syntactic differences arise only under the influence of transformations. But whereas the Port-Royal grammarians deduced the universality of grammar from the prior postulate according to which language is a representation of logical thought, the universalism of the Chomskyans presents itself as an empirical conclusion drawn from the study of languages and is thus not based on a postulated identification of deep syntax and logical reality. If the transformationalist thesis were to prove correct, one result would be the idea that the multitude of particular languages have as their common basis the universality of human nature (this would in a sense contradict the thesis of arbitrariness); but one could represent this natural basis of languages as a linguistic faculty with its own specific features, as compared with other faculties, in particular those that govern logical thought. We glimpse then a possible conciliation between the affirmation of the natural character of language and the affirmation of the irreducible originality of the linguistic order.

Linguistic Units

The most radical way to affirm linguistic arbitrariness consists in maintaining that the minimal units utilized by a particular language are not capable of being defined independently of that language. This thesis itself includes at least three distinct phases:

a) In the first phase, it is affirmed that the units used by languages (phonemes, distinctive features, semes, grammatical notions) are based on nothing other than their linguistic utilization: no physical or physiological constraint predisposes the multitude of sounds that can be pronounced in French as realizations of the vowel *a* to constitute a single and unique phoneme. Similarly, the set of color nuances designated by the word *green* does not have, from the viewpoint of physical or psychological reality, any objective unity (see the discussion about the word *courage* above, p. 93). Thus the slicing of extra-linguistic reality into linguistic units would not be inscribed, filigree-like, within things but would manifest rather the free choice belonging to language.

● This thesis of the originality of **linguistic segmentation** is presented in part 2, chapter 4, of Saussure's *Course in General Linguistics*; it has been taken up again by most phonologists and, in a general way, by the entire structuralist school. See, for example, L. Hjelmslev, *Prolegomena to a Theory of Language*, trans. F. J. Whitfield, rev. ed. (Madison, 1961), pp. 54–60. This thesis has been spared up to now by the transformationalist reaction against structuralism.

b) The second phase would consist in saying that the segmentations effected by language in extra-linguistic reality vary from language to language; thus they are not due to a general linguistic faculty, but to a free decision of the particular language. In an attempt to prove this, it has been shown for example to what extent the phonemes vary from language to language (A. Martinet, *Elements of General Linguistics*, trans. E. Palmer [London and Chicago, 1964], pp. 54–55) and how the same semantic reality is organized differently in different languages.

● The method of analysis of **semantic fields** developed by the German J. Trier makes it possible to demonstrate that the articulation of a given notional region may vary according to the language or to the successive states of a single language (*Der deutsche Wortschatz im Sinnbezirk des Verstandes* [Heidelberg, 1931]). B. L. Whorf maintains even more precisely that each language—or language group—is indissolubly linked to a representation of the world that is inconceivable outside of that language. Whorf studied in particular the concept of time and change incorporated in the Amerindian languages, which turns out to be very different from the Indo-European conception. Whorf's principal works have been collected by J. B. Carroll under the title *Language, Thought, and Reality* (Cambridge, Mass., 1956). On the use of the notion of semantic field in modern linguistics, see A. Lehrer, *Semantic Fields and Lexical Structure* (Amsterdam, 1974).

The adversaries of this thesis will reply that the alleged variations stem from a superficial analysis and that a thorough analysis would bring to light linguistic universals that would bear witness to a natural linguistic faculty. There would thus be a universal repertory of semantic or phonetic elements in which each language would choose the basic elements for its combinatorial. This thesis is currently defended by most transformationalists. According to them, each of the two components, phonological and semantic, must describe utterances in a universal metalanguage, whose symbols would thus designate **substantial universals,** which might be found in the most disparate languages.

● In the area of phonetics, the transformationalists have taken up R. Jakobson's ideas. If it is true that the phonemes differ from language to language, each phoneme is in itself nothing more than a group of distinctive features. Now these distinctive features, very limited in number, are the same for all languages (see R. Jakobson, C. Fant, and M. Halle, *Preliminaries to Speech Analysis*, M.I.T. Press Technical Report 13 [Cambridge, Mass., 1952], or N. Chomsky and M. Halle, *Sound Patterns of English* [New York, 1968]). In the area of semantics—less studied to date—the transformationalists think that although words do not have identical significations in different languages, their significations are nonetheless constructed on the basis of minimal semantic elements that are themselves universal. On this point, see the collections of J. H. Greenberg, ed., *Universals of Language*, 2d ed. (Cambridge, Mass., 1966); and E. Bach and R. Harms, eds., *Universals in Linguistic Theory* (New York, 1968).

c) In its most acute phase, the belief in linguistic arbitrariness is no longer grounded in the categorization of phonic or semantic reality by the various languages, but in the idea that the underlying nature of the linguistic elements is purely formal. As it has been elaborated by Hjelmslev, following certain of Saussure's leads [21], this thesis consists in affirming that linguistic unity is constituted above all by the relationships (syntagmatic and paradigmatic) that it maintains with the other units of the same language. In this perspective, each unit can only be defined by the system of which it is a part. It becomes contradictory then to discover identical units in different languages and to represent these different languages as being simply different combinatorials, constituted on the basis of a universal set of elements, given the human linguistic faculty. Since every element includes at its very center a reference to the linguistic system to which it belongs, the originality of each language is no longer a contingent phenomenon, but a necessary one that stems from the very definition of linguistic reality. A language then can no longer be anything but arbitrary.

● A. Martinet ("Substance phonique et traits distinctifs," *Bulletin de la société de linguistique de Paris* 53 [1957–58]: 72–85) discusses the Jakobsonian idea of universal phonological distinctive features, using arguments not far removed from the glossematic perspective. For him the distinctive features utilized by a language could not be described by a simple phonetic characterization, for they are only definable in terms of their relationship with the other distinctive features of the same language. Consequently, the question of their universality does not even arise. On the possible application of the Hjelmslevian conception to semantic questions, see O. Ducrot, "La Commutation en glossématique et en phonologie," *Word* 23 (1967): 116–20; J. Holt, "Contribution à l'analyse formelle du contenu linguistique," *Langages* 6 (June 1967): 57–69; and especially J. Kristeva, "Pour une sémiologie des paragrammes," *Tel Quel* 29 (1967): 53–75.

SYNCHRONY AND DIACHRONY

Although the terms "synchrony" and "diachrony" entered conventional linguistic terminology only with F. de Saussure, they can be defined independently of the Saussurian theses. A linguistic phenomenon is said to be **synchronic** when all the elements and factors that it brings into play belong to one and the same moment of one and the same language (that is, to a single **language state**). It is **diachronic** when it brings into play elements and factors belonging to different states of development of a single language. The application of this definition is relative in more than one respect. It depends on what is meant by "a single language." Is the same language spoken in Paris, Marseilles, and Quebec? It depends next on what is meant by "the same state." Do the French spoken in 1975 and that of 1960 belong to the same state of development of the language? And that of 1850? Proceeding by degrees in this way, why could we not say that French and Latin belong to the same developmental state of the Indo-European mother tongue? In the last analysis, every linguistic phenomenon is always linked to historical factors; the adjectives *synchronic* and *diachronic* qualify less the phenomena themselves than the viewpoint adopted by the linguist. Rigorously speaking, there is no such thing as synchrony; however, one may decide to exclude from consideration, when describing or explaining a phenomenon, everything that does not belong to a determined language state. (N.B. Although American terminology labels **descriptive linguistics** what is here called synchronic linguistics, it is not self-evident that the synchronic viewpoint cannot be explanatory (see the article on functionalism [24]). Conversely, certain diachronic research (like that of the comparatists [9]) is above all descriptive, for it is content to observe—and to formulate as simply as possible, with recourse to the "phonetic laws"—the resemblances and the differences between comparative language states).

It has taken linguistic reflection a long time to distinguish clearly between the synchronic and diachronic points of view. Thus etymological research hesitates constantly between two objectives: (*a*) setting one word in relationship with another word that gives it deep, hidden signification (for an example, see the etymology in the *Cratylus* [130]); and (*b*) setting one word in relationship with an earlier word from which it is said to derive (historical etymology [8]). It is not always easy to see whether the two types of research are regarded as independent or whether their convergence is held to be their common justification. Similarly, although since classical antiquity the particular relationships existing between certain sounds (*b* and *p*, *g* and *k*, and so on) have been noticed, they are often given synchronic and diachronic arguments—and these are not distinguished—as proof of this relationship. Thus Quintilian (cited in the *Grande Encyclopédie*, in the article "C") illustrates the relationship between the sounds *g* and *k* (the latter written as *c*) simultaneously by a synchronic fact (the Latin verb *agere* has as its participle *actum*) and by a diachronic fact (the Greek *cubernètès* became, in Latin, *gubernator*).

As for nineteenth-century linguistics, although it recognized the specificity of diachronic phenomena, it was progressively led to reabsorb synchronics into diachronics. This was the case for the comparatists, who concluded from the decline of languages that they had a right, indeed an obligation, to rediscover in the posterior state the organization of the anterior state [11]. It was also the case for the neogrammarians [13], according to whom a concept of synchronic linguistics is only meaningful to the extent that it can be interpreted in diachronic terms. Thus, for H. Paul, the statement that one word is derived from another (for example, *worker* from *work*) either has no precise meaning (that is, it is only a way to call attention to the resemblance between the words and to the greater complexity of the former) or else means that in a certain period the language included only the "source" word, and the "derived" word was constructed at a later point in time.

The absence of a sharp distinction, for the comparatists, between synchrony and diachrony is evident again in the way they treat the problem of classifying languages. This may be historical, genetic (grouping languages with a common origin), or **typological** (grouping languages that have similar phonic, grammatical, or semantic characteristics). Now the comparatists admit implicitly that a genetic classification, including for example a category for Indo-European languages, would be at the same time a typology, at least in the sense that the genetically related languages would necessarily have to be typologically similar; thus the Indo-European languages are of the inflectional type (see, above, the typology established by Schleicher and accepted, with variations, by most nineteenth-century linguists [12]). Such a belief is understandable, moreover, since this typology was based on a unique criterion, the internal organization of the word, and since the comparatist method implies that the languages among which one can demonstrate a genetic relationship construct words in the same way (this implication is developed above, on pp. 7ff.). Since the beginning of the twentieth century, many linguists have tried, on the other hand, to make typology independent of historical preoccupations; this effort has gone hand in hand with a broadening of the typological criteria. Thus Sapir recognized only a secondary role in the criterion of word construction. His essential criterion is based on the nature of the concepts expressed in the language. If all languages express "concrete concepts" designating objects, qualities, or actions (they are expressed by the roots [10] of nouns and verbs in the Indo-European languages), as well as "abstract relational concepts," establishing the principal syntactic relationships, certain languages have no "derivational concepts" that would modify the meaning of the concrete concepts (expressed in English for example by diminutives such as -*let*, prefixes such as *dis-* and *re-*, and endings such as the -*er* in *worker* or the -*ist* in *activist*) nor "concrete relational concepts" (number, gender). According to whether they express neither, one or the other, or both of these latter notional categories, languages can be grouped in classes that, given the nature of the criteria used, will no longer have a necessarily genetic character.

● See E. Sapir, *Language: An Introduction to the Study of Speech* (1921; reprint ed., New York, 1955), chap. 6. For an overview of the problem of typology, see E. Benveniste, *Problems in General Linguistics*, trans. M. E. Meek (Coral Gables, 1971), chap. 9; H. Birnbaum, "Typology, Genealogy and Linguistic Universals," *Linguistics* 144 (1975): 5–26; and E. Coseriu, "Sincronia, diacronia y tipologia," *Actas del 11ᵉ congreso internacional de lingüística y fonología románicas* (Madrid, 1968), vol. 1, pp. 269–83.

Saussure was doubtless the first to explicitly claim autonomy for synchronic research. He used various arguments:

1. H. Paul's view notwithstanding, it is possible to define synchronic relationships in a precise and rigorous fashion, *without any recourse to history*. A Saussurian, for example, will agree that there is a relation-

ship of **derivation** between two terms only if the passage from one to the other takes place according to a general procedure in the language under consideration, a procedure according to which a certain phonic difference produces a certain semantic difference. What validates the derivation *work / worker* is that it fits into the series *drink / drinker*; *fight / fighter*, a series distinguished by the fact that the verb in each pair is an action verb. In other words, the synchronic relationship is based on its integration into the overall organization—into the system—of language. Now language, for a Saussurian, *must* present itself, *at each moment of its existence, as a system* [16ff.].

2. Not only may the synchronic relationships be established apart from all diachronic considerations, but they may enter into conflict with the diachronic relationships. First, certain synchronic relationships are diachronically unjustified. In synchrony, we have, in French, the relationship *léguer / legs* ("to bequeath / legacy") (the *g* of *legs* is, for this reason, often pronounced), a relationship analogous to *donner / don* ("to give / gift"), *jeter / jet* ("to throw / throw"), and so on. Now there is no historical relationship between *léguer* and *legs* (which can be linked to *laisser* ["to leave"]); their association is a **popular etymology,** invented by speaking subjects because it could be readily integrated into the system of French. Conversely, many historically well-founded relationships have no synchronic reality, for they can no longer be integrated into the system of the contemporary language (consequently, they have been forgotten by the speakers of that language). Thus there is no connection, today, between the French *bureau* ("desk") and *bure* ("rough homespun cloth"), even though *bureau* was constructed from *bure* (it was a table covered with sackcloth).

3. Although it is true that phonetic changes often modify the expression of grammatical relationships, they only do so indirectly and by accident, never having this modification as their object. At a certain period in the evolution of Latin, the word for *honor* was *honos*, and a regular genitive was formed by the addition of *is: honosis*. Then a phonetic law transformed to *r*, in all Latin words, the *s* situated between two vowels; this produced *honoris*. The nominative-genitive relationship happened to be affected; however, it was not a specific target, since the rule concerned any *s* placed between two vowels. Given that this relationship was not specifically challenged, nothing prevented its reestablishment, and it is here that analogy intervenes [13]: using as a model the series of regular genitives (*labor / laboris*; *timor / timoris*), the Latins created a new nominative, *honor*, which little by little supplanted the old one and permitted the regular formation *honor / honoris*. Thus the system had sufficient resilience to produce a new word and to reestablish the general schema. We may conclude not only that analogical innovation is unable to modify a preexisting organization—which, on

the contrary, it presupposes—but also that analogy is a conservative element that may repair the damage done, accidentally, by phonetic laws.

The study of historical evolution thus confirms the arguments drawn from a reflection on synchronic relationships. The conclusion is that the state of a language at a given moment, insofar as its systematic organization is concerned, is never clarified—whether the attempt is to describe or to explain it—by a reference to its past. Synchronic research must be carried out apart from all diachronic considerations.

This thesis of the independence of synchronic investigation is currently accepted by almost all linguists, Saussurians as well as transformationalists. But it is not always clearly distinguished, in Saussure's work, from the reciprocal proposition, that is, from the idea that diachronics can be studied apart from all synchronic considerations. Certain arguments made in Saussure's *Course* do suggest this reciprocal proposition, however, since they assimilate historical change to the action that phonetic laws have on the elementary language sounds and since these laws —considered in the nineteenth century to be "blind"—are supposed to operate independently of the synchronic organization of the language, its "system." Many contemporary linguists are questioning this particular thesis (for reasons that are not always mutually compatible, however). Their common conclusion is that linguistic evolution may have one system as its starting point and another as its destination and that it must then be described as the transformation of one synchronic structure into another synchronic structure. While admitting that the synchronic organization of a language state must be established independently of any diachronic research, linguists believe that diachronic study must be based itself on prior knowledge of synchronic organizations.

This tendency is particularly clear in **diachronic phonology,** which considers it necessary, in order to understand the phonic evolution of a language, to distinguish two types of change. The phonetic changes are those that do not affect the phonological system of the language, for they only modify the variants through which the phonemes are manifested [171] (for example, the transformation of the pronunciation of the French *r* since the seventeenth century). The phonological changes, on the contrary, modify the phonological system itself:

Example 1. Suppression of a phonemic opposition. In contemporary French, even if a certain difference in pronunciation is maintained between *l'Ain* and *l'un*, this difference is used to distinctive ends less and less; the two pronunciations moreover are rarely still *heard* as different.

Example 2. Phonologization of a distinction that was formerly a combinatorial variant [171] imposed by the context. Toward the end of the sixteenth century in France, the difference between the sounds [ã] (the current pronunciation of the word *an* ["year"]) and [a] represented a combinatorial variant, the *a* being obligatorily pronounced [ã] before [m] and [n]; *an* and *Anne* were thus pronounced [ãn] and [ãnə], their distinction being assured by the *e* pronounced at the end of *Anne*. Later, when the final *e* was no longer pronounced, *Anne* was pronounced [an], as it is today (with the [ã] denasalized and the [ə] dropped), whereas *an* took on the contemporary pronunciation [ã] (with the [n] dropped), so that [ã] became a phoneme, endowed with distinctive power (the difference between the pronunciations [a] and [ã] allows us to distinguish *à* ["to"] and *an*).

Example 3. Displacement of an entire series of phonemes. When the Latin [kw] (as in the relative *qui*) gave the Italian sound [k] (as in the Italian relative *chi*), the Latin [k] (for example, the initial consonant of *civitas*) gave the Italian [č] (for example, the initial consonant of *città*), which made it possible to preserve all the distinctions between words.

In cases of phonological change, it is not only the material reality of the phonemes that is at stake, but their mutual relationships, that is, in Saussurian terms, their value, their systematic character [16]. Now, we could not hope to understand linguistic evolution without distinguishing phonetic change from phonological change. The former has extra-linguistic causes, either physiological (minimalization of effort) or social (imitation of one group by another). Phonological change, on the contrary, obeys an intra-linguistic causality. It is produced either by a sort of disequilibrium in the previous system, of which certain elements (phonemes or distinctive features [173], having become marginal, stop being supported by the pressure of others, or else, as Martinet says (the preceding examples were borrowed from him), by a global phenomenon of economy (a certain phonemic opposition may stop being viable *in a given language state*: in terms of a proportional relationship between its cost, in articulatory energy, and its return, in distinctive power, the opposition ends up costing too much more than the other oppositions of the same system or simply too much more than another opposition that has remained only potential until then and will now replace the first one). In any case, it is the overall organization of the linguistic state that is at stake in the transformation. Thus the phonic changes that, for Saussure, concerned only the elementary sounds and could not, as a result, involve the synchronic system of the language turn out in fact to provide examples of structural change in themselves.

● On diachronic phonology, see R. Jakobson, "Principles of Historical Phonology," in *Selected Writings I* (The Hague, 1962), pp. 202–20; A. Martinet, *Economie des changements phonétiques* (Bern, 1955); and idem, *Evolution des langues et reconstruction* (Paris, 1975), a collection of Martinet's articles. For an application to French, see G. Gougenheim, "Réflexions sur la phonologie historique du français," in *Etudes phonologiques dédiées à la mémoire de M. le Prince N. S. Trubetzkoy* (1939;

reprint ed., University, Ala., 1964), pp. 262–69; and A. G. Haudricourt and A. G. Juilland, *Essai pour une histoire structurale du phonétisme français* (Paris, 1949).

The partisans of generative grammar also attempt—but from a very different viewpoint—to reintroduce the consideration of synchronic systems into the study of linguistic change. Their research, not yet highly developed, is particularly concerned with the phonic aspect of language and focuses upon the following themes:

1. Phonetic changes, far from being "blind," often take into account the grammatical structure of the words to which they apply: the way in which a phoneme is modified depends on its grammatical function. This thesis, already maintained by the adversaries of the neogrammarians, as well as by those of Saussure, takes on particular importance in generative theory. Indeed, the "phonological component" [53] of the grammar, a component with purely synchronic value, has to take into consideration the grammatical function of the phonemes in order to translate the syntactic surface structure of sentences into a phonic representation: the application of the laws constituting this component is often conditioned by the syntactic role of the units that are subject to these laws; hence a first resemblance between the laws determining the evolution of phoneticism and those that constitute it in synchrony.

2. The laws constituting the phonetic component are ordered [233]. Let A be a syntactic surface structure. Its conversion into a phonetic representation B is not achieved by the successive modification of its various terminal elements a_1, a_2, a_3; rather, the thoroughgoing application of a first law to all the elements of A gives a representation A', then a second, applied to A', gives a representation A'', and so on until B is finally obtained. The component thus gives a series of different representations of the sentence that are further and further distant from the abstract structure A, closer and closer to the concrete form B. Now, according to the transformationalists, when a phonetic change occurs in a given state, it modifies directly not the concrete elements but the laws by means of which these elements are inserted into the final representation. What the change affects is thus the very system of the language, the system described in the laws of synchronic grammar.

3. Certain transformationalists have offered the hypothesis that (a) the phonetic change is quite often accomplished through the introduction of new laws into the phonological component and (b) when a law is introduced, it operates, in the order of application of the laws, *in the wake* of the preexisting laws (thanks to which we avoid pronunciation changes that would make comprehension impossible). One result of (a) and of (b) is that the synchronic order of the laws in the component reproduces, at least partially, the diachronic history of phoneticism. (N.B. This convergence is not presented as a theoretical principle, but as a

hypothesis to be verified empirically. [Verification requires that if the convergence is to be significant, there must be purely synchronic criteria for choosing and ordering the laws in the phonetic component.])

• On the application of generative phonology to the history of language, see *Langages* 8 (1967), particularly the articles by M. Halle ("Place de la phonologie dans la grammaire générative," pp. 13–36) and by P. Kiparsky ("A propos de l'histoire de l'accentuation grecque," pp. 73–93), as well as the bibliography, pp. 124–31. See also S. Saporta, "Ordered Rules, Dialect Differences and Historical Processes," *Language* 41 (1965): 218–24; P. Kiparsky, "Linguistic Universals and Linguistic Change," in *Universals in Linguistic Theory*, ed. E. Bach and R. Harms (New York, 1968); and idem, "Explanation in Phonology," in *Goals of Linguistic Theory*, ed. S. Peters (Englewood Cliffs, 1972), pp. 189–227.

In branches of linguistics other than phonology, attempts to construct a history of systems have unfortunately made much less progress, so the absolute dichotomy established by Saussure between synchrony and diachrony remains triumphant. It should be noted, however, that the analysis of semantic fields developed by J. Trier [135] has represented from the outset an attempt at structural history, since it shows how, in a given historical period, an overall semantic reorganization took place in a whole sector of the German lexicon.

• Theoretical indications can be found in E. Coseriu, "Pour une sémantique structurale," *Travaux de linguistique et de littérature* 2 (1964): 139–86, and examples of analysis may be found throughout E. Benveniste's *Indo-European Language and Society*, trans. E. Palmer (Coral Gables, 1973). See also P. Guiraud, *Structures étymologiques du lexique français* (Paris, 1967).

HISTORY OF LITERATURE

Definition

In order to dispel some frequent confusions, let us begin by defining the field of **literary history** in a negative way:

1. The object of literary history is not the genesis of works. J. Tynianov wrote as early as 1927: "The historical investigations of literature

fall into at least two main types, depending on the points of observation: the investigation of the genesis of literary phenomena, and the investigation of the evolution of a literary order, that is, of literary changeability" (in Matejka and Pomorska, eds., *Readings in Russian Poetics*, p. 67). We shall suggest as an initial approach that the specific object of literary history is this **variability**, not the **genesis** of works; although some still regard the latter as the object of literary history, it belongs in fact, in our view, to the psychology or the sociology of creation.

2. The history of *literature* must be clearly distinguished from *social* history. To substitute the latter for the former is to affirm that one can explain literary variability by social change: the answer is given even before the question has been formulated. This does not mean that the two series are independent: to differentiate does not mean to isolate; it is rather a question of establishing a hierarchical order in the object of the study, an order that has necessary repercussions on the form of the study itself.

3. Literary history does not coincide, either, with the immanent study —called reading or description—that seeks to reconstitute the system of the text. This latter type of study—which can embrace the system of an entire literary period—approaches its object in synchrony, we might say. History must be concerned with the passage from one system to another, that is, with diachrony [137ff.].

Literary history, therefore, cannot be the study of particular works that are unique specimens, affected by time only in that they are subject to differing interpretations according to the period. This latter problem belongs rather to the history of ideologies. We shall say, on the contrary, that literary history must study literary *discourse*, not works; thus literary history is defined as part of poetics.

Object

The first question that arises for the historian can be formulated in the following way: What is it, precisely, that changes within literary discourse?

In the nineteenth century (Brunetière), the answer was that the genres change: the novel, poetry, tragedy. This view betrays a subtle and dangerous shift from the concept to the word. For to declare that the novel changed between 1800 and 1900 is to say that the meaning of the word *novel* changed between these dates: the change in the extension of the concept brought about a change in its comprehension. But nothing authorizes us to postulate that common features relate two books separated by a century. Such identity is purely nominal; it resides in critical or journalistic discourse and nowhere else. Consequently, a study of the "life of the genres" is nothing other than a study of the life of the *names* of the genres, a task that may be interesting but is actually in the province of historical semantics. Works do not transform themselves; they are only signs of transformations. Genres do not transform themselves either; they are products of transformations, transforms. What changes has a still more abstract nature and is situated, in a way, "behind" or "beyond" the genres.

The Russian formalists proposed the following answer: literary devices change. B. Tomashevskii writes: "The specific devices, their combinations, their use and their functions have changed greatly in the course of literary history. Each literary period, each school is characterized by the system of devices which are present in the common style (in the broad sense of style) of the literary genres and preferences" (in Lemon and Reis, eds. *Russian Formalist Criticism*, p. 92). But here we confront the ambiguity of the term "device" (in Russian, *pzijom*) for the formalists. Tomashevskii gives as examples the rule of the unities, the happy or unhappy ending of comedies and tragedies. We see that the device in fact does not change: the ending is happy *or* unhappy, the rule of the unities is present *or* absent.

The first satisfactory (although imperfect) response is supplied by another formalist, Tynianov. What Tomashevskii calls devices, Tynianov calls forms, and he distinguishes these from *functions*, which are understood as relationships between forms. The functions are of two types: they can be defined either with respect to other, similar functions capable of replacing them (this is a relationship of substitution—for example, the lexicon of one text with respect to the lexicon of another text) or with respect to related functions capable of entering into combination with them (a relationship of integration—for example, the lexicon of a text with respect to the composition of this same text). For Tynianov, literary variability consists in the redistribution of forms and functions. *The form changes function, the function changes form.* The most urgent task of literary history is to study "the variability of the function of a given formal element, the appearance of a given function in a formal element, the association of the formal element with this function." For example, a certain meter (form) serves sometimes to introduce "higher" epic poetry, sometimes to introduce the vulgar epic (these are among its possible functions). The question Tynianov's schema fails to answer is whether there may not be two types of change one of which would be the introduction of new elements, the other their redistribution.

One of the marginal formalists, V. Vinogradov, suggests another requirement: "Dynamism must be presented either as the replacement of one system by another, or as a partial transformation of a single system whose central functions remain relatively stable" (translated from the conclusion of "O zadachakh stilistiki [Nabliudeniia nad stilem zhitiia protopopa Avvakuma]," in *Russkaia Rech'*, ed. L. Shcherba, vol. 1 [Petrograd, 1923]). Tynianov makes a similar affirmation: "The main concept for literary evolution is the mutation of *systems*" (in Matejka and Pomorska, eds., *Readings in Russian Poetics*, p. 67). Changes in literary discourse are not isolated; each of them affects the entire system, thus provoking the substitution of one system for another. We can thus define a literary period [151] as the time during which a certain system is maintained without major change.

● F. Brunetière, *L'Evolution des genres dans l'histoire de la littérature* (Paris, 1890); G. Lanson, *Méthodes de l'histoire littéraire* (Paris, 1925); A. N. Veselovskii, *Istoricheskaia poetika* (1940; reprint ed., with introduction by V. M. Zhirmunskii, The Hague, 1970); T. Todorov, ed., *Théorie de la littérature* (Paris, 1965); L. T. Lemon and M. J. Reis, eds., *Russian Formalist Criticism: Four Essays* (Lincoln, 1965); L. Matejka and K. Pomorska, eds., *Readings in Russian Poetics* (Cambridge, Mass., 1971); H. Cysarz, *Literatur-geschichte als Geisteswissenschaft* (Halle, 1926); M. Wehrli, "Zum Problem der Historie in der Literaturwissenschaft," *Trivium* 7 (1949): 44–59; R. Wellek, *Concepts of Criticism* (New Haven, 1963), pp. 37–53; G. Genette, "Poétique et histoire," *Figures III* (Paris, 1972); and R. Koselleck, *Geschichte-Ereignis und Erzählung* (Munich, 1973).

Models

The different types of transformational laws that have been identified may each, for the sake of convenience, be designated by a metaphor.

The first and most widespread model is that of the plant: an organicistic model. The laws of variability are those of the living organism; like it, the literary organism is born, flourishes, ages, and finally dies. Aristotle speaks of the maturity of tragedy; Friedrich Schlegel describes how Greek poetry grew, proliferated, flowered, matured, dried up, and turned to dust; Brunetière speaks of the adolescence, the maturity, and the old age of French tragedy. For this classical version of organicism another has recently been substituted, one that we find first with the formalists, then among the information theorists: the literary device, initially original, becomes automatic, then falls into disuse, which makes it once again improbable and consequently rich in information.

The second model, widespread in the literary studies of the twentieth century, is that of the kaleidoscope. This model postulates that the elements constituting literary texts are given once and for all and that change resides simply in a new combination of the same elements. This conception rests on the idea that the human mind is one and fundamentally invariable. For V. Shklovskii, "poets are much more concerned with arranging images than with creating them" (in Lemon and Reis, eds., *Russian and Formalist Criticism*, p. 7). According to T. S. Eliot, poetic originality is in large part an original way of assembling the most disparate and most dissimilar materials to make of them a new whole (*Selected Essays*, pp. 3–11). And for Northrop Frye, "there's nothing new in literature that isn't the old reshaped" (*The Educated Imagination*, p. 70).

Let us christen the third model of literary history "day and night." According to this model, changes are perceived as movements of opposition between yesterday's literature and today's. The prototype of all the versions of this metaphor is found in Hegel, in the formula thesis-antithesis-synthesis. The incontestable advantage of this model with respect to the first one is that it allows us to account not only for evolution but also for revolutions, that is, accelerations and decelerations in the rhythm of variability.

The formalists often lean on this Hegelian image. Tynianov writes, in this connection: "When people talk about literary tradition or succession, they usually imagine a kind of straight line joining a younger representative of a given literary branch with an older one. As it happens, things are much more complex than that. It is not a matter of continuing on a straight line, but rather one of setting out and pushing off from a given point. . . . Each instance of literary succession is first and foremost a struggle" (quoted in Eikhenbaum, "The Theory of the Formal Method," in *Readings in Russian Poetics*, ed. Matejka and Pomorska, p. 31). Shklovskii develops his theory of literary history by forging another metaphor: "The inheritance passes not from father to son, but from uncle to nephew." The "uncle" represents a tendency that does not enjoy a prominent position: what today is often called mass literature. The next generation will take up this secondary tendency, related and opposed to the preceding one, and "canonize" it: "Dostoevskii raises the devices of the dime novel to the level of the literary norm" (quoted in ibid., p. 32).

These models, as we can see at once, are neither very rich nor sufficiently elaborated. Because for too long it has confused its object with that of neighboring disciplines, literary history—the oldest branch among the disciplines of literary studies—today looks like a poor relation.

● L. T. Lemon and M. J. Reis, eds., *Russian Formalist Criticism: Four Essays* (Lincoln, 1965); L. Matejka and K. Pomorska, eds., *Readings in Russian Poetics* (Cambridge, Mass., 1971); E. R. Curtius, *European Lit-*

erature and the Latin Middle Ages, trans. W. R. Trask (1953; reprint ed., Princeton, 1967); T. S. Eliot, *Selected Essays* (New York, 1932); N. Frye, *The Educated Imagination* (Bloomington, 1964); and R. Wellek, *Concepts of Criticism* (New Haven, 1963), pp. 37–53.

LITERARY GENRES

The problem of genres is one of the oldest in poetics: from classical antiquity to the present the definitions of genres, their number, their mutual relationships have never ceased to give rise to discussion. Today this problem is considered to belong, in a general way, to the structural typology of discourse, of which literary discourse is only a particular case. Since this typology is not very well elaborated in its general aspects, however, it seems preferable to approach its study through the bias of *literary* genres.

First we must stop identifying genres with names of genres. Certain labels have always enjoyed great popularity ("tragedy," "comedy," "sonnet," "elegy"). It is nonetheless evident that if the concept of genre is to have a role in the theory of literary language, we cannot define it on the sole basis of denominations: certain genres have never been named; others have been merged under a single name in spite of differences in their properties. The study of genres must be undertaken on the basis of structural characteristics, not on the basis of names.

Although we have set aside this first confusion, we still have not resolved the question of the relationship between the structural entity and the historical phenomenon. In fact, we can see two radically different approaches in the course of history.

The first is inductive: it notes the existence of genres on the basis of the observation of a given period. The second is deductive: it postulates the existence of genres on the basis of a theory of literary discourse. Although certain aspects of the one can be found in the other, the methods, techniques, and concepts of these approaches are so different that one may ask whether their target is a single object or whether it would not be better to speak of **genres** in the first case and **types** in the second.

If, for example, we say that in the classical period in France contemporary tragedy was characterized by the "seriousness of the action" and by the "worthiness of the characters," it will be possible, on the basis of this starting point, to undertake two fundamentally different types of study.

The first consists in (1) establishing that categories such as "the action" or "the characters" are justified in the description of ·literary texts, whether they are present obligatorily or not; (2) showing that each of these categories can be specified by a finite number of properties organized in a structure—for example, that the characters may be of either "high" or "low" class; and then (3) elucidating the categories that have been thus discerned and studying their variety. *All* of the types of character (action, and so on) will be examined; the presence of one or the other, in a given combination, will indicate the literary types. These do not necessarily have a specific historical realization: they sometimes correspond to existing genres, sometimes to models of writing that have functioned at different periods; at still other times they do not correspond to anything—they are like an empty square in the Mendeleevian system that could only be filled by a literature to come. But we may observe then that there is no longer any difference between this typological study and poetics in general (*typological* becomes here a synonym for *structural*); the initial observation concerning genres is nothing other than a convenient point of departure for the exploration of literary discourse.

However, if we begin with the same initial observations concerning classical tragedy, we can follow a very different path. In a first phase we shall collect a certain number of works in which the properties described are found; these may be, for example, works representative of classical tragedy in France. The notion of **dominance,** used by the Russian formalists, finds its application here: if a certain work is to be declared a tragedy, the elements described must be not only present but dominant (even though, for the time being, we do not know very well how to measure that dominance). From this point on, we no longer inquire into the categories of literary discourse, but into a certain literary ideal of the period, which can be found both in the author (as a certain model of writing to which he refers, even if only to violate it) and in the reader (as a set of expectations or preexisting rules that orient his comprehension and allow him to appreciate the work). Within each period, the genres form a system; they can be defined only in terms of their mutual relationships. There is no longer a single genre known as tragedy: tragedy will redefine itself, at every moment of literary history, in relation to the other, coexistent genres. Here we leave behind general poetics to enter the area of literary history [144ff.].

The difference between type and genre reappears when we examine the relationship of each to individual works. Broadly speaking, three cases can be distinguished:

In the first case, the individual work conforms entirely to the genre and to the type. We speak then of **mass literature** (or popular novels). The good detective story, for example, does not attempt to be original (if it did, it would no longer deserve its name), but attempts, on the contrary, to apply the formula well.

In the second case, the work does not obey the rules of the genre. A work does not belong obligatorily to a genre: each period is dominated by a system of genres that does not necessarily cover all the works. On the other hand, a (partial) transgression of the genre is almost required; otherwise, the work would lack the minimal necessary originality (this requirement has varied a great deal according to the period). An infraction of genre rules does not profoundly affect the literary system. If tragedy implies, for example, that the hero must die at the end, then if in a particular case we have a happy ending, it is a case of transgression of the genre. This will usually be explained by a mixture of genres (in our example, a mixture of tragedy and comedy). The idea of the combined or mixed genre results from a confrontation between two genre systems: the mixture exists only when perceived from the earliest possible perspective; seen from the past, all evolution is degradation. But as soon as this blend is imposed as a literary norm, we enter a new system in which there is room, for example, for the genre of tragicomedy.

Finally there exists, although much less frequently, a transgression of the type. To the extent that the literary system is not eternal, given once and for all, but one in which the set of literary possibilities modifies itself, typological transgression is equally possible. In the preceding example, such a transgression would be the invention of a new category, neither comic nor tragic ("both X and not-X" would be a transgression of the genre, "neither X nor not-X" a transgression of the type). In other words, to transgress a genre rule is to follow a path already potentially present (but unrealized) in the synchronic literary system; on the other hand, the typological transgression affects the system itself. A novel such as *Ulysses* not only violates the rules of the preexisting novel but also discovers new possibilities for novelistic writing.

The opposition of type and genre may be very enlightening, but it must not be regarded as absolute. The passage from one to the other does not entail a rupture between system and history, but rather different degrees of inscription in time. This inscription is weaker in the case of the type, stronger in the case of the genre. As we have just seen, however, the type is not completely atemporal; and although the genre is in principle inscribed within an historical era, certain of its features are nevertheless conserved beyond the epoch in which they were established (for example, the rules of classical French tragedy were preserved in the eighteenth century). Finally, at the other extreme of this continuum, we find the **periods.** In fact, when we speak of romanticism or symbolism or surrealism, we are supposing, just as in the case of the genres, the predominance of a certain group of features peculiar to literary discourse. The difference is that the period may contain several genres; moreover, the period can by no means be separated from history: the period is not usually a purely literary notion, but one belonging also to the history of ideas, of culture, and of society.

● Bibliographies include I. Behrens, *Die Lehre von der Einteilung der Dichtkunst*, Beihefte zur Zeitschrift für romanische Philologie, no. 92 (Halle [Saale], 1940); and W. V. Ruttkowski, *Die literarischen Gattungen* (Bern, 1968). General discussions are in G. Müller, "Bemerkungen zur Gattungspoetik," *Philosophischer Anzeiger*, 1929, pp. 129–247; K. Vietor, "Probleme der literarischen Gattungsgeschichte," *Deutsche Vierteljahrschrift für Literaturwissenschaft und Geistesgeschichte* 9 (1931): 425–47; J. Tynianov, "On Literary Evolution," in *Readings in Russian Poetics*, eds. L. Matejka and K. Pomorska (Cambridge, Mass., 1971), pp. 70–71; B. Tomashevskii, "Thématique," in *Théorie de la littérature*, ed. T. Todorov (Paris, 1965), pp. 302–7 (this section was omitted from the English translation in L. T. Lemon and M. J. Reis, eds., *Russian Formalist Criticism: Four Essays* [Lincoln, 1965]; J. J. Donahue, *The Theory of Literary Kinds*, 2 vols. (Dubuque, Iowa, 1943–49), *I. Ancient Classifications of Literature, II. The Ancient Classes of Poetry*; P. van Tieghem, "La Question des genres littéraires," *Hélicon* 1 (1938): 95–101; J. Pommier, "L'Idée de genre," *Publications de l'école normale supérieure, section des lettres* 2 (1945): 47–81; E. Lämmert, *Bauformen des Erzählens* (Stuttgart, 1955), pp. 9–18; H.-R. Jauss, "Littérature médiévale et théorie des genres," *Poétique* 1 (1970): 79–101; T. Todorov, *The Fantastic: A Structural Approach to a Literary Genre*, trans. R. Howard (Ithaca, 1975), pp. 3–23; K. W. Hempfer, *Gattungstheorie* (Munich, 1973); and G. Genette, "Genres, 'types,' modes," *Poétique* 32 (1977): 389–421. The Polish journal *Zagadnienia rodzajow literackich* (in French, English, and German) and the American journal *Genre* are entirely devoted to the study of literary genres.

Typologies

An infinite number of genre classifications have been proposed, but they have rarely been based on a clear and coherent idea of the status of the genre itself. Two tendencies are particularly frequent: (1) the confusion of genres and types, or, more precisely, the description of genres (in the sense defined above) as if they were types; and (2) the reduction to simple oppositions between a single category and its contrary of what is in fact the conjunction of several distinct categories.

Furthermore, care has not always been taken to define the operative level of abstraction: it is evident that the genre may be characterized by a greater or lesser number of properties and that, on this basis, certain genres encompass others.

Let us review here some of the best-known classifications:

1. *Prose-poetry.* Although this opposition occurs very frequently, it is not very explicit. There exists even a certain ambiguity as to the meaning of the word *prose*: it signifies literary prose, as well as everything that is not literature. If we retain the first meaning (for the second refers to a functional typology, not a structural one [see p. 65]), we observe 'that the meaning given this opposition cannot be reduced to a single category. Is it a question of the verse-prose alternative, that is, of the rhythmic organization of discourse (the existence of free verse or of the prose poem then poses a thorny problem), or rather of that between **poetry** and **fiction,** that is, on the one hand a discourse that must be read on the literal level as a purely phonic, graphic, and semantic configuration and on the other hand a representative (mimetic) discourse that evokes an experiential universe? To this are added prescriptions of verbal style: the emotive, figurative, personal styles predominate in "poetry," whereas "fiction" is often characterized by the predominance of the referential style [302ff.]. It must be added that contemporary literature tends to cast off this opposition, and the contemporary "novel" requires a "poetic" reading, not as a representation of another universe, but as a semantic construction.

● See K. Hamburger, *The Logic of Literature*, trans. M. J. Rose, 2d ed., rev. (Bloomington, 1973); and M. Halle and R. Jakobson, *Fundamentals of Language* (The Hague, 1956).

2. *Lyric poetry-epic-drama.* From Plato to Goethe and Jakobson to Emil Staiger, attempts have been made to divide literature into three categories and to consider these as the fundamental or even the natural forms of literature. We may wonder, however, if a genre system peculiar to ancient Greek literature has been unjustifiably erected into a system of types. The theoreticians' efforts have been directed in this case (in the case of the prose-poetry distinction, they were not) toward the discovery of categories underlying the genres.

Systematizing Plato in the fourth century, Diomedes defined three basic genres: one including the works in which only the author speaks, another including the works in which only the characters speak, and a third including the works in which both author and characters speak. Since the eighteenth century, these three genres have been known, respectively, by the names **lyric, dramatic,** and **epic.** This classification has the advantage of clarity and rigor, but one can wonder whether the structural feature chosen is sufficiently important to serve as the basis for an articulation of this import.

Goethe distinguished the poetic "modes" (which correspond approximately to our genres: the ode, the ballad, and so on) from the "natural forms of poetry" (analogous to the types), and he affirmed that there were only three genuine natural forms of poetry: the "clearly telling," the "enthusiastically excited," and the "personally acting"—epic, lyric, and drama.

This formula can be interpreted as referring to the three protagonists of enunciation: *he* (epic), *I* (lyric poetry), *you* (drama); a similar juxtaposition is made by Jakobson, for whom the point of departure and the leading theme of lyric poetry are the first person and the present time, whereas those of the epic are the third person and past time.

In an important work devoted to the three "fundamental concepts" of poetics, Emil Staiger gives an essentially temporal interpretation of the genres, postulating the relationships lyric-present, epic-past, dramatic-future (this correspondence was first established by the German romantic J. Paul). At the same time, Staiger relates them to categories such as thrill (lyric), overview (epic), tension (dramatic). He contributes likewise to the dissociation of the types (designated by adjectives) and the genres (designated by substantives: lyric poetry, epic, drama). The three genres are thus grounded in language without being thereby reducible, as they were for Diomedes, to a feature situated at the surface of the text. But even supposing the pertinence of this tripartition, it remains to be proved that the categories that constitute it occupy a dominant place in the structure of the text (one that alone would justify their being called "fundamental concepts").

● See W. V. Ruttkowski, *Die literarischen Gattungen* (Bern, 1968); R. Jakobson, *Questions de poétique* (Paris, 1973); E. Staiger, *Grundbegriffe der Poetik* (Zurich, 1946); and G. Genette, "Genres, 'types,' modes," *Poétique* 32 (1977): 389–421.

3. *Tragedy-comedy*. Another very old and very widespread classification, although not as universal as the preceding ones, opposes tragedy and comedy. It is all the more evident here that these (historical) genres must be distinguished from the general categories of the **tragic** and the **comic**. Aristotle noted the opposition without explaining it. In Italian and French classicism, tragedy is characterized by the seriousness of the action, the worthiness of the characters, and the unhappy ending, while comedy is characterized by everyday actions, characters of low estate, and the happy ending. This definition is clearly generic. N. Frye sought a definition of types: the tragic designates the passage from the ideal to the real (in the very banal sense of a passage from desire to disappointment, from an idealized world to the discipline of reality); the comic designates the passage from the real to the ideal. Elsewhere, attempts

have been made to put on the same plane esthetic categories other than the tragic and the comic: thus the sublime, the grotesque, the marvelous.

Let us note here that comedy and tragedy are also subdivisions of the dramatic and that each of these categories can be subdivided in turn into farce, vaudeville, burlesque, and so on. The same holds true for the lyric (elegy, ode, sonnet) and for the epic (epic, novel, short story). These further subdivisions may be based on thematic properties (elegy, satire, ode), as well as on rhythmic and graphic characteristics (rondeau, sonnet, triolet).

● See R. Bray, *La Formation de la doctrine classique* (Paris, 1927); and N. Frye, *Anatomy of Criticism* (Princeton, 1957).

4. *Levels of style.* The theory of the three styles—**high, middle,** and **low**—goes back to the Middle Ages. Virgil's works often serve to illustrate it: the *Aeneid*, the *Georgics*, and the *Bucolics*, respectively. This theory deals, on the one hand, with vocabulary choice, syntactic constructions, and so on; and on the other hand, with the object of description, that is, with the social rank of the persons represented (warriors, peasants, shepherds). This distinction is thus at once literary (linguistic) and sociological; it has been obsolete since the romantic period.

● See E. Faral, *Les Arts poétiques du XIIᵉ et du XIIIᵉ siècle* (Paris, 1924).

5. *Simple forms.* André Jolles has attempted to base the genre-type "on nature"—that is, on language—by enumerating all of the **simple forms** in literature. The literary forms found in contemporary works would be derived from linguistic forms; this derivation is not produced directly, but through the intermediary of a series of simple forms that are found, for the most part, in folklore. The simple forms are direct extensions of linguistic forms; they themselves become basic elements in works of "great" literature. Jolles's system can be summarized in the following schema (which, however, never appears in his work):

	Interrogation	*Assertion*	*Silence*	*Imperative*	*Optative*
Realist	**case**	**saga**	**riddle**	**proverb**	**fable**
Idealist	**myth**	**memoir**	**joke**	**legend**	**tale**

Even though the description proposed by Jolles is inadequate, his concern for taking into account certain verbal forms, such as the proverb, the enigma, and so on, opens new paths to the typological study of literature. Moreover, genres as fixed as the fable, the essay, or the legend are doubtless not situated at the same level; but Jolles's multidimensional principle allows him to account for this, in a way that was impossible with the lyric-epic-dramatic triad.

- See A. Jolles, *Einfache Formen* (Halle [Saale], 1956), translated into French by A. M. Bugnet as *Formes simples* (Paris, 1972); M. Nøjgaard, *La Fable antique*, 2 vols. (Copenhagen, 1964–67); A.-J. Greimas, *Du sens* (Paris, 1970), pp. 309–14; S. Meleuc, "Structure de la maxime," *Langages* 13 (1965): 69–99; and P. Maranda and E. Köngäs-Maranda, " 'A Tree Grows': Transformations of a Riddle Metaphor," in *Structural Models in Folklore* (The Hague, 1971), pp. 116–39.

LANGUAGE ACQUISITION

Two phases are traditionally distinguished in the development of language activity. The first, pre-linguistic, covers approximately the first ten months of life. In the bucco-phonatory activity of this period, we recognize **wails** and **clicks,** which are respiratory manifestations; then, around the third month, come the **lallations,** which contain more extensive expressive possibilities than those used in language. The second linguistic phase begins toward the end of the first year. The child begins to manifest a certain comprehension of adult communicative behavior with respect to himself (at the beginning, the language signs of the adult doubtless have a role no less important than the role of the other expressive signals that accompany the adult's behavior). It is in the course of the second year that an indisputably linguistic activity is constituted.

Observing that every child, whatever his linguistic milieu, learns to speak spontaneously—except children who are deaf or who live exclusively with mute parents—people once concluded a bit hastily that the child acquires his mother tongue by simple imitation of the adult. It was once supposed that among the sounds that he produces spontaneously, the child recognizes those produced by the adult and is thus led in the end to produce only the latter. Language learning was thus represented as a series of attempts at imitation that were reinforced when they were similar to adult productions and eliminated when they were different. Through successive discriminations and through associations between sound patterns and situations or objects, then by associations among sound patterns, language learning found an explanation in conformity with the first psychological theories of behavior based on the notion of habits [69]. These habits, which can be more or less complex, had as a general representative schema that of the conditioned reflex.

More refined analyses of vocalic productions, of language productions at different ages, and of the conditions necessary for language acquisition and especially the fact that psychologists began to take into consideration linguistic studies on the structure of language all have led to a complete revision of the problematic embracing the development of intralinguistic coordinations such as the relationships between thought and language. Researchers are now asking how speakers acquire the capacity to "produce" sentences, both as encoders and as decoders.

The Auditory-Motor Aspect of Language

The analysis of infants' vocalic productions has shown that contrary to popular belief, during the first six months of life the vocalizations are the same whether the child is deaf or not and whatever the linguistic milieu. E. H. Lenneberg has described the acoustic features characteristic of these vocalizations, which differ considerably from the sounds produced in the second year. Around the third month **laryngeal modulation** and **control of phonation** begin to appear, but the structure of the formants [177] is ill-defined: vocalic resonance, glottal stops before the vocalic sounds, and formants identifiable with vowels are absent, and certain features [173] that do not belong to the language of the environment are present. The sounds of the language are produced only progressively, then. At this point the voice, the intonation, and a major part of the phonetic repertory of the deaf child become distinguishable from those of the normal child. It must be observed that the processes that will eventually allow the child to produce the phonemes of the language are extremely complex. It is essential to take into account the fact that the phoneme [171] is not a specific acoustic realization, but can be realized in different ways. The child must learn to identify classes instead of distinct elements.

In an attempt to account for this learning, A. M. Liberman has offered the hypothesis that the proprioceptive mediation of the place and the manner of articulation would play a decisive role. The fact that a child who is **anarthric** (physiologically unable to produce speech sounds) from birth can nevertheless develop a normal comprehension of language— a comprehension that necessarily includes the identification of phonemes —is not definitive evidence against this thesis; but it makes it necessary to specify the level at which the **auditory-motor coordinations** would take place.

In any case, the study of the motor coordinations in the course of word or sentence production by an adult shows that sound formation is programmed into the motor commands well before their emission and that the possibility of controlling this tangle of coordinations is a progressive acquisition.

● See R. Jakobson, *Selected Writings II* (The Hague, 1971); E. H. Lenneberg, *Biological Foundations of Language* (New York, 1967); and A. M. Liberman et al., "Motor Theory of Speech Perception: A Reply to Lane's Critical Review," *Psychological Review* 77 (1970): 3.

Syntax and Semantics

P. Guillaume pointed out as early as 1927 that the child commits errors that bear witness to the application of rules (the creation of verbs, for example). This brings up the problem of discovering what the child imitates or learns from adult language. We know that the simple repetition of a sentence is possible only if the form of this sentence corresponds to what the child is capable of producing spontaneously; otherwise the repetition is incorrect. However, if the utterance given as a model is understood or interpreted, the child will repeat it by transforming it to give a sentence in a form that he is able to produce spontaneously. At about two years of age, for example, repetition preserves the nouns, verbs, adjectives, and certain pronouns but omits the articles, prepositions, auxiliary verbs, and inflections. Repetition thus takes on the same telegraphic aspect as production (it should be noted that adult telegraphic style conserves inflections). Furthermore, the length of repeatable sentences, like that of spontaneous sentences, is limited (one word, then two, three, and so on), even though the child knows several dozen or several hundred words.

Finally, the order of acquisition of a certain number of very general rules of language use is the same for children of the same linguistic group, and the speed of acquisition is identical for all languages. These regularities have made possible the construction of global tests for developmental level based on sentence length and the order of acquisition of the parts of speech.

These facts have led researchers to regard language learning as the acquisition of a set of rules and to attempt to construct child grammars on the basis of spontaneous and induced corpuses (M. D. S. Braine, 1963; R. Brown, C. Fraser, and U. Bellugi, 1964; W. Miller and S. Ervin, 1964). R. Brown has subsequently criticized the characterization of child language in terms of lacunae—that is, its comparison with telegraphic style—as well as its characterization in terms of grammars that remain too close to the directly observed facts; these grammars claim not to be taking into account what the child means, whereas in reality, in order to construct such a grammar, the observer interprets utterances in relationship to the situation. We must, then, discover whether there exist different grammatical relationships (in terms of sentence structure) for different semantic structures. If we can show that there exists a deep structure for each sentence, we can probably better understand that period during which the child seems to grasp complex grammatical relationships that he does not yet know how to express.

But the chief problem remains that of knowing how to account in a coherent fashion for the progression of the acquisitions and for their order. F. Bresson hypothesizes—and demonstrates in specific instances—that a very small number of simple operators would allow us to account for the organization of the system at each stage of development and for the passage from one stage to another.

Language Development and Thought Development

In reality these considerations regarding the genesis of linguistic systems in the child raise the issue of the way the development of thought relates to that of language, a question that is being examined with renewed interest today. It had been more or less set aside when the viewpoint according to which language was only of interest as a tool of thought fell into disfavor.

Thanks to the genetic studies of J. Piaget and B. Inhelder, it has been understood for some time that the formation of thought is linked with the acquisition of the symbolic (or semiotic) function in general and not with the acquisition of language as such. P. Oléron has brought to light the development of symbolic thought in deaf-mutes, which is not considerably behind that of normal children. This does not at all mean that the semiotic function develops independently of language; B. Inhelder has shown the complex relationships between disorders in language acquisition and disorders in intellectual development manifested in the formation of figurative symbols. Moreover, the descriptions that children give of simple situations reveal the intimate connection between the form of utterances and the comprehension of situations (H. Sinclair, 1967). But we still know virtually nothing of the processes that allow the child to pass from the word-sentence to the utterance [323ff.].

The other side of the problem concerns the question of whether language, in its learning and its use, implies logical behavior. The comparison between the developmental stages of logical thought and those of the acquisition of syntactic rules shows that in both cases we are dealing with the acquisition of systems that cannot be attributed to the passive copying of a model, but require that the child put into play a complex activity of decoding realizations. Now, the acquisition of syntactic rules takes place very early. In other words, we are led to ask what hypotheses we can make about the systems with which the child is provided at the outset. Diverse hypotheses are possible; they are more or less innatist, that is, they endow the child with stronger or weaker preconstructed systems.

● Representative texts include U. Bellugi and R. Brown, eds., *The Acquisition of Language*, Monograph of the Society for Research in Child Development 29, no. 1 (1964); F. Bresson, "Langage et logique: Le Problème de l'apprentissage de la syntaxe," in *Psychologie et Epistémologie génétiques: Thèmes piagétiens* (Paris, 1966); M. Coyaud, "Le Problème des grammaires du langage enfantin," *La Linguistique* 2 (1967): 99–129; H. Sinclair, *Acquisition du langage et développement de la pensée: Sous-systèmes linguistiques et opérations concrètes* (Paris, 1967); D. McNeill, "On Theories of Language Acquisition," in *Verbal Behavior and General Behavior Theory*, ed. T. R. Dixon and D. L. Horton (Englewood Cliffs, 1968); N. Chomsky, *Language and Mind* (New York, 1969); F. Bresson, "Acquisition des langues vivantes," *Langue française* 8 (1970): 24–30; R. Brown, "Semantic and Grammatical Relations," in *A First Language: The Early Stages* (Cambridge, Mass., 1973); and N. Z. Smith, *The Acquisition of Phonology* (Cambridge, Mass., 1973). Reviews of particular questions and bibliographies are found the following: (*a*) before the war: D. McCarthy, "Language Development in Children," in *Manual of Child Psychology*, ed. L. Carmichael, 2d ed. (New York and London, 1954), pp. 492–630. (*b*) between 1958 and 1965: S. M. Ervin-Tripp and D. I. Slobin, "Psycholinguistics," *Annual Review of Psychology* 17 (1966): 435–74. (*c*) since 1965: B. de Boysson-de-Bardies et J. Mehler, "Psycholinguistique, messages et codage verbal. 1. L'Acquisition du langage," *L'Année psychologique* 69 (1969): 561–98; D. McNeill, "The Development of Language," in *Manual of Child Psychology*, ed. L. Carmichael, 3d ed. (New York: 1970-), vol. 1, pp. 1061–1161; and F. Smith and G. A. Miller, eds., *The Genesis of Language* (Cambridge, Mass., 1966).

LANGUAGE PATHOLOGY

Disorders of Verbal Communication

Since the middle of the nineteenth century a progressive differentiation of language disorders has taken place, reflecting, on the one hand, the evolution of psychological and linguistic conceptions of verbal behavior and, on the other hand, the evolution of anatomo-clinical conceptions of the relationships between cerebral lesions and behavior disorders.

Today we can provisionally distinguish three major types of disorders in verbal-communication behavior. This classification rests on linguistic and extra-linguistic criteria:

1. **Speech disorders,** which correspond to disorders of the peripheral organs of production (dysfunction in the synergy of the motor organs) or of reception (for example, a rise in the threshold of perception). We can include in this category disorders such as **stuttering** and **dyslexia;** but only certain of these latter disturbances have a confirmed auditory-motor origin.

2. **Language disorders,** which correspond to cerebral lesions that are focused (**aphasias**) or diffused (**schizophrenic aphasias**).

3. **Enunciation disorders,** which are manifestations, observed in utterances, of general modifications in the behavior of the subject toward the world; in certain cases (psychotics), there is a disorder in the schema of communication itself, bearing on the speaker-listener relationship, as well as on the speaker-referent relationships. In other cases (neurotics), the schema of communication is not destroyed, but undergoes a functional systematization that takes a specific form for hysterical discourse, obsessional discourse, and so on.

Speech disorders, when they occur in young children, have direct bearing on the study of the conditions of language acquisition. It is essential to realize that we do not know today how to identify clearly the level of disorders in verbal communication when they occur in young children; thus the term **dysphasia** covers a great variety of deficiencies from which we can exclude only the disorders stemming primarily from the articulatory component (**dysarthria** or **anarthria**). Enunciation disorders have received relatively little attention as yet. The aphasias, on the contrary, have been the object of numerous and systematic studies, inasmuch as they are thought to contain elements of information on the functioning of language. Various applications of linguistic methods have recently appeared (in particular in the wake of R. Jakobson, 1941, 1955); these were preceded by some earlier attempts such as those of

Alajouanine and Ombredane (1939), K. Goldstein (1933), and A. Luria (1947).

Disorders of Language

The type of language disorder that appears in subjects who have already mastered one or more languages is characterized by an anatomical focus; moreover, in the syndromes associated with these focused cerebral lesions (generally the left hemisphere for a right-handed person), disorders of verbal production and/or comprehension may be regarded as dominant with respect to other performative disorders in the subject. J. Baillarger (1865) and then H. Jackson (1868) were the first to regard aphasias as a disorder in propositional language.

There also exist disorders of the aphasic type in subjects with diffuse cerebral lesions: the disorganization appears not to be dominant but merely one element in the totality of behavioral disorders manifested by these patients (schizophrenic aphasia).

In fact, in spite of this apparent unity, and whatever the type of analysis undertaken, whatever the criteria of classification adopted, the varieties of disorders are very numerous. The classification that follows, borrowed from H. Hécaen and R. Angelergues (1965), uses anatomoclinical and psychological criteria first and linguistic ones second. They distinguish:

1. The **expressive aphasias,** in which the disturbance involves oral and written expression:

a) **Aphasia of phonic programming** (or **motor and graphic aphasia**), which involves phoneme production. Comprehension of the verbal message, oral or written, is intact or quasi-intact. Writing under dictation is disturbed, sometimes more clearly with the dictation of logatomes (unintelligible sequences) than with that of significative units.

b) **Agrammatical aphasia** (the term was introduced by J. Pick, 1913), in which difficulties in sentence development are manifested. Spontaneous language consists of isolated words perfectly pronounced and resembles telegraphic style. Spontaneous writing or writing under dictation is similar to that of aphasia of phonic programming.

c) **Aphasia of phrastic programming** (also called **conduction aphasia**), in which aural comprehension is intact. The concatenation of enunciated elements is disturbed. The difficulty increases with the length and the complexity of words and sentences; but the manipulation of the grammatical code remains intact on the whole, and patients are capable of spotting errors in ungrammatical sentences. Written language is disturbed in the same fashion. There seems also to be difficulty in the comprehension of written messages.

2. The **receptive aphasias** (or **sensory aphasias**), in which the reception of verbal signs is altered. The term **speech deafness** designates this more or less total elective deafness to language sounds. Recognition of musical airs or noises is most often intact. Disorders of production are necessarily involved: words are not always deformed, but they may be replaced by some other forms that make the meaning of the utterance incomprehensible (**paraphasias**), or the distortions and substitutions are mingled with stereotyped sentences (**jargonophasias**). The apparent disorders of syntax might be due to the fact that the paraphasias bring about a change in sentence schemas before the sentences are completed. Although the ability to read aloud is intact, comprehension of the text read is zero, or near zero. Written expression resembles oral expression (**agraphia** is characterized by deformation of words, substitution of one for another, and so on). Among these aphasics we often distinguish two groups: (1) those whose receptive disorder is not very pronounced and who are unconscious of their deficiency and (2) those whose verbal deafness predominates and who are conscious of their disorder.

3. **Amnesic aphasia,** in which the patient seems to have forgotten words. He often replaces the word he is seeking by a paraphrase (by the use of the object itself, for example) or by a term such as "thing" or else by gestures. This form of aphasia may be associated with the previously described types, or it may occur in an isolated form. It can be accompanied by spelling difficulties (**dysgraphia**), but rarely by difficulties with reading.

4. Aphasic disorders are encountered in subjects afflicted by **dementia** (schizophrenia) with diffused cerebral lesions. These subjects present a general intellectual deficiency. This category of language disorder has often been classified either with the aphasias described above or with psychotic disorders. It is characterized by the incoherence of the utterance, either because of an inadequacy in verbal responses to a situation or because of an inadequacy in logical connections in the sentence and the utterance. These **dyslogias** may at times end up in sets of words without any interconnections. Moreover, we may observe an automaticity of response, an impoverishment of the lexical stock, a difficulty in comprehension, and an unconsciousness of the disorders presented. Some recent linguistic studies carried out in a generative and transformational perspective [39ff.] (constitution of a message on the basis of a minimal sentence subjected to rules of phonemic and semantic interpretation [54]) have revealed fundamental differences between this form of aphasia and the preceding ones. Schizophrenic disorders would then reflect a disorder

concerning the semantic component [54]. In this linguistic optic, motor aphasia would concern phonemic interpretation, and the other aphasias would involve syntax, either in the constitution of minimal sentences or in their transformations.

Finally we can note some disorganizations in the written code unaccompanied by disorders in the spoken language:

a) Pure **alexia,** which designates either the impossibility of reading a word (**verbal alexia**) or the impossibility of recognizing a letter (**literal alexia**), while the subject can recognize all other types of drawings; that is why this disorder is also called **text blindness.** Alexia is not accompanied by notable agraphic disorder.

b) The agraphias, in which the disorder involves the motor schema of the letter or of words; but it is not simply a matter of disorder in actual motor function, since agraphia is also manifested in writing with ready-made letters.

The level of integrity of the intellectual processes of aphasics, with the exception of those suffering from schizophrenic aphasia, is quite variable. We will simply note that even in the most serious cases of receptive, expressive, or amnesic aphasia, one can sometimes observe that the ability to solve complex logical problems presented in various forms remains intact. But this integrity of logical competence does not rule out the presence of disorders of gnosis or praxis.

Language Disorders and Linguistic Analysis

Classifiers of aphasic disorders have had as a long-term goal the answers to two questions concerning language activity: What is disturbed? What is capable of being disturbed? The description of disorders is never neutral; it depends on the analytical model chosen. For the linguist, the first theoretical choice is that of the level of analysis at which to operate: at the level of verbal performances or at the level of functions. The distinction is important, for an identity of performances does not imply identity of functions or dysfunctions. The thesis according to which aphasic disorders would reproduce the stages of child language learning rests on that confusion.

Then comes the question of determining the type of analysis to undertake: Is it possible to establish **aphasic grammars**? Recently, still another positive response has been given to that question. This procedure can be juxtaposed to the one that consists in constituting **child grammars** on the basis of the language productions of young children. The regularity with which certain deviant rules are used by the child as well as by the aphasic has prompted the search for grammars capable of accounting for these rules. But from a theoretical point of view, adopting this procedure means prejudging the nature of the disorders. The problem of language acquisition and that of the aphasias are not presented in the same manner: the aphasic adult had, before the appearance of the disorder, a normal language; the child is in the process of constituting one. Considering that we do not know whether the performances of an aphasic correspond to a language and at what level the disorders are situated, it is not easy to see how to justify the elaboration of an aphasic grammar.

At the present time, the study of aphasia is presented as a search for the rules of deviance. The linguist proceeds as the anatomo-clinician does, undertaking a search for symptoms that would describe in a coherent fashion the disorders envisaged. Control of descriptive coherence is found in the possibility of predicting, on the basis of a set of anatomo-clinical symptoms, the corresponding linguistic symptoms, and vice versa, on the one hand, and on the basis of one part of a pathological corpus, another part that presents the same peculiarities, on the other hand.

Furthermore, the anatomo-clinical classification supplies the linguist with a frame of reference that allows him to study the relationship between linguistic systems and forms of disorder; one can thus compare aphasic disorders in different languages. One can also compare the disorganizations of the languages spoken by **polyglot aphasics.** But the question is a delicate one, since the attitude of the patient toward the languages he speaks and the details of their acquisition seem to be factors that cloud the role played by the linguistic structure itself.

Finally, the multidisciplinary classification of disorders permits a third type of comparison: diachronic analysis of a patient [137ff.]. This approach has made it possible to demonstrate that when a deficient system undergoes a series of readaptations, its disorganization nonetheless retains a consistent form.

This first symptomatological stage of linguistic analysis by no means satisfies, at this point, the criterion of predictability. This stems from the fact that while aphasic disorders are generally regarded as **performance disorders** [120ff.], we still do not dispose of models of the processes of production and comprehension, but only of models of language functioning, models that are based on the natural languages and put all the rules on the same plane. It is essential to see that there remains a certain ambiguity in what is meant by language function: this notion is sometimes assimilated to a model of the process of production and comprehension. The fact that certain disorders can be described in terms of disturbance of the operations of concatenation or of substitution, for example, has led to the belief that the processes of production and comprehension could be described at the same time by the same operations. In reality, the processes involved in concatenation and substitution may be multiple. Knowledge of these processes is for the moment quite meager, and studies of language pathology alone cannot contribute to it for the following reason: different dysfunctions in a set of mechanisms may give, for a certain level of analysis, the same type of observed disorder. Without a hypothesis about the normal functioning of these mechanisms, there can be no detection of a breakdown. Contrary to the idea that has long prevailed, the pathology of a system is not a natural experimentation: there is no possible interpretation of the disorders of a system without a knowledge of its normal functioning. This explains the extreme complexity of the study of disorders in language development.

● On the history of aphasia, see A. L. Benton and R. J. Joynt, "Early Descriptions in Aphasia," *Archives of Neurology* 3 (1960). Early texts have been republished in H. Hécaen and J. Dubois, *La Naissance de la neuropsychologie du langage (1825–1865)* (Paris, 1969). For a general study, see the Treatise by H. Hécaen and R. Angelergues, *Pathologie du langage* (Paris, 1965).

Important articles include J. de Ajuriaguerra et al., "Organisation psychologique et troubles du développement du langage: Étude d'un groupe d'enfants dysphasiques," in *Problèmes de psycholinguistique*, ed. J. de Ajuriaguerra et al. (Paris, 1963); J. Dubois et al., *Langages* 5 (1967): *Pathologie du langage*, which comprises articles on the linguistic approach to aphasia and enunciatory disorders and an annotated bibliography; W. Penfield and L. Roberts, *Speech and Brain Mechanisms* (Princeton, 1959); and A. V. S. de Reuck and M. O'Connor, eds., *Disorders of Language* (London, 1964), comprising articles on linguistics and psycholinguistics. See also in *Current Trends in Linguistics*, ed. T. A. Sebeok, 14 vols. (The Hague, 1963–76), vol. 12, pt. 11: A. R. Luria, "Basic Problems of Neurolinguistics," pp. 2561–94; O. L. Taylor and J. P. Fox, "Language Behavior and Disorders Associated with Brain Damage," pp. 2595–2639; and E. T. McDonald, "Speech Pathology," pp. 2641–56.

Representative articles reprinted appear in R. C. Oldfield and J. C. Marshall, eds., *Language* (Harmondsworth, 1968).

DESCRIPTIVE CONCEPTS

NONSIGNIFICATIVE UNITS

The invention of writing [193ff.], which permitted the notation of spoken words (and not merely of their meaning), and in particular the invention of alphabetic writing (which made it possible to note words sound by sound, not simply sign by sign), was tantamount to a discovery that all the words and signs used in oral language are obtained by combining a small number of elementary sounds each of which is represented, in principle, by a letter of the alphabet. This discovery eventually found its way into texts on linguistics, most of which include a description of the elementary language sounds. By discovering the phonetic laws [8], that is, by discovering that phonetic change takes place between sounds and not between words, historical linguistics seemed to give its definitive blessing to this method of analysis and thus endowed it with explanatory value.

● On the phonetic analysis of language in pre-scientific linguistics, see the articles in the *Grande Encyclopédie* devoted to the different letters of the alphabet.

Distinctive Units

It is a paradox of the history of modern linguistics that its founder, Saussure, at once condemned the analysis of words into sounds and formulated the principles that made possible its renascence. He condemned it—rather he excluded it from linguistics—inasmuch as he seemed to consider it self-evident that the elementary sounds are identical for all languages (each language is simply unable to use certain ones), whereas he argued that linguistic description should discover the specific character of the various languages. For Saussure, the abstraction delimiting the linguistic object—thus distinguishing language (*langue*) from speech (*parole* [118ff.])—had to be based on the notion of the sign: the linguist had only to study signs and their interrelationship. But at the same time, Saussure was opening the door to a new study of the nonsignificative units; for in reflecting on the sign, he attributed to it the nature of opposition [19], a nature to be recognized still more clearly by a later linguistics (especially phonology [24]) in certain elements of discourse that are not signs. Taking opposition itself, then, as a criterion of abstraction, Saussure's successors have extended linguistic investigation beyond signs to other areas.

- Saussure considered the study of language sounds to be only a preliminary to linguistic research proper (see his *Course in General Linguistics*, trans. W. Baskin [New York, 1959], appendix to the introduction). As it happens, he used the term **phonology** for this study, which he presented as pre-linguistic (he used the term **phonetics** for such a study undertaken from a historical point of view). His successors consider phonology a properly linguistic study, even though Saussure believed this to be impossible. (N.B. An isolated passage in the *Course*, however, hints at a phonology in the modern sense [ibid., pt. 2, chap. 4, sec. 3].)

In saying that a sign is oppositional, Saussure meant that what is important, both in its signification (signified) and in its phonic reality (signifier), is what allows it to be distinguished from the other signs of the language. Consider the description of the phonic aspect of the French word *dit* ("said"). We can point out, for example, what distinguishes its pronunciations from those of *du* (contracted article "of the") and *pie* ("magpie"), but not the absence of aspiration in the *d*, since no words in French are distinguished from others by the presence or absence of aspiration in the *d*. Rigorously applied, however, this method would complicate the description in a scarcely acceptable way. It would be necessary to leave aside the voiced character of the *d* of *dit* on the pretext that no sign is distinguished from *dit* by the absence of this sonority (since none is pronounced *ti*); on the other hand, the voiced character would be retained for the *d* of *doux* ("sweet"), since it distinguishes this word from *tout* ("all"). Such anomalies would be avoided if we were to apply the principle of opposition not directly to the signifiers of the signs (*dit* or *doux*) but to the elementary sounds composing these signifiers, for example, to *d*. We would then retain from each sound only those of its elements that could be used to distinguish one sign from another (the French *d* would be voiced, since that sonority allows *doux* to be distinguished from *tout*, but not unaspirated, since no sign is distinguished from another by the nonaspiration of the *d*). In this new approach, the elementary sounds can no longer be mistaken for universals (this fact would exclude them from linguistics proper, in Saussure's view), for, as a general rule, they will differ from language to language. It becomes impossible, for example, to assimilate any French vowel to a German vowel, for in contemporary French the length of the vowel has no contrastive value (although the *i* is sometimes long —as in *vide* ["empty"]—and sometimes short—as in *vite* ["quickly"]— this difference is never the means for distinguishing two words); thus

French vowels are not described as either short or long, while in German they are one or the other, since German uses this dichotomy to differentiate words. The nonsignificative units can thus be recuperated into a linguistics of Saussurian inspiration, provided that they are regarded as distinctive units and are defined only in terms of their distinctive power.

Phonemes

The first distinctive unit defined by phonologists, a **phoneme** is a phonic segment that (*a*) has a distinctive function, (*b*) cannot be decomposed into a succession of segments each having a distinctive function in turn, and (*c*) is defined only by those of its characteristics that have differentiating value, characteristics that phonologists call **distinctive** (in German, *relevant*; in French, *pertinents*). A few examples will show how these phonemes, by virtue of this definition, can be distinguished from the sounds themselves, which are the object of **phonetics** (in French, *phonétique*) and not of **phonemics** (in French, *phonologie*).

1. In German every word beginning with a vowel is preceded by a closing of the vocal cords (among other things, this prevents making a liaison between that vowel and the terminal consonant of the preceding word). Because this hard attack is necessary, it cannot have distinctive value, and by virtue of (*a*), above, it is not regarded as a phoneme. Nor do we count as phonemes, in English or in German, the aspiration that regularly follows the /p/, the /t/, and the /k/ in these languages. But this same aspiration, when it appears before a vowel, constitutes the phoneme /h/, which distinguishes, for example, in German, the words *Hund* ("dog") and *und* ("and").

2. In Spanish the phonic segment represented in the orthography by *ch* (for example, *mucho*, in which the *ch* is pronounced more or less like the *ch* of *much* in English, phonetically *tš*) is composed of two distinct sounds; but since *š* appears in Spanish only after *t*, the *t* of *tš* has no distinctive function, and by virtue of (*b*), the Spanish phonic group *tš* constitutes a single phoneme (the example is Martinet's).

3. The sounds /æ/ in the words *bad* and *bat*, phonetically quite different, constitute by virtue of (*c*) a single phoneme, since the features through which they differ are not distinctive (phonologists express this by saying that these sounds do not commute, that is, the substitution of one for the other cannot change one sign into another). To the extent that it is the presence of *d* and of *t* that produces, respectively, a long or a short /æ/, we say that the two sounds are **contextual** (or combinatorial, or determined) **variants** of the same phoneme.

4. The French *r* is either rolled or uvular, according to the region

or even the individual. But the two sounds do not commute (whereas they do so in Arabic). We then say, by virtue of (*c*), that there is a single French phoneme /r/: its two manifestations, rolled or uvular, since they are not determined by context, are called **free variants.**

In order to represent clearly the difference between sound and phoneme, it is customary to place a **phonetic transcription** (a transcription into elementary sounds) between square brackets, and a **phonemic transcription** (a transcription into phonemes) between slant lines. Thus we have, for *vide* and *vite*, the phonetic transcriptions [vi:d] (where *:* represents the lengthening of the *i*) and [vit] and the phonemic transcriptions /vid/ and /vit/.

- On phonemes, see N. S. Trubetzkoy, *Principles of Phonology*, trans. C. A. M. Baltaxe (Berkeley, 1969), esp. pp. 31–45; and the review article of W. P. Lehmann, "Observations on Trubetzkoy's Contributions to Phonological Studies," *Romance Philology* 29 (1975): pp. 40–57; W. F. Twadell, *On Defining the Phoneme*, Language Monographs (Baltimore, 1935); A. Martinet, *Elements of General Linguistics*, trans. E. Palmer (London and Chicago, 1964), secs. 3.5–3.17; M. Halle and R. Jakobson, *Fundamentals of Language* (The Hague, 1956), pt. 1 (including, in chap. 2, a critical review of the major conceptions of the phoneme); E. Buyssens, "Phonème, archiphonème et pertinence," *La Linguistique* 8, no. 2 (1972): 39–58. For a critique of commutation as a means of identifying the various occurrences of a given phoneme, see N. Chomsky, *Syntactic Structures* (The Hague, 1957), sec. 9.2. Several important texts are available in E. C. Fudge, ed., *Phonology* (Harmondsworth, 1973); see also *Langue française* 19 (1973): *Phonétique et Phonologie*, ed. J. Filliolet.

N.B. The distributionalist school [31ff.], which rules out the use of commutation [25] (to the extent that this includes a recourse to meaning), has sought a purely distributional procedure for identifying phonemes. This method would constitute a nonmentalist definition of the concept of the phoneme, that is, in neopositivist terminology, an "empirical reduction" of this concept. First step is the reduction: for the distributionalists, a phonetic description would make it possible to regroup the infinite number of phonic occurrences (the sounds pronounced in reality, here and now) into a finite number of classes each of which would correspond to an elementary phonetic sound. Second step: a phoneme is defined as a class of phonetic sounds. Two sounds belong to the same phoneme and are called **allophones** if they have either exactly the same distribution (that is, if they appear in the same contexts—they are then free variants) or **complementary distributions** (that is, if they never appear in the same context—they are then combinatorial variants).

- See B. Bloch, "A Set of Postulates for Phonemic Analysis," *Language* 24 (1948): 3–46 (the article is expanded in *Language* 29 [1953]: 59–61).

Distinctive Features

The definition of the phoneme implies (see above, condition 2) the impossibility of dividing it into *successive* distinctive units. But that does not prevent us from breaking it down into simultaneous distinctive units. Now, it happens that the characteristics that allow a particular phoneme to fulfill its distinctive function are few in number (thus the French /d/ has the feature *voiced*, which distinguishes it from /t/; the feature *oral*, which distinguishes it from the *nasal* consonant /n/; the feature *dental*, which distinguishes it from /b/ and from /g/). Furthermore, these characteristics are few in number in the language itself: at the most, we find about ten of these features, variously combined, in the thirty or so phonemes that a language possesses. Hence the interest in regarding the phoneme as a set of more elementary units, or **distinctive features** (in French, *traits distinctifs* or *traits pertinents*; Benveniste speaks of **merisms**).

Although there is agreement among phonologists on the principle of phonemic analysis, there is controversy as to the nature of the distinctive features, a controversy in which the opposing viewpoints of Martinet and Jakobson are prominent. Two questions in particular are much debated:

1. Are features **binary?** Can they then be grouped in pairs of opposed features each of which would represent, as it were, a phonetic dimension—implying that every phoneme, if it utilizes this dimension to distinctive ends, must possess one of the features of the pair? Such a pairing seems to impose itself for features such as *voiced* and *unvoiced* (describing, respectively, the presence or absence of vibrations of the vocal cords): the first occurs, in French, in /b/, /d/, and /g/; the second, in /p/, /t/, and /k/. (In the case of /l/, *voice* and *voicelessness* are not distinctive features; they only determine contextual variants.) For other phonetic dimensions, on the other hand, it seems natural at first to envisage a series of more than two terms: for example the point of articulation in the buccal cavity; thus /b/, /d/, and /g/ can be distinguished from each other by their articulations—labial, dental, and palatal, respectively. While Martinet recognizes both binary and other features (ternary, quaternary, and so on), Jakobson believes that every distinctive feature is binary. In characterizing the phonemes and looking for their distinctive features, he manages to make this thesis compatible with experience by using, not an articulatory description such as the one given above, but an acoustic description (based on the properties of sound waves), which allows him to discern binary distinctive properties more easily.

2. Do the features have a specifiable phonic reality? For Jakobson,

each feature corresponds to a specific property of the acoustic wave, a property that may be determined with precision through recordings (he recognizes, however, that a phenomenon of supplementation may intervene and that normally nondistinctive properties—known as re-dundant features—may be utilized by the speaker or the listener when the normally distinctive characteristics are blurred, in either production or reception). Jakobson can subsequently propose the hypothesis—subject to empirical verification—that the distinctive features are iden-tical for all languages (languages differ only through the way in which they combine these features into phonemes); there would then be **phono-logical universals.** Martinet, on the contrary, believes that a rigorous physical determination of the distinctive features is inherently impossible. For him, the existence in French of a feature *voiced* characterizing /b/, /d/, and /g/ and a feature *unvoiced* characterizing /p/, /t/, and /k/ does not imply an element common to all the occurrences of the first three that is absent from the occurrences of the other three. It signifies only that in a context c_1, the difference d_1 between /p/ and /b/ is iden-tical to that existing between /t/ and /d/ or between /k/ and /g/ and that the same holds true for the differences d_2, d_3, d_4 in the contexts c_2, c_3, c_4. But it remains possible that the differences d_1, d_2, d_3, d_4 may not be identical to each other. Thus one cannot provide a physical descrip-tion of the distinction *voiced / unvoiced* in French. To be sure, one can speak of the vibration of the vocal cords, which is its most frequent manifestation, but this is only a convenient way to express this distinc-tion. The linguistic reality is simply the correlation between the way in which the phonemes of the unvoiced series and those of the voiced series vary according to context. As a result, the hypothesis of universal dis-tinctive features is all the more unacceptable, since the distinctive fea-tures of a language cannot be defined without reference to the different contexts of phoneme use in that language.

● A. Martinet clarifies his position with respect to Jakobsonian phonology in "Substance phonique et traits distinctifs," *Bulletin de la société de lin-guistique de Paris* 53 (1957–58): 72–85.

Critique of Distinctiveness

While refusing to take recourse to commutation [25], distributional-ism used another method to try to find the same distinctive units that commutation brought to light. Generative linguistics [37ff.], on the other hand, questions the very importance of distinctiveness itself. **Generative phonology** denies that in the description of a language one must always single out distinctive units and properties. The phonological component of a generative grammar [54] is given the task of converting each string of morphemes generated by the syntax (strings accompanied by the trees that represent their internal organization, their structure) into a phonetic representation that describes the "standard" pronunciation of the corresponding sentence. At no stage of this process does there appear a representation of the sentence analogous to what would be its phonemic description (which would retain only the distinctive features).

a) The starting point is not phonemic: it represents above all the decomposition of sentences into morphemes (it is probable, for example, that the French adjective *grand* ["big"] would be represented with a final *d* that often has no phonetic or phonemic existence—cf. *grand garçon* ["big boy"]—since this *d* seems to belong to the morpheme, as the derivatives *grandeur* ["greatness"] and *grandir* ["to grow larger"] testify). (N.B. This does not prevent Chomsky from using the binary distinctive features defined by Jakobson to represent the morphemes [each morpheme is represented as a succession of phonemes, which themselves are represented as sets of features]. But he does so only because that notation appears economical, not because of any desire to represent the morphemes by whatever is distinctive at the moment of their realization in speech.)

b) The end result is not phonemic either: it represents the pronunciation itself. Thus the *l* of *alp* would be represented as unvoiced, as would the *t* of *tone*. In the case of *alp*, the unvoiced character is a combinatorial variant, determined by the proximity of *p* (by a phenomenon of **assimilation,** the voiced or unvoiced character of a consonant is transmitted to the sounds that surround it); in the case of *tone*, on the contrary, the unvoiced character is distinctive, opposing *tone* to *don* or *donor*.

c) Finally, Chomsky believes he can show that in the course of the operation of the phonological component, we shall not at any point obtain a representation of sentences corresponding to their description by phonologists; if we did, we would have to complicate the component deliberately and, what is worse, disallow the representation of certain rules in their full generality, rules (such as that of assimilation) whose existence seems incontestable. (N.B. This critique shows less the inadequacy of the phonological representation than its incompatibility with the generative model. The critique could thus be turned against the generative model itself if description in terms of distinctiveness were to prove necessary for other reasons. It will serve to remind us, however, that such a description—and the considerable degree of abstraction it implies—has no intrinsic legitimacy, but must be justified by its power to explain, for example, language-learning mechanisms, the poetic function, the historical evolution of language [141ff.].)

● On generative phonology, see N. Chomsky, *Current Issues in Linguistic Theory* (The Hague, 1964), and *Topics in the Theory of Generative Grammar* (The Hague, 1966), chap. 4. See also *Langages* 8 (1967), which contains an abundant bibliography; F. Dell, *Les Règles et les sons* (Paris, 1973); and S. A. Schane, *Generative Phonology* (Englewood Cliffs, 1973).

LINGUISTIC PROSODY

Phonematics and Prosody

Spinning off from the traditional meaning of the word *prosody* ("a set of rules pertaining to metrics"), a specialized meaning has developed with the birth of modern linguistics. Within prosody can be classified all the phonic phenomena that elude analysis into phonemes and distinctive features. This shift in meaning can easily be explained: Greek and Latin prosody (metrics) was based on the study of duration, pitch, and ultimately intensity, areas that are today the object of linguistic studies of prosody.

Thus most linguistic schools oppose (in the terminology used by Martinet and the phonological school) **phonematic** elements (phonemes [171] and features [173]) to **prosodic** elements, or (in the American terminology) **segmental elements** to **suprasegmental elements.** This opposition is often reinforced by the idea that prosodic characteristics are nondiscrete, that is, that they are capable of varying in a continuous fashion. (It is moreover the notion of discreteness that has allowed the segmental division of oral communication: division into phonemes, then into distinctive features.) By refusing to grant such a discrete character to the prosodic features, linguists have rapidly assimilated them to marginal phenomena—all the more so since while all languages have phonemes, the various prosodic possibilities are used much less generally and much less systematically. Whereas phonematic linking seems to be an indispensable base for linguistic communication, only a supplementary function is left to the prosodic phenomena. A distinctive role [171] is allotted to them only if no other way has been found to remove the ambiguousness of the phonetic form (message) produced by a speaker and addressed to an interlocutor: the missionaries or other observers who described African languages were most often concerned with variations in pitch only when such concern became indispensable in order to avoid listing too many homonyms. Even now, the study of accentuation appears useful particularly insofar as it helps to divide the utterance into elementary signs. It is granted a distinctive role only in very rare cases (in languages said to have free accent). As for intonation, it is most often regarded as redundant: a distinctive character is only attributed to it when syntax has proved incapable of explaining, without recourse to intonation, the different grammatical values that can be assigned to two strings of significant units that are otherwise identical.

- See A. Martinet, *Elements of General Linguistics*, trans. E. Palmer (London and Chicago, 1964), pars. 3.24ff.; I. Lehiste, *Suprasegmentals* (Cambridge, Mass., 1970); and P. R. Léon et al., eds., *Prosodic Feature Analysis—Analyse des faits prosodiques* (Montreal and Paris, 1970). On the distinctive character of the prosodic features, see E. Coseriu, "Determinación y entorno," in *Teoria del lenguaje y lingüística general* (Madrid, 1962), pp. 282–323.

The Physical Aspect of Prosodic Phenomena

Could the fact that the prosodic features are regarded as marginal be explained by their phonetic manifestations?

Timbre, pitch, intensity, and duration are the components generally recognized in the study of language sounds. The **timbre** of a sound is what opposes, for example, [a] to [i]. It is explained acoustically by the height of the zones of reinforced harmonics, or **formants,** and the relationships between these zones (relationships of frequency and intensity). Physiologically, it depends on the resonance of the cavities that come into play in phonation.

The **pitch** of a sound is explained by the frequency of vibrations of its fundamental. Physiologically, it is determined by the dimensions and the tensions of the vocal cords; this explains why the pitch of a sound varies with one's sex, age, height, and so on, and varies throughout discourse.

The **intensity** of a sound is due to the amplitude of the vibratory movement of the source: for greater amplitude, there is generally greater tension of the cords. This explains why intensity and pitch are linked in most languages: an accent of intensity is also manifested by a raising of the voice.

The **duration** of a sound is our perception of its production time. As far as speech sounds are concerned, a constant tension of the phonatory organs is difficult to obtain, and in the case of a prolonged sound its quality (that is, its timbre) is modified in the course of its production (as, for example, in diphthongization).

Thus defined, the prosodic characteristics are necessarily linked to all phonic activity; this explains why their study may be regarded as marginal or secondary from the linguistic viewpoint. Thus Martinet notes that the prosodic facts are "physical phenomena which are of necessity present in all spoken utterances. Whether the energy used in articulation is great or small, it is always present in some degree. As soon as voice is perceptible, the vibration of the glottis must have a certain frequency and this will impart a certain melodic pitch to the voice as long as it remains perceptible. Another feature capable of prosodic exploitation is duration, which naturally is an inescapable physical aspect of speech since utterances take place over a period of time. It will be understood that these facts cannot have linguistic value through their presence or absence at a given point, but rather by their modalities, which may vary from one part of the utterance to another" (*Elements of General Linguistics*, trans. E. Palmer [London and Chicago, 1964], p. 75).

Functions of the Prosodic Phenomena

Just as a phoneme is abstracted from the set of its phonetic manifestations, a set of *prosodemes* [23] can be posited, independently of the manifestations in which they are incarnated, but through analysis of the diverse functions of the prosodic features.

Since Trubetzkoy, it has been customary to differentiate three functions of the prosodic and phonematic phenomena, functions that may be distributed differently according to the language: the distinctive function, the demarcational function, and the culminative function.

A phonic element has a distinctive function (its major function, according to most phonologists) to the extent that it permits the differentiation of two significant units from each other. Thus there are languages in which two words can be distinguished according to whether, in one of them, we find an /í/, pronounced with a rising tone, or an /ì/, pronounced with a descending tone.

A phonic element that has a **demarcative** (or **delimitative**) **function** permits the recognition of word limits, or more generally, the limits of any linguistic unit whatsoever. This element may be phonematic (for example, phonemes that appear only in a fixed position in an utterance, such as the English /h/, which is always found in the initial position in a morpheme) or prosodic (for example, stress in languages with fixed accent: in Czech the accent, which is always on the first syllable of a word, permits division of an utterance into words).

The **culminative function** is that of a phonic element that allows us to "denote the presence in the utterance of a certain number of important articulations and thus facilitates the analysis of the message" (Martinet, *Elements of General Linguistics*, p. 83). An example is stress in languages with free accent.

- Regarding these functions, see N. S. Trubetzkoy, *Principles of Phonology*, trans. C. A. M. Baltaxe (Berkeley, 1969), pp. 27–28, 273–97. See also A. Martinet "Accents et tons," in *La Linguistique synchronique* (Paris, 1965), pp. 147–67.

On the basis of the foregoing functions, it is possible to define *tone, intonation,* and *stress*; their physical aspect would be envisaged only as the accidental manifestation of some function.

Tone. The pitch oppositions used in certain languages as distinctive units are called tones. These may make it possible to differentiate two phonemes in which all the distinctive features other than pitch are identical. Thus in Chinese /lì/ ("chestnut"), pronounced with a descending tone, is opposed to /lí/ ("pear"), pronounced with a rising tone. The pitch level at which an intoned element is pronounced is not very important: men and women, whose voices have different basic pitches, both respect the tonal oppositions in a particular language.

In languages that use tones as distinctive features, there are multiple possibilities and realizations. Alongside the punctual tones, in which only a point of the melodic curve (the highest, the lowest, or the midpoint) counts for identification, there are melodic tones, in which the slope of the tonal curve intervenes: rising tones, descending tones, rising-descending tones; we can also distinguish tones rising from a low level, tones rising from a middle level, and so on. The tonal system of a language may be very complex: certain Vietnamese dialects are said to include no fewer than nine tones.

- Concerning tones, in addition to the works by Martinet cited above, a comprehensive analysis can be found in K. L. Pike, *Tone Languages* (Ann Arbor, 1948); see also R. M. Brend, ed., *Studies in Tone and Intonation* (Basel, 1975).

Intonation. Pitch variations are not always attached to distinctive units such as phonemes. They may be attached to units belonging to another level (for example, to syntactic groups or to sentences); in this case we speak of intonation. The same physical phenomenon, relative to pitch, for example, may be the simultaneous manifestation of a tone (phonological level) and of an intonation (syntactic level); this makes analysis difficult and compels recourse to functional criteria. P. Kratochvil, for example, has shown (in *The Chinese Language To-Day* [London, 1968]) that in Chinese, accents, tones, and intonations with different functions are not mutually exclusive but can combine with each other.

Intonation understood in this way exists in all discourse and is due to the greater or lesser tension of the articulatory organs. It does not always have a distinctive linguistic value: in every sentence enunciation, the normal schema \ will simply manifest the relaxation of the organs at the end of the utterance; this allows an initial segmentation of a language as yet unanalyzed. However, intonation may be used as a significative linguistic means: it becomes significant as soon as the "normal" intonational curve is modified.

Intonation may be simply redundant [26] in an utterance in which what it expresses is already expressed in another way. It may become distinctive through the suppression of a grammatical morpheme in the utterance. Thus, in French, rising intonation that is redundant in

viens-tu?   (since the word order constitutes a sort of mor-
("are you coming?")   pheme that expresses interrogation)

becomes distinctive in:

tu viens?   (here the word order is common to affirmation
("you are coming?")   and interrogation).

It may be useful, in an analysis, to group significative pauses in the utterance and the phenomena of expressive stress with the intonational phenomena. As an example of a significative pause, let us cite the following French utterance:

/kabylanolaklanolakabylo/

which takes on meaning only when it is pronounced:

ka'by # 'lan # o'lak   # 'lan # o'lak   # aby'lo
(Qu'a bu   l'âne   au lac?   L'âne   au lac   a bu l'eau.)
["What did the donkey drink at the lake? The donkey at the lake drank the water."]

Intonation also will be distinctive in marking the grammatical distinction that exists in English between a restrictive relative clause and a nonrestrictive one:

"The children who have worked will be rewarded" (among the class of children, *only those who have worked* will be rewarded) and "The children, who have worked, will be rewarded" (certain particular children, *because they have worked*, will be rewarded).

This opposition is manifested graphically by punctuation marks (commas) and phonically by a pause after *children* in the second case.

● See P. Delattre, "L'Intonation par les oppositions," *Le Français dans le Monde* 8 (1969): 6–12.

As for the phenomena of emphasis achieved by the so-called expressive accent, they allow us to provide supplementary information in an utterance: compare the simple unaccented English sentence

"I will go"

with the accented sentences

"*I* will go" { *I* and not *you*

"I *will* go" (an action to be undertaken as a project, as the manifestation of a desire, as opposed, for example, to an *already accomplished* action

"I will *go*" (the action of *going* and not, for example, of *coming back* or of *remaining*.

It is possible to say, in French, "Je ne parle pas d'*im*pression mais d'*ex*pression"; similarly, in English, "I am not speaking of *im*pression but of *ex*pression."

These phenomena noticeably modify the intonational curve that we regard as normal. It may be useful to integrate them with the intonational phenomena and then to carry out an analysis of the resulting curve into discrete intonational units.

● For a systematic analysis of these facts, see K. L. Pike, *The Intonation of American English* (Ann Arbor, 1945), p. 21; Z. S. Harris, *Structural Linguistics* (1951; reprint ed., Chicago, 1960), esp. chap. 6; D. Bolinger, ed., *Intonation* (Harmondsworth, 1972); and R. Collier, "Intonation from a Structural Linguistic Viewpoint: A Criticism," *Linguistics* 129 (1974): 5–28. On intonation in English, see R. S. Wells, "The Pitch Phonemes of English," *Language* 21 (1945): 27–39; and D. Crystal, *The English Tone of Voice* (London, 1975). On intonation in French, see W. Zwanenburg, *Recherches sur la prosodie de la phrase française* (Leiden, 1964).

Stress. Diverse phenomena that vary from language to language are grouped under the single term "stress." No language is lacking in accentuation, but several sorts of stress are conceivable. We mean by stress, or **accent,** a manifestation of intensity of pitch and/or of duration that, operating on a syllable or **mora** (any segment of a syllable—a phoneme [171], for example—that can take an accent is called a mora; this is a useful notion in certain languages such as ancient Greek), emphasizes it with respect to its neighbors. The expressive accent mentioned above in connection with intonation emphasized a sign [100], that is, a unit with two faces. The accent with which we are dealing now, traditionally called tonic, physically strikes a syllable just as the expressive accent does, but it emphasizes this syllable as a figure [265] and not as a sign.

The basic function of the accent is the culminative function. But from the point of view of stress, two types of language can be distinguished, according to whether the supplementary function of accent is demarcational (as it is in languages with fixed accent, such as French or Czech, in which phonetic criteria determine where the accent falls) or distinctive (as it is in languages with free accent, such as English or German, in which the place of the accent is determined by morphological criteria).

The variety of its functions notwithstanding, stress obligatorily affects a nonsignificative unit, whether complex or simple (syllable or mora).

P. Garde spells out the perspectives of accentology as follows:

—A taxonomy will deal with the "accentual units" in the various languages.

—A functional syntax of language will determine what is "accentogenic," that is, what calls syntactically for an accent.

—A phonosyntax will specify the point at which the accent will be realized, that is, the "accented unit."

—Phonology will determine the "accentuable unit" in each language.

An "accentogenic unit" is one that requires the presence of an accent. The accentual unit is the morpheme, or group of morphemes, that encompasses an accentogenic element. The accent may fall upon a syllable or a mora; thus it is necessary to know which unit in a given language is accentuable. The accented unit (or accentophore) bears the physical expression of the accent. This latter is not necessarily the accentogenic unit: it may be a unit that, for a different reason, finds itself occupying the position of accent realization. Thus, in French, whose accentuable unit is the syllable, the accentual unit *Prends-le* ("Take it") includes an accentogenic unit *Prends* (*le* being nonaccentogenic, or "atonic"). But *le* is in fact the physical support of the accent and thus is the accented unit, to the extent that it occupies the position of accent realization (in French, the end of a group).

● On all these questions, see P. Garde, *L'Accent* (Paris, 1968). On the notion of level of analysis, see J. P. Rona, "Las 'partes del discurso' como nivel jeráquico del lenguaje," in *Litterae hispanae et lusitanae*, ed. H. Flasche (Munich, 1968), pp. 433–53.

We can specify the levels of analysis that will be common to suprasegmental and segmental elements by summarizing on a chart the principal distinctions to be drawn:

Levels	Segmental	Suprasegmental
1st level: phonemes (opposition)	Phonology	Tonology
2d level: morphemes (contrast)	Morphology	Accentology
3d level: propositions (opposition)	Syntax	Analysis of intonation
4th level: ? (contrast)	Stylistics	Analysis of expressive connotations

Although the prosodic features are in the first place **contrastive** phenomena (that is, they depend on the differences existing between successive elements in the speech chain) and are thus situated along the syntagmatic axis, they allow us to constitute paradigms [108] of units of different levels (units that are in opposition along the paradigmatic axis) by defining every paradigm by a common base plus a variable element (for example, if this element is $\emptyset$, then the paradigm would be $<Ax, Ay, Az, A\emptyset$, etc.$>$). If $<Domin\text{-}us, Domin\text{-}e, Domin\text{-}um$, etc.$>$ is a paradigm, then we can use a variable prosodic element on a common phonematic base to determine paradigms of units on the different levels established above. For example, the utterances

	tu viens	(interrogation)
and		
	tu viens	(affirmation)

form a paradigm consisting of units at the sentence level.

● See L. Prieto, "Traits oppositionnels et traits contrastifs," *Word* 10 (1954): 43–59.

Syntax and **prosody.** In support of the idea that syntax and intonation cannot be separated (see the chart given above), it should be noted that the problem of intonation was raised at the very beginning of the development of the theory of generative grammar [37ff.]. In 1957 Chomsky formulated the first postulates of the theory, and as early as 1960 R. P. Stockwell was studying the place of intonation in a generative grammar of English.

In an article published in *Language*, Stockwell posits intonation as an Immediate Constituent (IC) [32] and formulates the following syntagmatic rule [227ff.]:

$$S \to Nuc + IP$$

(that is, Sentence → Nucleus + Intonation Pattern).

Thus he proposes to treat intonation at the level of the sentence as a whole, and not separately for each *IC*. Therefore he specifies that the Intonation Pattern intervenes at the terminal level. He then proposes to study the constituent Intonation. He posits the rule:

$$IP \rightarrow C + JP$$

(that is, Intonation Pattern $\rightarrow$ Contour $+$ Juncture Point, where Juncture Point equals the end of the Contour morpheme). He defines the *JP* as being unchanged by certain transformations [242ff.] that will be applied to the *IP*, while *C* can be modified by these same transformations. In defining the constituents of the *IP*, he consequently defines at the same time the transformations that will be applied to them (although this is not spelled out, we find an underlying opposition "singulary transformations" / "generalized transformations," the singulary transformations being those that do not modify the *JP* but can modify the *C*). The *C* in turn will be analyzed in terms of the two essential functions of intonation: linking and rupture (continuity and discontinuity).

Once this taxonomic description of intonation contours has been carried out, a neutral, colorless *IP*, the base *IP*, is posited—just as in the grammatical component a kernel sentence is posited [244] (or at least it was posited at a certain stage of generative theory, at the time of Stockwell's article). And once this base *IP* has been chosen, we can formulate transformations at the level of the intonational component. These transformations are formulated in the context of the interplay of elements such as stress; thus they suppose a definition of these elements as well in the choice of the base intonation.

As soon as generalized transformations (the combination of two or more base *IP*s into a single *IP*) are posited, the analysis becomes excessively complex; it is here that the *JP* can also be modified and that the encounter between grammatical component and intonational component, avoided until now, becomes imperative.

The consideration of intonation as a sentence constituent with its own constraints leads to a new definition of transformations; the theory finds itself profoundly modified by the addition of this new IC. This is a logical consequence of the fact that in a generative syntax every element is defined in terms of the others, so the modification of any one entails a modification of the others.

The definition of transformations presupposed by the rewrite rule *IP* $\rightarrow$ *C* + *JP*, with the restriction that *JP* is unchanged for certain transformations, also presupposes a definition of *contour*; the latter is a function of the sentences obtained at the terminal level in the syntax and thus of the prior division effected in the grammatical component between base sentences and transformed sentences.

Stockwell's study, like all studies of intonation in generative grammar, deals with a particular language; we do not yet have a general systematic theory of intonation. But in this area more than in any other (because of the negligence with which the prosodic phenomena have been treated for so long), numerous individual studies are necessary before the general theory can be formulated.

It is very likely that the growing interest in prosodic features among contemporary linguists will have profound consequences. At the methodological level, certainly, but also at the theoretical level, the introduction of such important supplementary data implies a modification of the theoretical object, namely, the concept of language itself. After a formalist stage, it seems that language can no longer be analyzed simply as a formal system, but must be considered in terms of its communication function. This return to an ancient notion shows how difficult it is to abstract the object language from the whole set of enunciative processes.

● On the generative analysis of intonation in English, see R. P. Stockwell, "The Place of Intonation in a Generative Grammar of English," *Language* 36 (1960): 360–67. For a more general view, see S. A. Schane and A. M. Liberman, "Intonation and the Syntactic Processing of Speech," in *Proceedings of the Symposium on Models for Perception of Speech and Visual Form* (Boston, 1964); and P. Lieberman, *Intonation, Perception and Language* (Cambridge, Mass., 1967).

VERSIFICATION

We shall take *versification* to mean the set of phenomena that define the specificity of verse. We shall not concern ourselves here with another of its meanings, namely, "the set of rules which teach how to write verse." A synonym for *versification* in our sense might be *prosody*; but this term has taken on another meaning in contemporary linguistics [176].

The phenomena of versification are customarily divided into three major groups, linked to the concepts of meter, rhyme, and fixed forms, all of which depend on the same principle, which allows the distinction of verse from **prose** and has been given various names at different times: rhythm, periodicity, parallelism, or simply repetition. We can say, in a very general way, that the **parallelism** that is a constitutive element of verse requires that a relationship among elements of the speech chain reappear at a later point along this chain; this notion thus presupposes those of identity, temporal succession, and phonic form: We shall speak rather of **symmetry** when spatial disposition and graphics are at stake. According to the nature of the repeated elements, it is possible to distinguish precisely the three groups mentioned above.

This distinction does not of course imply that meter, rhyme and the fixed forms are independent of each other; none of them can be defined without reference to the others. This interdependence is also found in the relationships between the phenomena of versification and the other linguistic properties of an utterance: versification does not function in isolation from signification. One theory, popular at the beginning of the twentieth century (Saran, Verrier), held that the student of verse should put himself in the place of a foreigner, that is, he should exclude meaning from consideration, in order better to observe formal properties. The failure of this theory in the face of the real problems of versification is proof of the error in its postulate.

Studies of versification today do not try to set aside the significative nature of the utterance. But in spite of the existence of a very abundant literature (spread over two thousand years), the essential notions in the area of versification still lack rigorous definition. The discoveries of modern linguistics, and particularly of phonology, have made a number of old laws and rules obsolete and have not always replaced them with new ones.

When the repeated element is connected with accent [181ff.] or with quantity, we speak of **meter.** Meter can thus rest on three linguistic phenomena: the syllable, accent, and quantity. The **syllable** is a phonemic group constituted by a phoneme called syllabic and, optionally, by other nonsyllabic phonemes. The first constitutes the peak of the syllable, whereas the others form its margins. The syllable has linguistic reality only in a particular reading, that is called a **scansion.** In English, the vowels play the role of syllabic phonemes. As for accent, it is an emphasis involving the duration, the pitch, or the intensity of a syllabic phoneme and differentiating this phoneme from its neighbors. **Quantity,** finally, corresponds to differences in phonemic duration; these latter assume a distinctive function in certain languages.

Consequently we can distinguish three types of meter: **syllabic, accentual,** and **quantitative,** based, respectively, on the regular repetition of the number of syllables, of accents, or of quantities. Contrary to a widespread opinion, verse usually illustrates not just one of these three principles at a time, but two or even three (this is true of French verse, for example). A fourth type of meter is sometimes suggested: **tonematic** meter, which would be utilized in the tonal languages; but on the whole, linguists are content with the tripartite division proposed above.

A metric sequence of syllables forms a **line** of verse. The line is demarcated by the completion of a metric figure, which is manifested by a **metric pause;** the line is sometimes also marked by rhyme. Graphically, the line is set apart by a space that separates it (in Occidental poetry) from the right-hand margin of the page; but if the line is defined as a metric entity, it is apparent that one graphic line sometimes contains two or more metric lines, and vice versa.

It is said that a line has as many **measures** (or "feet") as it has syllables manifesting the repeated element. Consequently, in a purely syllabic line a distinction between measure and line would be impossible. In the case of accentual and quantitative lines, the number of measures equals the number of accented, or long, syllables. Classical versification codified the most frequent quantitative measures under names that have had widespread use and were also applied to accentual measures (with an assimilation of length and accent). Noting a long syllable by — and a short one by U, we can define the principal measures as follows: **iamb:** U—; **trochee:** —U; **anapest:** UU—; **amphibrach:** U—U; **dactyl:** —UU; **spondee:** — —; **tribrach:** UUU.

A pause that separates the line into two **hemistichs** is called a **caesura.** Since, however, the definition of the line also implies the existence of a metric pause, it is in fact impossible to distinguish rigorously between caesura and final pause and, consequently, between hemistich and line (unless the distinction is based on the written form). The existence of this pause is contradicted by the frequent phenomenon of **enjambment,** that is, of noncoincidence between metric pause and **verbal pause** (grammatical or semantic); moreover, enjambment could not exist if all the pauses were of the same nature. This noncoincidence allows two readings of lines that include enjambments: one, a *metric* reading, is performed to the detriment of meaning; the other, a *semantic* reading, is performed to the detriment of meter.

There have been frequent attempts to distinguish meter and **rhythm,** the former being the perfectly regular succession of accented and unaccented, long and short syllables; the latter, the realization of this schema in language. It is evident, however, that the difference lies only in the degree of abstraction. It is not necessary to reduce meter, for example, to the measures canonized by the classical writers and to require their regular repetition; that never happens. The metric description of a poem, of a period, or even of a national literature can be much more refined. Thus, recently, M. Halle and S. Kayser have given a new description of the classical English meter, one that allows them to account for almost all of the lines formerly considered to be irregular. Previous descriptions have thus been overly rough approximations, not descriptions of some other phenomenon; in both cases the same metric process is being described.

Metric theory has suffered numerous misinterpretations because of a confusion between the meter of a line and this same meter as it appears in the course of a particular recitation. R. Jakobson, in denouncing this confusion, introduces four distinct terms. On the one hand he opposes the **verse instance,** that is, the metric structure of a single line, to the **verse design,** which is the statistical result of all the verse instances within a poem, of the work of a poet, of a literary trend. On the other hand he distinguishes the verse instance from the **delivery instance** as it is realized in the course of a particular reading. Finally, we can seek the common denominator of diverse readings undertaken by the same person or by the same school or recitation; this will give us the **delivery model.** This distinction between verse and delivery already suggests the limits of any acoustical approach to versification.

Nor should we confuse the individual variants in the recitation of lines with the optional elements of versification. *Optional* does not mean "useless" or "meaningless"; the term designates here an element that is not necessary for the production of the phenomenon *line*. Certain poetic schools and certain poets make precisely these optional features obligatory. As for the nature of these features, they may be connected to all the other aspects of the verbal utterance. Thus, to cite some previously studied phenomena, R. Jakobson has shown the role that the distribution of the speech chain into words can play within the metric pattern: in Russian, an iamb of four measures is perceived differently according to whether the accent falls at the beginning or at the end of words. B. Eikhenbaum, in his *Melodika Stikha* (1921), was the first to study the distribution of intonations in poetry and to propose a typology of intonational organizations.

Free verse is situated at the limit of metric verse. According to some schools, it does not obey metric schemas; but this notion is obviously contradictory in itself. Either no meter exists, in which case we are probably dealing with a lyric prose in which the impression of poetry is produced by semantic or grammatical elements, or else a metric organization exists but the word *free* indicates that it cannot be described using terms such as "iamb" and "trochee"; however, we have seen that the inadequacy of our tools is not sufficient reason to conclude that we are confronting a different phenomenon. "Free verse" is then a synonym for **metric prose.**

Even the principles of metric description have varied a great deal during the last century. The classical method of description, which we might call *graphic*, has been maintained particularly within the academic tradition. The *musical* method, in which accents and quantities are marked by using musical signs, has represented an effort at renovation: its objective is to develop a unified science of metrics that would deal with music as well as with poetry. But the specificity of the linguistic meter seems much too powerful to justify such an enterprise, and in metric analysis it is never possible to put in parentheses the relation of meter to meaning or grammar. For the same reason, hopes for the *acoustic* method have been disappointed. By the use of spectrographs and other recording instruments, this method permits a detailed visual representation of word flow (**visible speech**); but we rediscover here a confusion between verse and delivery. With the work of the Russian formalists (Jakobson, Tomashevskii, Eikhenbaum, Zhirmunskii [82]), we can speak of the introduction of a *structural* method in the study of versification: they were beginning to study the linguistic components of the line of verse with respect both to the other elements of the poem and to the general structure of the language. Finally, the Bulgarian linguist M. Janakiev was the first to formulate an axiomatic theory of versification.

• See G. M. Hopkins, *The Journals and Papers* (London, 1959), an important precursor of modern studies of versification; E. Sievers, *Rhythmisch-melodische Studien* (Heidelberg, 1912), and M. Grammont, *Le Vers français* (Paris, 1913), the two leading promoters of versification studies at the beginning of this century; B. M. Eikhenbaum, "Melodika Stikha," first published in *Letopis' Doma literatorov*, no. 4, in 1921, and reprinted in book form as *Melodika russkogo liricheskogo stikha* (Petrograd, 1922); V. Zhirmunskii, *Introduction to Metrics: The Theory of Verse*, ed. E. Stankiewicz and W. N. Vickery, trans. C. E. Brown (The Hague, 1966); B. Tomashevskii, *O stikhe* (Leningrad, 1929), excerpts of which have been translated into French in *Théorie de la littérature*, ed. T. Todorov (Paris, 1965); W. L. Schramm, *Approaches to a Science of English Verse* (Iowa City, 1935), representative of the acoustic approach; W. K. Wimsatt and M. C. Beardsley, "The Concept of Meter: An Exercise in Abstraction," *PMLA* 74 (1959): 585–98; M. Ianakiev, *Bulgarsko stikhoznanie* (Sofia, 1960); R. Jakobson, "Linguistics and Poetics," in *Style in Language*, ed. T. A. Sebeok (New York, 1960), pp. 350–77; A. Kibedi Varga, *Les Constantes du poème* (The Hague, 1963); S. Chatman, *A Theory of Meter* (The Hague, 1965); M. Halle and S. J. Keyser, *English Stress: Its Form, Its Growth and Its Role in Verse* (New York, 1971); J. Thomson, "Linguistic Structure and the Poetic Line," in *Proceedings of the International Conference of Work-in-Progress Devoted to Problems of Poetics* (Warsaw, 1961); J. Roubaud, "Mètre et vers," *Poétique* 7 (1971): 354–75; W. K. Wimsatt, ed., *Versification: Major Language Types* (New York, 1972); P. Guiraud, *La Versification* (Paris, 1970); and *Langue française* 23 (1974): *Poétique du vers français*.

Rhyme is only a special case of sound repetition, a very widespread phenomenon in verse but one that occurs also, although less systemati-

cally, in prose. The systematic study of sound repetitions was undertaken .
by one of the Russian formalists, O. Brik, who distinguished the following factors: number of sounds repeated, number of repetitions, order of
sounds in each of the repeated groups, place of the repeated sound in
the metric unit. Taking an entirely different point of departure, F. de
Saussure also studied, in works that remained unpublished until 1964,
the repetitions of sounds in poetry, repetitions that, according to him,
obey the principle of **anagrams:** the sounds or the letters composing a
proper name would find themselves disseminated throughout the entire
poem.

This structural (and structuring) role of sounds must be distinguished
from the role traditionally attributed to them in the study of phonetic
symbolism [255]. In the latter case, there is a search for the intrinsic
meaning of sounds or a direct correspondence between the meaning of
words and the nature of the sounds of which they are composed. Such
a relationship exists, but in individual texts rather than in the language
in general; and it is proportional rather than direct. Beyond these local
correspondences, only extremely general (and therefore vague) patterns
can be established.

Rhyme is a sound repetition occurring at the end of a line. The notion of rhyme consequently implies that of line; at the same time, as we
have seen, rhyme is at the service of the line, marking its end in a particularly striking manner. However, unrhymed lines, called **blank verse,**
do exist.

Rhymes may be classified in a number of different ways, according to
the variable identified. The major systems of classification follow:

1. According to the degree of resemblance between the phonic sequences in question, we may have **assonance,** in which the vowel sounds
are identical but the surrounding consonant sounds differ (for example,
name, gain, fate, taste); **consonance,** in which the vowel sounds are
different but the consonant sounds following them are the same—the
preceding consonant sounds may be identical but need not be (for example, *nod, had, head, bid*); **true rhyme,** that is, "complete," "full," or
"perfect rhyme," also called "final" or **end rhyme** when it occurs at the
end of a line—by far the most commonly used rhyming device in English
verse—in which the final accented vowel sounds and subsequent consonant sounds are identical but the consonant sounds preceding the
vowels within the accented syllables differ (*bread, dead, said, ahead*);
or **rich rhyme,** that is, "perfect," "identical," or "echo rhyme," in which
the vowel sounds and both the preceding and the following consonant
sounds are the same, although the words in which these sounds appear
are different in meaning (*rain, rein, reign; alike, dislike*). The term **eye
rhyme** describes the case in which identical spellings appear but the

sounds differ (*hood, blood, brood*). The term **near rhyme** is sometimes used to describe some perceptible phonic resemblance between two words that, strictly speaking, do not rhyme (examples drawn from J. Shipley, ed., *Dictionary of World Literature* [Totowa, N.J., 1953]).

2. According to the number of syllables included in the rhymed sequence, a distinction is made between **masculine,** or one-syllable, rhymes (see the examples given above), and **feminine,** or two-syllable, rhymes (*broken, token; imploring, restoring*). Rhymes of more than two syllables are also known as feminine (*slenderly, tenderly*).

3. According to the location of the accent, we may identify **oxytonic rhymes** (the term "masculine" is also used here), in which the accent falls on the final vowel; **paroxytonic** (or "feminine") **rhymes,** in which the accent falls on the penultimate vowel; **proparoxytonic** (or **dactylic**) **rhymes,** in which the accent falls on the antepenultimate vowel; **hyperdactylic rhymes,** in which the accent falls on the fourth vowel from the last, and so on.

4. According to the types of combination between rhymes in the stanza (or, more precisely, in the quatrain), we identify **couplets,** in which the rhyme order is *aabb*; **enveloping rhyme,** in which the order is *abba*; **alternating rhyme,** in which it is *abab*. Other combinations, for example in the quintette (*ababb*), have no fixed nomenclature.

5. According to the relationship they maintain with the other elements of the utterance, **grammatical rhymes**—that is, those in which grammatically identical forms rhyme—are opposed to **antigrammatical rhymes;** and **semantic rhymes,** in which the sound resemblance creates an impression of semantic proximity, are opposed to **antisemantic rhymes,** in which the sound resemblance brings to light a contrast. Sound repetition generally creates the appearance of some semantic relationship.

6. The refinements of rhyme have been carried very far in France, especially in certain periods (the fourteenth and fifteenth centuries, for example). Consequently, it is possible to identify a large number of individual rhymes that are most often special cases or combinations of the types described above. As one example, we may cite the **equivocal rhyme,** which implies identity of the phonic word and difference in meaning, as in *le soir tombe / vers la tombe* ("night is falling / near the tomb").

● O. M. Brik, "Zvukovye povtory," in *Two Essays on Poetic Language* (Ann Arbor, 1964); J. Starobinski, *Les Mots sous les mots* (Paris, 1971); V. Zhirmunskii, *Rifma: Ee istoriia i teoriia* (1923; reprint ed., *Der Reim: Seine Geschichte und Theorie,* Munich, 1970); W. K. Wimsatt, "One Relation of Rhyme to Reason," in *The Verbal Icon* (Lexington, 1954), pp. 153–66; and P. Delbouille, *Poésie et sonorités* (Paris, 1961).

A succession of two or more lines is called a **stanza** (the upper limit is not fixed, but the term seems not to be used for more than fourteen lines). In a certain sense, the stanza is to the line what the line is to the measure: both require the repetition of a certain pattern in order to be considered complete. The stanzas of a poem often manifest the same pattern of rhyme and meter or an alternation of two patterns, and so on. If the entire text (the poem) is composed of a single stanza, it is not possible to speak of strophic organization. A stanza is said to be **isometric** if the lines that constitute it have the same number of measures; otherwise it is called **heterometric.** Moreover, according to the number of lines that constitute the stanza, we can distinguish the **distich,** or *couplet*; the *tercet*, or **triplet;** the **quatrain;** and so on. If the same stanza appears several times in the poem, it is called a **refrain.**

The combination of different types of stanzas has also been codified, producing certain **fixed forms.** Among those known best are the **rondeau,** constructed on two rhymes, the refrain being repeated in the middle and at the end; the **triolet,** always isometric, with eight lines, rhymed in the following order (the capital letters designate the repeated lines, that is, the refrain): ABaAabAB; the **ballad,** composed of three isometric stanzas and an envoy, in the Old French tradition (the stanzas usually have as many lines as there are syllables in each line; the envoy, half as many); and finally the best known of all, the **sonnet,** composed of fourteen lines, divided $4 + 4 + 3 + 3$ or $4 + 4 + 4 + 2$ (Shakespearean sonnet), and so on, with numerous variations in the rhyme scheme. These forms, very much alive in medieval and French classical poetry, are seldom used today.

● On English prosody, see L. Abercrombie, *Principles of English Prosody: Part I, The Elements* (London, 1923); G. R. Stewart, *The Technique of English Verse* (New York, 1930); N. Frye, *Sound and Poetry* (New York, 1957); S. Chatman, *A Theory of Meter* (The Hague, 1965); J. McAuley, *Versification: A Short Introduction* (East Lansing, 1966); G. S. Fraser, *Metre, Rhyme and Free Verse* (London, 1970); M. Halle and S. J. Keyser, *English Stress: Its Form, Its Growth and Its Role in Verse* (New York, 1971); and W. K. Wimsatt, ed., *Versification: Major Language Types* (New York, 1972). Some treatises on French versification are found in M. Grammont, *Petit traité de versification française* (Paris, 1960); J. Suberville, *Histoire et théorie de versification française* (Paris, 1956); and W. T. Elwert, *Traité de versification française* (Paris, 1965). Bibliographies are provided in J. Mazaleyrat, *Pour une étude rythmique du vers français moderne: Notes bibliographiques* (Paris, 1963); F. Deloffre, *Le vers français* (Paris, 1969); and M. Gauthier, *Système euphonique et rythmique du vers français* (Paris, 1974).

WRITING

Graphic Notation

Every visual and spatial semiotic system [103ff.] is, in the broad sense, **writing:** in the narrow sense, writing is a graphic system of language notation. More precisely, within writing taken in the broad sense we can distinguish *mythography* and *logography*, which coexist today but about which the question of historical precedence has often been raised.

Mythography is a system in which the graphic notation does not refer to (verbal) language, but forms an independent symbolic relationship. If semiotic systems are categorized according to the nature of the sense required for the reception of signs—sight, hearing, touch (taste and smell have not produced well-developed semiotic systems)—and according to the punctual or durative character of the signs, mythography brings together sign systems that are durative in character and address themselves to sight or to touch.

Mythography can be actualized in various forms. We can cite representation through objects (used as tropes [275] for what they signify): such was the famous message addressed to the Persians and composed of a mouse, a frog, a bird, and five arrows. This type of communication seems universal: in Sumatra, the Loutsou declare war by sending a piece of notched wood along with a feather, a chunk of ember, and a fish; this signifies that they will attack with as many hundred (or thousand) men as there are notches, will be as swift as a bird (represented by the feather), will devastate everything (the ember), and will drown their enemies (the fish). In the region of the Upper Nile, when an enemy enters their territory, the Azande place a cornstalk and a chicken feather on the road and an arrow on the roofpost of a house; taken together these mean: if you touch our corn and our chickens, you will be killed.

Another form of mythography is notation by means of knots on a string or ribbon, which is used especially in accounting; the knotted handkerchief is an example. And another: all the notches and marks whose function is either counting (for example the days of the year) or proclaiming ownership (brands on cattle). "Natural" signs such as animal or human footprints can also be incorporated into mythography.

The most important part of mythography is **pictography,** according to which figurative designs are used with a communicative function. A relatively elaborate system of pictograms is found among Alaskan Eskimos, who, when they leave home, leave a message-drawing on the door to indicate the direction they have taken and the nature of their activity. A precise meaning is considered attached to a drawing as soon as the drawing has become schematic and stylized and as soon as the type of event rather than the individual event has been represented. The historical position of pictography remains much in debate.

Mythographic systems can also be grouped, not according to their substance, as was suggested above, but according to the type of signification they establish. We then find the same dominant functions as in verbal language: denomination, permitting the identification of a *particular* object (brands and notches), and description (drawings and representative objects). But in no case is a relationship with verbal language necessary; indeed, very often it is impossible. There are no specific, unique words that must be attached to a given design or a given object; that is why the theory according to which pictograms correspond to sentences (as opposed to other signs that designate words or sounds) must be rejected: sentences, like words, are linguistic units; mythography is an autonomous, semiotic system.

In spite of its universal extension, mythography has never had a role as important as that of language. Mythographic systems cover only quite limited areas of experience, whereas language has a totalizing purport. This is probably because pictograms form open, unorganized series, whereas language can be conceived as a combinatorial system: a limited number of sounds produce a very large number of words; the latter in turn produce an infinite number of sentences.

Today (verbal) language coexists with mythographic systems; and there is no reason to seek to reduce the one to the other in human prehistory. However, it seems to be true that **logography,** the graphic system of language notation, developed for the most part out of mythography. The other source of logography, according to J. Van Ginneken, was gestural language. All writing systems, in the limited sense of the word, are included in logography.

In a complementary fashion, several logographic principles govern the different writing systems. No writing system of any people obeys one single principle; thus, in the framework of a general topology, we have to classify principles and not writing systems.

1. The first major principle is what can be called **morphemography,** in which the graphic sign denotes a meaningful linguistic unit. The term "morphemography" should be used instead of the misleading terms "ideography" and **ideogram:** in no case do the graphic signs directly denote ideas (this would be mythography); they denote morphemes or— as in the case of classical Chinese, where the two coincide—words. The

proof is that synonyms are not represented, in these systems, by similar signs. The morphemographic system, like every logographic system, denotes language, not "thought" or "experience."

2. The second major principle is **phonography,** in which the graphic sign denotes a nonmeaningful linguistic unit, that is, a sound or a group of sounds. When the unit is a sound, we speak of **alphabets;** when it is a group of sounds, of **syllabaries.** Historically, the two forms seem to be connected. We first encounter the Semitic syllabaries; then an intermediate form, the **consonantal alphabets** (of which the Phoenician alphabet is the most important). In the Semitic and Hamitic languages, the non-notation of vowels is "natural," since the latter correspond to our endings, while the consonantal skeleton corresponds to our root. The Greeks began to note systematically all the sounds, including the vowels (using for them Phoenician letters with consonant value), and thus formed the alphabet, in the narrow sense of the word. The most widespread alphabets in the world, most notably Latin and Cyrillic, are derived from the Greek alphabet.

The phonographic principle is historically related to the morphemographic one in the following way: the pure morphemograms (which were formerly called, as we have seen, ideograms or **hieroglyphics**), while functioning as signifiers of a morpheme, a language unit, are constructed so as to constitute a schematic image of the object or the act designated by this morpheme or as a kind of image of the gesture, "natural" or conventional, that accompanies a given activity. (It is important of course not to exaggerate either the resemblance of the image with the object—the design is stylized very rapidly—or the "natural" and "universal" character of the signs: Sumerian, Chinese, Egyptian, and Hittite hieroglyphics for the same object have nothing in common.) The same process applies to what are called **logical aggregates,** signs formed by two already meaningful units (as in our word *skyscraper*; in Chinese the word *quarrel* is designated by repeating twice the sign for *woman*; in Sumerian the word *eat* is designated by the sign for *bread* within the sign for *mouth*. Let us also note the presence of the type of symbolization known as metaphorical, in which the sign for *sun* also designates *brilliant*; here it is actually a question of synecdoche).

Now it is the impossibility of generalizing this principle of representation that has introduced, even into fundamentally morphemographic writing systems such as Chinese, Egyptian, and Sumerian, the phonographic principle. We might almost conclude that every logography grows out of the impossibility of a generalized iconic representation; proper nouns and abstract notions (including inflections) are then the ones that will be noted phonetically.

The introduction of phonography has followed various paths:

a) Through **rebus** (the device that seems to have played the most important role), which consists in noting one word by using the sign for another because the two are homophones. For example, in Sumerian, the sign for *arrow*, pronounced *ti*, also serves to designate *life*, which is also pronounced *ti*. This rebus principle does not imply perfect equivalence; for example, in Egyptian, *master* is pronounced *nb* and is noted by using the same sign as the one for *basket*, pronounced *nb. t*, the *t* being the sign of the feminine. Once the homographic relationship has been established, the speaker also (probably) senses a resemblance in meaning: if in Chinese *sorcerer* and *liar* are both designated by *won*, speakers forget that they are dealing with a rebus and, following the well-known principle of popular etymology [140], see instead a kinship. In proper nouns, several hieroglyphs may be combined for their phonetic value, always according to the rebus principle. For example, the Aztec proper noun *Quauhnawac*, meaning "near the forest" (*quauh*, "forest"; *nawac*, "near"), is denoted by the signs for *forest* and for *speech*, since the latter word is pronounced *naua-tl* (here again we have an approximation). It is curious to note that this device has influenced even mythographic systems: if *ring* and *return* are designated by the same word in a language, a ring is sent to an exile to call him home.

b) Through borrowing from foreign languages. Knowing that a given hieroglyph is pronounced in a certain way in a neighboring language, one can use it in one's own language in order to note the same sounds, while giving it a different meaning. The Akkadians borrowed Sumerian signs in this way.

c) Through **acrophony,** in which each hieroglyph takes on the value of the initial sound of the word that it designates. Thus the hieroglyph for *steer* begins to be read as *a*, first letter of the word *aleph*, which signifies *steer* (this would explain the names given to the letters in Hebrew, Greek, and so on). The widespread application of this device has been often debated, and here again it may well be a matter of a popular etymology: the name of the letter is often a mnemotechnic device (like the words which help us "spell" a telephone number) for which motivation is sought after the fact.

3. A widespread device in writing systems in which the morphemographic element dominates is what historians of writing call **semantic determiners** (or keys). These are graphic signs added to the elementary hieroglyph that permit the distinction of homonyms and the specification of a word's precise meaning (in our Western languages, suffixes assume this second function: thus *worker* is distinguished from *working*, while both include the "idea" of work). In Sumerian the sign for *plow* signifies, with the sign for *wood* as a determiner, the instrument itself; with the sign for *man* as a determiner, it signifies the one who plows. This analysis can be carried quite far in Chinese writing, where there

are 214 determiners that divide words into classes along the lines of semantic categories such as animate-inanimate; the determiners are not pronounced. Such a categorization evidently presupposes a logical analysis of the language, which justifies Meillet's remark that "the men who invented and perfected writing were great linguists; it is they who created linguistics." The alphabet, for its part, presupposes the equivalent of a phonological analysis of language.

No national writing system is the pure incarnation of a single principle or writing procedure. Contrary to what is affirmed in numerous speculations about Chinese writing, the latter is not exclusively morphemographic; indeed, the vast majority of Chinese signs are used for their phonetic value. Similarly, the deciphering of the Egyptian hieroglyphics was floundering until Champollion discovered that certain of them had phonetic value. Conversely, the Occidental alphabets are not, as one might easily think, entirely phonetic: a single letter designates several sounds, and a single sound is designated by several letters; certain phonic elements (for example, intonation) have no graphic equivalent, while certain graphic elements (for example, the comma) have no phonetic equivalent; certain graphic signs (such as numbers) function in the manner of hieroglyphs, and so on.

● Basic works include H. Jensen, *Sign, Symbol and Script: An Account of Man's Efforts to Write*, trans. G. Unwin (New York, 1969); J. Février, *Histoire de l'écriture*, 2d ed. (Paris, 1959); I. J. Gelb, *A Study of Writing: The Foundations of Grammatology*, 2d ed. (Chicago, 1963); M. Cohen et al., eds., *L'Ecriture et la psychologie des peuples* (Paris, 1963), proceedings of a colloquium sponsored by the Centre International de Synthèse, Paris, May 1960; A. Leroi-Gourhan, *Le Geste et la Parole* (Paris, 1964–65). For a bibliography, see M. Cohen, *La Grande Invention de l'écriture*, 3 vols. (Paris, 1958), vol. 2, *Documentation et index*. On the origins of writing in gestural language, see Chang Chêng-ming, *L'Ecriture chinoise et le geste humain* (Paris, 1937); and J. Van Ginneken, *La Reconstruction typologique des langues archaïques de l'humanité* (Amsterdam, 1939). Studies of writing in the framework of structural linguistics are J. Vachek, "Zum Problem der geschriebenen Sprache," in *Etudes phonologiques dédiées à la mémoire de M. le Prince, N. S. Trubetzkoy* (1939; reprint ed., University, Ala., 1964), pp. 94–104; H. J. Uldall, "Speech and Writing," *Acta linguistica* 4 (1944): 11–16; D. Bolinger, "Visual Morphemes," *Language* 22 (1946): 333–40; and J. Vachek, *Written Language: General Problems and Problems of English* (The Hague, 1973).

Toward a Grammatology

Studies of writing systems have almost always taken the form of a history unless they have been devoted to the problems of deciphering:

more than one writing system still remains incomprehensible to us today (Mayan, that of Easter Island, and so on). The project of writing the history of writing borders on the impossible, since history presupposes writing, in the broad sense: it is unthinkable without the existence of durative signs.

Unfortunately, all the histories of writing to date accept as postulates certain affirmations that contemporary linguistics or even simple common sense make suspect. Thus the evolution of language and of writing is always envisaged as a movement of the concrete toward the abstract; such a movement is, at the very least, problematical. It suffices to consider numbers, attested from the very earliest documents. Or else the existence of a teleological movement is postulated: from mythography toward logography, from morphemography toward phonography, in the name of some principle of efficacity that has not been made very explicit. But mythography continues to exist today, and Chinese writing is no more phonetic today than it was a thousand years ago. These postulates result from an ethnocentric vision, not from observation of the facts.

The historical phase of the accumulation of facts needs to be transcended by the elaboration of a **grammatology,** or science of writing. Grammatology's tasks will include the discovery of evolutionary laws, as well as the definition of the very phenomenon of writing among the other semiotic activities and the typology of graphic principles and techniques. The only outline of this positive science to date is found in I. J. Gelb's *A Study of Writing: The Foundations of Grammatology* (1952). In France this study has been carried forward in the direction of a philosophical critique of the fundamental concepts of writing and language together [349ff.].

It goes without saying that the study of writing must be envisaged in a perspective that is also ethnological. Even more than speech, writing seems linked to magic, religion, and mysticism.

- Philosophical studies include M. V. David, *Le Débat sur les écritures et l'hiéroglyphe aux XVIIe et XVIIIe siècles* (Paris, 1965); and J. Derrida, *Of Grammatology*, trans. G. C. Spivak (Baltimore and London, 1976). Ethnological studies include F. Dornseiff, *Das Alphabet in Mystik und Magie*, 2d ed. (Berlin, 1925); and A. Bertholet, *Die Macht der Schrift in Glauben und Aberglauben* (Berlin, 1949).

SIGNIFICATIVE UNITS

Until the end of the eighteenth century, most Occidental linguists tacitly agreed that the smallest linguistic unit that was at once meaning-bearing and materially present in the speech chain was the **word**. Sentences are made up of clauses that are themselves made up of words. If a word is broken down in turn, it is broken into nonsignificative units (syllables, letters). The definition of the word, moreover, remains generally implicit. The decomposition of an utterance into words seems to be somehow self-evident, and this allows us to dispense with all explicit determination. This division into words rests in fact not only on a graphic tradition solidly established since the Renaissance, but on indisputable phenomena of pronunciation: the word is the unit of accentuation [181ff.] (the accentual languages generally attribute only one accent, or at least only one strong accent, to each word); moreover, certain modifications are produced only at word boundaries (for example, in German, the distinction of the sounds *d* and *t* is annulled at the end of a word and there alone).

The advent of comparative linguistics brought with it a dissociation of the word into more elemental units of meaning. In fact, the relationship between two different languages cannot be determined by comparing words, but only by comparing parts of words.

● Turgot had already pointed out (in his article "Etymologie," in the *Grande Encyclopédie*, p. 99, col. 1) that in the case of a derived word, the etymologist must "bring it back to its root, ridding it of the apparatus of endings and grammatical inflections which disguise it; if it is a compound, the different parts must be separated." In the same spirit Adelung (*Mithridates*, 4 vols. [Berlin, 1806–17], vol. 1, p. xii) made fun of those who related the German *packen* ("to take") to the Greek ἀπαγω ("to take away") without noticing that, as soon as the second word is broken down into two parts, ἀπ-αγω, neither of its elements has anything in common with the German verb.

The discovery of the relationship between most of the contemporary Indo-European languages and Sanskrit was also a determining factor. In Sanskrit, in fact, the internal organization of the word is particularly striking: its various elements are often juxtaposed to each other in a transparent fashion; this has sometimes led to the conclusion that the lesser distinction of these elements in the contemporary languages is only an accident, attributable to the vagaries of phonetic evolution. Most comparatists are thus led to distinguish two types of components within the word: (*a*) elements designating notions and categories relative to reality (in French, *mange* ["eat"] in *mangeront* ["they will eat"]); and (*b*) grammatical marks designating the categories of thought, the intellectual viewpoints imposed on reality by the mind. The former are called, in German, **Bedeutungslaute,** in French **sémantèmes** or *radicaux,* in English **roots;** the latter are called **Beziehungslaute,** or **morphemes.** For certain philosophical grammarians the union of these two elements in the word reflects the association of an empirical content and of an *a priori* form that, according to the Kantian tradition, characterizes every act of understanding. As for the morphemes themselves, it has become customary to distinguish among them **inflections,** which enter into systems of conjugation or declension, and **affixes,** which are more independent of each other; for example, *retrenchments,* in which *trench* is the root, *re* and *ment* are derivational affixes, and *s* is an inflectional affix. Moreover, depending on whether the affix appears before or after the root, it is considered to be either a **prefix** (*re-*) or a **suffix** (*-ment*).

While they retain the idea that word decomposition is necessary, most modern linguists reject the preceding classification, alleging that it is valid at the most for the languages of classical antiquity, that it is introduced into the modern Indo-European languages through the projection of the past into the present (contrary to the principle of a purely synchronic description [141]), and, finally, that it has hardly any meaning in most of the non-Indo-European languages. It has also become customary to call by a single name all the significant components of the word: American linguists use in this sense the terms **morpheme** and **formative;** Europeans speak either of morphemes or of *formants.* The determination of morphemes, minimal meaningful units, confronts, in practice, the difficulty that the morpheme must at once be a material element—a segment of the speech chain—and bear meaning. Now it is often the case that materially distinct segments carry in a quite evident way the same meaning (thus, in French, the *i* of *ira* ["he will go"] and the *all,* phonetically [al], of *allons* ["we are going"], both of which designate the concept *aller* ["to go"] and between which the choice is automatically determined by the person and the tense of the verb; or the two forms *peux* and *puis* [both meaning "I can"] of the present tense of the verb *pouvoir* ["to be able"]). On the other hand, an unanalyzable phonic element is frequently charged at one and the same time with several clearly distinct meanings (such as the *a* of the Latin *bona* ["good"], which indicates simultaneously that the adjective is of the feminine gender, in the nominative case, and singular in number). This divergence between the phonic and the semantic facets of morphemes has led certain Americans to modify their terminology. They call **morph** any meaningful phonic element that cannot be broken down into smaller meaningful phonic elements (thus *i, al, a,* in the preceding examples, are morphs). The morpheme is thus redefined as a class of morphs:

intuitively, it is a class of morphs giving the same semantic information; this intuitive "sameness of semantic information" can be distributionally described as follows: if two morphs belong to the same morpheme, either their substitution is never possible in the same context or it is possible in any context. Morphs belonging to the same morpheme are called **allomorphs** (for example, *i* and *al*, which can never be substituted one for the other, since they are imposed by the person and the tense of the verb; and *peux* and *puis*, which can always be substituted one for the other). As for the morph charged with several bits of information at the same time, while it remains unanalyzable into smaller meaningful units, it is considered as a member of several different morphemes (it has become traditional to call it a **portemanteau morph**).

● On the notion of morpheme in American linguistics, see C. F. Hockett, *A Course in Modern Linguistics* (New York, 1958), chap. 32; and E. P. Hamp, *A Glossary of American Technical Linguistic Usage, 1925–1950* (Utrecht, 1966). Methods for identifying morphemes are given by Z. S. Harris, *Structural Linguistics* (1951; reprint ed., Chicago, 1960), chaps. 12–19. Harris calls a **morphemic segment** that which has been designated here as a morph, and a **morpheme alternant** that which here has been called an allomorph. On the set of problems posed by morpheme analysis, see C. E. Bazell, "Phonemic and Morphemic Analysis," *Word* 8 (1952): 33–38, and "Meaning and Morpheme," *Word* 18 (1962): 132–42; and P. H. Matthews, *Morphology: An Introduction to the Theory of Word Structure* (London, 1974). L. Hjelmslev's use of the word *morpheme* ("Essai d'une théorie des morphèmes," in *Essais linguistiques* [Copenhagen, 1951], pp. 152–64) must be carefully distinguished from all the uses presented above. Hjelmslev's morphemes are elements of meaning, units of content (the term "formant" is reserved to designate their material expression). Furthermore, like the morphemes of the French tradition, Hjelmslev's are units whose value is basically grammatical and are in opposition to units of lexical value (the pleremes). Finally, for Hjelmslev, morphemes and pleremes both belong to the form of language [22]; thus they are defined only by the relationships linking them with other morphemes and pleremes, respectively. The characteristic feature of the morphemes—as opposed to the pleremes—is thus that their presence may determine (or be determined by) the presence of other morphemes outside of the syntagma to which they themselves belong (in Latin, a preposition may determine the presence of a certain case ending in some later word).

Certain European linguists have found a degree of gratuitousness— and some artifice—in the effort of American linguists to maintain that the morpheme is a phonic unit, while accepting the idea that it satisfies semantic criteria. This is why A. Martinet has elaborated the notion of **moneme.** The moneme is neither phonic nor semantic in nature: it represents a certain type of choice effected by the speaking subject during an act of enunciation. The moneme constitutes, among the choices that are directly determined by the content of the message to be communicated, the elementary choice (unanalyzable in terms of simpler choices). Thus the *a* of *la* in *La soupe est bonne* ("The soup is good") does not correspond to a moneme, since it is not chosen, but imposed by the gender of the word *soupe*. The same is true for the *s* of *soupe*, since it is not directly determined by the content: it is only chosen to produce the word *soupe* rather than *loupe* ("magnifying glass") or *coupe* ("cup"), and it is only through the intermediary of the word *soupe* that it participates in the intention to communicate. The choice of *la soupe*, finally, is not a moneme, since it is analyzable, since it can be understood on the basis of the choice of the definite article *la* and of *soupe*. Considered now in a positive light, our example would consist of five monemes, corresponding to the choice of (1) the definite article, (2) the noun *soupe*, (3) the verb *être*, (4) the present indicative tense, and (5) the adjective *bon* (we could also envisage—but here the question is more open to debate—a sixth moneme, representing the choice of the singular number).

The definition of the moneme as a unit of choice also allows us to describe without difficulty the phenomena for which American linguists have created the concepts of allomorph and of portemanteau morph. For nothing prevents us from recognizing that the same choice may be represented by different segments of the speech chain, according to the context in which it appears: thus the single moneme *definite article* will be manifested either by *le* or by *la*, according to the gender of the noun that follows; or the choice corresponding to the signification *aller* will be phonically realized sometimes as [i], sometimes as [al]. And nothing prevents two distinct choices from resulting in an unanalyzable segment of the speech chain; in this case, the two monemes are said to be **amalgamated** (for example, the monemes *verb "être"* and *present indicative* are amalgamated in the segment *est*). Martinet manages furthermore to recuperate the difference between the semantemes and the morphemes of the French grammatical tradition. He distinguishes in fact two types of monemes:

a) **Grammatical monemes** (such as *present indicative* or *definite article*), which "belong to closed inventories," in the sense that the appearance of a new article or of a new tense would lead necessarily to the modification of the value of existing articles or tenses; and

b) **Lexical monemes,** "which belong to open inventories" (the appearance of a new food name would *not* necessarily lead to a modification of the value of *soupe*).

The usefulness of the notion of minimal unit of meaning, even in the very supple form Martinet gives it, is currently being questioned by certain linguists.

For transformationalists, the monemes, in spite of their abstractness, are still much too close to the superficial structure of utterances. If we grant that the true semantic choices of speaking subjects are situated at the level of deep structure [244], then their relationship with the surface structure is still more indirect and complex than the relationship of manifestation that, according to Martinet, links the monemes to the speech chain.

Moreover, once the possibility of amalgams (in which several significative units are manifested by a single phonic segment) has been recognized, how can we distinguish clearly the minimal significative units from the minimal semantic elements (semes), of which semanticists such as B. Pottier or A.-J. Greimas [265ff.] speak? Why not say that the phonic segment *soupe* manifests—while amalgamating—the semantic choices *food, liquid, salty.* In short, the major difficulty encountered in an analysis into minimal meaningful units explains why, at a given moment, the analysis is ended.

● On moneme analysis, see in particular chapter 4 of Martinet's *Elements of General Linguistics,* trans. E. Palmer (London and Chicago, 1964). The idea that this analysis is based on the notion of choice is explicitly presented in Martinet's "Les Choix du locuteur," *Revue philosophique* 91 (1966): 271–82. A transformationalist critique of Martinet's linguistics, particularly of the notion of the moneme, is found in P. M. Postal, "Review Article (André Martinet, *Elements of General Linguistics*)," in *Foundations of Language* 2 (1966): 151–86.

PARTS OF SPEECH

The search for a regular order within a language seems very often to require, among other tasks, the classification of the elements of that language. If the word is taken as the fundamental linguistic element, one of the linguist's first duties must then be to establish a classification of words. The Greek and Latin grammarians called **parts of speech** (μερη του λογου, *partes orationis*) the principal word classes that they were led to distinguish. The determination and the definition of these classes were the object of numerous discussions throughout classical antiquity; the distinctions that seem clearest today have been perceived and elaborated only very gradually.

- Among the principal participants in this elaboration seem to have been Aristotle (*Poetics* 1457a), the Stoic philosopher Chrysippus, the Alexandrian grammarian Aristarchus (for the two latter figures, see Quintilian *De Institutione Oratoria* I. 4. 18ff.), Apollonius Dyscolus (fragments of his work are found translated into Latin throughout Priscian's *Institutiones grammaticae*), and Varro (*De lingua latina* 6. 36; 8. 44–45). A very original theory of parts of speech was developed by J. Harris, in *Hermes, or A Philosophical Inquiry Concerning Language and Universal Grammar* (London, 1751). On the history of the theory of parts of speech, see V. Brøndal, *Les Parties du discours* (Copenhagen, 1948), intro.; for the summary of this history up to Varro, given in chart form, see J. Collart, *Varron: Grammairien latin* (Paris, 1954), pp. 158ff. See also I. Michael, *English Grammatical Categories and the Tradition to 1800* (London, 1970).

In his treatise *De octo orationis partibus*, the Latin grammarian Aelius Donatus (fourth century) established a list that has undergone, in fifteen centuries, only minor alterations of detail: his list, with few changes, was used by the *Port-Royal Grammar* and until quite recently served as the basis for many French grammar textbooks. It contains the following eight classes: noun, pronoun, verb, participle, conjunction, adverb, preposition, interjection. Rather than discussing this classification in detail, it may be more useful to bring to light, in connection with it, the general difficulty raised by any theory of the parts of speech, a difficulty that concerns its conditions of validity. What guarantees that one list of the parts of speech is the right one, or even that it is better than another?

a) A first possible answer would be that a theory of the parts of speech, in order to be valid, must be universal, that its categories must be represented in all languages. It is significant that the ancient grammarians did not raise this question of universality explicitly. This is because for them, it went without saying that their classification had universal value: they conceived of it as the necessary framework for all possible linguistic description (in today's terminology, we would say that their classification appeared to them to be a principle of "general linguistics," an element of "linguistic theory"). Now, a certain dose of artifice was necessary to defend this thesis, even while staying within the comparison of Greek and Latin, languages that resembled each other relatively closely. Thus, since Latin possessed no articles, the Latin grammarians had to squeeze into their pronoun category two classes, article (ἄρθρον) and pronoun (ἀντωνυμια), which Greek grammarians such as Aristarchus carefully distinguished. For even more obvious reasons, the consideration of "barbaric" languages would have made it very difficult to uphold the universality of the classification. It is difficult to see, moreover, how it could be otherwise: for a classification established on the basis of particular languages to be adapted in a natural way to fit all languages, a good deal of luck would be necessary. On the other hand, how else can we define parts of speech but by studying particular languages?

It is to avoid this dilemma that the Danish linguist V. Brøndal abandons inductive procedures in his search for a universal theory of the parts of speech. He proposes an inverse method that consists in constructing an intrinsically justifiable classification whose applicability to the real languages would be necessary *a priori*. Brøndal starts from the idea that languages all have a logical foundation that, given the universality of logic, must be identical for all of them. But in order to be compatible with experience, this thesis requires certain restrictions. It implies, according to Brøndal, neither that all the parts of speech need be found in reality in all languages nor even that certain of them need be; rather it requires defining, through reasoning, an inventory of all the possible parts of speech and then showing that the real languages always choose their parts of speech within this inventory. An analysis of the intellectual operations brings to light four fundamental categories: relationship, object, quantity, and quality. Each of these categories taken separately and, on the other hand, all the logically coherent combinations of several categories allow us to define the possible categories of discourse (there are fifteen, according to Brøndal). The categories actually represented in the languages will never be anything but manifestations of these possible categories: thus the class of French prepositions manifests the category of relationship; that of pronouns, the combination of the category of object and that of quantity (since pronouns represent indeterminate objects, characterized only as quantifiable). It is apparent that the difficulty raised by Brøndal's categorization is precisely the inverse of the one raised by the traditional classification: its applicability to particular languages is likely to be not too difficult, but rather too easy, given the level of generality of the definitions of the categories.

b) Let us suppose that a classification of parts of speech abandons the pretention to universality and limits itself to the description of a given language. By what criteria can we then recognize its validity? How can we be sure that the distribution proposed reveals some intrinsic features of the language described? An interesting confirmation would be that the classification established can be justified from several different points of view and, for example, that semantic, morphological, and syntactic considerations converge to impose the same distribution of words into classes. In order for this test to have indisputable value, however, it would have to be possible to effect the distribution according to each of these viewpoints independently, in which case their agreement, impossible to predict *a priori*, would prove that this distribution corresponds to a sort of natural articulation of the language. In reality, unfortunately, the traditional classification of the parts of speech is obliged to take recourse *simultaneously* to different viewpoints; since it makes heterogeneous criteria intervene in a *complementary* fashion, it is no longer capable of receiving that sort of confirmation that the agreement of independent criteria would provide.

Thus it happens that morphological criteria are the ones used [51]: Varro distinguished the noun from the verb by virtue of the fact that the noun is declined (takes case endings), while the verb is conjugated (takes tenses). This is doubtless the reason that the participle was considered an autonomous part of speech and not as one of the forms of the verb (the participle, in Latin and Greek, is capable of taking both case and tense). But distributional criteria [32] are employed at the same time: the way in which words are arranged with respect to each other in a sentence is taken into consideration. Thus the preposition is defined by the fact that it precedes the noun. At other points, only the syntactic function intervenes; thus the conforming function, shared by all coniunctions, does not imply a common position in the arrangement of the discourse. The Middle Ages elaborated the notion of the adjective, unknown in classical antiquity, essentially to emphasize the fact that most adjectives designate qualities and most substantives designate objects. But since morphological criteria failed to distinguish substantives and adjectives in Latin or Greek (they are declined in the same way), and since syntactic criteria were also lacking (in Latin at least, where the adjective may function as subject of a verb), a compromise was sought by making them two subclasses of the noun category. This continued hesitation over criteria is suggested in the fact that one of the first distinctions established, that of the noun (ὄνομα) and the verb (ρῆμα), seems to have been based originally on the different roles played by these two classes in the activity of enunciation (the one serves to designate objects, the other to affirm something with regard to these objects). This is approximately the way modern logicians distinguish subject and predicate [269]; but one can no longer coherently maintain that the two classes are word classes, that they are thus parts of speech, for the function of the ρημα may be accomplished in many ways besides the use of a verb in the grammatical sense. And that is why Plato (*Cratylus* 399*b*) presents the expression Δι φιλος ("friend of God") as a ρημα, even though it includes no verb.

There remains the question of whether this heterogeneity of criteria belongs to the traditional classification alone or is linked to the very project of establishing parts of speech, that is, a classification of words. Most contemporary linguists would opt for the second hypothesis. For them, words are units whose nature is much too composite to allow all the words of a language to be classified according to one and only one criterion, even less so according to several independent and convergent criteria. This composite nature seems to prevent, in particular, the use of the semantic criterion. If for example we analyze a word into morphemes—as has become customary since the end of the eighteenth century [199]—it is perhaps only among the morphemes that a semantically interesting classification can be established. Thus certain comparatists—for example, F. Bopp (*Grammaire comparée des langues indo-européennes*, trans. M. Bréal, 2 vols. [Paris, 1866], vol. 1, pp. 221–22)—believed they had established that the Indo-European roots (that is, the morphemes of the Indo-European mother tongue) are distributed in two opposing classes, the **nominal roots** (which have come to form, in the later languages, the radicals of nouns, verbs, and adjectives) and the **pronominal roots** (which constitute in these languages, on the one hand, the grammatical marks of verbs, nouns, and adjectives and, on the other hand, the grammatically independent words—pronouns, conjunctions, prepositions). In this perspective, a semantic classification of words can never be coherent, since it will have to put on the same level grammatically simple words such as prepositions (which express a grammatical signification in the pure state) and semantically composite words such as verbs (which express a blend of grammatical and lexical signification).

The semantic classification of words is made difficult not only by the presence of grammatical marks within words but also by the presence of derivations. Thus the *Port-Royal Grammar* sought to oppose adjectives and substantives in terms of meaning and proposed to consider the former as the expression of properties (for example, *white*) and the latter as designating classes of objects or substances (for example, *man*). The distinction seems to be all the more solid in that there is a correspondence between the nature of the property (which is always a property of something) and the syntactic behavior of the adjective (which must always be related to a substantive, as epithet or attribute). But at once we confront the counterexample of substantives such as *whiteness* (obviously designating a property) and adjectives such as *human* (having no less to do with substances than the substantive *man*). Port-Royal's solution was to consider words such as *whiteness* and *human* as derived substantives and adjectives; as such, they cannot pretend to the semantic characteristics possessed by basic substantives and adjectives such as *man* and *white*. The situation is in fact more complicated still, for, as the *Port-Royal* grammarians noted, the creation by the language of the substantive *whiteness* leads to presenting the quality white as a sort of substance; and the adjective *human* tends to show up, as a sort of property, the fact of being a man. Thus we do not even have the solution of considering derived adjectives and substantives as false substantives and adjectives. The semantic characterization of a class of words such as the adjective then becomes a speculative matter.

● See *Grammaire générale et raisonnée* (1660; reprint ed., Paris, 1969), Eng. trans., *A General and Rational Grammar* (1753; facsimile reprint ed., Menston, England, 1968), pt. 2, chap. 2. A commentary on this text is found in "Linguistique," in *Panorama des sciences humaines* (Paris, 1971).

Similarly, transformational grammar leads to despair over every semantic classification and every syntactic classification of words. A large number of words are in fact regarded by this school as the residue in surface structure of very different deep configurations. This is the case, for example, when a **nominalization transformation** produces a nominal group in surface structure on the basis of a complete utterance in deep structure [244]. Let us thus suppose that "the construction of the dam is under way" has as its origin "the dam is constructed" and "it is under way." It would not make much sense then to put in a single category the noun *construction*, which corresponds to a verb in deep structure, and the noun *dam*, which is already a noun in deep structure. They cannot have the same semantic value, since the latter, according to Chomsky, is read in the deep structure. And their syntactic properties will also differ, since they are largely tied to the configuration of the underlying utterance (thus *construction*, coming from a passive verb, may have as complement of agent *by the men*, which is not the case for *dam*).

● A detailed discussion of the nominalization transformation and of the syntactic and semantic properties of the resulting nouns is found in P. Chapin, "On the Syntax of Word Derivation in English," (Ph.D. diss., M.I.T., 1967). A more nuanced position is presented by Chomsky in his "Remarks on Nominalization" (1967), available in R. Jacobs and P. S. Rosenbaum, eds., *Readings in English Transformational Grammar* (Waltham, Mass., 1970), pp. 184–221. See also J. S. Bowers, "Some Adjectival Nominalizations in English," *Lingua* 37 (1975): 341–61. On nominalization in French, there is considerable information in J. Dubois, *Grammaire structurale du français*, 3 vols. (Paris, 1965–69), vol. 3, *La Phrase et les transformations* (1969); and in M. Tutescu, *Le Groupe nominal et la nominalisation en français moderne* (Paris, 1972).

SYNTACTIC FUNCTIONS

In the terminology used in many French grammar textbooks, to analyze a clause (to perform a so-called grammatical analysis) is to indicate the functions fulfilled by the words or word groups in that clause (that is, to identify the subject, direct object, and so on). Similarly, to analyze a sentence (a so-called logical analysis; the Port-Royal theorists speak of this in their *Logic* [A. Arnauld, *La Logique de Port-Royal* (Paris, 1660), translated as *Logic; or, The Art of Thinking* (1865; reprint ed., London, 1965)], pt. 2, and not in their *Grammar*) is to indicate the functions fulfilled by its clauses. The two exercises both presuppose that the constituents of an utterance possess different **syntactic functions;** this idea itself includes several underlying theses:

1. From the syntactic point of view, the totality constituted by a sentence is not a pure agglomeration of elements, that is, a set (in the mathematical sense). If no particular structure is added to a set, the relationship of the element to the whole is the same for all the elements. Syntax, on the contrary, defines certain relationships between the elements of the sentence and the totality of the sentence such that two distinct elements find themselves in a different relationship with respect to the sentence as a whole (e.g., the one is subject, the other complement).

2. The particular relationship that unites a constituent to the sentence as a whole can be described in finalist terms as a role: it is recognized that the sentence, taken in its entirety, has an end and that each constituent is distinguished from the others by the role that it plays in achieving this end. As in a biological or social organism, in a sentence each part is supposed to bring its specific contribution to the accomplishment of the collective task.

3. The function of an element is not directly determined by its nature: two elements that are different in nature may have the same func-

tion (for example, two words described as different parts of speech may play the same role: a substantive and an adjective may both be attributes). Conversely, constituents of the same nature may have different functions (a substantive may be either subject or complement). These two types of phenomena seem to attest to the reality and the autonomy of the syntactic function, just as the reality of a function is attested, in biology, by the polyvalence of the organs and by the possibility that one may supplant another in the same function. The study of syntactic functions would thus be to the study of parts of speech what physiology is to anatomy.

● On the distinction between the study of parts of speech and that of functions, see L. Tesnière, *Eléments de syntaxe structurale* (Paris, 1965), chap. 49; O. Jespersen, *Philosophy of Grammar* (London and New York, 1924), pp. 96ff.; and idem, *Analytic Syntax* (Copenhagen, 1937), chap. 31.

4. Finally, in order to maintain that the syntactic functions belong to the sphere of language and in order to distinguish them from the indefinitely variable intentions of speaking subjects, it must be admitted that for a given language (or, ultimately, for all languages) there is a fully determined inventory of syntactic functions and that the same ones can appear in the most widely differing utterances.

Two functions were identified as early as classical antiquity: the **subject** (indicating the object about which one is speaking) and the **predicate** (affirming something about the subject); the Port-Royal grammarians reaffirmed this fundamental distinction (*Logic*, pt. 2, chap. 1). But to the extent that the analysis of a sentence into subject and predicate leaves no residue (one part of the utterance has the subject function, all the rest is predicate), this distinction has long been an obstacle to the discovery of other functions.

Two texts—the articles "Construction" and "Régime" in the *Grande Encyclopédie*—seem to have inaugurated a functional analysis surpassing the distinction of subject and predicate; they achieved this by introducing the notion of **complement.** Until this point, the problems of the internal organization of the sentence seemed to be limited particularly to the problems of **construction** (meaning the linear arrangement of words), assimilated by Port-Royal to syntax, under the pretext that *syntax* signifies, etymologically, "putting together," and to the problems of agreement (one word "governs" another when it imposes on it a certain form, for example, case or gender). The notion of syntactic function, in order to be used systematically, has thus had to be distinguished (*a*) from the notion of agreement (the function *object complement* remains identical whether this complement takes a particular case, as in Latin, or no case at all, as in English); and (*b*) from the notion of construction (this distinction is well-drawn in the article "Construction" in which Dumarsais defends the idea that the Latin utterances *Accepi litteras tuas* and *Tuas accepi litteras,* although different in construction, since they are different in word order, have the same syntax, since the relationships of the words among themselves are the same). Considered positively, what functions can the elements of a proposition fulfill aside from those of subject and predicate? Beauzée replied, in the article "Régime", by using the notion of complement, a notion he owed to Dumarsais. Words are related to each other to the extent that certain ones are there in order to complete the meaning—in itself deficient—of certain others. Whence the distinction of two sorts of complements: **relational complements,** which designate the object of a relationship that is part of the meaning of the completed word ("the author of the *Misanthrope*," "the mother of Coriolanus," "necessary to life"); and **determinative complements,** which merely adds determinations specifying that which, in the completed term, is left indeterminate: if someone eats, he eats something, at a certain time, in a certain place, and so on; and each type of determination of this sort makes possible a particular type of complement (object, place, time).

● On the elaboration of the notion of syntactic function in the seventeenth and eighteenth centuries, see J.-C. Chevalier, *Histoire de la syntaxe* (Geneva, 1968). Chevalier shows that the development of French grammar in this period appears as a gradual evolution of the concept of complement.

This broadening of the notion of function that followed upon the work of Dumarsais and Beauzée has remained almost unquestioned by subsequent linguists, notwithstanding certain differences in presentation. The notion appears indispensable for the description of numerous languages, moreover, for it establishes the concept of **syntactic coordination,** according to which two segments of an utterance are coordinated if they have the same function (this is the case for *in the evening* and *before lunch* in "Call me in the evening or before lunch"). Now we cannot dispense with coordination if we wish to describe certain conjunctions such as *and* and *or,* which can only connect coordinated segments: one cannot say, without a peculiar stylistic effect, "He reads in the evening and his book" or "He works in the evening and in London."

What poses problems, in Beauzée's theory, is the juxtaposition of two types of completely heterogeneous functions: on the one hand the functions *subject* and *predicate,* which seem tied to the very nature of the act of judgment (one always judges something about something); on the other hand the functions of complementation, which have a basis of another sort, namely, the impossibility of expressing a complete idea with a single word. Tesnière, for example, will attempt to suppress this heterogeneity: for him, the opposition of subject and predicate can only be justified from the logical point of view, which is unacceptable in linguistics. In every function he will thus see complementation, or, if we agree to say that the complement *depends* on the completed term, a relationship of **dependency.** To describe the syntactic functions actualized in an utterance is thus to indicate the dependencies existing among the elements of this utterance. Given that a term is never both completed by another and also a complément of that other, and given also that the unity of the sentence is manifested by the existence of an element that is itself a complement of nothing, Tesnière can represent the network of dependencies organizing an utterance by a sort of tree, which he calls a **stemma,** in which the complement is always placed underneath the completed term and linked to it by a line. What follows, for example, is what would be the stemma of "Today Peter bought an electric train for his son."

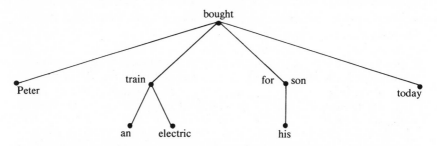

The upper term, which serves as keystone for the sentence, and is not the complement of anything, is the **predicate** (in languages that possess this part of speech, this is generally a verb). It should be observed in this connection that having defined the function through dependency, one can no longer really speak of a function *predicate*, since the predicate does not depend on any other term. Moreover, for Tesnière, the predicate is a particular word, whereas for the Port-Royal grammarians it was a much longer segment of the utterance (everything other than the subject).

Once the stemma has been constituted, the nature of the relationships of dependency actualized in the utterance must be indicated. Tesnière initially distinguishes (1) the relationships of the first level (between the predicate and its direct dependents) and (2) the relationships of the following levels. In the second group, he does not make an explicit classification, but in the first he establishes several subdivisions. For the sentence represents, for him, a sort of little drama, in which the predicate represents the action (in the theatrical sense), or process, of which the dependents of the predicate are the major elements. These elements are of two sorts: the **actants** (designating the characters) and the **circumstants** (designating the situation). While there may be any number of circumstants (in our example there is only one, *today*, but we could add as many as we liked to give indications of place, goal, cause, and so on), there can be only three actants: actant 1, the subject (here *Peter*); actant 2, the object of an active verb (*train*) or the agent of a passive verb; and actant 3, the beneficiary (*son*). At the same time, then, that Tesnière reduces the predicate to the status of a simple sentence element (it is no longer the totality of what is said about the subject), he takes away from the subject the sort of privilege it previously enjoyed: it is now merely one of the actants. Thus the systematic utilization of the notion of complement has exploded the traditional analysis based on the opposition of subject and predicate.

A. Martinet has attempted a sort of synthesis between the two conceptions. For him, as for Tesnière, the **predicate** is a particular element of the utterance, the one toward which all the relations of dependency converge; to this extent it has no function, properly speaking, for an element's function is always defined by the type of relationship linking it to the predicate, directly—if it is a primary constituent (actant or circumstant, according to Tesnière)—or indirectly—if it depends first on another constituent. But at the same time, Martinet tries to do justice to the preeminence that has long been granted the subject, and he does so without recourse to an analysis of judgment, which would take him out of the realm of linguistics. The solution is provided by the theory of **expansion.** Any term or group of terms in an utterance that can be removed without taking away from the utterance its nature as utterance and without modifying the mutual relationships of the remaining terms is called an expansion. That which remains after all the expansions have been removed is called a minimal utterance, or **nucleus** (in our example the nucleus is "Peter bought"). In certain languages (English and French, but not Basque) the nucleus always has at least two elements. One is the predicate, the center of all the sentence's relationships; the other, Martinet calls the **subject.** To say that a language includes the subject function is thus to say that there is in that language an obligatory complement. The existence of this obligatory complement allows us to oppose the subject to all the other complements without recourse to the "logical" criteria of traditional grammar.

The notion of expansion that allows Martinet to recuperate the subject allows American distributionalists [31ff.] to rediscover, sometimes inadvertently, the notions of function and dependency. The finality implied by the idea of function seems completely incompatible with the antimentalist attitude of this school. Thus the word hardly ever appears in their works (even though Bloomfield sometimes uses it [see *Language* (New York, 1933), p. 169]). They prefer, as does Hockett, to speak of **construction.** Let us suppose that we have succeeded in segmenting into immediate constituents [32] all the utterances of a language and that we have furthermore grouped into classes all the immediate constituents having (more or less) the same distribution. We may speak of a construction [*A, B; C*] if we have established that by joining in a certain way an element of the class *A* to an element of the class *B*, we obtain an element of the class *C*. Thus we may speak of a construction [*nominal group, predicate; clause*].

But the traditional duality between functions of the subject or predicate type and functions of complementation (verb / verbal complements; noun / epithet) reappears, to some extent, within the study of constructions. It constitutes in fact a particular case of the distinction between two types of constructions: **exocentric,** in which *A* and *B* are both different from *C* (this is the case for the construction that brings together subject and predicate), and **endocentric,** in which one of the two constituent classes is identical to the resulting class. Thus the construction [*nominal, adjective; nominal*] is endocentric: *good bread* is a nominal by the same token as *bread*. The term "center," or "head," designates the element that is at once constituent and result of the endocentric construction: *nominal* is the head of the preceding construction. Such a construction corresponds fairly well to the intuitive notion of dependency (*good* depends on the head word *bread*). Similarly, we can redefine in terms of construction the notion of coordination (relationship among words with the same function). Coordination is an endocentric construction where $A = B = C$; thus the three segments *my aunt, my uncle,* and *my aunt and uncle* belong to the same class, *nominal group*.

The theory of constructions raises the same problems as those raised by distributionalism in general. In order to be applied in a reasonable fashion, does it not suppose a recourse, explicit or not, to meaning? Is it possible to see two different constructions in "He reads nights" and "He reads books" if one does not require—in order to say that two segments represent the same construction—that the meaning effect produced by the conjunction of terms in each be identical? But is this meaning effect that accompanies a certain mode of syntactic combination very different from function, in the traditional sense?

Since one of the objectives of generative grammar is to give precise formulation to the concepts of traditional grammars, Chomsky has had to be concerned with expressing the notion of **syntactic function** in terms of generative grammar even though the tree describing a sentence represents above all its distribution into immediate constituents. Given the tree corresponding to a sentence, how can we deduce from it the functions connecting the words or morphemes of the sentence? Take the following tree, corresponding (approximately) to sentence (1), "Peter bought a book":

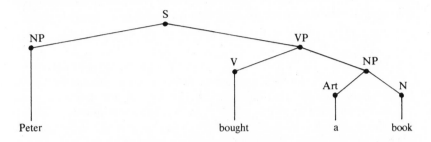

How can we read here that *Peter* is the subject and *book* the object complement without adding information foreign to that contained in the rules that generated the sentence? It suffices, for example, to posit as a definition that a segment *X* is subject of a sentence if it is dominated by a node *NP*, which is immediately dominated by the node *S*, which dominates the sentence. *Peter* is thus the subject of sentence (1). We shall define in an analogous manner the relationship "to be the main verb of a sentence," and a simple examination of the tree will show that *bought* is the main verb of sentence (1). In order to obtain the desired result, namely, that *Peter* is the subject of *bought*, it suffices to postulate that if *X* is the subject of a sentence and *Y* is the main verb of the same sentence, then *X* is the subject of *Y*.

Generative grammar thus finds itself explicitly reintegrating this notion of function that is often rediscovered only implicitly by the distributionalists. However, some differences between this view and the traditional concept remain.

1. For Beauzée, Tesnière, or Martinet, the notion of function is the basis for syntax; in the Chomskyan perspective, on the contrary, function is a derived notion. The divergence reflects two rather different conceptions of sentence organization. For the first group, this organization results from an attraction that the elements exercise on each other. For Chomsky, on the other hand, it manifests a set of abstract schemas, summarized in the grammar rules, that are independent of the words or morphemes that eventually complete them.

2. For a follower of Chomsky, the syntactic representation of an utterance is double (according to whether we take into consideration the tree representing deep structure or the one representing surface structure); it is thus possible to recognize two levels of function as well. Thus the passive utterance "A book was bought by Peter," whose deep structure is approximately the same as that of sentence (1), will have

as surface subject *a book* and as deep subject *Peter*. For most linguists, a word has, on the contrary, only one function, the one that Chomsky would call its surface function (let us note however the traditional distinction, in French, between the real subject [*il*] and the apparent subject [*place*] in *Il reste une place* ["There is one seat left"]).

● On the idea of syntactic function in modern linguistics, see for example L. Tesnière, *Eléments de syntaxe structurale* (Paris, 1965), pt. 1; N. Chomsky, *Aspects of the Theory of Syntax* (Cambridge, Mass., 1965), chap. 2, sec. 2; A. Martinet, *Elements of General Linguistics*, trans. E. Palmer (London and Chicago, 1964), chap. 4, and *La Linguistique synchronique* (Paris, 1965), pp. 206–29, as well as *Studies in Functional Syntax* (Munich, 1975). On the fairly closely related notion of construction, as it is used by Bloomfield's disciples, see C. F. Hockett, *A Course in Modern Linguistics* (New York, 1958), secs. 21 and 22; and R. S. Wells, "Immediate Constituents," *Language* 23 (1947): 93–98. The tagmemic theory, developed by K. L. Pike, achieves a sort of reconciliation between distributionalism and a traditional theory of functions. For an introduction to tagmemics, consult R. E. Longacre, *Some Fundamental Insights of Tagmemics* (The Hague, 1965); see also the bibliography on pp. 36–37, above.

MOTIF

The search for the smallest meaningful **unit** of a text reveals, more directly than any other undertaking, the choice of initial postulates, which is itself based on philosophical presuppositions. In contemporary studies of discourse (and particularly of literary discourse), two fundamental attitudes can be identified. One consists in regarding the text as a full presence, irreplaceable in its essence; this attitude attempts to discover an organization *in the text itself*. The other postulates that textual organization is situated *outside the text*, that it is placed at a level of abstract elaboration, and that the text is the manifestation of a structure that is inaccessible to direct observation.

The first attitude, which is both more empiricist and more respectful of the literality of discourse than the second, has nevertheless shown little concern for describing its own working instruments and, consequently, its basic units. Rather than focusing our attention on the sentence or the word, linguistic units whose discursive pertinence is uncertain, we shall be oriented here toward the **lexie**, a unit of reading that, as R. Barthes has written, "will sometimes include only a few words, sometimes a few sentences"; it is defined as "the best possible space in which one can observe meanings." The dimensions of the lexie are thus a function of the type of reading adopted. On the one hand, lexical analysis is related to that of sonority, rhythm, grammatical or stylistic structures, to the extent that it is attached to the verbal aspect of the text, to the linguistic forms present; on the other hand, it touches on narrative and thematic analysis, since it has to do with meaning [294ff.].

The other attitude, that of abstraction, has been adopted much more frequently: attempts have been made from time immemorial to divide the whole of a text into smaller and more intelligible units; and this distribution has most often followed linguistic divisions (at the level of the signified and at that of the signifier). Thus a novel is divided into chapters or episodes; a poem into stanzas and sentences; impelled by the desire to obtain simple and indivisible units, some critics have sought to push the analyses further and further. Tomashevskii went as far as the clause ("each clause has its own motif," that is, it has what is the "smallest particle of thematic material"). Propp showed that each word within a clause could correspond to a different motif. Greimas extends the analysis to the distinctive semantic features, that is, to the semantic categories whose conjunction forms the meaning of the word.

The distinctive semantic feature, or seme, may well be accepted as the semantic atom of the text, just as it is within the linguistic sentence. But in order to be applicable to discourse analysis, this notion needs to be made more specific.

To the extent that the distinctive semantic feature is the product of an analysis, the aim of ending with undecomposable elements is not sufficient. It is also necessary to spell out the perspective in which the analysis is situated. When we observe the relationships of contiguity and of linkage that are established between units of meaning, we place ourselves in a syntactic perspective and seek to establish a list of **predicates.** When, on the other hand, we do not take into account the relationships of contiguity and immediate causality, but attempt to uncover those of resemblance (and thus of opposition) between units often widely separated from each other, the perspective is semantic, and we obtain **motifs** as a result of the analysis. The same words or the same sentences will thus be described by means of different semantic features, according to the type of observation adopted.

● B. Tomashevskii, "Thematics," in *Russian Formalist Criticism: Four Essays*, ed. L. T. Lemon and M. J. Reis (Lincoln, 1965); A.-J. Greimas,

Sémantique structurale (Paris, 1966); E. Falk, *Types of Thematic Structure* (Chicago, 1967); and R. Barthes, *S/Z*, trans. R. Miller (New York, 1974).

Syntactic decomposition is a frequent theme in the work of the Russian formalists. Thus Tomashevskii was concerned with the study of the smallest syntactic unit (he called it motif and had it coincide with the clause). He proposed an initial subdivision of predicates classifying motifs according to the objective action that they describe: "motifs which change the situation are *dynamic* motifs; those which do not are *static*" ("Thematics," p. 70). Greimas picks up the same opposition: "The division of the class of predicates must be introduced, along with the postulation of a new classematic category, the one which actualizes the opposition *staticity/dynamism*. According to whether they include the seme [semantic feature] of *staticity* or that of *dynamism*, the predicative sememes are capable of supplying information about either the states or the processes in which the actants are involved" (translated from *Sémantique structurale*, p. 122). This dichotomy makes explicit the grammatical opposition between adjective and verb (the third lexical component of discourse, the substantive, is assimilated here to the adjective). Let us note also that the adjectival predicate is given as anterior to the process of denomination, whereas the verbal predicate is seen as contemporaneous with that same process; as Sapir would say, the first is an "existent," the second an "occurrent."

The notion of narrative predicate is also applicable to all the lexemes of a sentence; the only element not included within it is the subject of the narrative proposition (that is, in the simplest case, the character's name) [221ff.]. We can further specify the subclasses of predicates at this level and bring to light the relationships of discursive transformations that exist between them [289ff.].

This examination of predicates has as its limit the framework of the clause. Now, it is possible to adopt instead the framework of a larger narrative unit, the sequence, and to classify the predicates according to the role played by the clauses that contain them. Once again Tomashevskii proposes a dichotomy: "Usually there are different kinds of motifs within a work. By simply retelling the story we immediately discover what may be *omitted* without destroying the coherence of the narrative and what may not be omitted without disturbing the connections among events. The motifs which cannot be omitted are *bound motifs*; those which may be omitted without disturbing the whole causal-chronological course of events are *free motifs*" ("Thematics," p. 68).

R. Barthes has reworked this opposition, calling Tomashevskii's bound motifs **functions** and the free motifs **indices**. The latter are not free in the sense that they could be absent; they simply do not participate in the immediate causal chain and are interconnected at more or less remote points in the text. This is why Barthes speaks of distributional units in the case of the indices and of integrative units in the case of the functions. He further subdivides each of the classes into two: the functions are nucleii, or catalyses; the former "constitute actual hinges of the narrative (of a fragment thereof)" ("An Introduction to the Structural Analyses of Narrative," pp. 247–48), the latter "only 'fill in' the narrative space separating the hinge-type functions" (ibid., p. 249). The indices, in turn, are *indexes* properly speaking, "referring to a personality trait, a feeling, or an atmosphere (e.g., suspicion), a philosophy," or "*bits of information* used to identify or pinpoint certain elements of time and space."

A predicate may be charged with several roles; it may be, for example, at once function (signifying an action in immediate causal relationship with the following action) and index (qualifying a character): the polysemy of syntactic units is the rule rather than the exception.

The predicates may be classified according to other viewpoints, for example, that of genre; the list of constant and variable predicates may then be established. This is the path chosen by J. Bédier and Propp.

● See B. Tomashevskii, "Thematics," in *Russian Formalist Criticism: Four Essays*, ed. L. T. Lemon and M. J. Reis (Lincoln, 1965); V. Propp, *Morphology of the Folktale*, trans. L. Scott (Bloomington, 1958); A.-J. Greimas, *Sémantique structurale* (Paris, 1966); R. Barthes, "An Introduction to the Structural Analysis of Narrative," *New Literary History* 6 (1975): 237–72; T. Todorov, *Grammaire du Décameron* (The Hague, 1969); and G. Prince, *A Grammar of Stories: An Introduction* (The Hague, 1973).

The description of units of thematic analysis is not very well elaborated as yet. The term "motif" is borrowed from the study of folklore, in which it is used, however, in a different sense (see below); here it will designate the minimal thematic unit. Most of the time, the motif coincides with a word present in the text. But it can sometimes correspond to a part (of the meaning) of the word, that is, to a semantic feature; at other times, it corresponds to a syntagma, or a sentence, in which the word by which we designate the motif does not appear.

The motif must be distinguished from the **theme**. This latter notion designates a semantic category that may be present throughout an entire text or even in the whole of literature (the theme of death); motif and theme are thus distinguished above all by their degree of abstraction and consequently by their capacity for denotation. For example, glasses are a motif in Hoffmann's *Princess Brambilla*; vision is one of the themes. It is rare, but not impossible, to find the theme presented also by a word in the text.

When the motif returns frequently in the course of a work and assumes a specific role there, we may speak, by analogy with music, of a **leitmotif** (for example, Vinteuil's little phrase in *A la Recherche du temps perdu*). If several motifs form a stable configuration that returns often in literature (without necessarily being important within a given text), it is designated as a **topos**; this is precisely what is called motif in folklore studies. Certain *topoï* characterize all of Occidental literature, as E. R. Curtius has shown (the world turned upside down, the aged child, and so on); others belong to a literary trend (those of romanticism are particularly well-known). The presence of a given *topos* (or of any motif, generally speaking) in two works does not mean, of course, that the same theme is likewise present in both cases; motifs are polyvalent, and the presence of a theme can be recognized with certainty only after an analysis of the text in its entirety.

In the face of this limited technical apparatus, numerous attempts at substantial, rather than formal, description of thematic units have been made. But here literary analysis touches on one of its greatest difficulties: How can we speak of themes or ideas in literature without reducing their specificity, without making of literature a system of translation? Currently almost all thematic systems are inspired by one psychoanalytical tendency or another: the Jungian theory of archetypes; Bachelard's theory of the material components of the imagination (the four elements); Frye's theory of the natural cycles (the four seasons; the hours of the day); G. Durand's theory of the Occidental myths (Narcissus, Oedipus). These constructions, as ingenious as they are fragile, hold literary specificity in continual jeopardy: seeking to encompass all of literature, they encompass more than literature; on the other hand, to refuse to recognize the existence of thematic elements in the literary text does not solve the problem either. It will be essential to find a way to show the resemblance between literature and the other sign systems while demonstrating at the same time the specific originality of literature; this task remains to be accomplished.

● See W. Kayser, *Das sprachliche Kunstwerk* (Bern, 1948); E. R. Curtius, *European Literature and the Latin Middle Ages*, trans. W. R. Trask (Princeton, 1967); G. Bachelard, *The Poetics of Space*, trans. M. Jolas (New York, 1964); N. Frye, *Anatomy of Criticism* (Princeton, 1957); G. Durand, *Le Décor mythique de la "Chartreuse de Parme": Contribution à l'esthétique du romanesque* (Paris, 1961); R. Girard, *Deceit, Desire and the Novel: Self and Other in Literary Structure*, trans. Y. Freccero (Baltimore and London, 1966); and T. Todorov, *The Fantastic: A Structural Approach to a Literary Genre*, trans. R. Howard (Ithaca, 1975).

CHARACTER

Definition

The category of the character has paradoxically remained one of the most obscure in poetics. One reason for this is doubtless the fact that this notion is of little interest to writers and critics today, in reaction against the total submission to the character that was the rule at the end of the nineteenth century. (Arnold Bennett: "The foundation of good fiction is character creating, and nothing else.")

Another reason for this state of affairs is the presence, in the notion of character, of several different categories. The character cannot be reduced to any one of these but participates in each. Let us enumerate the major ones:

1. *Character and person.* A naive reading of works of fiction confuses characters and living persons. "Biographies" have even been written of characters, going so far as to explore the parts of their lives absent from the book ("How did Hamlet spend his student years?"). It is forgotten in these cases that the problem of the character is first and foremost linguistic, that the character does not exist outside of words, that it is a paper being. However, to reject all relationship between character and person would be absurd: characters *represent* persons, according to modalities appropriate to fiction.

2. *Character and vision.* Twentieth-century criticism has sought to reduce the problem of the character to that of vision [328ff.] or point of view. This confusion is all the easier in that, since Dostoevsky and H. James, the characters are less objective creatures than they are subjective consciousnesses: in place of the stable universe of classical fiction, we find a series of visions, all equally uncertain, that inform us much more about the faculties of perceiving and understanding than about a supposed reality. It remains nonetheless true that the character cannot be reduced to the vision that he himself has of his surroundings and that numerous other devices are necessarily linked to him, even in modern novels.

3. *Character and attributes.* In a structural perspective there is a tendency to equate character and attributes, that is, those of the predicates that are characterized by their staticity [218]. Once again, the relationship between the two is incontestable; however, it is essential, on the one hand, to observe the kinship of the attributes with all the

other predicates (the actions) and, on the other hand, to emphasize the fact that the characters, although endowed with attributes, are not reduced to them.

4. *Character and psychology.* The reduction of the character to psychology is particularly unjustified; this is what has provoked the rejection of the character among twentieth-century writers. To appreciate the arbitrariness of this identification, we have only to think of the characters of ancient, medieval, or Renaissance literature: do we think psychology when we say *Panurge*? The psychology is not in the characters, nor even in the predicates (attributes or actions); it is the effect produced by a certain type of relationship among propositions. A psychic determinism (which varies with time) makes the reader postulate relationships of cause and effect among the various propositions, for example, "*X* is jealous of *Y*," so "*X* is hurting *Y*." The process of making this interpropositional relationship characterizes the "psychological novel"; the same relationship may be present without being explicit. But the character does not necessarily imply an intervention of psychology.

What definition must we give of the term "character" if we wish it to keep its value as a descriptive and structural category? To answer this question, we have to place ourselves within the framework of the propositional analysis of narrative [296]; then we will be able to describe the **character** at several successive levels. Thus:

a) The character is the subject of the narrative proposition. As such, he is reduced to a pure syntactic function, without any semantic content. The attributes, as well as the actions, play the role of predicate in a proposition and are only provisionally linked to a subject. It will be convenient to identify this subject by a proper name that incarnates him in most cases, insofar as the name identifies a spatio-temporal unity without describing its properties (we put into parentheses, for such an identification, the descriptive values of the proper name [see below]). Certain theoreticians of the narrative see more than a syntactic function in the narrative proposition; we would have then, alongside the subject, functions such as *object, beneficiary*, and so on (see below).

b) In a narrower sense, we can call character the set of attributes that have been predicated for the subject in the course of a narrative. This set may or may not be organized; in the former case, several types of organization may be observed. Attributes are combined differently in Boccaccio, in Balzac, and in Dostoevsky. Moreover, this organization may be the object either of explicit indications by the author (the "portrait") or of a series of indications addressed to the reader, who has to accomplish the task of reconstitution; finally, it may be imposed by the reader himself, that is, it may not even be present in the text—

hence the reinterpretation of certain works in function of the dominant cultural codes of a later period.

c) In every representational text, the reader "believes" that the character is a person; this interpretation takes place according to certain rules that are inscribed in the text. One rule (variable according to the period) comes from prevailing conceptions concerning the structure of the personality. Another implies a certain equilibrium of resemblance and difference among the predicated attributes: the actions of a given character must be sufficiently varied to justify mentioning them and sufficiently consistent to allow the character to be recognized; in other words, resemblance is the cost of the character, difference his value. It is of course possible to transgress this equilibrium in one direction or the other: a Sinbad is always varied, a Beckett character always consistent.

● See W. J. Harvey, *Character and the Novel* (Ithaca and London, 1965); R. Barthes, *S/Z*, trans. R. Miller (New York, 1974); and P. Hamon, "Pour un statut sémiologique du personnage," in R. Barthes et al., *Poétique du récit* (Paris, 1976).

Various efforts have been made to constitute typologies of character. Among these attempts we can distinguish those based on purely formal relationships and those that postulate the existence of exemplary characters recurring throughout literary history.

1. *Formal typologies.*

a) Characters who remain unchanged throughout a narrative (static characters) are opposed to those who change (dynamic). It must not be supposed that the former are characteristic of a more primitive narrative form than the latter: they are often encountered in the same works. A particular case of the static character is the one called a **type:** not only do his attributes remain the same, but they are extremely few in number and often represent the highest degree of a quality or a defect (for example, the miser who is only miserly).

b) According to the importance of their role in the narrative, characters may be either major (the **hero,** or **protagonist**) or minor (granted only an episodic function). These are only two extremes, of course, and numerous intermediate cases exist.

c) According to their degree of complexity, the **flat** characters are opposed to the **round.** E. M. Forster, who insisted on this opposition, defined the two types of character as follows: "The test of a round character is whether it is capable of surprising in a convincing way. If it never surprises, it is flat" (*Aspects of the Novel*, p. 78). Such a definition obviously refers to the reader's opinions concerning normal human psychology; a sophisticated reader will be less easily surprised. Depth in characters should rather be defined by the coexistence of contradictory attributes; in this, the "deep" characters resemble the dynamic characters, although in the latter, such attributes are inscribed in time.

d) According to the relationship maintained between the propositions and the plot, we can distinguish between characters subjected to the plot and those who, on the contrary, are served by it. H. James calls those of the first type *ficelles*: they appear only to assume a function in the causal chain of actions. Those of the second type belong to the psychological narrative: the principal aim of the episodes is to spell out the properties of a character (we find fairly pure examples of this in Chekhov).

2. *Substantive typologies.* The most famous of these typologies is found in the *commedia dell'arte*: the characters' roles and personalities (that is, their attributes) are established once and for all (like their names: Harlequin, Pantalone, Colombine); only their actions change according to the occasion. The same constellation of roles, which derives from Latin comedy, reappears in France in the classical period. Later, in the *théâtre du boulevard*, a new typology is created: the leading man, the ingenue, the soubrette, the noble father, the deceived husband, and so on; these are **standard roles** whose traces can still be found today.

This spontaneous typology reaches the level of theory for the first time with Propp: starting with the analysis of Russian fairy tales, he ends by establishing seven "spheres of action": the *villain*, the *donor*, the *helper* of the *sought-for person* and her *father*, the *dispatcher*, the *hero*, and the *false hero*. These spheres of action each combine a precise number of predicates; they correspond, in other words, to **roles.** A role does not necessarily coincide with a character (a proper name); Propp spells out the three possible cases: one role, several characters; one role, one character; several roles, one character.

A similar task was accomplished (some twenty years later) by E. Souriau, working with the theater. Souriau distinguished character from role (which he called dramatic function) and glimpsed the possibility of an irregular distribution of the two classes. His roles are the following: "the *oriented Thematic Force; the Representative of the desired object, of the orienting value; the potential Obtainer of this object* (the one for whom the oriented Thematic Force is working); the *Opponent*; the *Arbiter*, attributor of the good; the *Rescuer*, double of one of the preceding forces" (translated from *Les Deux Cent Mille Situations dramatiques*, p. 117; emphasis added).

A.-J. Greimas has reworked the two preceding analyses, trying to synthesize them; he has also attempted to bring together this role inventory and the syntactic functions in language [209ff.], and, following Tesnière, he has introduced the notion of **actant.** Greimas's actants are as follows:

subject, object, sender, receiver, helper, and *opponent;* the relationships that they maintain form an *actantial model.* The structure of narrative and the syntax of languages (which retains certain of these functions) thus become two manifestations of a single model. Greimas's actants bring to light a difference between Souriau's and Propp's conceptions of roles. Propp identifies each role with a series of predicates; Souriau and Greimas, on the other hand, conceive of roles outside of any relationship with a predicate. In Greimas's system we are led thereby to oppose roles (in Propp's sense) and actants, which are pure syntactic functions (like the term "subject" in our first definition, above).

● See W. J. Harvey, *Character and the Novel* (Ithaca and London, 1965); E. M. Forster, *Aspects of the Novel* (New York, 1927); B. Tomashevskii, "Thematics," in *Russian Formalist Criticism: Four Essays,* ed. L. T. Lemon and M. J. Reis (Lincoln, 1965); V. Propp, *Morphology of the Folktale,* trans. L. Scott (Bloomington, 1958); E. Souriau, *Les Deux Cent Mille Situations dramatiques* (Paris, 1950); and A.-J. Greimas, *Sémantique structurale* (Paris, 1966).

Characters are manifested in several ways. First, they are manifested by the name that announces in advance the properties that will be attributed to a character (for the proper name is only ideally nondescriptive). Here we must distinguish between the allegorical names of the comedies, evocations through milieu, the effect of phonetic symbolism, and so on [255]. Moreover, names either may entertain purely paradigmatic relationships with the character's personality (the name designates the character, such as Sade's Noirceuil) or else may be implicated in the syntagmatic causality of the narrative (the action is determined by the meaning of the name, as in Raymond Roussel's work).

The characterization of an individual, on this basis, follows two possible paths, direct or indirect. The characterization is direct when the narrator tells us that *X* is courageous, generous, and so on; when another person describes *X;* or when the hero describes himself. It is indirect when it is incumbent upon the reader to draw the conclusions, to name the qualities: either on the basis of the actions in which the character is involved, or through the way in which this same character (who may be the narrator) perceives the others. Flaubert systematized the procedure of characterizing an individual by means of a material detail concerning him (characterization through synecdoche).

One special device for characterization is the use of the **emblem:** an object belonging to the character, a way of dressing or speaking, the place where the character lives—these are evoked each time the character is mentioned and thus assume the role of distinctive mark. This is an example of metaphorical use of metonymy: each of these details acquires symbolic value.

- See B. Tomashevskii, "Thematics," in *Russian Formalist Criticism: Four Essays*, ed. L. T. Lemon and M. J. Reis (Lincoln, 1965); R. Scholes and R. Kellogg, *The Nature of Narrative* (New York, 1966); W. J. Harvey, *Character and the Novel* (Ithaca and London, 1965). On the use of proper nouns, see E. Berend, "Die Namengebung bei Jean Paul," *PMLA* 57 (1942): 820–50; E. H. Gordon, *The Naming of Characters in the Works of Dickens*, University of Nebraska Studies in Language, Literature and Criticism (Lincoln, 1917); and C. Veschambre, "Sur les *Impressions d'Afrique*," *Poétique* 1 (1970): 64–78.

GENERATIVE RULES

In the perspective of the Chomskyan school, the total description of a language (that is, of its grammar) includes a generative component, capable of generating all the sentences (strings of morphemes, in the American sense) judged acceptable in that language. (For Chomsky, this generative component is the syntax. Phonology and semantics are, for their part, interpretative: they merely convert the morpheme strings generated by the syntax into representations that are phonetic and semantic, respectively.)

In order to generate the set of strings constituting a language, we shall provide (*a*) a finite set of symbols, an alphabet that includes, in particular, all the morphemes of the language; (*b*) within this set, an initial symbol, the **axiom** (the letter S is conventionally chosen); and (*c*) a set of **rules**, also called **productions**. Each rule describes a certain operation that may be performed on any string of symbols. The first part of the rule indicates the strings on which the operation may be carried out; the second part indicates the result obtained.

We speak of the **generation** of a string of symbols A if:

1. No rule permits us to act further on A (A is then called a **terminal string**).

2. A series $x_0, x_1, \ldots, x_n$ can be constructed in such a way that (*a*) each x_i is a string of alphabetical symbols; (*b*) $x_0 = S$; (*c*) $x_n = A$; (*d*) for each pair x_i, x_{i+1}, there exists a rule allowing us to go from x_i to x_{i+1}.

The multitude of possible rules can be classified in two categories, rewriting rules and transformational rules. (These two expressions have been chosen arbitrarily, and they must be understood in terms of the technical definitions that will be given here, not in terms of their meaning in ordinary language; in the ordinary sense, in fact, every rule effects a transformation on the string to which it is applied, and it ends up furthermore by rewriting that string in some other way.)

1. The **rewrite rules** (*RR*). The general formula of rewriting rules is $A \rightarrow B$ (*A* and *B* each represent a string of symbols possibly reduced to a single symbol). A rule of this type indicates that in every string of which the substring *A* is an integral part, we can replace *A* by *B*. Let us take, for example, *abc* and *ed* for *A* and *B*, respectively. The rule *abc* → *ed* thus gives us the right to construct, on the basis of the string *fgabcd*, the string *fgedd*. It is obvious that such rules make it possible to carry out a great variety of transformations. They allow us to delete symbols, as well as to add them; they even allow us to modify a discontinuous symbol sequence (thus the rule *afb* → *cfd* leads to the replacement of one discontinuous sequence, $a - b$, by another, $c - d$).

An important Chomskyan hypothesis is that the natural languages bring into play only one particular category of rewriting rule, that of the **phrase structure (PS) rules,** or **syntagmatic rules** (through misuse of the terminology these are sometimes confused with the entire class of which they are a subcategory, and they are defined in the same way as the rewriting rules in general). The *PS* rules allow only one, well-defined type of manipulation, which consists in replacing a single symbol of a string by one or several others (on this basis, they represent formally the empirical concept of expansion used in distributional linguistics [32]). As a general formula for the *PS* rules, we have $VXW \rightarrow VYW$, in which *X* is a single alphabetical symbol and *V, Y,* and *W* may be strings of several symbols (*V* and *W* may even possibly be null). Given a string containing the symbol *X*, surrounded by *V* and *W*, the manipulation permitted by a rule of this type consists in replacing *X* with *Y*. Take for example a rule *efag* → *efbcg* (in which *ef* corresponds to the *V* of the general formula, *a* to *X*, *g* to *W*, *bc* to *Y*); it allows us in particular to constitute the string *mnefbcgo* on the basis of the string *mnefago*.

The *PS* rules are divided into two subcategories. On the one hand we have **context-sensitive rules,** defined by the condition that *V* and *W* are not both null; thus they posit that the substitution of *X* for *Y* can only be made in a certain context. On the other hand there are **context-free rules** (*CF*), in which *V* and *W* are null. These rules thus give us the right to replace *X* by *Y* in any string in which we encounter *X*. Chomsky has shown that the distributional description of a language, if it is rigorous, could be translated by a *CF* generative grammar, which would generate all the sentences of the language and those alone.

If a grammar contains only *PS* rules (*CF* or not), the **derivation** of a string (that is, the chain $x_1, x_2, \ldots, x_n$ that links it to *S*) can be represented by a particular type of mathematical graph called a **tree.** Take for example the following set of rules (in which each expression—*NP, VP, ate, the, horse, hay*—must be considered as a single symbol):

$$S \to NP \quad VP$$
$$NP \to Det \quad N$$
$$VP \to V \quad NP$$
$$V \to ate$$
$$Det \to the$$
$$N \to horse$$
$$N \to hay$$

These rules, which may be regarded as a fraction of the generative grammar of English, allow us to generate the terminal string "The horse ate the hay" by constructing the following derivation:

S, NP VP, Det N VP, Det N V NP, Det N V Det N, "the" *N V Det N,* "the horse" *V Det N, . . . ,* "The horse ate the hay." We can represent this derivation by the following figure—which constitutes a tree—if we inscribe under each symbol those that are substituted for it through the application of a rule and connect the substituted symbols to the initial ones by lines:

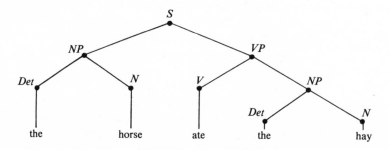

N.B. This tree representation allows us to see the linguistic interpretation to be given to the symbols used in the rules and the derivations. Thus *S*, the axiom, situated at the first stage of the derivation, and therefore at the top of any tree, necessarily dominates the whole of the generated string: it must be interpreted as "sentence" (hence the initial *S*). In the symbol *NP* (noun phrase), the two letters chosen remind us that it always dominates, in the tree, what linguists call a "nominal syntagma" (that is, a noun plus its satellites). And the *VP* (verb phrase), which dominates the predicate of the sentence, in the traditional sense of the term predicate [210], is interpreted as a "verbal syntagma." Similarly, *Det* must be interpreted as "determiner," *N* as "noun," *V* as "verb." It is important to realize, however, that these interpretations, which are not definitions, do not intervene at all in the mechanism of sentence generation, which is purely formal. The mechanism is undoubtedly chosen in view of linguistic interpretation, but once chosen, its application is entirely independent of this interpretation.

A derivation can also be represented by a series of **embedded parentheses** if we write within each parenthesis a segment of the terminal string the elements of which are all attached, directly or indirectly, to the same symbol of the tree (they are said to be dominated by the same node). We would then obtain, for the preceding tree:

$$\Big(\big[\text{(the) (horse)} \big] \quad \big[\text{(ate)} \quad \big(\text{(the) (hay)} \big) \big] \Big)$$

Furthermore, if we index each parenthesis by the symbol that dominates its content in the tree, we produce **labeled parentheses:**

$$\Big(_S \big[_{NP}(_{Det}\text{the}) (_N\text{horse}) \big] \quad \big[_{VP}(_V\text{ate}) \quad \big(_{NP}(_{Det}\text{the}) (_N\text{hay}) \big) \big] \Big)$$

This notation contains, in linear form, all the information that the tree presents in a two-dimensional space. We use this transcription especially when we need to represent only a single level of the tree. We can thus achieve a sort of transverse section in the derivation:

$$\Big(\big[_{NP}\text{the horse} \big] \quad \big[_{VP}\text{ate the hay} \big] \Big)$$

A special case of *CF* rules arises with rules of the type $X \to Y$, in which X is a single symbol and Y is either (*a*) a **terminal symbol** (that is, it is not the left-hand element of any rule) or (*b*) a string constituted by both a terminal symbol and a nonterminal symbol. If the rules of a grammar are all of this type and if, furthermore, in all of those that satisfy condition (*b*), the order of succession of the terminal symbol and the nonterminal symbol is identical, the grammar is called **regular,** a **Kleene's grammar,** a **finite-state grammar,** or a **finite automaton.** The trees then have a characteristic form. Given the following regular grammar

$$S \to aX$$
$$X \to bY$$
$$Y \to cZ$$
$$Z \to d$$

the string *abcd* can be generated according to the following tree:

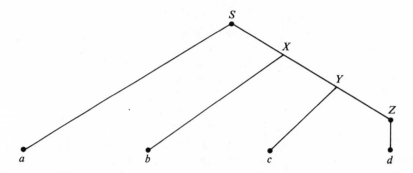

With each application of a rule, we write a symbol of the terminal string, according to the linear order of the string—the first application produces the symbol furthest to the left, the second the following one, and so on (the string would be written from right to left if, in the rules, the terminal symbol were to the right and not to the left of the nonterminal symbol). Chomsky has shown that there exist in English (and in many other languages) certain types of sentences that cannot be generated by this sort of grammar.

In order for a *PS* grammar to generate an infinite number of sentences, while including only a finite number of rules, it is mathematically necessary for certain symbols to be able to dominate themselves in the trees corresponding to the derivations, so that we may have, for example, branches such as those shown below:

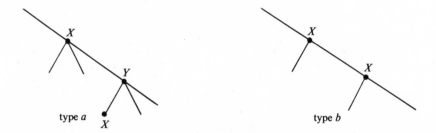

Such symbols—*X* in this case—are called **recursive.** We have direct recursiveness if the symbol is immediately below itself (type *b*), indirect in the other cases (type *a*). Most generativists currently recognize that the only directly recursive symbol is *S* (to be interpreted as "sentence") and that if another symbol is used in an indirectly recursive fashion, an *S* is always present at an intermediate level between these two occurrences. This latter possibility is found in the following branch, which would correspond to the syntagma "the fact that John left" (the two *NP*s are connected by an *S*; *Comp* corresponds to "complementizer"):

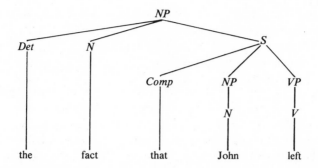

The syntactic complexity of an utterance would thus have as its essential cause the embedding of subordinate sentences (called **constituents**) within a principal sentence (called the **matrix**).

2. The **transformational rules** (*TR* or *T*). A rule is called transformational if its applicability to a string depends not only upon the structure of that string but also upon the way in which that string has been derived (that is, upon its "derivational history"); this was not the case for any of the rules described earlier. The *TR* are thus rules that operate, not on strings, but on trees. To this general definition we must add some clarifications that are not necessarily implied by the notion of *TR* itself, but stem from the actual practice of generative linguistics.

a) Not only do the *TR* start with trees but they also end up with trees (this is because they are used for converting a deep structure into a surface structure [244]).

b) The applicability of a *TR* to a string usually does not depend on the totality of the derivation of the string, but on a single stage. The statement of the *TR* thus need not always specify the total tree of the starting string, but may specify only a particular level of a tree. It is convenient, then, in formulating a *TR*, to fall back upon the notion of **analyzability.** A string X is said to be analyzable into $(a_1, a_2, \ldots, a_n)$, in which the symbols are nonterminal, if we can subdivide X into a series of n successive segments $x_1, x_2, \ldots, x_n$, such that, in the tree representing the derivation of X, at a certain level x_1 is dominated by a_1, x_2 by $a_2, \ldots, x_n$ by a_n. Thus the terminal string "The horse eats the hay" (see p. 228) is analyzable into (*NP, VP*) or into (*Det, N, V, NP*). It is evident that if X is analyzable into $(a_1, a_2, \ldots, a_n)$, there must be at a certain level a representation of X which consists in a series of labeled parentheses, $a_1, a_2, \ldots, a_n$.

Most *TR* can thus be formulated as follows: convert each string $x_1, \ldots, x_n$, analyzable into $(a_1, \ldots, a_n)$, into a string $y_1, \ldots, y_m$, analyzable into $(b_1, \ldots, b_m)$. (N.B. It is possible for n to be equal to m.)

c) To denote the analysis of the strings to which the *TR* is applied, the following notational system is often used:

$$a_1, a_2, \ldots, a_n,$$
$$1 \quad 2 \qquad n$$

in which $a_1, a_2, \ldots, a_n$, are the nonterminal symbols that must dominate the first, second, . . . , nth segments of the string.

d) If certain segments can be indifferently dominated by any node and may even, ultimately, be null, we write, above the numbers that represents them, the variables *X, Y,* and so on. Thus the formula

$$X \quad NP \quad V \quad NP \quad Y$$
$$1 \quad\ 2 \quad\ \ 3 \quad\ 4 \quad\ \ 5 \tag{1}$$

indicates that the *TR* is applied to every string whose analysis includes a nominal syntagma followed by a verb that is followed in turn by a nominal syntagma, independently of what precedes the first nominal syntagma and of what follows the second.

e) We often refrain from indicating the analysis of the string at which we arrive, either because it appears evident or because it can be deduced from general laws indicated elsewhere in the grammar, and we only indicate which segments will constitute it. Those segments that already belong to the initial string are represented by the numbers that they had there; for the others, we indicate the constituent morphemes. Supposing that the starting point of a *TR* for French is given by formula (1), its end point might be, for example:

$$1 \quad\ 2 \quad\ se \quad\ 3 \quad\ 5. \tag{2}$$

This means that the first two segments of the initial string are to be reproduced as is, that the morpheme *se* must then be inserted, the third segment reproduced, the fourth destroyed, and the fifth reproduced. Formulas (1) and (2) thus constitute, very approximately, a description of the *TR* of reflexivization in French. They allow us in fact to pass from

Quelquefois Voltaire contredit Voltaire à deux lignes d'intervalle
$$1 \qquad\ 2 \qquad\ \ 3 \qquad\ \ 4 \qquad\qquad 5$$

("Sometimes Voltaire contradicts Voltaire at two-line intervals") to:

Quelquefois Voltaire se contredit à deux lignes d'intervalle
$$1 \qquad\ 2 \qquad\ 3 \qquad\qquad 5$$

("Sometimes Voltaire contradicts himself at two-line intervals").

f) As the preceding analysis shows, it is sometimes necessary to add to the analysis of initial strings a special condition concerning the lexical form of the morphemes. In order to constitute the *TR* of reflexivization, the two nominal groups must have lexical identity. This condition can be written as 2 = 4. (In practice, to avoid obtaining *un auteur se contredit* ["an author contradicts himself"] on the basis of *un auteur contredit un auteur* ["an author contradicts an author"], it is often required that 2 and 4 refer to the same object. This raises some difficulties: can we say, properly speaking, that *un auteur* refers to anything at all?)

g) Given that the only rewriting rules Chomsky uses are syntagmatic (phrase structure) rules, we shall always fall back upon transformations in order to delete a morpheme (if, for example, we want to generate the structure corresponding to "Bill ate" on the basis of the one corresponding to "Bill ate something"). Similarly, we shall use transformations to deal with the phenomena of discontinuity, for example, to bring to light the morpheme *plural* in three different, noncontiguous places in the French *les animaux mangeront* ("the animals will eat").

Transformational universals. As the definition of the *TR* is not very restrictive, it may seem immediately evident that every language can be described by using *TR*: this would rule out presenting the transformational model as an empirically verifiable hypothesis about the structure of human language. To compensate for this drawback, generatists have sought to reinforce the model by formulating more precise hypotheses on the way in which the *TR* operate (in any language at all). Here, as a sample, is the **tree-pruning rule.** If, after the application of a *TR*, a given node *A* no longer dominates more than a single node, *A* must be deleted. Thus, in the tree below, *A* must be deleted, and *D* must be directly attached to *B*:

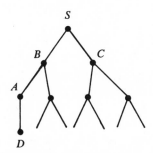

Rule ordering. Whether it is speaking of *PS* rules or of *TR*, a generative grammar must indicate whether the rules may be applied in any order whatsoever or whether a particular order is required. In practice, in generative grammar certain principles seem to impose themselves:

a) The *PS* rules are applied before the *TR*; the latter operate on strings that, from the viewpoint of the *PS* rules, are terminal. This implies (1) that the *TR* are applicable to strings that already correspond to complete sentences; and (2) that the operation of the *PS* rules and that of the *TR* belong to two different levels of the grammar, levels that are interpreted as producing, respectively, the deep structure and the surface structure [244] of utterances.

b) It is frequently the case that no order is *explicitly* imposed on the *PS* rules (but even in this case a certain order may in fact be necessary, for we may lack the opportunity to apply a given rule until we have first applied some other one).

c) Generally speaking, there is an explicit order for the *TR*.

d) Many authors presently classify the *TR* in two groups; each group is ordered, and they operate one after the other.

e) The first group constitutes a **transformational cycle.** Let us suppose, for example, that it consists of the three *TR A, B,* and *C* (so ordered). Let us further suppose that the application of the *PS* rules has produced the tree sketched below, in which a secondary sentence S_2 is embedded within the principal sentence S_1 (the numbers attached to *S* would not appear in the grammar itself; they serve only to simplify the presentation which follows):

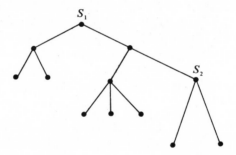

If *A, B,* and *C* form a cycle, all three must first be applied to S_2 (thus we apply *A* to S_2, then *B* to the resulting output, then *C* to the new resulting output, then *A* again, . . . , until S_2 no longer allows for any of these transformations). Then *A, B,* and *C* are applied in the same way to S_1. The *TR* of a cycle are thus first each applied in turn to the lowest level of the tree, then to the immediately higher lever, and so forth.

f) The second group of *TR*s has a **linear** mode of application. If *A, B,* and *C* form such a group, we first apply *A* to S_2, then to S_1, then similarly *B*, and finally *C*. The *TR* of a non-cyclic group thus operate one after another, according to their own order, each one exhausting all the possibilities of application offered by the sentence at the time it is applied. It has been shown that very different results are obtained according to whether the same transformations operate cyclically or in linear fashion.

The following diagram summarizes the classification proposed for the generative rules:

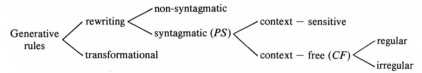

- On the technical apparatus of generative grammar, see N. Chomsky, "Three Models for the Description of Language," in *Readings in Mathematical Psychology*, ed. R. D. Luce, R. R. Busch, and E. Galanter (New York, 1965), vol. 2; M. Gross and A. Lentin, *Introduction to Formal Grammars*, trans. M. Sakoff (New York, 1970); and G. Fauconnier, "La Grammaire générative; La description d'un mécanisme," in *Comprendre la linguistique*, ed. B. Pottier (Verviers, Belgium, 1975), chap. 8. The tree-pruning rule is proposed by J. R. Ross, in *A Proposed Rule of Tree-Pruning*, Harvard Computation Laboratory, National Science Foundation Report 17 (Cambridge, Mass., 1966). For examples of the application of cyclic transformations in syntax, see J. R. Ross, "On the Cyclic Nature of Pronominalization," in D. Reibel and S. Schane, ed., *Modern Studies in English* (Englewood Cliffs, 1969), pp. 187–200; and R. S. Kayne, *French Syntax: The Transformational Cycle* (Cambridge, Mass., 1975). On the technical problems posed by the detailed justification of a rule, see P. M. Postal, *On Raising* (Cambridge, Mass., 1974).

SURFACE STRUCTURES AND DEEP STRUCTURES

Generative linguistics was the first to grant the status of technical term to the expressions "surface structure" and "deep structure." The notions covered by these expressions, however, may be regarded as coextensive with reflection on linguistics. They are connected in fact with the feeling—with the astonishment, one might say—in which this reflection originates, a feeling that there is no correspondence between the perceptible form of utterances and their real function: utterances that are apparently perfectly analogous may in fact be very different, and vice versa. Hence the idea that the underlying function of utterances cannot be read in their visible make-up, but only in an underlying organization: what is apparent is only superficial.

Synonymy and Homonymy

The phenomena of homonymy and synonymy constitute the most spectacular forms of this divergence. Two expressions (words, groups of words, utterances) are called **synonymous** if they have the same meaning, even though they are materially different. To be sure, the intervention of the notion of meaning prevents for the moment (and may always prevent) a rigorous definition of synonymy. Is there synonymy between "pediatrician" and the expression "children's doctor," between "I shall come after you leave" and "You will leave before I come," between "Go away!" and "Clear out!"? The question is far from resolved (see below, pp. 287ff.). However, the uncertainties do not affect our feeling that there is a semantic proximity between certain sentences that does not exist between others and that this proximity is rarely apparent in the material constitution of these sentences. For speaking subjects to be able to sense this, they must possess some representation of sentences very different from the one that constitutes their perceptible appearance. Whether "pediatrician" and "children's doctor" are synonymous or not, it is certain that at some moment of their interpretation, there come into play identical elements that have no counterpart in the material nature of the words themselves.

An analogous paradox arises with the phenomena of **ambiguity** or **homonymy:** radically different meanings may correspond to a single phonic reality (*post* may signify a stake of wood, a military base, a mail delivery system; "he made Bill *cross*" may mean that someone forced Bill to cross the street, that someone made Bill ill-tempered; and so on). In order to discover what may be problematic in homonymy, this phenomenon must be distinguished from ones that are similar, but different in nature; for example, from **contextual determination,** which stems from the fact that the situations in which an expression is used may inflect its meaning in different directions. "This store *is open Mondays*" will be interpreted to mean that the store is open even on Mondays (if Monday is a day when stores are usually closed); in other situations it will be understood to mean that the store is open only on Mondays. We do not speak of homonymy here, for the different meanings have a common core (that is, that the store is open on Mondays) to which the situation adds an element of overdetermination. Furthermore, we shall speak of **polysemy** rather than of ambiguity when relatively general laws allow passage from one meaning to another and allow us to foresee the variation. Thus we understand, through the rhetorical figure of metonymy [278], that the word *violin* designates sometimes the musical instrument, sometimes the musician. (N.B. In practice, there are borderline cases: the figure that connects the meanings may not be [or may no longer be] perceived as such. Is there homonymy or polysemy if *bureau* designates both a piece of furniture and an administrative office?) Ambiguity must also be distinguished from semantic **extension:** most expressions have a very general signification that allows them to describe very different situations. But the word *vehicle* is not considered ambiguous just because it can be used for a bicycle as well as a truck, nor the verb *to love*, on the grounds that one can love one's father and love jam. In these examples, in fact, a general meaning seems common to all the uses of the same expression; it is simply a very broad and abstract meaning. The same thing can be said when this abstraction becomes **indeterminacy** (the English philosophers speak of **vagueness**). Many expressions not only describe very different situations but leave unresolved, in certain cases, the problem of whether or not they should be used: in innumerable borderline cases we can neither deny nor affirm that someone is bald, happy, successful, and so on. But this undecidability in borderline cases does not preclude the existence of cases that allow the unequivocal characterization of an expression within a certain sphere.

● On ambiguity, see D. François and F. François, "L'Ambiguïté linguistique," *Word* 23 (1967): 150–79; and H. Weydt, "Le Concept d'ambiguïté en grammaire transformationnelle et en linguistique fonctionnelle," *La Linguistique* 8 (1972): 41–72. On the notion of vagueness, see M. Black, "Vagueness: An Exercise in Logical Analysis," *Language and Philosophy* (Ithaca, 1949), pp. 23–58; and G. Lakoff, "Hedges: A Study in Meaning Criteria and the Logic of Fuzzy Concepts," *Journal of Philosophical Logic* 2 (1973: 459–506. Y. Gentilhomme has defined mathematically the notion of **fuzzy set** (in French, *ensemble flou*), making it possible to describe the zone of application of these vague notions, in "Les Ensembles flous en linguistique," *Cahiers de linguistique théorique et appliquée* (Bucharest, 1968), pp. 47–65.

To conclude this list of pseudo-ambiguities, let us finally point out what might be called **oppositional signification.** Given that there are small elephants, as well as small microbes, we might declare that the adjective *small* is ambiguous. But we shall not do so if we recognize, with Saussure, that linguistic reality does not lie in the term itself but rather in the opposition of terms [19] and if we note that the opposition "small elephant" / "large elephant" is analogous to the opposition "small microbe" / "large microbe." What interests the linguist is the opposition *small / large*, which is not ambiguous.

● An analogous problem is examined by P. T. Geach in "Good and Evil," *Analysis* 17 (1957): 33–42.

Contrary to the situations pointed out above, authentic homonymy, or ambiguity, supposes that between the different meanings of the same expression there is neither a common core nor even continuity; this makes it impossible either to explain any one by the others or to derive them all from one basic signification. Consequently, if an ambiguous expression has the two meanings *a* and *b*, its use in sense *a* and its use in sense *b* correspond to two choices that are as distinct as if two different expressions were involved. This makes the divergence between the appearance and the reality of language all the more flagrant. Choices that in reality have nothing in common lead us, on the surface, to choose the same expression.

Descriptive Level

The intuition of this divergence is doubtless at the origin of a belief that is as old as linguistics: namely, that in order to describe an utterance, we must place ourselves, successively, at different **levels** (in French, *niveaux*; in German, *Ebenen*). In other words, the linguist has to give several distinct representations for each utterance, and these representations must be hierarchically arranged according to their greater or lesser depth. This idea is institutionalized, in a sense, in our distinction, within linguistic description, of several components [51ff.] each of which has the function of supplying representations of utterances at a specific level.

It is possible in fact to justify the existence and the independence of the various levels on the basis of the phenomenon of ambiguity. Let us suppose that at a level L_1 we have a single representation for an utterance U_1 perceived as ambiguous; we can see that we have to construct another level L_2 that gives as many representations to the utterance as it has meanings. And in the case that neither the rules of L_1 nor those of L_2 attribute to another utterance U_2 as many representations as it has meanings, we shall construct L_3, and so on.

Let us take for L_1 a phonetic representation, that is, a representation according to which a sequence of phonetic symbols corresponds to each utterance; this will give only one representation for U_1, "He made me cross." Hence the necessity of constructing L_2, which represents the utterance as a sequence of words (or morphemes), while indicating the parts of speech to which the words belong (or the nature of the morphemes). Now let us take U_2, "He killed the man with the gun." Its ambiguity is not representable in L_2, since whatever its meaning, U_2 is still composed of the same words (or morphemes). We must thus imagine L_3, which takes into consideration the syntactic functions [209ff.] and gives two representations for U_2, one in which *with the gun* is adjectival in function, the other in which it is adverbial. In order to demonstrate the existence of a supplementary level, L_4, we have only to think of a conversation such as "John loves his wife." "So do I." It seems that the ambiguity of "So do I" cannot be attributed to a difference in syntactic function. It has its source rather in the logico-semantic organization of the utterance "John loves his wife," which is double, according to whether we attribute to John the property "to love John's wife" or "to love one's own wife." Not only does the phenomenon of homonymy require us then to distinguish between the apparent and the real value of utterances, but it requires us to institute between these two extremes a whole series of intermediate levels (the four preceding ones are only examples).

Syntactic Transformation

Is it necessary to distinguish different levels even within the type of description generally regarded as syntactic? In other words, must an utterance be given several superposed syntactic representations? Many linguists answer in the affirmative, although they often start with quite dissimilar preoccupations. We find an affirmative answer, for example, among certain grammarians concerned with defining the possible syntactic functions within an utterance. Compare, in French, *la maison paternelle* ("the family home"), *la maison du père* ("the father's house"), and *la maison qui appartient au père* ("the house that belongs to the father"). In spite of their patent differences, *paternelle, du père,* and *qui appartient au père* seem in fact to play the same role in the sentence, namely, that of determining the substantive *maison*. It was in order to represent the possible functional analogy between expressions that are very different in other respects that Bally defined the notion of **functional exchange,** or **transposition,** and Tesnière defined the very similar notion of **translation.** These terms designate procedures that in some way change the syntactic nature of words or word groups. Thus, for Tesnière, a translation would give the adjectival function (symbolized by A) to the proposition *elle appartient au père.* The underlying analogy between *paternelle* and *qui appartient au père* and, at the same time, their superficial difference would thus be represented by schemas (stemmas [212ff.]) such as the following:

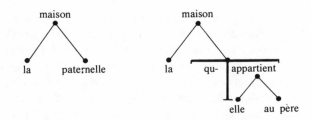

The *T* of the right-hand schema indicates that there has been a translation and that, in this case, we have to distinguish between *elle appartient au père*, which is the **transferend,** and *qu-,* which is the **translative.** Although Tesnière's schemas represent both fundamental syntactic dependencies and translations, the two concepts have, for him, an entirely different status and correspond to two distinct descriptive levels. This duality appears in the very organization of Tesnière's book, which treats first the elementary syntactic functions, defined independently of the fact that they are fulfilled by single words or by transferred complex expressions, and then the different possible types of translation.

● See L. Tesnière, *Eléments de syntaxe structurale* (Paris, 1965), pt. 3. On the relationships between this theory and generative grammar, see P. Guiraud, "Lucien Tesnière and Transformational Grammar," *Language Sciences* 15 (1971): 1–6. For C. Bally's similar conception, see *Linguistique générale et linguistique française*, 4th ed., rev. (Bern, 1965), secs. 179–96.

An analogous but more prudent conception can be found in O. Jespersen (*Analytic Syntax* [Copenhagen, 1937], chap. 35). Comparing word groups that he calls **junctions** (for example, "the furiously barking dog") and utterances that he calls **nexus** (for example, "the dog barked furiously"), he notes that the same hierarchy can be found in both: in the two preceding examples, *dog* is always the principal term, on which *barking* (or *barked*) depends; *furiously* in turn depends on this latter term. Jespersen expresses this by assigning, in both cases, **rank** 1 to *dog,* rank 2 to *barking* (or *barked*), rank 3 to *furiously*. But he does not go so far as to conclude from this possible invariance of rank in the nexus and the junctions that the latter would be derived from the former, or vice versa.

It is remarkable that certain distributional linguists [31ff.] have arrived at similar results. Their starting point is in fact entirely different, since they reject the notion of function as intuitive and finalist and are interested above all in the combinatorial possibilities of elements within utterances. But a combinatorial study may lead us to group in classes not only the elements that have identical combinatorial properties but also types of construction, of sentence structures, that are capable of being filled by the same elements. This is why Z. S. Harris, whose earliest work grew out of a distributionalism that could be called atomistic (since it had the elements of the language as its object), arrived at a structural distributionalism that led him to the notion of **transformation.** Take for example the two sentence schemas (*a*) *Noun*₁ *Verb Noun*₂ and (*b*) *Noun*₂ is *Verb by Noun*₁. We can construct an entirely acceptable sentence ("The wolf eats the lamb") on the basis of (*a*) by replacing *Noun*₁ by *The wolf*, *Verb* by *eats*, and *Noun*₂ by *the lamb*. If we make the same substitutions in (*b*), we obtain another acceptable sentence (with the adjustment of a few details): "The lamb is eaten by the wolf." Let us now make in (*a*) a substitution such that the sentence obtained will be much less acceptable (for example, "The table respects Peter"). The result of this same substitution in (*b*) will be just as unacceptable ("Peter is respected by the table"). Even more generally, if a substitution S_1, operated in (*a*), gives a more acceptable result than another substitution S_2, the result of S_1 in (*b*) will be more acceptable than that of S_2. It is this equivalence of two structures in terms of the degree of acceptability of the substitutions that defines, for Harris, the transformations between structures. We can now say that two sentences are transformations of each other if (1) their underlying structures are transformations of each other and (2) they are obtained by the same substitution. Thus there is transformation between an utterance in the active voice and the corresponding passive utterance, between a sentence and its nominalizations [208], and so on. (N.B. The translation that served as the example in Tesnière's presentation would be described by Harris as a transformation, or rather as an amalgam of several transformations. The usefulness of this notion of transformation is readily apparent. It allows us to show schematically, on the basis of strictly distributional considerations, that syntactic structures that at first appear very different may have an underlying kinship. It thereby becomes possible to use linguistics in **content analysis.** The latter aims in fact at defining mechanical, or mechanizable, procedures that permit the discovery of the organizational structures of relatively large texts. To achieve this aim, one must be able to recognize the diverse occurrences of a single idea in divergent forms. By permitting linguists to go beyond the literal appearance of the text, the notion of transformation increases the power they bring to the task of discourse analysis.)

● Harris defines transformations in "Co-occurrence and Transformation in Linguistic Structure," *Language* 33 (1957): 283–340, and in various articles reprinted in his *Papers in Structural and Transformational Linguistics* (Dordrecht, 1970). For a formalization of this notion, see H. Hiż, "Congrammaticality, Batteries of Transformations, and Grammatical Categories," in *Structure of Language and Its Mathematical Aspects*, .ed. R. Jakobson (Providence, 1961), pp. 43–50. Harris's notion of transformation is applied to the study of French by M. Gross in *Grammaire transformationnelle du français: Syntaxe du verbe* (Paris, 1968), and in *Méthodes en syntaxe* (Paris, 1975). In *String Analysis* (The Hague, 1962), Harris explicitly presents transformational analysis as the discovery of a syntactic *level* that is superimposed in particular on the distributional level (see, for example, par. 1.3).

Transformations in Generative Grammar

(N.B. In what follows, *sentence* shall be understood, not as a sequence of sounds, phonemes, or letters, but as a string of meaningful units analogous to Martinet's monemes [201] or to the morphemes of American linguistics [200]; the perceptible manifestation of these units will be excluded from consideration. We shall thus consider as a sentence the string *definite article-house-present-be-beautiful,* corresponding to "the house is beautiful.")

In order to understand the role of the notions of **transformation** and of deep syntactic structure in generative grammar as it stands today, we must reintegrate them into the evolution of that theory. Chomsky's first work (*Syntactic Structures* [The Hague, 1957]), while it introduced transformations, did not speak of deep structure. It distinguished between two moments in the syntactic generation of a sentence:

In the first, syntagmatic rules, or *PS* rules [227], come into play; these rules, through successive derivations, generate a sequence of morphemes known as a **kernel string.** Associated with this string is the tree [228ff.] that represents the process according to which the string has been generated; this association makes possible the string's decomposition into embedded substrings and thus allows us to attribute to it an immediate constituent structure [32]. However, the strings generated in this way are not sentences of the language described (even in the already abstract sense in which *sentence* is used here). Chomsky thought he could show, in fact, that even if it were possible to generate the sentences of a language directly by means of *PS* rules, there would be serious drawbacks.

1. The generative grammar obtained would not be able to represent the underlying kinship between sentences organized in apparently very dissimilar ways (for example, between *Peter-present-love-Paul* and *Paul-present-be-love-en* [past participle]-*by-Peter*). In fact, if we had only *PS* rules, the generative processes leading to these sentences would be very different: they would have almost nothing in common but their first stage; from the second stage on, they would diverge. (N.B. To conclude from this that a *PS* grammar could not represent the proximity

existing between these two sentences is to suppose that the proximity of two sentences has as its *only* possible representation in a generative grammar the fact that their derivations are, at the outset and during a certain number of stages, identical—in other words, that their trees overlap in part; this is a strong hypothesis, for at first glance we can imagine many other modes of representation.) Conversely, many ambiguous expressions, such as "the fear of the policeman," could only be generated, according to Chomsky, in a single way in an exclusively *PS* grammar.

2. As a corollary of this first inadequacy, a *PS* grammar would be redundant. If, for example, the active sentence and its corresponding passive sentence are generated independently of each other, we have to state two distinct rules to say, for example, (*a*) that the name of an inanimate being may not be the subject of the verb *to see* and (*b*) that it may not be the agent of the passive verb *to be seen*. Now it is intuitively clear that we are dealing here with a single phenomenon. (N.B. This argument supposes that we are describing *in the syntax* the distributional restrictions in question; now this is a decision—perhaps a correct one— that must be justified.)

In order to reduce these disadvantages of a uniquely *PS* grammar, Chomsky distinguishes a second moment in sentence generation, that is, a second syntactic level in generative grammar. After the *PS* rules (which do not generate sentences, but kernel strings), rules of an entirely different type come into play, namely, transformational rules [231ff.], which transform these strings into sentences. We can thus imagine that the same kernel string, since it is subject to two different transformations, gives either the active or the passive sentence; this allows us on the one hand to represent the proximity of the kernel strings and on the other hand to formulate at a single point (the one at which the strings are generated) the distributional restrictions that are valid for both the active and the passive. We are thus led to consider two types of transformations: (1) **obligatory transformations,** to which every kernel string must be submitted in order to become an acceptable grammatical sentence (thus a **reflexivization transformation** creates, from the kernel string *John-present-detest-John*, the sentence *John-present-detest-himself*); and (2) **optional transformations,** which are not needed to obtain a sentence and thus correspond to a choice on the part of the speaker: most of these add semantic indications not included in the kernel string. The optional transformations are divided into two classes: (*a*) **singular transformations,** which have as their starting point a single string (for example, passivization, the transformations that introduce interrogation or negation, and so on); and (*b*) **generalized transforma-**

tions, which amalgamate several kernel strings into a single string (for example, nominalization [208]: starting with two strings, it transforms one into a noun, which is then introduced, as subject or complement, into the second). (N.B. Sentences that have not undergone optional transformations are called **kernel sentences.**)

With Chomsky's second major work (*Aspects of the Theory of Syntax*), a considerable modification was introduced into the economy of the doctrine, a modification connected with the idea of deep structure. In the wake of the work of E. S. Klima, in particular, it appeared useful to abandon the idea of optional transformations. Thus two different kernel strings are given for an active sentence and its corresponding passive, in such a way that the difference between the strings is less marked than in their surface organization, since it is reduced to the presence of a particular symbol within the string corresponding to the passive. Obligatory transformations, then, acting on these two strings, which are different even though analogous, would produce two sentences that are distinctly different in organization. In the same way, symbols of interrogation and negation would be introduced at the level of the kernel strings. The optional generalized transformations are also abandoned. Let us take, for example, the nominalization "John's leaving satisfies me." It will have only one kernel string, approximately: *it-John's-ing-leave-present-satisfy-me*. Its generation according to the *PS* rules will thus be a single process, representable by a single tree (which will include, as a subtree, the tree corresponding to *John's-ing-leave*). The transformations will then come into play only to delete *it* and to reorder and combine the initial elements, producing the sentence "John's leaving satisfies me."

Discarding the optional transformations—the only ones with semantic content—necessitates in turn an overall reworking of the doctrine. Transformations are henceforth semantically neutral; thus all elements with semantic value will be introduced at the point of sentence generation by the *PS* rules. If two sentences are identical at the level of these rules, they must be synonymous, and if a sentence is ambiguous, it is at the level of these rules that it must have two different derivations (perhaps even two different kernel strings). We can therefore say that the kernel string and the tree representing its derivation constitute, for each sentence, its **deep structure** and that the transformations, reduced to simple mechanisms, produce only a **surface structure.** (If we hypothesize that the *PS* rules are identical for all languages—languages would then differ only in the lexicon and the transformations—we arrive at the idea that the deep structure of language manifests a linguistic faculty innate in man.) The two structures produced by the syntactic component will have in effect very different functions: the deep structure serves as an entry to the semantic component [54], which brings into correspondence with it a phonetic description. From this we get the following schema:

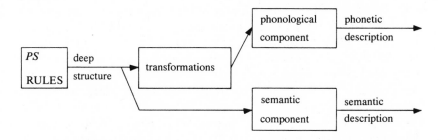

This schema can be compared with the one that would represent Chomsky's first theory; the latter would take one of two forms, according to whether the derivation of a sentence does or does not undergo optional transformations. Thus:

1. For kernel sentences

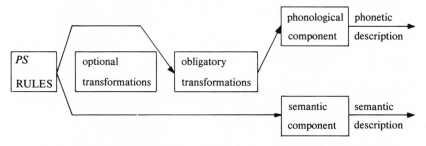

2. For complex sentences

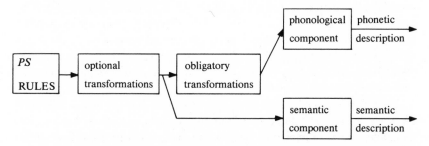

- On the second Chomskyan theory, see N. Chomsky, *Aspects of the Theory of Syntax* (Cambridge, Mass., 1965); J. J. Katz and P. M. Postal, *An Integrated Theory of Linguistic Description* (Cambridge, Mass., 1964); and N. Ruwet, *An Introduction to Generative Grammar*, trans.

N. S. H. Smith (Amsterdam, 1973), chap. 6. For E. S. Klima's contribution, see especially his "Negation in English," in *The Structure of Language*, ed. J. A. Fodor and J. J. Katz (Englewood Cliffs, 1964).

This harmonious construction has very rapidly proved incompatible, however, with a considerable number of facts (pointed out, and in some cases discovered, by the Chomskyans themselves). In particular, it has become clear that certain modes of expression whose semantic value is incontestable seem to need to be introduced by transformations (this is the case for intonation, which may give the sentence "I won't be the first president to lose a war" two very different meanings and seems, however, to be a typical transformational phenomenon; the same is true for word order, which, like intonation, often plays a decisive part in determining the presuppositions [272] of an utterance [compare, for example, "I saw Bill" and "It was Bill that I saw"]). In the face of facts of this sort, three solutions are possible:

a) We may say that the semantic differences in question concern not the true meaning of an utterance but the pragmatic value [338]. This supposes a dichotomy between the meaning of an utterance and the speech acts that it allows us to accomplish.

b) We may admit that transformations can modify meaning (this is the solution finally adopted by Chomsky). But then the expression "deep structure" loses part of its intuitive content (in which *deep* would be synonymous with *semantic*).

● This solution has led to the development of a third Chomskyan theory, the "extended standard theory"; M. Ronat, ed., *Langue, théorie générative étendue* (Paris, 1977), includes an article by Chomsky, "Introduction à la théorie standard étendue," which has not yet appeared in English.

c) We may decide to introduce into the base constituent (*PS* and lexical rules) everything that has a semantic implication, even if we have no syntactic justification for this. This is the solution adopted by the proponents of generative semantics [56]. Generative semantics thus rejoins certain discourse-analysis research, which aims at constituting a semantic metalanguage in which all the meanings borne by the language might be translated: the deep structure of a sentence would then be its translation into this metalanguage.

If we choose the third solution, we are certainly not led to abandon the idea—which is related to all linguistic research—that there are in language, and even in syntax, deeper and more superficial aspects; but we are led to relativize this distinction (the choice of a linguistic structure may or may not have semantic implications, depending on the intentions of the user of language). Thus the frontiers between surface structure and deep structure may well depend largely on the point of view chosen by the person describing them. The same problem arises for discourse-analysis. Is it sufficient to construct a single metalanguage, or is it necessary to construct several, each devoted to one particular aspect of meaning (one for the expression of logical relationships, another for the expression of affective values, and so on)?

● On the passage from deep syntax to semantic translation, see I. Bellert, "A Semantic Approach to Grammar Construction," in *To Honor Roman Jakobson* (The Hague, 1967), pp. 165–73. On discourse analysis, see M. Pêcheux, *Vers l'analyse automatique du discours* (Paris, 1969); and idem, ed. *Langages* 37 (1975): *Analyse du discours, langue et idéologie.* Pêcheux develops the theoretical presuppositions of his analysis in *Les Vérités de la Palice* (Paris, 1975). Examples of the analysis of political discourse can be found in *Langages* 23 (1971) and 41 (1976). See also R. Robin, *Histoire et linguistique* (Paris, 1973).

REFERENCE

Since linguistic communication often has extra-linguistic reality as its object, speakers have to be able to designate the objects that constitute this reality; this is the **referential function** of language (the object or objects designated by an expression form its referent). This reality is not necessarily, however, *the* reality, *the* world. The natural languages in fact have the power to construct the universe to which they refer; they can thus give themselves an imaginary **discursive universe.** Treasure Island and Grand Central Station are possible objects of reference.

Philosophers, linguists, and logicians have often insisted on the necessity of distinguishing the referent [101] of a sign and its signified [100] (or meaning). Thus Saussure stresses that the sign connects "not a thing and a name, but a concept and a sound-image" (*Course in General Linguistics*, trans. W. Baskin [New York, 1959], p. 66). The signified of *horse* is thus neither a horse nor all horses, but the concept "horse." Saussure even specifies a bit later that those concepts that constitute the signifieds are "purely differential and defined not by their positive content but negatively by their relations with the other terms of the system. Their most precise characteristic is in being what the others are not" (ibid., p. 117). In the signified of a sign we thus find only the distinctive features that distinguish it from the other signs of the language, and not a complete description of the objects that it designates. Thus the signified of *mutt* will include a pejorative feature (by virtue of which *mutt* is opposed to *dog*), even though this feature has no existence in the referent itself. Conversely, many of the referent's properties have no place in the signified, for they do not come into play in the classifications inherent in the language: thus, to take the Aristotelian example, the signified of *man* doubtless does not include the feature *without feathers*, since it happens that the natural classification incorporated into English does not oppose *man* and *bird* within the category *biped*, but *man* and *beast* within the category *animal*.

Philosophers of language such as P. F. Strawson have arrived at the sáme conclusion, but for different reasons. They note, for example, that, rigorously speaking, meaning and reference may not even be attributed to the same linguistic reality. When we speak of a sign, it is always necessary in fact to specify whether we are speaking of a particular occurrence of this sign—that is, of the unique event that was its use by a certain person at a given moment in space and time (sign token)— or of the sign considered in itself, independently of the fact that it is or is not utilized (sign type). The sign in itself generally has no assignable referent. (To what do the signs *I, you, that boy, John, the car coming up the hill* refer?) With a few exceptions, it is only the sign token— the use of the sign by a specific speaker in specific circumstances—that has referential value. As for the sign itself, we can only give it a "meaning." What do we call "to understand the meaning of a sign"? This is tantamount to possessing a method for determining to what each occurrence of the sign refers (to know the meaning of *I* is to be capable of knowing, when a person says *I*, to whom that person is referring). There is an obvious relationship between this definition of meaning as the mode of determination of the referent and the Saussurian definition of the signified, which regards the latter as a set of distinctive features, that is, finally, as the system of criteria maintained by the language in order to discriminate a certain type of object among all things existing in reality.

The Saussurian opposition of signified and referent recalls as well certain distinctions that logicians have used in different periods. As early as the Middle Ages, for example, the terminist school (Peter of Spain and Albert of Saxony, among others) made a radical distinction between two possible relationships between the word and nonlinguistic reality:

a) There is a relationship of "signification" (**significatio**) between words and the intellectual representations (in Latin, *res*) that correspond to them: thus *white* signifies the idea of whiteness, and *man*, that of humanity.

b) The term "supposition" (**suppositio**) refers to the relationship that unites the word with the exterior object (in Latin, *aliquid*) that it serves to designate. Thus the possibility of supposition belongs only to certain words, the substantives (*Socrates, man*); adjectives and verbs are excluded, even though these all possess meaning.

The analogy with Saussure is clear when certain authors specify (see Peter of Spain, *Traité des suppositions,* lines 30–35) that signification precedes supposition and that it is never the material reality of the word (*vox*) that possesses a supposition, but the term, that is, the whole constituted by the *vox* and what it signifies.

About six hundred years later, the German logician G. Frege established an analogous distinction between the referent of a sign (**Bedeutung**) and its meaning (**Sinn**). Frege's initial problem is the following. By definition, if two objects are identical, everything that is true of one is true of the other. Thus, if Faulkner wrote *The Sound and the Fury,* it must also be true that the author of *Sartoris* wrote *The Sound and the Fury.* Or again, if the morning star is smaller than the earth, it must also be true that the evening star is smaller than the earth, since the morning star and the evening star constitute a single object, the planet Venus. But there exist certain contexts (called "oblique" or "opaque") in which we cannot substitute *evening star* for *morning star* without running the risk of modifying the truth value of the proposition. Thus "Peter knows that Venus is the morning star" may be true even when "Peter knows that Venus is the evening star" is false. To resolve this paradox, Frege distinguishes the referent of an expression, that is, the object that the expression designates, from its meaning, that is, from the way in which it designates this object, from the information that it gives about the object in order to allow it to be located. *Morning star, evening star,* and *Venus* thus have a common referent but different meanings. We can then define **oblique** (or **opaque**) **contexts** as those in which the substitution of two terms with identical referent and different meaning may involve a change in truth value; and this happens because in these contexts the meaning of the expressions is in question, not their referent. The similarity between the opposition *meaning / referent* and the Saussurian opposition *signified / referent* becomes striking when we know that for Frege, knowledge of the meaning of an expression is part of the knowledge of the language (which is not the case for knowledge of the referent). (N.B. The *meaning-referent* opposition does not coincide with the *comprehension-extension* opposition of formal logic. The extension of a term is the set of objects that it designates; its comprehension is the set of features common to all these objects. Fregian *meaning*—or the Saussurian *signified*—retains only those features of comprehension that serve, *in the language used*, conventionally to locate the referent.)

● On the opposition of meaning and referent, see P. F. Strawson, "On Referring," *Mind* 59 (1950): 320–44; and G. Frege, "Über Sinn und Bedeutung," *Zeitschrift für Philosophie und philosophische Kritik* 100 (1892): 25–50. Frege's thesis is outlined and discussed in detail in L. Linsky, *Referring* (London, 1967). The medieval theory of supposition is presented, for example, by P. Bühner in *Medieval Logic* (Manchester, Chicagó, and Toronto, 1952), pt. 2, chap. 2.

What means for referring to objects are provided by a language?

Definite descriptions. By "definite descriptions" is meant, following Bertrand Russell, expressions including a nominal form (noun, noun plus adjective, noun plus relative, noun plus complement, and so on) accompanied by a definite article ("the book," "the book that I bought," and so on). Even without changing this definition, we can include nominals introduced by a possessive in the category, by interpreting "my book" as "the book that is mine." The meaning of expressions of this sort can be read in the nominal form, which gives a description of the referent. The use of a definite description is considered abnormal if there exists no object satisfying the description ("the current king of France") or if several exist (in an utterance such as "The train has just left," the uniqueness of the object is assured by a situational implication: "the train you are talking about" or "the train that we are supposed to take"). If we recognize that the existence of the object is presupposed [272] by the use of a definite description, we understand that such descriptions serve frequently to present some imaginary discursive universe (for example, at the beginning of a science fiction novel: "The inhabitants of Mars were celebrating the departure of their third terrestrial rocket").

● The problem of definite descriptions is discussed most notably by B. Russell in "On Denoting," *Mind*, n.s. 14 (1905): 478–93; and by P. F. Strawson in "On Referring," cited above, and in "Identifying Reference and Truth-Values," *Theoria* 30 (1964): 96–118. On the relationship between definite descriptions and reference, see K. Donnellan, "Reference and Definite Descriptions," *Philosophical Review* 75 (1966): 281–304; J. R. Searle, *Speech Acts* (London, 1969), chaps. 4 and 7; and O. Ducrot, *Dire et ne pas dire* (Paris, 1972), chap. 8.

Proper nouns. Grammarians use the term "proper nouns" for nouns that apply only to a single being (*God, Milton, London*). It has been objected that such names are very rare and that there are countless Miltons and many Londons. The *Port-Royal Grammar* responds (pt. 2, chap. 3) that this plurality of referents is accidental in the case of proper nouns, whereas it is essential for common nouns. We would say today that if there are several Londons, it is through ambiguity (the existence of homonyms), whereas the existence of different men does not prove any ambiguity in the word *man*. From the fact that the referent of a proper noun is normally unique, the conclusion is sometimes reached that the proper noun is a simple label attached to a thing, that it has a referent but no meaning, or as J. S. Mill says, a denotation but no connotation. Frege maintains to the contrary that no reference is possible without meaning. For this reason, he recognizes no logical difference between grammatical proper nouns and definite descriptions and regards both categories as **logical proper nouns.** What meaning can linguistic observation discern in a **grammatical proper noun?** It should first be noted that it is considered inappropriate to use a proper noun if one does not think that the interlocutor has any knowledge about the bearer of this name. We can thus regard as the meaning of a proper noun for a given collectivity certain information relative to the bearer of the name, information that every member of the collectivity is reputed to possess at least in part. Moreover, a tendency to specialize certain types of proper names for certain species will be noted: *Fido* is a dog's name, *Cadichon* a donkey's name in French; in many countries, there is also a distinction between plebeian and aristocratic names. In all these cases, the proper name incorporates at least a hint of description.

● Considerable information about the problem of proper nouns is found in A. H. Gardiner, *The Theory of Proper Names* (London, 1954). The viewpoints of Frege and Mill are discussed by J. S. Searle, in *Speech Acts* (London, 1969), pp. 162–74.

Demonstratives. When the condition of uniqueness required for the use of definite descriptions is not fulfilled, we take recourse to demonstratives. These are linguistic elements that accompany a gesture of designation (often demonstratives in the grammatical sense: *this, that*) or definite articles (for example, "The dog!" said to attract the attention of the listener to the dog that is being pointed out). Would a demonstrative that is not accompanied by a description, explicit or not, other than the gesture of designation, suffice to accomplish the act of reference? Russell thinks so; for this reason he regards the pronouns *this* and *that* as proper nouns (for Mill, they denote without connoting). This thesis is inadmissible in Frege's perspective. And indeed, it is evident that *this* or *that*, even if we take into account the gesture of designation, cannot suffice to delimit an object. How can I know whether that which is being pointed out to me on the table is the book as a whole, its cover, its color, the contrast between its color and that of the table, or the particular impression that it is making on me at this moment? A substantive, if only an implicit one, is necessary to accomplish the act of reference, for substantives divide the perceptible continuum into a world of objects (*substantive* should not be understood in the sense of substance; the object to which I refer may be that whiteness, that impression). Neither the demonstrative nor the gesture of designation is thus in itself referential, and *this* and *that* must be interpreted as "the book that I am showing you," "the color of the wall," and so on. (N.B. What precedes leads to a justification of the opposition between **adjectives** and **substantives.** The adjective does not have the substantive's power to constitute objects. Supposing that English syntax allowed us to say "this small," if a substantive were not implied, the expression would not suffice to tell us, even if we were simultaneously shown a point in space where there was only a book, whether it was a question of the book itself qualified as small, of a small portion of the book, of its small value, and so on. For such reasons the substantive, as opposed to the adjective, has long been known as an "appellative noun." To be sure, the adjective may participate in the description of an object, but this description itself can only be used for reference if it includes a substantive.)

● On the role of the substantive in reference, see P. T. Geach, *Reference and Generality* (Ithaca, 1963), chaps. 2 and 3.

Deictics. "Deictics" are expressions whose referent can only be determined with respect to the interlocutors (R. Jakobson calls them **shifters, embrayeurs**). Thus the pronouns of the first and second persons designate, respectively, the person who is speaking and the person spoken to. In many languages there exist pairs of expressions whose elements are distinguishable only through the fact that just one is deictic (the first of each pair in the list that follows):

here (the place where the dialogue is occurring) / *there*
yesterday (the day before the day on which we are speaking) / *the day before*
at this time (the time when we are speaking) / *at that time*

E. Benveniste has shown that deictics constitute an irruption of discourse within language, since their very meaning (the method used to find their referent), even though it depends on language, can only be defined by allusion to their use.

We may ask whether an act of reference is possible without the use, explicit or not, of deictics. The demonstratives, as we have defined them here, include deictics, as do proper nouns ("Smith" as the Smith whom you know). Finally, definite descriptions may not be able to satisfy the condition of uniqueness unless they contain either deictics or proper nouns and demonstratives.

● On deictics, see E. Benveniste, *Problems in General Linguistics*, trans. M. E. Meek (Coral Gables, 1971), chap. 5; and R. Jakobson, "Shifters, Verbal Categories and the Russian Verb," in *Selected Writings II* (The Hague, 1971), pp. 130–47. On the logical aspect of deictics, see Y. Bar-Hillel, "Indexical Expressions," *Mind* 63 (1954): 359–79. The relationships between personal pronouns and demonstratives were described in a systematic way as early as 1904 by K. Brugmann, who offers a general theory of deixis (*Die Demonstrativpronomina der indo-germanischen Sprachen* [Leipzig, 1904]). In modern linguistics, an overview of the problem of deixis can be found in C. J. Fillmore, *Santa Cruz Lectures on Deixis*, Indiana Linguistic Club, 1975.

Determiners. The *Port-Royal Grammar* (pt. 2, chap. 10), noting that a common noun in itself designates nothing and refers only to a concept (we would say that it has a meaning and no referent), calls for "determiners," elements that must be added to the noun to allow us to fix its "extension," that is, to bring into correspondence with it a certain sector of reality (allowing the passage from meaning to referent). This role may be played by the definite article, the possessives, the demonstratives, but also by nouns of number or by the indefinite articles and adjectives (*some, certain, all*). Thus we would be accomplishing an act of reference not only by saying "*the* friend," or "*this* friend," but also by saying "*a* friend," "*some* friends"; this raises certain problems, for it is difficult to see what is designated by these latter expressions.

● A theory very close to that of the Port-Royal grammarians is found in C. Bally, *Linguistique générale et Linguistique française*, 4th ed., rev. (Bern, 1965), chap. 3. For a critique of that theory from the logical point of view, see P. T. Geach, *Reference and Generality* (Ithaca, 1963), chap. 1 (Geach calls it a "doctrine of distribution"). A critique from the linguistic point of view is offered by O. Ducrot, in "Les Indéfinis et l'énonciation," *Langages* 17 (1970): 91–111.

TYPOLOGY OF THE PHENOMENA OF MEANING

The complexity of the problems related to meaning has two sources. On the one hand, the meaning of a word or of a sentence is in itself already complex: we can break it down into meaning and reference

[247ff.], into semantic features [265], or into explicit and presupposed content [272] or we can follow the various routes opened by a polysemic term [236]. On the other hand, this same meaning, taken in its entirety, can be viewed in relation to other facts that are different in nature but nonetheless depend on linguistic linkage. It is with the enumeration and the description of these allied phenomena that we shall be concerned here.

1. A first perspective according to which we can distinguish several varieties of meaning is the degree of **encoding** of meaning. The strongest degree is appropriately called **linguistic,** and the dictionary bears witness to this: the linguistic meaning of a word is present in every use of the word and constitutes its very definition. The next degree is that of **cultural** encoding: within a given society, which may or may not be coextensive with a linguistic community, and during a given period, other meanings are added to the properly linguistic meaning; for example, we associate dogs with faithfulness, although this quality does not constitute part of the linguistic (lexicographic) meaning of the word. Linguists are reluctant to concern themselves with this type of signification, under the pretext that it is impossible to treat it rigorously; however, the meanings do not cease to exist by virtue of being ignored. The weakest degree of encoding is **personal** association, according to which, for example, a dog evokes for me my brother, who once had a dog. This type of signification and the modalities of its production are studied in a psycholinguistic perspective.

A second perspective in which several types of signification can be distinguished is that of the existence or nonexistence of a direct relationship between the linguistic utterance and the act of its enunciation [323ff.]. Language always functions simultaneously in two ways: (1) as an abstract system of symbols and (2) as an activity occurring in a particular context. Certain elements of this context are coded and integrated into the language: for example, information concerning the identity and the status of the two interlocutors, the time and place of the enunciative act, the modalities of enunciation. But the signs linked to the enunciative act establish a new relationship of signification: we say, after Peirce, that these are indexes, as opposed to symbols [86]. The modalities of enunciation, that is, the speaker's attitude concerning what he is speaking about, the way he is speaking about it, his interlocutor, thus in turn produce a signification, but one of a specific nature. Linguists have given it various names—expressive value (Bally), expressive function (Bühler), emotive and conative function (Jakobson), modes (Empson). Diverse linguistic forms can carry this type of signification—words, semantic features, syntactic constructions, intonation, punctuation marks.

People have often sought for words a meaning that would be derived from the intrinsic signification of the sounds (or letters) of which they are composed (**phonetic symbolism**). This signification would depend on the conditions of articulation and, ultimately, of perception. For example, *i* would signify acuteness; *a*, roundness; and so on. In spite of the statistical and psycholinguistic studies devoted to this problem, it is not possible to affirm the universality of such meanings. It is certain, however, that within a linguistic community, stable associations are created between a sound and its meaning.

Finally, studies of word frequency in a vocabulary bring to light yet another dimension of meaning: interlocutors perceive a word as rare or hackneyed, and they customarily postulate the presence of "more meaning" in the first case. It would be more precise to speak of more **information,** as the term is used in information theory, according to which this notion is an inverse function of frequency. But in all cases, a supplementary signification of the type "rare," "precious," "old," and so on, is perceived by the interlocutors.

● See G. Stern, *Meaning and Change of Meaning* (Göteborg, 1932); J. R. Firth, *Papers in Linguistics 1934–1951* (London and New York, 1957), pp. 190–215; R. Jakobson, "Linguistics and Poetics," in *Style in Language*, ed. T. A. Sebeok (New York, 1960), pp. 350–77; C. Bally, *Traité de stylistique française* (Paris and Geneva, 1909), pp. 140–84; E. A. Nida, *Toward a Science of Translating* (Leiden, 1964); E. Stankiewicz, "Problems of Emotive Language," in *Approaches to Semiotics*, ed. T. A. Sebeok (The Hague, 1964); P. Delbouille, *Poésie et sonorités* (Paris, 1961); J. M. Peterfalvi, *Recherches expérimentales sur le symbolisme phonétique* (Paris, 1970); I. Fónagy, "Les Bases pulsionnelles de la phonation," *Revue française de psychanalyse* 34 (1970): 101–36; and T. Todorov, "Le Sens des sons," *Poétique* 11 (1972): 446–62.

2. The moment a word is used, significations perceived as secondary sometimes graft themselves onto the principal meaning. As we have just seen, they may be the product either of cultural conventions or of the immediate context; they do not appear in the dictionary, but they are nonetheless perceived by the speakers. Saussure observed that a word "can always evoke everything that can be associated with it in one way or another" (*Course in General Linguistics*, trans. W. Baskin [New York, 1959], p. 126). Diverse attempts have been made to classify these *associations;* we shall limit ourselves to one, purely formal association that is based on the existence of several levels in the structure of the word (signifier / signified) and of several types of relationship between the first and second meanings (resemblance / contiguity). *First* must be understood here, not in a historical sense, but in a synchronic sense (it is synonymous with *principal*).

a) *Resemblance between signifieds.* When we speak of a resemblance between signifieds, we are speaking of the phenomenon of *synonymy*: at the time of use, a word may evoke its synonyms, either by its very nature or because of a particular context.

b) *Resemblance between signifiers.* Perfect resemblance between signifiers is termed "homonymy"; in the case of partial resemblance, we speak of **paronymy,** or more specifically, of "alliteration" and "consonance." This is fairly close to phonetic symbolism: impelled by a desire to motivate signs, the speaker associates similar meanings with similar sounds. The tendency described by the term "popular etymology" comes from this: we hear the French verb *broder* ("to embroider") in *brodequin* ("half-boot"), even though the real origin of the latter word is entirely different [140]. This relationship is very frequently exploited in poetic texts, which has led Jakobson to introduce the notion of "poetic etymology": a text may suggest on the basis of the resemblance between the signifiers, a kinship between two words. Rhyme falls into this category: rhyme words are placed in a semantic relationship.

c) *Contiguity of the signifiers.* The use of a word of any moment in time evokes its previous uses and thus its previous contexts, especially if the latter can be systematized in some way. Hence we have, in everyday discourse, what Bally called effect by **evocation of milieu:** certain words or syntactic constructions are perceived as designating the milieu in which they appear with particular frequency—for example, slang words or expressions, "poetic" turns of phrase, and so on. In literary discourse, differentiation of "poetic" words from others is not enough; certain words or expressions are identified with literary trends or periods, even with authors and particular works. When a word thus marked by previous contexts is used to perform a function analogous to its previous one, we have **stylization;** with the inverse function, we have **parody** (Bakhtin). No word entirely escapes this type of supplementary signification, although degrees can be observed between the "neutral" and the "colored" term.

d) *Contiguity of the signifieds.* The cases we described earlier under the name of "cultural significations" are arrayed here. For example, the properties of an object are evoked when someone mentions the name of this object: milk evokes whiteness; the lion, courage; and so on. English linguists, following in the path of J. R. Firth, have described this phenomenon under the name of "signification by collocation"; it must not be forgotten, however, that the context evoked is not linguistic (contiguity of the signifiers) but cultural (contiguity of the signifieds): the expression "white milk" is probably extremely rare, since it is perceived as a pleonasm. O. Ducrot has isolated some cases of this type of signification under the name of understood meanings, cases in which the supplementary meaning grows out of the very existence of the enunciative act ("if I say something, it is because I attach importance to it"). This group of secondary meanings is sometimes called connotation, sometimes implication.

● See Ullmann, *The Principles of Semantics* (Glasgow, 1951); C. Bally, *Traité de stylistique française* (Paris and Geneva, 1909), pp. 203–49; M. Bakhtin, *Problems of Dostoevsky's Poetics*, trans. R. W. Rotsel (Ann Arbor, 1973);. R. Firth, *Papers in Linguistics 1934–1951* (London and New York, 1957), pp. 190–215; O. Ducrot, "Présupposés et sousentendus," *Langue française* 4 (December 1969): 30–43; W. Empson, *The Structure of Complex Words* (London, 1951), pp. 1–40; and M. Black, *Models and Metaphors* (Ithaca, 1962), pp. 48–63.

3. Another problem is raised by the relations that the various meanings maintain with each other, no longer in the perspective of derivation (as in 2, above) but in that of their simultaneous functioning. According to the medieval theory of interpretation, an utterance has always and only four meanings: *literal, allegorical, tropological* (or moral), and *anagogic*; these meanings coexist but keep their autonomy. For certain modern semanticists, on the contrary (Katz and Fodor, for example), a word normally has one meaning and only one (in a particular occurrence): amalgamation rules always oblige us to choose among the different meanings of the word; the irreducible ambiguities are regarded as forming a quite special case.

When the meanings are *different* in nature (for example, symbolic and indicial signification, or symbolic signification and signification by evocation of milieu), they seem to coexist without mutual interaction. Nevertheless, proportional relationships can be observed: Jakobson and Tynianov have noted that the effect of stylistic evocation of a word is all the stronger when its meaning is unusual (this effect reaches its maximum in incomprehensible words).

If the meanings are *similar* in nature (as are the ones enumerated in a dictionary for a given word), the process is more complex (there is a new product, not simply a new sum). W. Empson has proposed a first formulation of this relationship: if two meanings of a word can be evoked simultaneously when the word is included in a sentence, their relationship can be described by using a new sentence, "*A* is *B*," in which *A* is one of the meanings, *B* the other. Language (poetic language in particular) postulates, as we have seen, the identity of meanings in cases in which there is identity of sound. But the assertion "*A* is *B*" is not in itself univocal: it may signify "*A* is a part of *B*," "*A* is like *B*," "*A* implies *B*," "*A* is typical of *B*." To describe these variations, Empson uses two oppositions: subject / predicate, and **head meaning** of a word (outside of any context) / **chief meaning** of the same word (in the sentence in question). The relationships of meaning at the level of the sentence have been studied by Empson in another work dealing with ambiguity.

● See N. Frye, *Anatomy of Criticism* (Princeton, 1957), pp. 71–128; J. J. Katz and J. A. Fodor, "The Structure of a Semantic Theory," *Language* 39 (1963): 170–210; R. Jakobson, "On Realism in Art," in *Readings in Russian Poetics*, ed. L. Matejka and K. Pomorska (Cambridge, Mass., 1971), pp. 38–46; J. Tynianov, *Le Problème de la langue du vers* (Paris, 1977); W. Empson, *The Structure of Complex Words* (London, 1951), pp. 41–82; and idem, *Seven Types of Ambiguity* (London, 1930).

Theoreticians of literature have often tried to define its specificity by observations concerning the status of meaning in literary texts. According to a tendency represented at the beginning of the nineteenth century by Goethe and Coleridge, the literary text functions as a symbol, as opposed to an **allegory.** As Goethe wrote in his "Maxims and Reflections": "There is a great difference, whether the poet seeks the particular for the general or sees the general in the particular. From the first procedure arises allegory, in which the particular serves only as an example of the general; the second procedure, however, is really the nature of poetry: it expresses something particular, without thinking of the general or pointing to it" (Maxim 279, quoted by R. Wellek in *A History of Modern Criticism, 1750–1950,* 4 vols. to date [New Haven, 1955–], vol. 1, p. 211). We could interpret these lines as marking the necessity of a relationship of participation between signifier and signified (which thus coincide with the particular and the general, respectively). On this basis, the signifier acquires an essential irreducibility; it is not purely transparent. On the other hand, the imprecision of the signified seems a necessary condition for the existence of the symbol. For Coleridge, the "symbol is a sign included in the idea which it represents" (*Aids to Reflection* [London, 1913], p. 173n). "The Symbolical cannot be better defined in distinction from the Allegorical than that it is always itself a part of that, of the whole of which it is the representative" ("Lecture VIII," in *Miscellaneous Criticism* [London, 1935], p. 99). In rhetorical terms, this means that the symbol-synecdoche is characteristic of poetry, whereas the allegory-metaphor is excluded from it.

Tynianov proposed a somewhat different description: if we distinguished the principal meaning of a word (its dictionary definition) from its contextual meanings, which only come forth on the occasion of a particular use, literary discourse would be characterized by the preponderant role accorded to contextual significations at the expense of the principal signification. A supplementary, positional correlation characterizes any sequence of poetic discourse: the meaning of each word results from its orientation toward the neighboring word. J. Mukařovský retains this idea of a different discursive orientation of the word in poetry but does not seek to situate it in a segmentation of meaning; for him, the difference corresponds to two functions of discourse, one representative, the other autonomous (esthetic). In the poetic text, "the link between the designation and the surrounding contexture comes to the fore" ("Poetic Designation," p. 67). N. Frye pursues the same idea, affirming the existence of two types of signification: centrifugal and centripetal, external and internal; poetry is characterized by the predominance of the second type. "In literature, questions of fact or truth are subordinated to the primary literary aim of producing a structure of words for its own sake, and the sign-values of symbols are subordinated to their importance as a structure of interconnected motifs" (*Anatomy of Criticism*, p. 74).

From Goethe to Frye, we observe the same feature of poetic discourse: linguistic signs cease to be transparent, cease to be simple instruments serving the circulation of meaning; they acquire importance in themselves (the differences of opinion that we have evoked concern the explanation of the fact, not its existence). This importance is attached, in the simplest case, to the sounds themselves; but in a general way, the poetic text is characterized by an accentuation of meaning, to the detriment of reference. The text of fiction conserves the representational orientation of the words, but the secondary symbolic system formed by these words (the narrative) possesses the autonomous, noninstrumental character of the poetic text.

- See Fletcher, *Allegory* (Ithaca, 1964), pp. 1–23; J. Tynianov, *Le Problème de la langue du vers* (Paris, 1977); J. Mukařovský, "Poetic Designation and the Aesthetic Function of Language," in *The Word and Verbal Art*, trans. J. Burbank and P. Steiner (New Haven and London, 1977), pp. 65–73; and idem, "Art As a Semiotic Fact," in *Structure, Sign, and Function*, trans. J. Burbank and P. Steiner (New Haven and London, 1978), pp. 82–88.

THE DISCOURSE OF FICTION

When certain linguistic utterances refer to particular extra-linguistic circumstances, they are said to denote a referent [247]. This property, important as it is, is not a constitutive property of human language: some utterances possess it, others do not. But there also exists a type of discourse known as **fictional,** in which the question of reference arises in a radically different fashion: it is explicitly indicated that the statements made describe a fiction, and not a real referent. Literature is the best-studied area of this type of discourse (even though not all literature is fiction) [153].

Discussions devoted to this relationship have almost always been tied to the concept of **realism,** which has to be examined here. However, like most of the key terms of literary theory, the term "realism" includes a very considerable polysemy. Even without taking into account cases in which it serves to designate a period of literary history (coinciding roughly with the nineteenth century), we have to distinguish between several uses of the term:

1. It is essential first to avoid confusing "realism" and "truth" in the sense of formal logic. For logicians, truth is a relationship between the individual occurrence of a sentence and the referent about which the sentence affirms something. Sentences constituting literary discourse have no referent; they present themselves as expressly fictional, and the question of their truth is without meaning. It is in these terms that G. Frege describes literary discourse: "In hearing an epic poem, for instance, apart from the euphony of the language we are interested only in the sense of the sentences and the images and feelings thereby aroused. The question of truth would cause us to abandon aesthetic delight for an attitude of scientific investigation. Hence it is a matter of no concern to us whether the name 'Odysseus,' for instance, has reference, so long as we accept the poem as a work of art" (*Translations from the Philosophical Writings of Gottlob Frege*, p. 63). To question a literary text on its "truth" is not appropriate; it amounts to reading the text as a nonliterary work.

2. Thus it is not truth that is in question in the innumerable discussions devoted to realism. The Russian formalists vigorously denounced this confusion, on the basis of specific examples. In his study of Gogol's "The Overcoat," B. M. Eikhenbaum comments on the detailed descriptions of Petrovitch's fingernail and of his snuffbox and wonders about its meaning: "Naive readers will tell us that this is realism, description, etc. It is useless to discuss the matter with them, but they might contemplate the fact that we are informed at length about the fingernail and the snuffbox, whereas about Petrovitch himself we are told only that he was in the habit of drinking on every feast day, and about his wife, simply that he had one and that she wore a bonnet. This is an obvious device of grotesque composition: accentuate the least important details, leave out those which would deserve greater attention" (translated from "Kak sdelana 'Shinel' ' Gogolia," in *Literatura: Teoriia, kritika, pole-*

mika [Leningrad, 1927]). Shklovskii evokes similar examples: "In the period of the *Sturm und Drang* in Germany, for five years the great majority of plays dealt with the motif of fratricide. This is nevertheless not proof that during this period in Germany fratricides were occurring on a massive scale" (translated from *O teorii prozy* [Moscow, 1925]).

If a given motif appears in a work, it is because it belongs to the tradition to which the work is attached. If a given device is found, it is because the latter belongs to the rules of the genre—that of the grotesque, for example. The elements constituting a work obey an internal logic, not an external one. The notions we need here are those of **conformity to genre** and **conformity to type.** Every work falls within the sphere of a type, that is, every work possesses a certain configuration of structural properties [150]; furthermore, most works of a period belong to a genre, that is, they can be related by contemporary readers to other, already known works [150ff.]. Genre rules constitute a code that is necessary for the correct interpretation of the literary work. Once again, there is no reason to refer to truth.

In an article devoted to the problems of realism, R. Jakobson makes some supplementary distinctions. First, the genre to which the work is attached by the author and by the reader may not be the same; thus what is a realist work for one may not be so for the other. Furthermore, the genre to which the work is related may be in harmony or in contrast with the reigning tradition; the claim of realism may just as well betray a revolutionary tendency as a conservative one. These distinctions underline the imprecise character of the notion and explain the contradictory uses that have been made of the term: "Classicists, sentimentalists, the romanticists to a certain extent, even the 'realists' of the nineteenth century, the modernists to a large degree, and, finally, the futurists, expressionists and their like have more than once steadfastly proclaimed faithfulness to reality, maximum verisimilitude—in other words, realism—as the guiding motto of their artistic program" ("On Realism in Art," in *Readings in Russian Poetics*, p. 39).

Two related problems arise here:

a) Given the representational character of the great majority of literary texts, we may also examine the **modes of representation** employed. The question is no longer one of finding out how a preexisting reality is described, but one of how the illusion of such a reality is created. E. Auerbach sees in the succession of different modes of representation the key to an internal history of literature. R. Kellogg proposes to see in representation and illustration the two extremes—mimetic and symbolic—of a single continuum.

b) We must not conclude from the foregoing that literature maintains no relationship with the other levels of social life. Rather, we must establish a hierarchy among all these levels. Tynianov stresses that every element of a work has (in his terms) a constructive function that permits its integration into the work. The latter, in turn, possesses a literary function that allows it to be integrated into contemporary literature. This last, finally, has a verbal function (or orientation) thanks to which it can be integrated into the whole set of social phenomena. "A separate work must be related to a literary order before one can talk about its orientation" ("On Literary Evolution," in *Readings in Russian Poetics*, p. 75). "It would be methodologically fatal to consider the correlation of systems without taking into account the immanent laws of each system" ("Problems in the Study of Literature and Language," in *Readings in Russian Poetics*, p. 87). The relationship between the literary order and other orders is one, not of reflection, but of participation, of interaction. In the study of this relationship, we must again establish a hierarchy: the relationship "can be established and investigated only through the study of closely-related conditions, without the forcible incorporation of remote, though major, causal orders" (Tynianov, "On Literary Evolution," p. 75). Thus we should begin with the study of the relationship between literature and the general verbal behavior of a society.

● On literature and logical truth, see P. T. Geach and M. Black, eds., *Translations from the Philosophical Writings of Gottlob Frege*, 2d ed. (Oxford, 1960); R. Ingarden, "Les Différentes Conceptions de la vérité dans l'oeuvre d'art," *Revue d'esthétique* 2 (1949): 162–80; M. C. Beardsley, *Aesthetics: Problems in the Philosophy of Criticism* (New York, 1958); T. Todorov, "Note sur le langage poétique," *Semiotica* 1 (1969): 322–28; G. D. Martin, *Language, Truth and Poetry* (Edinburgh, 1975). On modes of representation, see E. Auerbach, *Mimesis: The Representation of Reality in Western Literature*, trans. W. R. Trask (Princeton, 1953); and R. Scholes and R. Kellogg, *The Nature of Narrative* (New York, 1966), pp. 82–105. On literature and social life, see L. Matejka and K. Pomorska, eds., *Readings in Russian Poetics* (Cambridge, Mass., 1971), pp. 38–46, 66–81; and V. Voloshinov, *Marxism and the Philosophy of Language*, trans. L. Matejka and I. R. Titunik (New York, 1973).

Owing to its representational character, literary fiction is also confronted, consciously or not, with the system of collective representations that dominate a society during a given period; in other words, it is confronted with ideology. The latter is not the referent any more than the genre rules are; it is yet another discourse, but one that is diffuse in character and discontinuous and one of which we are rarely conscious. We can envisage two relationships between the literary text and the set of representations that constitute an ideology: either the text seeks to disguise its conformity to the genre as conformity to the ideology or else it is content with the former, without seeking to assimilate itself to the latter and even, ultimately, proclaims its independence. The formalists designate the first relationship by the term **motivation** of the device, the second by the expression **laying bare.** According to Tomashevskii, laying bare a device corresponds to using it apart from its usual motivation; the device becomes a demonstration of the literary character of the work. In the first case (motivation), the very existence of the book is justified in order to make it still "truer"—it is a manuscript found by chance, a correspondence, or the memoirs of a historical character. In the second case, the illusion is constantly being destroyed in order to remind us that we are reading a fiction and that we must not mistake it for reality.

Motivation is thus a variant of realism. It is not conformity to the genre, but a cloak that the text casts prudently over the rules of the genre. G. Genette describes in the following way the articulation of the two: "From the viewpoint of narrative economy there is . . . a diametrical opposition between the function of a unit and its motivation. If the function is (loosely speaking) that for which a unit is *used*, its motivation is what it *needs* in order to dissimulate its function. In other words, function is a profit, motivation is a cost. The return of a narrative unit, or, to put it another way, its *value*, will thus be the difference supplied by the following subtraction: function minus motivation" (translated from *Figures II* [Paris, 1969], p. 97).

The desire to provide a narrative with full motivation is not unrelated to the arbitrariness of the sign [130ff.]. Signs are arbitrary; names are not inscribed in things. But any user of a sign system tends to naturalize it, to present it as though it were self-evident. The tension resulting from this opposition gives rise to one of the dominant currents of literary history.

Thus the question of the relationship between literature and life splinters in fact into several questions—more modest, to be sure, but also more precise—that fit within the framework of a general theory of discourse.

- See L. Matejka and K. Pomorska, eds., *Readings in Russian Poetics* (Cambridge, Mass., 1971), pp. 38–46; L. T. Lemon and M. J. Reis, eds., *Russian Formalist Criticism: Four Essays* (Lincoln, 1965), pp. 80–83; *Communications* 11 (1968): *Recherches sémiologiques: Le vraisemblable*; and P. Stewart, *Imitation and Illusion in the French Memoir Novel* (New Haven, 1969).

SEMANTIC COMBINATORIAL

Belief that the semantic linguistic description of a language is possible amounts to a judgment that it is reasonable to attribute to each utterance a meaning—or several meanings if the utterance is ambiguous—without denying, of course, that this meaning may then either be modified or clarified by the situation in which the utterance is used. It implies a belief, moreover, that one can calculate the total meaning of an utterance if one knows the meaning of the significative units (words or morphemes) that appear in it and the syntactic relations that unite them (from a Chomskyan standpoint, the units and relations of deep structure [244]). But even though this **semantic combinatorial** takes syntactic organization as its point of departure, many linguists think that that organization is no more than a point of departure, that it supplies nothing but guidelines. This implies not only that semantic relations are defined differently from syntactic relations, that they have their own content, but especially that they cannot be placed in a one-to-one correspondence with the syntactic relations, that the two networks do not overlap, that there may be a relation of one type without a parallel relation of the other type. In other words, the semantic combinatorial, although it depends on the syntactic combinatorial, is not a simple reinterpretation of the latter.

● Some recent attempts to constitute a semantic combinatorial—understood as a calculation of the meaning of utterances on the basis of their syntax—are found in: (*a*) J. J. Katz and J. A. Fodor, "The Structure of a Semantic Theory," *Language* 39 (1963): 170–210, research that is carried out in the generativist perspective and that tends to consider the semantic component as interpreting syntax alone (see Chomsky's second theory [244ff.]); (*b*) U. Weinreich, "Explorations in Semantic Theory," in *Current Trends in Linguistics*, ed. T. A. Sebeok, 14 vols. (The Hague, 1963–76), vol. 3, *Theoretical Foundations* (1966), pp. 395–478; and (*c*) all the research carried out by R. Montague and the logicians whose work is based on his goal of constituting a formal calculus that would make it possible to determine the logical value (truth conditions) of an utterance on the basis of the words of which it is composed. This research is based on the principle, formulated by Frege, according to which in a well-constructed language, the meaning of a compound utterance ought to be a function of the meaning of its constituents. See the references on p. 287, below.

Semantic Units

A possible indication (not a proof) of the originality of the semantic combinatorial stems from the lack of correspondence between the minimal units of syntax and those of semantics. Hjelmslev was one of the first linguists to insist on this fact: not only do the minimal linguistic units (words or morphemes), which are the basic elements of syntax, most often have a complex semantic content but their breakdown into simpler semantic units may be based upon strictly linguistic considerations. It suffices to apply to the realm of meaning the method of commutation [25] that phonologists apply to the realm of sound. If phonologists see three units /b/, /æ/ and /n/ in the English morpheme /bæn/ (*ban*), it is because each unit may be replaced by another unit, and each of these replacements will produce a difference in meaning (we have for example *tan, bun, bang*). The same commutation can be applied to morpheme content. Thus we may say that the verb *wish* contains, among others, the semantic units *absence* and *good*; in fact, if we replace *good* by *bad*, the meaning obtained has to be expressed by another verb, for example, *dread*. If we replace *absence* by *presence*, the resulting meaning resembles that of *appreciate*. The units thus discerned, although they are elements of the signified of *wish*, cannot be considered as signifieds in themselves, since there is no signifier that corresponds to them (to be sure, we can find words of the language to describe them approximately—for example, *absence* and *good*—but the mode of presence of these units in the verb *wish* is independent of the words used to name them). Hjelmslev, who uses the term **figure** for every linguistic element that is neither a signified nor a signifier, calls the minimal semantic units content figures. French linguists often speak, with Pottier and Greimas, of **semes;** the usual English term is **semantic feature.**

The search for these units is called **semic analysis** or **componential analysis.** Its method is above all the comparison of words (as we have compared *wish* with *dread* and *appreciate*), and in the end it does no more than perfect the older method of semantic fields [135]. But instead of merely listing all the words from the same area of the lexicon to which a given word can be opposed, linguists who use this method first find pairs of words whose difference appears minimal, deciding that each of these differences stems from the opposition of two semantic atoms, or distinctive semantic features (semes). Then they describe the more complex differences as combinations of minimal oppositions (they posit that the words compared differ in several distinctive semantic features).

To the extent that semic analysis bears only upon elements of the lexicon (morphemes or words—Pottier says **lexemes**), to the extent that they represent bundles of semes, this analysis does not suffice to ensure the originality of the semantic combinatorial. For it remains possible that semantic relations deal with each of these bundles as a whole, in which case they could have the same beginning and end point as syntactic relations, which are directly applied to the lexemes. If semic analysis is to imply the irreducible character of the semantic combinatorial, it must deal not only with the content of lexical units but, like that of Greimas, with the content of larger segments of utterances, indeed with meaning effects (called **sememes**), that is, with significations tied to a certain context or to a certain discourse situation. Since the distinctive semantic features are no longer connected then to words or morphemes, the relations that unite them can no longer be parallel to the syntactic relations. But in this case the border between the semantics of a language and the analysis of discourses carried out in that language is blurred.

● On semic analysis, see L. Hjelmslev, *Prolegomena to a Theory of Language*, trans. F. J. Whitfield, rev. ed. (Madison, 1961), chap. 14 (and A. Martinet's critique, "Au sujet des fondements de la théorie linguistique de L. Hjelmslev," *Bulletin de la société de linguistique* 43 [1946]: 19–42); A.-J. Greimas, *Sémantique structurale* (Paris, 1966), esp. pp. 50–54; B. Pottier, "Vers une sémantique moderne," *Travaux de linguistique et de littérature* 2, pt. 1 (1964): 107–37; T. Todorov, "Recherches sémantiques," *Langages* 1 (1966), secs. 2–3 (this issue contains other important texts and a bibliography); and E. A. Nida, *Componential Analysis of Meaning* (The Hague, 1975).

Certain partisans of generative grammar believe they can justify by "purely syntactic" arguments the attribution of semantic features to the morphemes of the language. Let us suppose in fact that it is incumbent upon syntax to account for **selectional restrictions**, that is, for the fact that not all the elements of a grammatical category A combine with all the elements of a grammatical category B, whereas these two categories normally enter into combination (to use one of Chomsky's examples, we do not say "Sincerity admires John," even though we can usually make a sentence by combining a noun, a transitive verb, and a proper noun). In order to describe this fact, we will attribute to certain morphemes **intrinsic semantic features** (thus *sincerity* has the feature *non-animate*, represented [—animate]) and to others, **contextual semantic features,** that is, the indication of intrinsic features that must be possessed by the morphemes with which they combine (thus *admire* has the feature *requires an animate subject,* represented symbolically by +[[+animate]—]). And a general rule of the grammar will preclude combining morphemes whose intrinsic and contextual features are incompatible.

● It was not until *Aspects of the Theory of Syntax* (Cambridge, Mass., 1965) that Chomsky introduced the idea of semantic features. This notion has given rise to numerous controversies; see S. Y. Kuroda, "Remarques sur les présuppositions et sur les contraintes de sélection," *Langages* 14 (June 1969): 52–80. The problem was taken up again by Chomsky, in relation to the discussions on generative semantics: *Studies on Semantics in Generative Grammar* (The Hague, 1972).

Semantic Relationships

For certain linguists, the different distinctive semantic features composing the semantic content of an utterance constitute a set, in the mathematical sense, that is, a simple collection, without internal organization, without specified relationships among its elements. As a result, if two units have the same distinctive semantic features, they are synonymous. It becomes difficult then to distinguish *garage* and *trunk* (of a car), since both words possess the features *storage* and *automobile*. We shall be obliged, in order to escape from this dilemma, to make use of distinctive semantic features such as *for automobiles* and *in automobiles*.

● Such a conception of linguistic description is found, implicitly, in J. J. Katz and J. A. Fodor, "The Structure of a Semantic Theory," *Language* 39 (1963): 170–210. It is also found—modified by the notion of contrastive features [29]—in L. Prieto, *Principes de noologie* (The Hague, 1964). It is the basis, moreover, for the documentary languages known as a-syntactic, which represent an object only by a collection of independent marks (an example of such a language might be the system of key words sometimes used to summarize, on notecards, the content of a book or an article, the key word being to the work summarized what the distinctive semantic feature is to the word).

A systematic critique of this thesis has been propsed by U. Weinreich. According to Weinreich, distinctive semantic features can be associated in two different ways in the content of a significative unit. There is additive association (**cluster,** agglomeration) if the features have no particular relationships among themselves. Thus *boy* is a cluster composed of the features *child* and *male* and will be represented as (*child, male*); the criterion is that a boy is at once a child and a male. From this we must distinguish the **configuration,** which institutes a particular relationship between distinctive semantic features. *Dwarf*, a configuration connecting *man* and *small*, will be represented as (*man* → *small*); the criterion is not that a dwarf is at the same time small and a man but that he is small for a man. On the basis of these elementary definitions, Weinreich tries to characterize the principal semantic relationships between meaning-bearing units (words or morphemes) according to the type of grouping that they institute between constituent units.

a) **Linking** describes an association of units that constitutes a new cluster. This is generally the case for the association of adjective + substantive: *nice boy* = (*child, male, nice*); *nice dwarf* = ((*man* → *small*), *nice*). This is also the case for certain compound words such as *wolfhound*. (N.B. Complex maneuvers are required to present as a linking an expression such as *fast driver*, for at first glance it appears that no new cluster has been created: the fast driver is not someone who is (1) a driver or (2) fast, but someone who is fast as a driver.)

b) A nonlinking relationship does not create new clusters. This is the case, for example, for **transitive relationships,** which associate a verb and its complements. If *buy* is represented by a grouping (*v, u*) and *car* by (*x, y*), then *buy* (*a*) *car* will have to be represented by ((*v, u*) → (*x, y*)). Certain compound words are constructed, semantically, on this model (*carryall, drop-leaf*).

● See U. Weinreich, "Explorations in Semantic Theory," in *Current Trends in Linguistics*, ed. T. A. Sebeok, 14 vols. (The Hague, 63–76), vol. 3 (1966). The linking-nonlinking distinction is fairly close to that established by eighteenth-century French grammars between the two types of grammatical agreement: the first type, *accord de concordance*—between adjective and substantive, for example—is based on the fact that the two terms designate the same object; the second, *accord de rection*—between the verb and its complements, for example—is based on the fact that a relationship between different objects is established.

The so-called generative-semantics school [56], which pursues and extends Weinreich's approach, currently tends to abandon the very idea of cluster and to represent the content of every meaning-bearing unit of a configuration. Thus most words and morphemes of a language will be regarded as simple abbreviations, in surface structure [244], of a much more complex real structure, analogous to the syntactic structure of complete sentences. Thus the verb *break* would be the superficial trace of a deep organization analogous to that of an expression like "to be the cause, by a shock, of an object becoming in pieces." To justify this paraphrase, which might be considered as arbitrary as it is awkward, it is alleged that this paraphrase alone can make understandable the ambiguity of "He almost broke the vase" (which could mean "he nearly broke it—but he didn't" or "he cracked it; it's almost broken"). The ambiguity stems from the fact that the modifier *almost*, applied on the surface to the single word *break*, may in deep structure be applied at other places in the complex semantic organization represented by this word (the example is borrowed from J. D. McCawley). Similarly, we may observe that the features *human* and *young* present in the word *child* seem to be in a semantic relationship analogous to that of substantive and adjective in a sentence. If we apply in fact the restrictive word *only* to a group formed of substantive + adjective, the restriction concerns only the adjective: "He has only light beer" = "as for beer, the only kind he has is light." In the same way, "There are only children here" = "as for humans, there are only young ones here" (and not the inverse, which would be "as for young creatures, there are only human ones here").

● See J. D. McCawley, "Semantic Representation," in *Grammar and Meaning* (Tokyo, 1973), pp. 240–56. To construe the lexical items as the superficial traces of complex deep structures entails, in many cases, the supposition that these structures, before being replaced by the lexical items, have already been the object of transformations. This thesis— which is contrary to the principle according to which lexical insertion occurs before the transformations—is characteristic of the theory known as generative semantics (see G. Lakoff, "Linguistics and Natural Logic," in *Semantics of Natural Language*, ed. D. Davidson and G. Harman [Dordrecht, 1972], pp. 545–665). This thesis is discussed in terms of a particular example by J. A. Fodor, in "Three Reasons For Not Deriving 'Kill' from 'Cause to Die,' " *Linguistic Inquiry* 1 (1970): 429–38, and, in general terms, by R. S. Jackendoff, in *Semantic Interpretation in Generative Grammar* (Cambridge, Mass., 1972).

The Semantic Organization of the Utterance

Do utterances have a semantic structure? In other words, do the formulas describing the meaning of utterances all have to be constructed on the same model, or at least on a small number of well-defined models? Although currently no one claims to have resolved the question, we can point out certain distinctions that ought to appear in many semantic descriptions of utterances but whose articulations with each other are still hard to see.

1. It seems that all assertive utterances (affirmative and negative) must be described as the attribution of a certain property to a certain object. Thus their semantic description must include two parts: a **logical subject,** designating the object about which something is affirmed, and a **logical predicate,** indicating the property affirmed. Even more importantly, in many languages there seems to be a distinction corresponding to the subject-predicate one in the syntactic structure of utterances: the grammatical subject, when it exists, may often be described as designating the object of the affirmation (as identical, consequently, to the logical subject). The object of an affirmation *A* has, for example, the property of being also the object about which something is affirmed in the negation of *A* (Peter is the object both of "Peter has come" and "It is false that Peter has come"). Now negation, in most languages

possessing the syntactic function *subject*, may be effected by an operation that leaves the syntactic subject unchanged and bears upon another segment (the verb, for example): "It is false that Peter has come" has as its equivalent "Peter has not come." The connection between grammatical subject and logical subject allows us to understand, moreover, that the passive transformation of an utterance can radically modify its meaning: "Only Peter loves only Mary" does not have the same meaning (nor the same truth conditions) as "Only Mary is loved only by Peter." This divergence is explained if the grammatical subject designates that about which something is affirmed. For it is necessarily different to affirm that (*a*) Peter is the only one with the property *love only Mary* and (*b*) Mary is the only one with the property *be loved only by Peter*.

● The irreducible logical properties of the grammatical subject were pointed out by N. Chomsky as early as *Syntactic Structures* (The Hague, 1957), pp. 100–101; according to S. Y. Kuroda, a language such as Japanese, in which the existence of a grammatical subject is in doubt, possesses certain particles that make it possible to attribute to a single word of the sentence the logical properties possessed by the subject in the Indo-European languages ("Jugements catégoriques et jugements thétiques," *Langages* 30 [1973]: 81–110).

It may seem arbitrary to attribute a single object to each affirmation and, for example, to decide that (1) "Peter loves Mary" has as its object *Peter* rather than *Mary*. We must take recourse then to a breakdown of the utterance into **predicate** and **arguments.** We may say that (1) affirms the predicate *love* of the pair of arguments (*Peter* and *Mary*). (Nothing prevents us, moreover, from having a predicate with more than two arguments.) Appearances notwithstanding, this analysis represents an expansion of the preceding one, rather than its abandonment. It was noted earlier, for example, that the object of an affirmative utterance is also the object of the corresponding negative utterance. Similarly, the arguments of an affirmation are also those of its negation. ("It is false that Peter loves Mary" has the same arguments, *Peter* and *Mary*, as (1).) If it is true, furthermore, that this new analysis leads us to recognize several arguments where there is only a single grammatical subject, it does not prevent us from representing, in a certain way, the logical properties of the grammatical subject. However, we shall have to proceed indirectly, establishing an asymmetry between the different positions in the predicate and attributing particular properties to one of them, the one, in fact, that is filled by the argument corresponding to the grammatical subject.

    2. Whereas the distinction between what is affirmed and that about which the affirmation is made is based on the logical functioning of lan-

guage, the distinction between **topic** and **comment** is psychological in nature. The topic (in French, *thème*) of an act of enunciation is what the speaker is talking about, the object of discourse, or as linguists at the beginning of the century used to say, the **psychological subject;** the comment (in French, *propos*) is the information that the speaker means to convey relative to the topic, what used to be called the **psychological predicate.** By saying "Peter has come," we may intend to give information, not about Peter, but about the people who have come, or more generally, about what has happened. Thus even though *Peter* is both the semantic and the grammatical subject, it may not represent the topic of the conversation. What allows us to determine the topic is the question that the utterance answers or that it is supposed to answer ("What has Peter done?" or "Who has come?" or "What has happened?"). Up to now we have presented the topic-comment distinction as relating to enunciative acts. But it seems that this distinction may sometimes be established within the utterance; the latter will then possess marks that permit distinction of the topic and the comment. This is the case for certain intonations and for certain forms of repetition. An utterance like "Peter, he came" can hardly have any topic other than Peter.

(N.B. An expression that is stressed, or **emphasized** [certain transformationalists also speak of expressions being put into **focus,** or focused], does not necessarily represent the comment. To be sure, the emphasis placed on *Peter* in "It is Peter who has come" is very often accompanied by a tendency to take *Peter* as the comment: we are speaking of the person who has come, and we announce that it is Peter. But such an interpretation is difficult in certain contexts, for example, if the sentence in question is integrated into an entire discourse on Peter's activities. "It is Peter who has talked, it is Peter who has worked, it is Peter who has come, it is he again who. . . ." Moreover, there are forms of emphasis in which the term stressed may not represent the comment, such as the utterance "*Peter* came," in which a division into topic and comment would be quite arbitrary.)

● The topic-comment distinction is prefigured in the opposition of the psychological subject and the psychological predicate as they are used, for example, by H. Paul (*Principien der Sprachgeschichte*, 2d ed. [Halle, 1886], p. 99). It is taken up again and refined by the linguists of the Prague circle, especially V. Mathesius (see "O tak zvaném aktuálním členění větmém," available in a collection of Mathesius's texts, *Čeština a obecný jazkopyt. Soubor statí* [Prague, 1947], pp. 234–42). See also Mathesius's "Verstärkung und Emphase," in *A Prague School Reader in Linguistics*, ed. J. Vachek (Bloomington and London, 1964), pp. 426–32. Mathesius's theses are presented by J. Firbas, in "On Defining the Theme in Functional Sentence Analysis," *Travaux linguistiques de Prague* 1

(1964): 267–80, and in F. Daněs, ed., *Papers on Functional Sentence Perspective* (The Hague, 1974). On the importance of not confusing the distinction of psychological subject and predicate with that of the logical subject and predicate, J. L. Austin makes some essential points in "How to Talk?" *Philosophical Papers* (Oxford, 1961), pp. 181–200. Generative grammarians often speak of a topicalization transformation (see N. Ruwet, *An Introduction to Generative Grammar*, trans. N. S. H. Smith [Amsterdam, 1973], pp. 280–84). The topic-comment opposition is used by J. M. Zemb to study negation, in *Les Structures logiques de la proposition allemande* (Paris, 1968).

3. We must also distinguish the opposition of what is **affirmed** and what is **presupposed** from the two preceding oppositions. The utterance "Jack continues to act foolishly" affirms both (*a*) that Jack has acted foolishly in the past and (*b*) that he is acting foolishly in the present. Now affirmations (*a*) and (*b*) seem to have to be separated within the global description of the utterance, for they have different properties. Thus (*a*) is still affirmed when (*b*) is denied ("It is false that Jack continues to act foolishly") or when it is the object of an interrogation ("Is Jack continuing to act foolishly?"). The same does not hold true for (*b*). Moreover, (*a*) is not affirmed in the same way as (*b*): (*a*) is presented as self-evident or as already known and impossible to put in doubt; (*b*), on the contrary, is presented as new and ultimately debatable. Thus we call (*a*) a presupposition and (*b*) an affirmation. Although there is general agreement on the properties of affirmations and presuppositions, it is very difficult to find a general definition of the phenomenon. The effort may be made along three lines:

a) From the logical point of view: the presupposition will be defined by the fact that if it is false, the utterance can be called neither true nor false (the falseness of the presuppositions establishes a "hole" in the truth table of the proposition).

b) From the viewpoint of use conditions: the presuppositions must be true (or regarded as true by the hearer) in order for the use of the utterance to be "normal"; otherwise it is unacceptable. But this "deontology" of discourse to which we are then referring remains to be more precisely defined.

c) From the viewpoint of the intersubjective relationships in the (pragmatic [338]) discourse: the choice of an utterance introduces a certain modification in the relationships among the interlocutors—according to the presupposition included in the utterance. Presupposing would then be a speech act with illocutionary value [343ff.]), by the same token as promising, ordering, interrogating.

● The notion of presupposition, found implicitly in the *Logique de Port-Royal* (Paris, 1660), pt. 2, chap. 10, is used explicitly by:

Figure 273

—logicians: G. Frege, "Uber Sinn und Bedeutung," *Zeitschrift für Philosophie und philosophische Kritik* 100 (1892): 25–50; L. Karttunen, "Presuppositions and Linguistic Context," *Theoretical Linguistics* 1 (1974): 182–94; and R. R. Hausser, "Presuppositions in Montague Grammar," *Theoretical Linguistics* 3 (1976): 245–80. The latter two deal with the problems posed by the integration of presuppositions into a formal semantics.

—philosophers: R. G. Collingwood, *An Essay on Metaphysics* (Oxford, 1940); and P. F. Strawson, "Identifying Reference and Truth-Values," *Theoria* 30 (1964): 96–118.

—linguists: E. H. Bendix, *Componential Analysis of General Vocabulary* (The Hague, 1968); O. Ducrot, "La Description sémantique des énoncés français," *L'Homme* 1 (1968): 37–53; and C. J. Fillmore, *Entailment Rules in a Semantic Theory*, Ohio State University Research Foundation Project on Linguistic Analysis, no. 10 (1965), pp. 50–82. There is considerable bibliographical information in *Langages* 19 (1970): 119–22.

General studies of presupposition are to be found in O. Ducrot, *Dire et ne pas dire* (Paris, 1972); R. Zuber, *Structure présuppositionnelle du langage* (Paris, 1972); R. M. Kempson, *Presupposition and the Delimitation of Semantics* (Cambridge, 1975); and P. Harder and C. Kook, *The Theory of Presupposition Failure* (Copenhagen, 1976). See also the collection of J. S. Petöfi and D. Franck, eds., *Präsupposition in Philosophie und Linguistik* (Frankfort, 1973).

FIGURE

The most widespread, most tenacious definition of the **figure** describes it as a deviation, a modification of a primary expression regarded as normal. A sentence including an inversion is opposed to the same sentence without an inversion; the metaphorical use of a word is related to its "ordinary" use—the operative notion here is one of substitution. The figure's value lies in providing a single principle for explaining a variety of phenomena; historically, it has made possible some interesting explorations of the nature of certain figures. But it encounters several objections, which may be summarized as follows:

1. Is every figure really a deviation? If the definition of figure is to

avoid being tautological, figures must be identifiable without its help. Now if we take as an appropriate sample the figures identified and described in any one of the classical treatises of rhetoric, we find that "figures" are included that, for the reader, do not contradict any particular rule. For example, an asyndeton is a coordination by juxtaposition; a polysyndeton, a coordination with repeated conjunctions. Which is a deviation—the first, the second, both? We may of course posit a rule that excludes them both from the norm; but this rule will not be situated at the same level as the one that proscribes the spelling *phynance*, to recall the favorite figure of Père Ubu. It turns out, in fact, that deviation passes from the position of original cause to that of final cause: numerous figures are only deviations with respect to an imaginary rule according to which language should be without figures.

2. Although it is difficult to prove that all figures are deviations, it is entirely obvious that not all deviations are figures. The definition of the figure as deviation remains incomplete so long as its specific difference from the norm is not identified. And this question has remained without a valid response to date.

3. Particular difficulties arise around the notion of norm [124ff.]. For, to all appearances, figures are neither rare, incomprehensible, nor strictly limited to literary language. Modern linguistics maintains that this norm corresponds to language, in the sense of a body of abstract rules [118ff.]; but to postulate that language excludes metaphor, for example, is to provide a singularly impoverished image of language. The metaphorical process, on the contrary, seems to be one of the most important characteristics of human language [104], a fact that has often led philosophers and linguists to see in it the origin of language itself. To get around this difficulty, we may compare the figures, not to the norm of language, but rather to the norm of another discourse: thus J. Cohen confronts examples of French symbolist poetry with the prose of contemporary scientists. But then another question arises: If there are two distinct types of discourse, why take one as the norm and the other as a deviation? Would it not be more accurate to suppose that each obeys its own norm? Or, as I. A. Richards put it humorously, must water be considered a deviation from ice?

The figures thus seem to form a set in intersection with (rather than included in) that of the linguistic infractions. This fact of course does not invalidate all the observations made in the name of deviation. If, for example, a figure has been described as repetition, we can retain this feature without necessarily postulating that the norm excludes repetitions; the deviation theory fails at the level of explanation, but it has some successes to its credit at the level of description.

Figure   *275*

The classic definition of the figure as deviation, as exception, has provoked a "romantic" reaction (almost as old as the definition itself) according to which the exception is credited with the same role as the rule: all language is metaphorical, as Vico, Hamann, Rousseau, and Nietzsche, among many others, have remarked. Adherents to this thesis base their judgment on the fact that a large number of words perceived today as nonmetaphorical are in fact extinguished metaphors. But this theory visibly confuses diachrony and synchrony: whatever the origin of language may have been, it remains true that in its use at a given moment, certain expressions are perceived as figures, while others are not. The question of the figure first requires a synchronic solution.

It is not certain, moreover, that all figures can be reduced to a single principle. The classical rhetorics usually distinguish **tropes,** or figures in which there is change of meaning, from the others, which would be the figures proper. And certain theories make it possible to account for the tropes without including the figures.

Thus I. A. Richards, resolute adversary of the figure as deviation, proposes this definition: "When we use a metaphor, we have two thoughts of different things active together and supported by a single word, or phrase, whose meaning is a resultant of this interaction" (*The Philosophy of Rhetoric*, p. 93). Neither of the two meanings is privileged with respect to the other; the metaphor grows out of their simple coexistence (interaction). This theory depends on the thesis (also professed by semanticist-critics such as Tynianov, Winkler, Empson) that the word does not have fixed and mutually exclusive meanings, but a potential semantic nucleus that is actualized differently in each context. Metaphor thus loses its specificity and is only one instance of polysemy [236].

It could be objected that in this theory, as in the theory of deviation as final cause, we are describing an object by the effects that it produces. The metaphor is a linguistic mechanism one effect of which is the establishment of a relationship between several meanings of a single word.

Whereas the foregoing theory deals exclusively with tropes, another conception seems particularly applicable, on the contrary, to figures in the narrow sense. This view originated in classical rhetoric, but we find it again among certain representatives of the Linguistic Circle of Prague. Figures would be nothing other than language perceived as language, that is, a use of language in which the latter more or less ceases to fulfill its signifying function (that is, its function of referring to something absent) and takes on an opaque character. This general effect is achieved by means of numerous devices, such as repetition, omission, quasi-geometrical formations (antithesis, gradation), and so on. Such a conception of the figures obviously does not account for the particular case of the tropes among the figures.

Some examples of problems never (or very rarely) touched upon in work on the figures follow:

First, the question of the nature of the relationship on which the figure is based has never been clearly raised. Aristotle defined *metaphor* as "transferring to one thing a name which designates something else," that is, as a change in the meaning of a word. But in place of that relationship, rhetorical tradition has surreptitiously substituted another: a relationship between *two* words that have the same meaning. Hence the desire, in the works of classical rhetoric, to name the expression itself, to translate metaphors. The first (Aristotelian) relationship alone corresponds to the linguistic process proper; the second is a metalinguistic elaboration of the describer: the handicap of all semantics—namely, that we can only speak about words by using words—has here become a source of confusion.

Second, rhetoric has always been content with a paradigmatic view of words (one in place of another), without attempting to interrogate their syntagmatic relationship (one next to the other). By the mid eighteenth century Dumarsais had already been able to assert (in the *Traité des Tropes*) that words take on metaphorical meaning only by a new union of terms. There would thus be another perspective, complementary to the first, in which metaphor, for example, would be defined not as a substitution but as a particular combination. Works that are linguistic (and, in particular, syntactic) in inspiration have begun to point out this possibility, but it remains to be explored.

A third question, already mentioned, would be that of the relationship between two meanings of a word that forms a figurative expression. For centuries rhetorical treatises have affirmed that one meaning replaced (supplanted, and so on) the other. Not until Richards's and Empson's research did there emerge the hypothesis of a relationship of interaction as opposed to a relationship of substitution [257].

If the theory of figures still includes so many obscure points, it is because the figure is a phenomenon of linguistic semantics (a fact that has not always been understood), and semantics itself is still far from resolving (or even raising) all its own problems.

● General and historical overviews are H. Konrad, *Etude sur la métaphore* (Paris, 1939); C. D. Lewis, *The Poetic Image* (London, 1947); and H. Meyer, *Die Metapher* (Zurich, 1964). Some recent works devoted to the problem of the figures are I. A. Richards, *The Philosophy of Rhetoric* (New York and Oxford, 1965); C. Brooke-Rose, *A Grammar of Metaphor* (London, 1958); S. Levin, "Deviation—Statistical and Determinate

Figure 277

—in Poetic Language," *Lingua* 12 (1963): 276–90; J. Cohen, *Structure du langage poétique* (Paris, 1966); T. Todorov, *Littérature et signification* (Paris, 1967), pp. 91–118; J. Dubois et al., *Rhétorique générale* (Paris, 1970); and *Communications* 16 (1970): *Recherches rhétoriques.*

The rhetorical figures have been categorized in countless ways. In order to make the principles of classification intelligible, we shall name some twenty of those most frequently listed and give their definition along with characteristic examples in English and in French.

Alliteration: a repetition of the same sounds. "But day doth daily draw my sorrows longer" (Shakespeare, sonnet 28); "Pour qui sont ces serpents qui sifflent sur vos têtes?"

Antanaclasis: a repetition of the same word with a different meaning. "We must all *hang* together, or most assuredly we shall all *hang* separately" (B. Franklin); "Proculeius reprochait à son fils qu'il *attendait* sa mort, et celui-ci ayant répliqué qu'il ne *l'attendait* pas, eh bien! reprit-il, je te prie de *l'attendre.*"

Antithesis: a comparison of two antonyms (that is, words including opposed semantic features). "Drown desperate *sorrow* in dead Edward's grave, / And plant your *joys* in living Edward's throne" (Shakespeare, *Richard the Third*); "Quand je suis tout de *feu*, d'où me vient cette *glace?*"

Chiasmus: the repetition and—simultaneously—inversion of the relationship between two words in the course of the sentence. "The *fool* doth think he is *wise*, but the *wise* man knows himself to be a *fool*" (Shakespeare, *As You Like It*; "Il faut *manger* pour *vivre* et non pas *vivre* pour *manger.*"

Ellipsis: the suppression of one of the elements necessary for a complete syntactic construction. "And he to England shall along with you" (Shakespeare, *Hamlet*); "Déjà vibraient les rires, déjà les impatiences."

Gradation: a succession of (at least three) syntactically equivalent terms that possess one or several semantic features in common and among which at least one feature is repeated with quantitative changes. " . . . knowing that *tribulation* worketh patience; and *patience,* experience; and *experience, hope. . .* " (Romans 5:3–4); "Un *souffle,* une *ombre,* un *rien,* tout lui donnait la fièvre."

Hyperbole: a quantitative augmentation of one of the properties of an object, a state, and so on. "His legs *bestrid the ocean*; his rear'd arm / *Crested the world. . .* " (Shakespeare, *Antony and Cleopatra*); "Les flots couverts de morts *interrompent leur course.*"

Inversion: a permutation of the elements of a syntactic construction. "Achilles wrath, to Greece the direful spring / Of woes unnumbered, Heavenly goddess, sing" (Pope); "Flottait un nocturne archipel / Dans le jour ruisselant de ciel."

Irony: the use of a word to express the meaning of its antonym. " 'It *grieves* me much,' replied the Peer again, / 'Who speaks so *well* should ever speak in vain' " (Pope, *The Rape of the Lock*); "Comme vous êtes *courageux!*"

Litotes: a quantitative diminishing of one of the properties of an object, state, and so on. "*Nor are thy lips ungraceful, Sire of Men, / Nor tongue ineloquent*" (Milton, *Paradise Lost*); "Va, *je ne te hais point.*"

Metaphor: the use of a word to express a meaning resembling, yet differing from, its habitual meaning. "Eye, *gazelle,* delicate *wanderer,* / *Drinker* of horizon's fluid line" (Spender); "Le remords *dévorant* s'éleva dans son coeur."

Metonymy: the use of a word to designate an object or a property occurring in an existential relationship with the habitual reference of this same word. "*Bell, book* and *candle* shall not drive me back" (Shakespeare, *King John*); "Je ne décide point entre *Grèce* et *Rome!*"

Oxymoron: the establishment of a syntactic relationship (coordination, determination) between two antonyms. "Eternity, thou *pleasing, dreadful* thought" (Addison); "Cette *obscure clarté* qui tombe des étoiles."

Paralipsis: a formula by means of which one declares that one is not saying what one is saying in the sentence itself. "Let but the commons hear this testament / Which (pardon me) I do not mean to read. . . " (Shakespeare, *Julius Caesar*); "Je ne vous peindrai point le tumulte et les cris, / Le sang de tous côtés ruisselant dans Paris."

Paronomasia: the juxtaposition of words that have the same sound but different meanings. "Were it not *here apparent* that thou art *heir apparent*" (Shakespeare, *Henry IV*, Part 2); "Il a compromis son *bonheur* mais non pas son *honneur.*"

Repetition: a re-use of the same word or group of words. " . . . O, now, for ever / *Farewell* the tranquil mind! *farewell* content! *Farewell* the plumed troops and the big wars / That make ambition virtue! O, *farewell!*" (Shakespeare, *Othello*); "*J'ai vu, j'ai vu* couler des larmes véritables."

Simile: the establishment of a parallelism between two meanings through the intermediary of *like* or *as* [in French, *comme*] or a substitute. "Pleasures are *like* poppies spread— / You seize the flow'r, its bloom is shed" (Burns); "Le bonheur des méchants, *comme* un torrent s'écoule."

Syllepsis: the use of a single word that has more than one meaning and participates in more than one syntactic construction. "At a word, *hang* no more about me. I am no gibbet for you" (Shakespeare, *Merry Wives of Windsor*); "Je souffre . . . brûlé de plus de *feux* que je n'en allumai."

Synecdoche: the use of a word in a broadened sense that includes the

Figure   279

ordinary meaning as one aspect. "Give us this day our daily *bread*" (*Matthew* 6:11); "Depüis plus de six mois, éloigné de mon père / J'ignore le destin d'une *tête* si chère."

Zeugma: the grammatical coordination of two words that possess opposed semantic features—for example, *abstract* and *concrete*. "Here though, great Anna! whom three realms obey, / Dost sometimes *counsel take*—and sometimes *tea*" (Pope, *The Rape of the Lock*); "On croirait voir deux femelles grises, *habillées de loques et de découragement*."

- A classical treatise in French, recently reprinted—P. Fontanier, *Les Figures du discours* (Paris, 1968)—has a much more extensive catalogue. In English, see, for example, J. W. V. Macbeth, *The Might and Mirth of Literature* (New York, 1875). For a recent treatment, with examples from political discourse, see S. Chaneles, *"That Pestilent Cosmetic, Rhetoric"* (New York, 1972).

These figures, like numerous others (which, for the most part, are subdivisions of the ones cited), have been categorized according to quite diverse principles that have of course influenced the definitions proposed. Unlike the classical rhetoricians, authors with a linguistic orientation seek to formalize the logical matrices of which the figures would be a manifestation; in other words, they seek to present the figures as the products of a combinatorial system whose constitutive categories are to be determined. A first category is immediately apparent, namely, the nature of the linguistic units in which the figure is actualized. This category can be subdivided at once, moreover, according to whether the dimensions of each unit or its level is observed (according, then, to whether the syntagmatic or the paradigmatic viewpoint is adopted) [108ff.]. In the first case the following degrees can be identified: (1) the sound (or letter) isolated; (2) the morpheme (or word); (3) the syntagma; and (4) the sentence (or utterance). In the second case we can distinguish (1) sounds or spelling; (2) syntax; and (3) semantics; within this latter class, syntagmatic semantic relationships (as in metaphor) can be opposed to paradigmatic semantic relationships (as in irony). Of course, certain figures bring into play several categories at a time; for example, repetition involves sounds (letters) and meaning simultaneously.

A second undertaking, much more difficult than the first, attempts to systematize the constitutive operations of each figure. The Liège group (J. Dubois et al.) and J. Durand have proposed retaining four logical operations: adjunction, suppression, substitution (that is, suppression *and* adjunction), and permutation. Such a division is irreproachable from a logical standpoint, but we may wonder to what extent it corresponds to the operations actually brought into play and to what extent it is more than a simple mnemotechnic device. Other dimensions are doubtless required for this analysis, but they are much less evident, and for the moment there is no agreement as to what they might be. J. Durand has shown that in the relationship between two terms, identity, similarity, difference, and opposition can be distinguished; the Liège group qualifies operations as "simple," "partial," "complete," and so on. It is equally possible to use as a basis more properly linguistic categories such as ambiguity, coordination, and so on; the distinction between affirmed and presupposed meaning may also be taken into account. Perhaps the difference between certain figures will prove to be less considerable than had been thought: the Liège rhetoricians have shown, for example, that metaphor is nothing but a double synecdoche.

Another question concerning the figures has to do with their use. Since the Middle Ages, they have been pointed out in literature in particular, and people have tended to see a relationship of mutual implication between poetic language and figurative language. But objections have been raised at least since the time of Dumarsais, who affirmed that popular language contained as many figures as any other, if not more. And in our day several theoreticians of literature (V. Shklovskii, I. A. Richards, R. Jakobson) have insisted on the (inverse) existence of a literature without images (which is not the same as a literature without figures). The affinity of literary and figurative language remains in fact incontestable.

Since the emergence of the social sciences in the nineteenth century, it has been observed that the grid formed in language by the rhetorical figures occurs elsewhere as well. Psychological associations are often classified in terms of "resemblance" and "contiguity," and these same terms are found in protocols concerning magic (Frazer, Mauss) or dreams (Freud); Saussure, after Kruszewski, finds them again in the very organization of language. Several researchers are currently trying to describe symbolic systems other than language in rhetorical terms and thus are contributing to the development of semiotics [84ff.]. R. Jakobson has attempted to relate two important rhetorical figures—metaphor and metonymy—and two fundamental categories of language—selection and combination [111]—by speaking of the "metaphoric and metonymic poles" that dominate linguistic structure.

● See R. Jakobson, "Two Aspects of Language and Two Types of Aphasic Disturbances," in *Selected Writings II* (The Hague, 1971), pp. 239–59; J. Cohen, *Structure du langage poétique* (Paris, 1966); T. Todorov, *Littérature et signification* (Paris, 1967), appendix; J. Dubois et al., *Rhétorique générale* (Paris, 1970); J. Durand, "Rhétorique et image publicitaire," *Communications* 15 (1970): 70–95; and idem, "Rhétorique du nombre," *Communications* 16 (1970): *Recherches rhétoriques*, pp. 125–133.

SEMANTIC RELATIONSHIPS AMONG SENTENCES

Anaphor

A segment of discourse is termed anaphoric if one must refer to another segment of the same discourse in order to interpret it (even literally). The segment to which the anaphoric term refers is called the interpretant (Tesnière proposes the expression **semantic source.** The term **antecedent** is often used, for the interpretant generally precedes the anaphor; furthermore, etymologically speaking, the anaphor is that which refers back). The anaphor and its interpretant may belong either to the same sentence or to two successive sentences; it is this latter possibility that allows us to consider the anaphor as a potentially transphrastic relation. In the examples that follow, the anaphor is in italics and its interpretant is in capitals.

(1) If *he* comes, PETER will be happy.

(2) I ran into SOME FRIENDS $\left\{ \begin{array}{l} \textit{. These} \text{ friends} \\ \textit{. They} \\ \textit{who} \end{array} \right\}$ spoke to me about you.

(3) Peter TOLD ME THAT THE WEATHER WOULD BE NICE. Jack *too.*

(4) Peter knows my HOUSE, but not *yours.*

(5) PETER DETESTS PAUL, and $\left\{ \begin{array}{l} \textit{the reverse is also true.} \\ \textit{vice versa.} \end{array} \right\}$

(6) PETER, PAUL, AND JACK came. $\left\{ \begin{array}{l} \textit{They} \text{ were } \textit{all} \text{ happy.} \\ \textit{None of them} \text{ was happy.} \end{array} \right\}$

It is clear from these examples that the interpretant may have widely varying dimensions and, furthermore, that anaphors may be found in very different parts of speech [203] (but especially in the category of pronouns; this is why the Greek grammarian Apollonios, one of the first to speak of anaphors, used the notion to distinguish those pronouns that refer to objects—the deictics—from those that refer to segments of discourse—the anaphorics. Except for the terminology used, this distinction is similar to F. Brunot's: for him, pronouns may be either **nominal**—when, as nouns do, they designate things—or **representative**).

Anaphor and Syntax. Many linguists tend to exclude the anaphor from the syntactic phenomena. This stems from the fact that the syntactic function of the anaphoric expression is completely independent of its interpretant and may be determined without reference to the latter (in [1], above, for example, *he* can only be a subject, whatever its interpretant). This is why Tesnière says that the anaphor is a "supplementary semantic connection with no corresponding structural connection" (translated from *Eléments de syntaxe structurale*, p. 85). In the same way, Martinet assigns the pronouns, on the same basis as he does the articles, to the category of **modalities** (monemes that—although they are grammatical [202]—cannot serve to mark functions); this is because, for him, the only syntactic functions are those that link constituents to the predicate, directly or indirectly [213].

We could raise the following objections to this exclusion:

a) That the anaphor plays an essential role in the phenomena of agreement and that we must take it into account in order to explain the impossibility of certain utterances, such as "Mary does not know how to laugh at himself." Martinet would answer that agreement is a superficial phenomenon (morphological and not syntactic [53]).

b) That the **relative pronoun,** which seems typically anaphoric, has an essential role to play in the organization of the relationships of dependency within the sentence, since it allows us to connect one clause to another. The *Port-Royal Grammar* gives a partial answer: it separates the two functions of the relative pronoun, which would be, simultaneously but independently, conjunction and anaphor ("The soldiers who were afraid fled" = "The soldiers fled *if* they were afraid"). Tesnière takes up the same idea in his description of the relative as a sort of amalgam of two distinct units. For him, in fact, a relative clause (he calls it an **adjectival clause**) is the product of a translation [239] that has put a clause in the role of adjective (the relative clause is the epithet of its antecedent). Thus we have to distinguish, in the relative pronoun, (1) a translative, which has syntactic value and marks the existence of the translation; and (2) an anaphoric pronoun, which has as its interpretant the noun to which the relative is attached as epithet. This separation may well appear artificial. Is it really by chance that it is in fact an anaphoric that transforms a clause into an adjective? One can hardly define the function of the adjective without recognizing that an anaphor underlies it: to say that one is buying the red book is to say that one is buying a book and to say at the same time, in a way, that *that* book is red.

● L. Tesnière deals with anaphors in general in *Eléments de syntaxe structurale* (Paris, 1965), chaps. 42 and 43. On relative pronouns, see ibid., chaps. 241 and 242; and the *Port-Royal Grammar*, pt. 2, chap. 9.

The quarrel over whether the anaphor is syntactic or not has echoes within generative theory. Chomsky deals with anaphorics in his description of the syntactic component [54] of grammar. More precisely, he attributes two different deep structures to the utterance (7) "Peter said I could see him," according to whether *him* is anaphoric, referring back to Peter, or deictic, designating a third party. In the first case, the deep structure is "Peter said I could see Peter" (and a later transformation will suppress the repetition of *Peter*). In the second case, it is "Peter said I could see he" (with a subsequent transformation of agreement). This thesis is currently much debated, for in the case of a slightly more complicated anaphor, it may be difficult to determine what the deep structure should be. Some transformationalists suggest that a single syntactic structure should be recognized in (7); the job of foreseeing the two possible interpretations (and of foreseeing also that only one is appropriate to "Mary said I could see him") would fall to the semantic component. The same objections may be offered to this approach as to Tesnière's; in any case, the generativists have to treat phenomena analogous to the anaphor in deep structure, especially the type of anaphor implied in the adjective (since they give as deep structure for "I have bought the red book" something like "I have bought the book—the book is red"), and in order to suppress the repetition, they use a transformation analogous to the one with which Chomsky generates the anaphoric pronoun.

● On the problem of pronouns in generative grammar, see J. R. Ross, "English Pronominalization," in *To Honor Roman Jakobson* (The Hague, 1967); R. C. Dougherty, "A Theory of Pronominal Reference," *Foundations of Language* 5 (1969): 488–519; P. M. Postal, "A Global Constraint on Pronominalization," *Linguistic Inquiry* 3 (1972): 35–59; and G. Fauconnier, *La Coréférence: Syntaxe ou sémantique?* (Paris, 1974).

The Semantic Nature of the Anaphor. The difficulty with the anaphor stems not only from its situation on the borderline between syntax and semantics but at least as much from the fact that its semantic nature is far from clear. A widespread approach consists in representing the anaphor as a substitution: the anaphoric expression "stands for" its interpretant, whose repetition it avoids (a particular application of this approach is found in the traditional definition of the pronoun as a replacement for a noun; this definition arose from a truncated quote from Apollonios, in whose text the pronoun is said to replace the *proper noun*). According to the *Port-Royal Grammar*, a desire for elegance is at the origin of the anaphor (repetition is tedious); modern grammarians consider themselves more scientific because they speak of a desire for economy. This view of the anaphor as a substitution gives rise to serious difficulties the least of which is the following: we would often obtain an ungrammatical sentence if we were to replace the anaphoric expression purely and simply by its interpretant (cf. utterances [4] and [5], above). The basic problem is that substitution, even when it is possible without grammatical alterations, may involve serious modifications in meaning. This is the case when the interpretant is an indefinite expression: "I ran into some friends; they spoke to me about you" does not have the same meaning at all as "I ran into some friends; some friends spoke to me about you" (we gain nothing by arguing that the interpretant of *they*, has to be changed into *these friends* in order to be substituted for *they*, for *these* is itself an anaphoric expression).

Thus we are led to another description in which we may say, for example, that the anaphoric, when it serves to designate an object, designates the same object as its interpretant (certain English philosophers describe this role of the pronoun as that of picking up the reference of the antecedent). In the same spirit, F. Brunot described the pronoun as a "representative." This view resembles that of certain medieval grammarians, for whom the pronoun designated the substance of the thing, separated from its accidents (*substantiam solam*: when the interpretant is a description of an object, the pronoun then represents purely and simply the object of this description). Some difficulties remain, however. Does it mean anything to say that *some friends* designates objects [253] that would subsequently be represented by *they*? Furthermore, it is not at all clear what particular objects are designated by *he* in "And no one knows himself so long as he has not suffered," "A child may cry when he is afraid," or "Only Peter said that he would come." In all these cases, the anaphoric pronoun seems to have a much more complex role than that of representative: it seems to play the role of the variable in logico-mathematical language; in other words, it only marks the place of the arguments in the predicate. A unified theory dealing with all the modes and functions of the anaphor—assuming that such a project is legitimate—still remains to be elaborated.

• On the notion of the anaphor as substitute, see, for example, J. Dubois, *Grammaire structurale du français*, 3 vols. (Paris, 1965–69), vol. 1 *Nom et pronom* (1965), pt. 3. On the anaphor as representative, see F. Brunot, *La Pensée et la langue* (Paris, 1922). On the relationship between the pronoun and the variable, see W. V. Quine, "Logic As a Source of Syntactical Insights," in *Proceedings of Symposia in Applied Mathematics*, vol. 12, *Structure of Language and Its Mathematical Aspects* (Providence, 1961); and T. Wasow, "Anaphoric Pronouns and Bound Variables," *Language* 51 (1975): 368–83. On the history of pronoun theory up to the eighteenth century, see G. Sahlin, *César Chesneau Du Marsais et son rôle dans l'évolution de la grammaire générale* (Paris, 1928), chap. 8. An attempt at a unified theory of the anaphor is in H. Hiż, "Referentials," *Semiotica* 2 (1969): 136–66. On the problem of the pronoun in English, see P. M. Postal, "On So-called Pronouns in English," in *Modern Studies in English*, ed. D. Reibel and S. Schane (Englewood Cliffs, 1969).

Semantic Coordination

Alongside syntactic coordination [211], which is the relationship among segments having the same function, C. Bally introduced the idea of semantic coordination. If the latter must be distinguished from the former, it is because semantic coordination is based above all on the acts of enunciation accomplished on the occasion of sentence production and because, furthermore, it has no obligatory grammatical marks.

A and *Z* are semantically coordinated if (*a*) *A* is independent of *Z*, in the sense that it is the object of a complete act of enunciation (it thus includes a topic and a comment [271]), or if (*b*) *Z* is presented as a comment whose topic has been provided by *A*, as a judgment on the occasion of *A*. Thus there is coordination in the successive enunciation of *A*, "It is freezing," and *Z*, "We won't go out"; *Z* is presented as drawing the consequences of *A*. We do not have coordination, however, in an enumeration of independent statements (even if they are of the same nature) such as "Yesterday I went to the movies. The day before yesterday I stayed home." Here condition *b* is not met. On the other hand, it is condition *a* that precludes the existence of semantic coordination when two propositions are joined together in a single enunciative act. This would be the case for the enunciation of the sentence "I only went to see him so he could tell me the news." Here we have a single act of enunciation corresponding to a single (avowed) intention: to state the goal of the visit. Bally speaks of **linked sentences.** (N.B. It is not the existence of a subordinating conjunction that prevents semantic coordination, for there may be semantic coordination in "I went to see him so that he could tell me the news," especially if there is a pause between the two clauses.)

There is doubtless a close relationship between the phenomenon of the anaphor and that of coordination. Bally points this out by imagining a child language that would include only two "words": *Coucou* ("I see a bird") and *Frtt* ("I hear wings flapping"). If the sequence *Coucou Frtt* is understood as a coordination, the second word being regarded as a comment concerning the first, it will probably be interpreted as "I see a bird. *It* is flapping its wings." A coordination is perhaps also the basis for the following anaphor: "I ran into some friends. They spoke about you." *They* designates the persons whose existence was affirmed by the first sentence and who will be the topic of the second. It is not without importance that those anaphors that impose the representation of the pronoun as variable always appear within a linked sentence; thus it should be possible to distinguish two major types of anaphor, one corresponding to coordination, the other corresponding to the linked sentence.

● On coordination, see C. Bally, *Linguistique générale et linguistique française*, 4th ed., rev. (Bern, 1965), pt. 1, chap. 2 (cf. the much more concise description given by A. Sèchehaye, in *Essai sur la structure logique de la phrase* (Paris, 1926), chap. 2, sec. 1). On the application of this theory to the problem of the anaphor, see O. Ducrot, "Les Indéfinis et l'énonciation," *Langages* 17 (1970): *L'Enonciation*, ed. T. Todorov, pp. 91–111. A syntactic theory of coordination (but based on semantics) is presented in S. C. Dik, *Coordination* (Amsterdam, 1968).

Logical Inference

Whereas the anaphor and coordination are relationships internal to a given text that connect the utterances of a discourse with one another, inference and paraphrase relate utterances without regard to the texts in which they occur. Utterance A is said to be inferred from the set of utterances U if it is contradictory, for logical (and not empirical) reasons —that is, independently of all factual knowledge—to accept the utterances of U and not utterance A (U may consist of a single utterance). When we attempt to describe the utterances of a language semantically, must we indicate the utterances of which they may be either the conclusion or the point of departure? Three attitudes are possible:

1) We may maintain (as do most linguists in the Saussurian tradition and quite a few philosophers of the Oxford school [95]) that the factors determining the inferential properties of an utterance have a very loose relationship with its linguistic organization. We may even ask whether it is possible, given the semantic indeterminacy [237] with which most utterances are afflicted, to attribute to them a fixed inferential value. Moreover, this value would not belong, most of the time, to the utterance itself, but to its enunciation by one particular speaker, given that in many cases the referent [252] depends upon the speaker's identity (*I* and *here* do not refer to the same person and the same place if they are pronounced by different speakers) and that the inferential value is often tied to the referent.

2) Conversely, it may be argued that the meaning of an utterance, or an essential part of it, is constituted by the set of inferences that it allows (this thesis could be called **logicistic**): if we are not capable of inferring "Certain viviparous animals are serpents" from "Certain serpents are viviparous," it is because we have not understood these sentences (we have failed to grasp the value of *certain* or that of the subject-attribute relationship). Thus we have failed to describe a lan-

guage if we have not provided the means to predict, for each utterance, what can be inferred from it.

3) An intermediate position would consist in the following:

a) We would refuse to recognize that the inferential value of an utterance is *ipso facto* constitutive of its meaning; thus we would refuse to include automatically in the description of the elements of a language the indication of their effect in inference. At the very most, we might admit that for certain particular turns of phrase, certain possibilities of inference, felt particularly strongly by speaking subjects, are an integral part of their meaning or tend to become so.

b) We would require of the linguist that his semantic description of utterances not render their use in reasoning incomprehensible. In other words, even if we grant that the laws of inference are not those of language, the linguistic description of utterances must allow us to comprehend that logical laws may have some control over them.

● On the relationships between logic and languages see Y. Bar-Hillel, "Logical Syntax and Semantics," *Language* 30 (1954):230–37, for an uncompromising presentation of the logicistic thesis. On more recent developments of the problem, see *Langages* 30 (1973): *Logique et langage*, ed. R. Zuber; and E. L. Keenan, ed., *Formal Semantics of Natural Language* (Cambridge, 1975). Certain contemporary logicians, disciples of R. Montague, believe that they are able, owing to the most refined logical techniques, to express the semantics of natural languages in the framework of a theory of logical inference and logical truth, without sacrificing any of the specific features of natural languages. Two essential texts, from this point of view, are M. J. Cresswell, *Logics and Languages* (London, 1970); and R. Montague, *Formal Philosophy* (New Haven, 1974), which has a very useful introduction by R. Thomason. The intermediate position mentioned above (attitude 3) has led to the development of a theory of argumentation that aims to be better adapted to ordinary language than a theory of inference; see O. Ducrot, *La Preuve et le dire* (Paris, 1973), chap. 13; and J.-C. Anscombre and O. Ducrot, "L'Argumentation dans la langue," *Langages* 42 (1976): 5–27.

Paraphrase

The comprehension of a language implies that we can establish a correspondence between each utterance and other utterances of the same language that are considered synonymous, or semantically equivalent (at least from a given viewpoint); that is, it implies that each utterance is capable of paraphrase, of being translated into the same as an integral (and doubtless essential) part the construction of an algorithm of paraphrase, that is, of a mechanical procedure, a calculation allowing the prediction, on the basis of any utterance, of the set of its possible paraphrases. They even believe that this algorithm of translation might have a simpler mathematical structure than that of sentence production that constitutes the generative grammars (for Chomsky, on the contrary, the study of paraphrase belongs to the semantic component [54]; that is, it comes after the construction of the sentence-generating syntactic component).

● On this view of linguistic description, see H. Hiż, *The Role of Paraphrase in Grammar*, Monograph Series in Language and Linguistics, no. 17 (Washington, D.C., 1964), pp. 97–104; and idem, "Aletheic Semantic Theory," *Philosophical Forum*, n.s. 1 (1969): 438–51. On the general problems raised by paraphrase, see *Langages* 20 (1973): *La paraphrase*, ed. D. Leeman; and R. Martin, *Inférence, antonymie et paraphrase* (Paris, 1976).

A basic difficulty with this view stems from the very notion of paraphrase, of semantic equivalence, which is not easy to define. If we refuse to content ourselves with the simple intuitions of speaking subjects (synonymous sentences are sentences that speaking subjects are willing to use interchangeably), we may seek logical criteria. Different possibilities then come to mind, but there are problems with each one. Two examples of definition follow:

a) Two utterances are synonymous only if they have exactly the same truth conditions, if neither can be true unless the other is true. This definition has relatively unacceptable consequences. All **tautological utterances** (for two plus two equals four, the Pythagorean theorem, any truism) would be synonymous, since by definition they are all always true. The same could be said of contradictory utterances (which are never true). By the same token, two utterances differing only in the expression they use to designate the same person would be synonymous (for example, "The author of *Hamlet* did not scorn comedy" and "The author of *Much Ado About Nothing* did not scorn comedy"). The synonymy of these two utterances would be shocking, since the former is usually understood to mean " . . . nevertheless did not scorn. . . ," and the latter, " . . . thus did not scorn. . . . "

b) Two utterances U_1 and U_2 are synonymous if one of them—U_1, for example—is a component of a larger utterance U_3 and if, when we replace U_1 by U_2 in U_3, the resulting utterance U_4 still has the same truth conditions as U_3 (in other words, U_1 and U_2 are interchangeable, *salva veritate*). In the sentence, "Peter knows that two plus two equals four," for example, let us replace "two plus two equals four" by the statement of the Pythagorean theorem; the truth value of the sentence may well be modified. But it is still not clear that this definition is not too restrictive, that it does not run the risk of suppressing all synonymy (even if we decide never to take as U_3 utterances of the type "Peter said . . . ," *veritate*). This second definition enables us to escape the difficulties that arise from the first one. In the sentence, "Peter knows that two plus two equals four," for example, let us replace "two plus two equals four" by the statement of the Pythagorean theorem; the truth value of the sentence may well be modified. But it is still not clear that this definition is not too restrictive, that it does not run the risk of suppressing all synonymy (even if we decide never to take as U_3 utterances of the type "Peter said . . . ," utterances which, *a priori*, would render synonymy impossible).

- For a discussion of synonymy, see, for example, W. V. Quine, *From a Logical Point of View* (Cambridge, Mass., 1953). Two viewpoints more directly related to linguistic description are in H. G. Schogt, "Synonymie et signe linguistique," *La Linguistique* 8, no. 2 (1972): 5–38; and R. Harris, *Synonymy and Linguistic Analysis* (Oxford, 1973).

DISCURSIVE TRANSFORMATIONS

When we undertake to analyze a text, we obtain a series of propositions each of which consists of at least a subject (argument) and a predicate (function). We can then seek to specify the nature of the predicates and thus to state the static-dynamic (adjective-verb) opposition [218]. We can also explore the relationships between propositions, taken in pairs (independently of their relationship in contiguity), and, more particularly, between their predicates; we shall discover that the latter often have common elements and can thus be regarded as **transformations** of each other. This undertaking was first developed in linguistics with Z. S. Harris—whose objects were particular lexical sequences—and, at about the same time, but in a different way, in anthropology with Lévi-Strauss's analysis of myths. In the case that concerns us here—propositional analysis of discourse [296]—interest centers around the relationships between terms that are introduced by the observer and that may represent units of variable dimensions within the real text. Thus we may say that "X is working" and "X is deciding to work" are in a relationship of transformation: these two propositions must always designate events evoked by the discourse, but it is not necessary that they appear there literally.

The derivation described here is purely logical, not psychological: we may say that "X is deciding to work" is a transformation of "X is working," even though, psychologically, the relationship is the inverse. Psychology intervenes here as an object of knowledge, not as a working tool: most of the time, the transformations designate either psychic operations or the relationship between an event and its representation.

There appear to be two restrictions on transformations. On the one hand, we cannot yet speak of transformation if the difference in predicates cannot be clearly established. On the other hand, we can no longer speak of transformation if, instead of two transforms of the same predicate, we find two autonomous predicates. An example of a relationship similar to the one between transformed predicates—but which does not fall within the category of transformation—is that of actions that are consequences of each other (relationships of motivation, implication, presupposition). This is the case for the propositions "*X* has no money" and "*X* is beginning to work": they do not have a common predicate, and the relationship between them is not one of transformation. A case that is even more closely related, in appearance, is that of actions designated by causal verbs: "*X* incites *Y* to work," "*X* makes *Y* work," and so on; even though such a sentence calls to mind the relationship of transformation, we are dealing here with two independent predicates and with a consequence. The possible confusion with transformation comes from the fact that the first action is almost entirely set aside; we have retained only its objective (we are not told how *X* "incites," or "makes," and so on).

A more attentive examination allows us to distinguish two major types within the category of transformations, according to the form of the relationship between base predicate and transformed predicate.

The first type is *simple transformation* (or **specification**), which consists in replacing a certain operator determining the predicate (modality, negation, and so on, are examples of operators). The base predicates may be regarded as endowed with a zero operator. This process evokes what is, in language, the process of auxiliation, in the broad sense, in which a verb accompanies the main verb and limits its meaning ("*X* is beginning to work"). In English, this operator may come from other linguistic forms as well—adverbs, particles, other lexical terms.

The second type is *complex transformation* (or **reaction**), which is characterized by the appearance of a second predicate, which is grafted onto the first and cannot exist independently of it. Whereas in the case of the simple transformation there is only one predicate and consequently a single subject, in the complex transformation the presence of two predicates may correspond to that of one or two subjects. "*X* thinks that he has killed his mother" is, like "*Y* thinks that *X* has killed his mother," a complex transformation of the proposition "*X* has killed his mother."

If we are no longer concerned with the form of the relationship between base predicate and transformed predicate, but rather with its very definition, we can discern several transformational classes within each of the two preceding types. The list of these classes, which is purely logical, should be at the same time universal; but the insufficiency of our knowledge in this area obliges us to be satisfied for the moment with a simple enumeration of the most representative transformations (and those that are the easiest to observe in English). The verbs grouped within a single class of transformations are linked by the relationship that they imply between the base predicate and the transformed predicate. They diverge, however, in terms of what their meaning presupposes: for example, "*X* confirms that *Y* is working" and "*X* reveals that *Y* is working" operate the same descriptive transformation; but *to confirm* presupposes that this fact was already known, while *to reveal* presupposes that *X* is the first to affirm it.

Simple Transformations

1. *Transformations of* **mode.** Transformations of mode, which concern the possibility, the impossibility, or the necessity of an action, are put into play by the language through modal verbs such as *can* and *must* or one of their substitutes. *Example*: "*X* must commit a crime."

2. *Transformations of* **intent.** In transformations of intent, the intention (on the part of the subject of the proposition) to accomplish an action is indicated, but not the action itself. This operator is formulated in the language by verbs such as *try, plan, premeditate. Example*: "*X* is planning to commit a crime."

3. *Transformations of* **result.** Whereas in the transformation of intent the action was seen in the incipient stage, the transformation of result formulates it as accomplished. In English this action is designated by verbs such as *succeed in, manage to, achieve*; in the Slavic languages, the perfective aspect of the verb plays this role. The transformations of intent and result, preceding and following the same zero-operator predicate, have been described by C. Bremond as "triads." *Example*: "*X* succeeds in committing a crime."

4. *Transformations of* **manner.** All the other classes of simple transformations—which specify the way in which an action takes place—could be characterized as transformations of manner; yet, certain more homogeneous groups may be examined separately. The language operates this transformation chiefly by means of adverbs, but we frequently find auxiliary verbs in the same function—*hasten, dare, excel at, persist in*. A relatively coherent group is formed by the indices of intensity such as those found, for example, in the comparative and the superlative. *Example*: "*X* hastens to commit a crime."

5. *Transformations of* **aspect.** In English, aspect finds its least ambiguous expression in the progressive construction (the imperfective aspect

is marked in the auxiliary by the elements *be —ing*) and in auxiliating verbs such as *begin to* (inchoative aspect), *continue* (continuative aspect), and *finish* (terminative aspect). Other aspects include the iterative (repetition of an action or state), the suspensive (interruption), and so on. We may note the referential proximity of the inchoative and terminative aspects to the transformations of intent and result, respectively, but these phenomena are categorized differently, since the ideas of finality and will are lacking in these aspects. *Example*: "*X* is beginning to commit a crime."

6. *Transformations of* **status.** The term "status," used in the Whorfian sense, designates the replacement of the positive form of a predicate by its negative or its opposite form; negation is expressed in English by *not*; opposition, by a lexical substitution. This group of transformations had already been pointed out, very briefly, by Propp; Lévi-Strauss refers to the same type of operation when he speaks of transformations (he suggests that we could treat the violation as the inverse of the prohibition and the latter as a negative transformation of the ·injunction). *Example*: "*X* is not committing a crime."

Complex Transformations

1. *Transformations of* **appearance.** Transformations of appearance indicate the substitution of one predicate for another, the latter passing for the former without really being equivalent to it. The verbs *feign, pretend, claim, disguise* customarily designate this action. In all such cases, the action of the primary predicate is unaccomplished. *Example*: "*X* (or *Y*) pretends that *X* is committing a crime."

2. *Transformations of* **knowledge.** As opposed to these *trompe l'oeil* cases, we can image a type of transformation dealing with acquired knowledge of the action denoted by another predicate. Verbs like *observe, learn, guess, know, lack knowledge of* describe the different phases and modalities of knowledge. Aristotle had this transformation in mind when he spoke, in the *Poetics*, of *recognition*; Propp also noted the autonomy of such actions but did not grant them much importance. In the case of lack of knowledge, the subject of the two verbs is generally different, but it is not impossible for it to be identical; this refers us back to stories relating a memory loss, unconscious actions, and so on. *Example*: "*X* (or *Y*) learns that *X* has committed a crime."

3. *Transformations of* **description.** Transformations of description find themselves in a complementary relationship with the transformation of

knowledge: the former are destined to promote knowledge. A subset of the verbs of communication appears most often in this function in English: the constative verbs of communication and the performative verbs denoting autonomous actions, such as *tell, say, explain. Example*: "*X* (or *Y*) reports that *X* has committed a crime."

4. *Transformations of* **supposition.** A subset of descriptive verbs refers to actions that have not yet been accomplished, such as *foresee, anticipate, suspect, expect.* This subset deals with predictions; contrary to what happens in the other transformations, the action designated by the base predicate in transformations of supposition is situated in the future, not in the present. It should be noted that a variety of transformations may denote common situational elements. For example, the transformations of mode, intent, appearance, and supposition all imply that the denoted event has not taken place, but a new category intervenes each time. *Example*: "*X* (or *Y*) anticipates that *X* will commit a crime."

5. *Transformations of* **subjectivization.** Transformations of subjectivization refer to actions denoted by the verbs *believe, think, have the impression, consider.* Such a transformation does not really modify the main proposition; rather, it attributes it, as a statement, to some subject: "*X* (or *Y*) thinks that *X* has committed a crime." The base proposition may be true or false: I may believe in something that has not really taken place.

6. *Transformations of* **attitude:** Transformations of attitude refer to the state provoked in the subject by the action described, while it is going on. Similar to the transformations of manner, they are distinguished by the fact that their supplementary information concerns the subject, not the predicate; thus in the transformations of attitude, there is a new predicate, and not an operator specifying the first predicate. *Examples*: "*X* enjoys committing a crime," or "*Y* is horrified by the fact that *X* is committing a crime." The transformations of attitude, like those of knowledge or subjectivization, are particularly frequent in what is conventionally known as the psychological novel.

The conjunction of several transformations is often designated by a single word in the lexicon of the language; we must not conclude from this that the operation itself is indivisible. For example, the acts of condemning and congratulating can be decomposed into a value judgment and a speech act (transformations of attitude and description).

● See Z. S. Harris, *Mathematical Structures of Language* (New York, 1968); C. Lévi-Strauss, *Mythologiques*, 4 vols. (Paris, 1965–71)—the first two volumes are available in English, as *Introduction to a Science of Mythology,* trans. J. Weightman and D. Weightman (New York, 1969 and 1973); T. Todorov, *Grammaire du Décameron* (The Hague, 1969); and L. Doležel, "Narrative Modalities," *Journal of Literary Semantics* 5 (1976): 5–14.

TEXT

The Text

Linguistics limits its object of investigation to the sentence; in an extreme case, as with Saussure, what is linguistically knowable ends with the word or the syntagma. Classical *rhetoric* sought to codify the rules for the construction of a discourse, but both its normative intent and its neglect of concrete verbal forms prevented it from passing on many usable teachings. Finally, *stylistics,* in Bally's wake, is more interested in the interpenetration of the utterance and the enunciative process than in the organization of the utterance itself. Thus there is a gap in the theory of the text that has not yet been filled by disparate remarks on the part of literary scholars.

The notion of the **text** is not situated on the same level as that of the sentence (or the clause, the syntagma, and so on); in this sense, the text must be distinguished from the **paragraph,** a typographical unit of several sentences. The text may coincide with a sentence, as well as with an entire book; it is defined by its autonomy and by its closure (even if, in another sense, certain texts are not "closed"); it constitutes a system that must not be identified with the linguistic system, but related to it, both in contiguity and in resemblance. In Hjelmslev's terms, the text is a connotative system, for it is secondary with respect to another system of signification. We distinguish the phonological, syntactic, and semantic components of the verbal sentence; we shall distinguish just as many components in the text, although not on the same level. Thus with regard to texts, we shall speak of the **verbal aspect,** constituted by all the linguistic elements proper of the sentences that make up a text (phonological, grammatical, and so on); of the **syntactic aspect,** which refers not to the syntax of sentences, but to relationships among textual units (sentences, groups of sentences, and so on); and finally, of the **semantic aspect,** a complex product of the semantic content of the linguistic units. Each of these aspects has its own problematics and is the basis for one of the major types of textual analysis—**rhetorical, narrative,** and **thematic.**

We should first take care to note that the global study of the text thus conceived is not reduced to what certain representatives of distributional linguistics [32ff.] (Z. S. Harris and his students) have called **discourse analysis,** which consists in dividing the text into elements (generally of one or several syntagmas in length) that are grouped into equivalence classes (a class is constituted by the elements that may appear in an identical or similar context; whether the elements have the same meaning or not is of no concern). Certain sentences (including equivalent and nonequivalent elements) will henceforth be described as being in relationships of transformation among themselves (a notion to be distinguished from the generatist transformations and the discursive transformations). Parallel research has been undertaken on sentence elements containing a reference to the preceding sentence—articles, pronouns, and so on [281ff.].

The semantic and verbal aspects of a text raise problems that must be studied in their own context [219ff., 301ff., 329ff.]. We shall simply point out here that one of the few analyses dealing with the semantic aspect of the text is situated in the perspective of tagmemics [36.]. A. L. Becker analyzes discourses of the exposé type and discerns two basic schemas: topic-restriction-illustration and problem-solution. Each of these may be varied by means of operations such as suppression, permutation, addition, and combination; they may be repeated or alternated.

In the following pages our study will be limited to the syntactic aspect of the text. Before beginning this analysis, we should note that for several years researchers working in France in a semiotic perspective (notably J. Kristeva) have been attempting to elaborate a global theory of the text in which this notion is given a more specific meaning and can no longer be applied to every organized sequence of sentences [356].

● See Z. S. Harris, *Discourse Analysis Reprints* (The Hague, 1963); *Langages* 13 (1969): *L'Analyse du discours,* ed. J. Dubois and J. Sumpf; W. O. Hendricks, *Essays on Semiolinguistics and Verbal Art* (The Hague, 1973); R. Harweg, *Pronomina und Textkonstitution* (Munich, 1968); E. U. Grosse, ed., *Strukturelle Textsemantik* (Freiburg, 1969); *Probleme der semantischen Analyse literarischer Texte* (Karlsruhe, 1970); A. L. Becker, "A Tagmemic Approach to Paragraph Analysis," in *The Sen-*

tence and the Paragraph (Champaign, 1966), pp. 33–38; T. Todorov, "Connaissance de la parole," *Word* 23 (1967): 500–18; J. Kristeva, *Semeiotikè* (Paris, 1969); T. A. Van Dijk, *Some Aspects of Text Grammars* (The Hague, 1971); W.-D. Stempel, ed., *Beiträge zur Textlinguistik* (Munich, 1971); W. Raible, *Satz und Text* (Tübingen, 1972); and C. Grivel and A. Kibedi Varga, eds., *Du linguistique au textuel* (Assen, Neth., 1974).

The study of the syntactic aspect of the text is based on **propositional analysis,** through which discourse is reduced to logically simple propositions constituted by an agent (subject) and a predicate, according to the propositional model adopted. The presence of two predicates—which may be either attributes or verbs—implies the presence of two propositions. Thus the sentence "The child is crying" is only a linguistic form, an amalgam, from the logical viewpoint, of two successive propositions: "*X* is a child," and "*X* is crying." The proposition corresponds to what J. Dubois calls the minimal sentence. The relations established between propositions can be studied in this light.

These relations may be of three types, each of which defines a textual order (often all three are present within a single text). The **logical order** groups all the logical relationships among propositions—causality, disjunction, conjunction, exclusion, inclusion. Causality, particularly frequent in narrative, is not a simple notion, moreover; it combines conditions of existence, consequences, motivations, and so on. Relations such as inclusion are particularly frequent in didactic discourse (as when a rule is illustrated by an example).

The **temporal order** is constituted by the succession of facts evoked by the discourse; it will thus be present only in the case of referential (representational) discourse, which takes the temporal dimension into account, as do history and narrative; it will be absent both from nonrepresentational discourse (for example, lyric poetry) and from descriptive discourse (for example, synchronic sociological studies). Certain types of texts, such as the logbook, the diary, memoirs, and autobiography (or biography), are dominated by the temporal order.

Finally, **spatial order** is defined by a relationship among propositions that is neither logical nor temporal, but one of similarity or dissimilarity; this type of relationship at the same time inscribes a certain "space." Poetic rhythm is an example of spatial order.

- See E. Muir, *The Structure of the Novel* (London, 1928); R. Jakobson, "Poetry of Grammar and Grammar of Poetry," *Lingua* 21 (1968): 597–609; J. Dubois, *Grammaire structurale du français,* 3 vols. (Paris, 1965–69), vol. 3, *La phrase et les transformations* (1969); and T. Todorov, *Poétique* (Paris, 1973).

The Case of the Narrative

Groups of more than one proposition have been studied in only one type of discourse: the **narrative** (in French, **récit**), which will be examined here at some length. The narrative is a referential text in which temporality is represented. The unit higher than the proposition that can be located in narrative is the **sequence,** which is constituted by a group of at least three propositions. Contemporary narrative analyses inspired by Propp's study of folk tales and Lévi-Strauss's study of myths agree that in every minimal narrative it is possible to identify two attributes—related but different—of at least one agent and a process of transformation or mediation, which allows passage from one attribute to the other. Attempts have been made to break down this general matrix in several ways.

1. E. Köngäs-Maranda and P. Maranda categorize narratives according to the result obtained in the mediation process. They distinguish four subtypes: (1) absence of a mediator; (2) failure of the mediator; (3) success of the mediator, resulting in nullification of the initial tension; and (4) success of the mediator, resulting in reversal of the initial tension. Ethnological research seems to prove that the subtypes are distributed according to geographic region.

2. C. Bremond's typology of narrative sequences is based on the different ways in which a mediation, itself unchanging, is actualized. He first sets up an opposition between the processes of amelioration and degradation, according to whether there is passage from an unsatisfactory state to a satisfactory one (for the character), or the reverse. The processes of amelioration, in turn, are subdivided into the accomplishment of a task by the protagonist and the receipt of assistance from an ally. In order to distinguish, in a later phase, among the various accomplishments of the task, the following factors are taken into account: (1) the moment, in narrative chronology, at which the protagonist acquires the means permitting him to arrive at his goal; (2) the internal structure of the act of acquisition; and (3) the relationship between the protagonist and the former possessor of these means. If the analysis is made still more detailed (without however reducing it to a mere enumeration; it always remains an exposure of the structural possibilities of the plot), it becomes possible to characterize quite accurately the organization of each individual narrative.

3. It is similarly possible to specify the nature of the mediation itself. Initially, narrative analyses sought to discover in the process of mediation an inversion from positive to negative, or vice versa. However, numerous other transformations can be observed: the passage from obligation or desire to action, from ignorance to knowledge, from knowledge

to its enunciation, from an act to its evaluation, and so on [291ff.]. Moreover, the sequences are made more complex not only by means of subdivision but also through the addition of optional propositions.

The combination of several sequences lends itself easily to a formal typology. The following cases are possible: **linking,** in which the sequences are arranged in the order 1-2; **embedding,** in which the order is 1-2-1; and **interweaving** (or alternation), in which it is 1-2-1-2. These three fundamental types can be combined further among themselves or with other instances of the same type. The global linking of sequences within a text produces the **plot:** this notion is often applied exclusively to texts dominated by the causal order.

These analyses have the advantage of being explicit and systematic, but they always run the risk of bogging down in excessive generality. Their contrast with the more traditional tendencies in literary studies will be more readily apparent when the foregoing analyses are confronted with a classification that sums up a considerable number of earlier works and reflects the variety of problems that present themselves to the "narratologist" of the future. This classification, the work of N. Friedman, is a characteristic example of a formal descriptive undertaking that has not yet been theorized.

1. *Plots of fortune*
   a) The action plot. The only question the reader asks is, What happens next? The plot is organized around a problem and its solution: to catch a gangster, discover the murderer, find a treasure, reach another planet. It is particularly frequent in popular (mass) literature. *Example*: Stevenson's *Treasure Island.*

   b) The pathetic plot. A series of misfortunes befalls an attractive but weak protagonist; he does not deserve them. The narrative has an unhappy ending and inspires the reader's pity. This plot is common in the nineteenth-century naturalist novel. *Example*: Hardy's *Tess of the D'Urbervilles.*

   c) The tragic plot. The protagonist, still attractive, is in some way responsible for his own misfortune, but he does not discover this until too late. The reader then experiences catharsis. *Examples*: Shakespeare's *Oedipus Rex, King Lear.*

   d) The punitive plot. The protagonist does not have the reader's sympathy, even though he is admired for certain of his qualities (often satanic); the story ends with the failure of the protagonist. *Example*: Molière's *Tartuffe.*

   e) The cynical plot (this class is not mentioned by Friedmann but follows logically from his categories). A "wicked" central character triumphs in the end, instead of being punished. *Example*: P. Allain and M. Souvestre's *Fantomas.*

f) *The sentimental plot* (this is, in its conclusion, the inverse of the melodramatic plot). The protagonist, attractive and often weak, undergoes a series of misfortunes but triumphs in the end.

g) *The admiration plot* (the counterpart of the tragic plot). The protagonist, strong and responsible for his actions, undergoes a series of perils but conquers them in the end. The reader's response combines respect and admiration.

2. *Plots of character*

a) *The maturing plot.* The protagonist is attractive but inexperienced or naive; events allow him to mature. *Example*: Joyce's *Portrait of the Artist as a Young Man.*

b) *The reform plot.* As in the foregoing, the attractive protagonist changes for the better. In this plot, however, he himself is responsible for the misfortunes that punctuate his career. Thus, during part of the story, the reader denies him compassion. *Example*: Hawthorne's *The Scarlet Letter.*

c) *The testing plot.* All of the protagonist's initiatives fail one after the other; in the wake of these failures, he himself renounces his ideals. *Example*: Chekhov's *Uncle Vania, The Sea Gull.*

3. *Plots of thought*

a) *The education plot.* Improvement in the outlook-of the attractive protagonist. This plot resembles the maturing plot, but in this case the psychic change does not influence the character's actual behavior. *Examples*: Tolstoy's *War and Peace*, Twain's *Huckleberry Finn.*

b) *The revelation plot.* At the beginning, the protagonist does not know his own condition.

c) *The affective plot.* The protagonist's attitudes and beliefs change, but not his philosophy. *Example*: Austen's *Pride and Prejudice.*

d) *The disillusionment plot* (opposed to the education plot). The character loses his fine ideals and dies in despair. At the end of the book, the reader no longer sympathizes with him.

This classification, which of course is not an authentic one, shows fairly clearly the difficulties of plot categorization. Every plot is based on change; but the nature and the level of change remains to be studied rigorously before the typology of plots can be established.

- See V. Propp, *Morphology of the Folktale*, trans. L. Scott (Bloomington, 1958); A. Jolles, *Einfache Formen* (Halle [Saale], 1956); P. Maranda and E. Köngäs-Maranda, *Structural Models in Folklore* (The Hague, 1971); C. Bremond, *Logique du récit* (Paris, 1973); and N. Friedman, *Form and Meaning in Fiction* (Athens, Ga., 1975). For a survey, see P. Hamon, "Mise au point sur les problèmes de l'analyse du récit," *Le Français moderne* 40 (1972): 200–221.

STYLE

Definition

In order to define *style* as an operative term, we shall first set aside several current meanings of the word.

1. People often speak of the style of a period, of an artistic movement: the romantic style, baroque style, and so on. It would be preferable to refer to concepts such as period, genre, type [149ff.].

2. When the style of a work is discussed, its unity, its coherence is usually in question: "This work has a style, that one does not." But this category of unity is much too general and abstract to be usable in the study of discourse.

3. Style is sometimes regarded as a deviation with respect to a norm. But V. Hugo's style, for example, cannot be said to be a deviation with respect to his period, for (1) the establishment of a norm raises insurmountable problems, and (2) what characterizes Hugo is not necessarily what distinguishes him from the common usage.

4. It is superfluous to use the term "style" here to designate a functional type of language [65]—for example, journalistic style, administrative style, and so on.

Style will be defined rather as the choice that every text necessarily makes among a certain number of possibilities included in the language. Style thus understood is equivalent to the registers of the language, to its subcodes; this is what is meant by expressions such as "figurative style," "emotive discourse," and so on. And the stylistic description of an utterance is nothing but the description of all its verbal properties.

One medieval theory distinguished between low, middle, and elevated styles. This division has little meaning today, but it is based on the same principle as the one being advanced here: none of the three styles can be regarded as deviant with respect to the others; the styles are in the language, and not in the psyche of language users; style remains a structural property, not a functional one. And although the chart of styles that can be presented today is much more complex, based as it is on knowledge of language provided by linguistics, it is nevertheless no different in its aim.

- Bibliographies include H. A. Hatzfeld, *A Critical Bibliography of the New Stylistics*, 2 vols. (Chapel Hill, 1953–66). *I. 1900–1952* and *II. 1953–1965*; and L. T. Milic, *Style and Stylistics: An Analytical Bibliography* (New York, 1967). Surveys are found in H. A. Hatzfeld, "Methods of Stylistic Investigation," in *Literature and Science* (Oxford, 1955); N. E. Enkvist, *Linguistic Stylistics* (The Hague, 1973); and P. Guiraud, *La*

Stylistique (Paris, 1970). For collections of texts, see S. Chatman and S. R. Levin, eds., *Essays in the Language of Literature* (Boston, 1967); P. Guiraud and P. Kuentz, eds., *La Stylistique: Lectures* (Paris, 1970); S. Chatman, ed., *Literary Style: A Symposium* (London and New York, 1971); R. Fowler, ed., *Style and Structure in Literature* (Oxford, 1975); and H. A. Hatzfeld, ed., *Romanistische Stilforschung* (Darmstadt, 1975). For style as register, see M. A. K. Halliday, A. McIntosh, and P. Strevens, *The Linguistic Sciences and Language Teaching* (London, 1965), pp. 87–94; and T. Todorov, *Poétique* (Paris, 1973), pp. 39–48.

In order to capture the stylistic characteristics of a text in a rigorous way, we must approach the text on two levels: at the level of the utterance, that is, at the level of its verbal, syntactic, and semantic aspects [294ff.], as well as the divisions that fix the dimensions of the units—from the distinctive features, phonic or semantic, to the entire utterance; and at the level of enunciation, that is, at the level of the relationship defined among the protagonists of the discourse (speaker, listener, referent).

At the Level of the Utterance

1. The verbal aspect (which directly concerns the phonic and/or graphic signifier) of an utterance has been studied in particular at the level of the minimal units. A text may be characterized by the number and the distribution of the phonemes (or graphemes) that constitute it; even the distinctive features of these phonemes may be taken into consideration. Word length, too, is a characteristic feature of style. To study the verbal aspect at the level of the sentence or the utterance is to look for its rhythmic and melodic properties. The disposition of a text on the page is also an aspect of style (we have only to think of the poems of Mallarmé and Apollinaire).

● See B. Eikhenbaum, *Melodika russkogo liricheskogo stikha* (Petrograd, 1922); W. Winter, "Styles as Dialects," in *Proceedings of the Ninth International Congress of Linguists*, ed. H. G. Lunt (The Hague, 1964), pp. 324–30; and N. Ruwet, "Sur un vers de Charles Baudelaire," in *Langage, musique, poésie* (Paris, 1972), pp. 200–209.

2. The syntactic aspect can be studied at the level of the sentence by techniques developed in the framework of generative grammar [226ff.]. The syntactic structure of a sentence can be presented as the result of a series of transformations beginning with one or more nuclear propositions. The nature and number of these transformations determine the "syntactic style." Within the sentence (and, in poetry, often within an entire text), the distribution of grammatical categories (gender, number, person, case, and so on) may also characterize a style.

At the level of the (transphrastic) utterance, three types of relationships among sentences may be observed. The logical relationships (of implication, inclusion, and so on) characterize at one and the same time a good deal of fiction, everyday discourse, and scientific discourse. Temporal relationships (of succession) are encountered in the pure state in the logbook or the chronical. Spatial relationships (of symmetry, opposition, gradation) are particularly frequent in poetry [153].

• See R. Jakobson, "Poetry of Grammar and Grammar of Poetry," *Lingua* 21 (1968): 597–609; R. Ohmann, "Generative Grammars and the Concept of Literary Style," *Word* 20 (1964): 423–39; and T. Todorov, *Poétique* (Paris, 1973), pp. 67–77.

3. As for the semantic aspect—the least studied to date—we may note a progressive penetration of the sentence by several categories that are never simply present or absent and whose dosage determines the style of each utterance.

a) **Representationality.** At one extreme, we find sentences that describe facts and events and thus have a maximum denotative capacity; at the other, sentences that enunciate eternal truths, abstract reflections, maxims.

b) **Figurativeness.** Since the figure is nothing other than language's capacity to be perceived in and of itself [275ff.], every expression is potentially figurative. The various linguistic anomalies offer one way among others to render language perceptible.

c) **Multivalence.** Discourse evokes not only its immediate reference but also, always, other discourse. The pastiche and stylization are characterized by the uniqueness of the text evoked; but the one inverts, ironically, the tendency of the discourse imitated, while the other conserves it. The effect of evocation by milieu [256] is distinguished, on the other hand, by the reference to a global mass of discourse used in particular circumstances (in dialectal speech, social jargon, and so on). The different parts of a single text may also refer to each other (for example, the words of the characters and those of the narrator).

• See J. Cohen, *Structure du langage poétique* (Paris, 1966); T. Todorov, *Littérature et signification* (Paris, 1967); C. Bally, *Traité de stylistique française*, 3d ed. (Geneva, 1951); and M. Bakhtin, *Problems of Dostoevsky's Poetics*, trans. R. W. Rotsel (Ann Arbor, 1973).

At the Level of Enunciation

1. To describe the phenomenon of enunciation itself gives rise to **reported discourse;** according to whether certain grammatical transfor-

mations have been effected or not, we speak of **indirect style** or **direct style**.

2. The spatio-temporal situation of the protagonists of the discourse is most often indicated—although not always—by entire morphemes (personal pronouns, demonstratives, possessives; adverbs; verb and noun endings). Their distribution and frequency allow us to measure stylistic differences.

3. The speaker's attitude toward his discourse and/or its reference is perceptible by virtue of distinctive semantic features (semes). Several cases can be differentiated:

a) The **emotive style** places the emphasis in the relationship between the speaker and the reference of the discourse on the speaker. The clearest example is provided by interjections: *Ah!* does not evoke the object provoking the astonishment, but rather this astonishment itself on the part of the speaker.

b) The **evaluative style** emphasizes references in this same relationship between speaker and reference, for example, in expressions such as "a *good* table," "a *beautiful* woman."

c) In the **modalizing style,** the speaker passes judgment on the truth value of the discourse, that is, on the relationship between the discourse and its reference (or its context). This judgment is manifested by expressions such as "perhaps," "doubtless," "it seems to me."

● See *Langages* 17 (1970): *L'Enonciation*, ed. T. Todorov; E. Benveniste, *Problems in General Linguistics*, trans. M. E. Meek (Coral Gables, 1971), pp. 195–246; E. Stankiewicz, "Problems of Emotive Language," in *Approaches to Semiotics*, ed. T. A. Sebeok (The Hague, 1964); and V. Voloshinov, *Marxism and the Philosophy of Language*, trans. L. Matejka and I. R. Titunik (New York, 1973).

Stylistics has often been preoccupied with certain syncretic categories that group together more than one style. The best-studied case is **free indirect style** ("represented speech" or "narrated monologue"—in French, *style indirect libre*; in German *erlebte Rede*). This is a discourse that presents itself at first glance as an indirect style (that is, it includes marks of time and person corresponding to a discourse on the part of the author) but is penetrated, in its syntactic and semantic structure, by enunciative properties, thus by the discourse of the character. These same two properties may meet, moreover, in another combination—for example, in a remark by a character that is in direct style but manifests all the properties of the authorial discourse (this combination does not have a specific name).

Another pair of terms used to designate syncretic styles is that of **monologue** and **dialogue.** Monologue can be described by the following features: emphasis on the speaker; little reference to the allocutionary situation; single frame of reference; absence of metalinguistic elements; frequency of exclamations. Dialogue, on the contrary, can be described as a discourse that emphasizes the person addressed; refers abundantly to the allocutionary situation; plays simultaneously on several frames of references; and is characterized by the presence of metalinguistic elements and by the frequency of interrogative forms. The opposition, as we can see, is far from simple.

- On free indirect style, see M. Lips, *Le Style indirect libre* (Paris, 1926); *Readings in Russian Poetics*, Michigan Slavic Materials, no. 2 (Ann Arbor, 1962); M. Friedman, *Stream of Consciousness: A Study in Literary Method* (New Haven, 1955); R. Humphrey, *Stream of Consciousness in the Modern Novel* (Berkeley and Los Angeles, 1962); D. Cohn, "Narrated Monologue," *Comparative Literature* 18 (1966): 97–112; D. Bickerton, "Modes of Interior Monologue: A Formal Definition," *Modern Language Quarterly* 28 (1967): 229–39; and G. Genette, "Le Discours du récit," in *Figures III* (Paris, 1972), pp. 67–282. On monologue and dialogue, see J. Mukařovský, *Kapitel aus der Poetik* (Frankfort, 1967), pp. 108–49; and T. Todorov, "Les Registres de la parole," *Journal de psychologie* 64 (1967): 265–78.

TIME AND MODALITY IN LANGUAGE

The two categories discussed in this article are among the most resistant to linguistic reflection; their very delimitation is controversial. One reason for this is doubtless that their means of expression are disconcertingly varied. They cannot be described in any case by means of the usual grammatical or lexical categories; semantics finds little support in grammar here. Moreover, the subject of the enunciative act [323ff.] frequently appears as the necessary point of reference for notations of time or modality. Post-Saussurian linguistics, for fear of confusing language (*langue*) and speech (*parole*) [118ff.], has always hesitated to bring the speaker into the description of language; hence it manifests a certain suspicion in the face of the categories of time and modality, which have often served to label unresolved problems. These categories have something else in common, however, besides this unfortunate privilege; this other shared feature, which accounts for their being grouped together here, will be brought to light in the discussion that follows. It is a question of their potential for transcending the division of the utterance into subject and predicate [210] (or arguments and predicate [271]) and thus for being attached to the totality of the utterance, of which they constitute something like the general framework.

Time

The semantic notion of **time** will be our object. Thus we shall not be dealing with a physical reality (the one that interests the natural sciences) nor with the psychological phenomenon of lived time. Nor shall we be concerned with the grammatical concept used to classify the various forms of the verb (tense). We are situated at an intermediate level between physics and psychology on the one hand and grammar on the other. What interests us is how human experience of time is manifested through linguistic activity. We shall first examine—among other topics in this article—the role indications pertaining to time play in the internal semantic organization of the utterance. In the following article we shall show how time is manifested in discourse.

Take, for example, the following sentence, which might inaugurate an account of D-day, 1944: "At dawn on June 6 the first troop transports had already left England several hours earlier; some had even started the night before." The time indications included in this sentence can be organized in three categories:

A. Some indications of time (expressed with precision by *At dawn on June 6*, and more vaguely by the fact that the verb is in a past tense) specify the period in question in the utterance, the period that constitutes its topic. As for the events described in the sentence (the departure of the first convoys), chronologically anterior to this period, these do not constitute the object that is in question but are mentioned to the extent that they are necessary for our comprehension of the moment on which the utterance focuses, that is, dawn of June 6. What indicates this moment is thus not, properly speaking, a constituent of the subjects (*the first troop transports, some*), nor of the predicates (*had left England several hours earlier, had started [to leave England] the night before*) but is situated at a level beyond that of the subject-predicate distinction.

B. Other temporal indications (those concerning the events reported in the sentence) are distributed, on the contrary, between the subjects and the predicates. Thus the adjective *first* is related to a subject: it serves to locate the reality designated by the latter, situating it with respect to a sequence. On the other hand, the groups "several hours earlier" and "the night before," which specify in temporal terms the process (to leave England) whose agent is designated by the subject, must be linked to the predicates. In the same category will be classified the succession of presence and absence implied by the verb *to leave*; this is in fact a temporal indication (which has meaning only in terms of a chronological order), and it constitutes the semantic core of the predicate group.

C. The third category—the least obvious, but as essential as the others—concerns the relationship established in the utterance between indications of types A and B. In our example, it is represented by the choice of a compound tense and also by the adverb *already*. Their combination indicates that the events reported by means of the subjects and predicates (and determined temporally by B) precede the moment in question in the utterance (a moment defined by A) and that their consequences persist into this moment and mark it: to say that the dawn of June 6 follows upon the fleet's departure is to characterize this moment internally.

1. The notion that certain time indications (type A) are coextensive with the totality of the sentence is confirmed by numerous semantic phenomena. Compare, for example, the utterances "In the morning, I work" and "I work in the morning." In the first, the temporal indication *In the morning* is of type A and supplies a part of the topic of the sentence, which is presented as a description of the speaker's morning activities, in answer to the question, What do you do in the morning? Thus this utterance in no way implies that the speaker does not work at other times. In the second utterance, however, *in the morning* is of type B and part of the predicate attributed to the subject *I*. The temporal topic of the sentence is indicated, very imprecisely, by the present tense of the verb. Thus in a general way, the question here is one of the speaker's current schedule, which includes, according to his statement, a stint of work in the morning. It is now apparent that if this sentence were produced in isolation, without complement or correction, it might convey the impression that the speaker works only in the morning.

Another illustration of the same phenomenon is found in the semantic indeterminacy of an utterance like "Last year her car was blue," which may mean that since last year the subject either (*a*) has had her car painted or (*b*) has changed cars. This uncertainty stems from the fact that the chronological indication *last year* applies to the entire sentence, and not just to the predicate. First the hearer is asked to imagine himself situated in the previous year, and then, within this past period, a certain quality is attributed to a certain object. It is thus not clear whether the referential expression *her car* (that is, the expression designating the object of predication) should be understood in terms of the present speech situation (from which meaning [*a*] derives) or in terms of the period envisaged in the utterance (which gives rise to meaning

[*b*]). If meaning (*b*) is possible, it is because the attribution of the predicate to the subject has as a framework not only the present speech situation but also a sort of temporal background lodged in the utterance itself.

2. Indications of type C correspond to what is generally called **aspect.** They concern the relationships between the period that is the topic of the utterance and the one in which the process is situated ("process" is the action or the qualification expressed by the subject-predicate group). The aspect thus indicates the relationships between A and B. Two aspectual oppositions are particularly clear-cut.

First is the opposition between the **perfective aspect** and the **imperfective aspect,** which is clearly expressed by the Slavic languages; thus almost all Russian verbs have different forms for each of the two aspects in each tense. In spite of the great diversity in the descriptions proposed for these terms, it seems possible, at the cost of a certain oversimplification, to reduce them to the following general definitions. The perfective aspect is one in which the process is internal to the period the speaker is talking about, that is, to the topic:

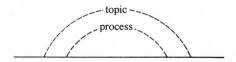

The imperfective aspect is the inverse of the perfective: in it, the process is, at the very least, coextensive with the topic; ordinarily, in fact, the former encompasses the latter. This is why the speaker's chosen viewpoint (which determines the topic) appears to cut a slice, or to light up a zone, within the factual development of the process. And if this zone happens to be identical to the entire course of development, it appears to be a chance coincidence, not dependent on the mode of presentation chosen. Hence the schema:

The opposition of the two viewpoints may produce quite varied semantic effects. The difference sometimes has consequences that may be objectively located. Compare the following:

"When Peter arrived, John screamed." (perfective)
"When Peter arrived, John was screaming." (imperfective)

This opposition, which in English is rendered by the progressive form, is expressed more directly in the Romance languages, which have two simple past tenses: the simple preterite, or aorist, which expresses the perfective aspect, and the imperfect, which expresses the imperfective. But whatever grammatical means are employed, the semantic effect of the opposition remains the same. In order to describe it on the basis of the foregoing schemas, we shall suppose that Peter's arrival determines the topic, the point of view chosen with respect to reality, and that John's screams constitute the process. It is thus predictable that the first utterance should situate John's screams within the period characterized by Peter's arrival. In the second utterance, however, the arrival takes place while the screams are going on: the topic selects one moment of the event (without ruling out the possibility that, by chance, this moment may coincide with the event taken in its entirety).

Sometimes the effects of the opposition are largely subjective. This is the case if one compares "Last year I moved in," and "Last year I was moving in." Objectively, it is apparent that the moving (process) took up only a part of the year (topic). But in the second sentence this process is *presented* as at least coextensive with the year. Hence the impression that it was the problem of the year and that it marked the year from one end to the other.

This variety of effects is particularly obvious in the Slavic languages, in which the opposition of the two aspects generally appears in each tense and each mood, producing, in every context, a particular difference in meaning. But cutting across this variety, we find the fundamental difference illustrated by the two schemas provided above [210]. Thus, in the past tense, the opposition existing in Russian between *ja vypil* (perfective) and *ja pil* (imperfective) seems analogous to the one presented above that separates the aorist and the imperfect in the Romance languages, or, in English, the preterite and the past progressive ("I drank" and "I was drinking").

In the present tense this opposition, while unchanged, is used toward other ends: the present imperfective (progressive) designates the moment of enunciation, whereas the present perfective serves to mark the future (which has no form of its own in Russian): *Ja piju* ("I am drinking") and *Ja vypiju* ("I shall drink"). Now this affinity of the future and the perfective is easily understood (without it being possible, of course, to assert that the present perfective must inevitably serve to express the future): since the future event exists, at the moment when I speak of it, only in my discourse, it cannot extend beyond the sighting I am taking of it. On the contrary, it is necessarily internal to, or, at the most, coextensive with, my temporal perspective. Similarly, there is an understandable affinity between the imperfective and the expression of present events, that is, events that are contemporaneous with the speech act. For, if the temporal topic of my discourse is the moment at which I am speaking, there is every chance that the events I am describing extend beyond this moment: given its inherent narrowness, the time period envisaged when the present tense is used is almost necessarily situated within the period spanned by the observed events. This explains why languages that include the form known as progressive (in English, "to be writing"; in Portuguese, *estar escrevendo*), whose essentially imperfective aspect has been demonstrated, use it, in combination with the present tense, to report events observed at the very moment the report is being made ("he is writing"; *está escrevendo*).

Finally, the effect of aspect on the Russian infinitive and, more generally, on the verb, considered here apart from all spatio-temporal specifications, can be explained in the same way: *pit'*, imperfective ("to drink"); *vypit'* ("to drink to the last drop"). The perfective infinitive presents the action as stopping because it has obtained a result that makes its continuation impossible. Here again we can establish a link with the earlier schema. It suffices to propose the not unreasonable hypothesis that the infinitive presents the action in a pure state, isolated from its possible environments. We know, moreover, that the perfective outlook maintains the process inside the speaker's field of vision and therefore requires that the process itself be represented at the same time as is its end. If all external historical determination is set aside—which is the case for the infinitive—the end of the action must then result, as it were, from the action itself, which would exhaust its own possibilities in the course of its development. (We may arrive at an approximate understanding of the nuances contributed to the Russian imperative by the perfective and imperfective aspects if we compare expressions such as "finish one's work" and "stop one's work": only the first attributes the cessation of work to the fact that the work has achieved its goal.)

Another clear-cut aspectual opposition is the one between the **completed aspect** and the **uncompleted aspect,** especially in ancient Greek, in which the completed aspect is expressed by the verbal tenses known as *perfect*. The uncompleted aspect describes at least partial simultaneity between the reported process (that is, the attribution of predicate to subject, as in indications of type B, above) and the period dealt with in the enunciative act (as in indications of type A). This is the case for the utterance "Yesterday Peter worked all evening": the process (Peter's work during the evening) overlaps partially with the temporal topic (expressed by "yesterday"). There is a completed aspect, on the contrary, if the process is anterior to the period in question and yet the speaker wishes to signal the trace of the process in that period, as in the following schema:

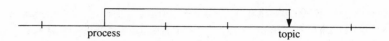

An example of the latter situation can be found in the sentence about D-day studied above. We could even use an utterance such as "By closing time at the casino, he had lost his entire fortune" (the topic is the gambler's state at closing time, and this is characterized by what happened earlier).

(N.B. a. The French *passé composé* is ambiguous. [a] It may have as its topic the past, taken in the uncompleted and perfective aspects. *Hier, il a dîné à 8 heures, puis s'est couché*, corresponding to the English preterite, "Yesterday he had dinner at 8:00, then went to bed." [A paraphrase is thus possible, in written French, by use of the *passé simple*: *Hier, il dîna à 8 heures, puis se coucha*]. [b] Or it may have as its topic the present moment, characterized, in the completed aspect, by a past event: *Maintenant, j'ai mangé*, corresponding to the English present perfect, "I'm no longer hungry."

b. If the utterance has a single temporal topic, the perfective aspect necessarily stems from the uncompleted aspect, according to our definitions. The situation is in fact more complicated than this, for the same sentence often includes a hierarchy of temporal perspectives; thus numerous aspectual combinations are possible.

c. The ordinary terminology concerning aspects is very loose: perfective and completed are sometimes confused, if only because in ancient Greek the completed aspect appears in the "perfect" tenses.)

3. Finally, we shall look at the temporal indications of time [B] that concern the process itself. In this area, even more than in that of aspect, it is impossible at the moment to present a systematic overview; we must content ourselves with some isolated remarks.

a) All the parts of speech [203] are capable of conveying indications relative to time—not only verbs and adverbs but also substantives (such as *predecessor, successor*) and adjectives (such as *old, former*). Moreover, it is clear that the same nuance may often be expressed in each of these categories. Thus it is possible to paraphrase certain temporal adjectives by verbs and adverbs: "my *former* friend" means "someone who once was and is no longer my friend"; "my *old* friend" means "someone who has been my friend for a long time."

b) The most obvious temporal indications are specifications of date and hour ("He ate *at seven o'clock*"), frequency ("He goes to the movies *often*"), duration ("I've known that *for a long time*"), succession ("He reads *before* going to sleep"). We should like to stress a more hidden category, one that involves the way a process develops in time, the way it occupies the time that is its own. To the extent that this category is situated within the description of the process and thus serves to provide factual information, it must be distinguished from the category of aspect as we have defined it here. The latter relates process and topic, that is, the reported fact and the speaker's outlook; it can only play an informative role in an indirect way. But this basic difference does not preclude, as we shall see, certain (largely negative) analogies grounded in the fact that neither of the two categories is concerned with questions of dating and chronology. This is why grammarians sometimes call the indications with which we are dealing here **objective aspects** (as opposed to the true aspects, called **subjective**). German linguists also use the term **Aktionsart,** or **mode of action.**

Some examples of these distinctions—which concern the way in which a process (action or quality) occupies the time of its manifestation— follow: Uniform development may be opposed to intermittent development (*fly / flutter*; *shine / sparkle*). Or processes may be categorized according to whether they comprise a beginning, a passage from nonbeing to being (they are then called **inchoative**); a continuation (they are called **continuative**); or an ending, passage from being to nonbeing (**terminative**). These distinctions produce the following three categories: (1) *begin, take, win, find, build, enter*; (2) *continue, hold, keep, maintain, remain*; and (3) *finish, stop, let go, lose, destroy, go out, abandon, leave.* (This tripartite categorization is less obvious, less natural, less imposed by reality than it might seem at first, for every beginning is also an end, every entry a departure.) Let us mention, in addition, the resultative aspect, often marked, in German, by the prefix [200] *er-,* which indicates that an action has reached its end: *steigen* ("climb"), *ersteigen* ("reach the summit"), *schlagen* ("beat"), *erschlagen* ("kill by beating"). The resultative semantic nuance, as we may recall, is also obtainable by means of subjective aspects: the perfective often produces the same signification, but in an indirect, derivative manner and as a result of a much more complicated interpretative mechanism.

In this category of objective aspect we also find the difference established in the Iberian languages (that is, Spanish and Portuguese) between two different modes of attributing a quality to an object. These languages have in fact two verbs corresponding to the single English verb *to be.* The one (in Portuguese, *estar*) signifies that the quality is introduced from the outside (this does not prevent it from being durable, even permanent); thus the Portuguese translation of "He is happy" is *Está contente,* that of "He is sick," *Está doente* (the possibility that these two states may persist is not excluded: we may say *Está sempre doente,* or "He is always sick"). The second *to be* (in Portuguese, *ser*) implies that the quality belongs intrinsically to the nature of the object, at the moment when it is being considered; the quality is not added on as a supplement to the object (thus "He is intelligent" and "He is sickly" are translated, respectively, by *E intelligente* and *E doente*). This does not rule out the possibility of using *ser* to express states subject to variation or even inherently transitory states (*Era doente* means "He was sickly at one time"; *E jovem*, "He is young"), so long as they are not perceived, at the moment of observation, as produced by an external agent. The two verbs thus represent two relationships between an object and time: it would be possible to speak of an external time, modifying being, and of an internal time, expressing it.

Similar oppositions may exist in other parts of speech. This observation emerges from E. Benveniste's study of names of agents in the ancient Indo-European languages. In ancient Greek, the names of agents may be formed by means of two suffixes [200], -*ter* and -*tor*, which are added to verbal roots designating a type of action. The suffix -*tor* seems to have the same effect on actions as the verb *estar* has on qualities: it gives them an accidental character, as if they were simply added on to the agent. The suffix -*ter* (comparable to the verb *ser* in this respect), on the contrary, presents the action as the accomplishment of a function or a vocation, as if it were attached, so to speak, to being itself. Thus we have *dotor* (the person who gives or has given) and *doter* (the person charged with giving), *botor* (the person who guards the herd, if only sporadically) and *boter* (the herdsman). Benveniste suggests an analogy between -*ter* and the English suffix -*er*: a *shaker* is the person whose function it is to shake or the instrument destined to be shaken (-*er* may be related, moreover, to the Portuguese verb *ser*: a *shaker* is a person inclined, by temperament, to tremble).

From these examples one can see the great diversity of the temporal nuances that are marked in languages and, at the same time, the heterogeneity of the means used to express them. This density accounts for the fact that this area is one of those in which it is so difficult to achieve systematization at the present time and also one of those that have provided material for the greatest number of systems.

● Since there is considerable literature on time, tense, and aspect, we shall limit our list here to certain basic works: A. Meillet, "Sur les caractères du verbe," a text from 1920 reprinted in his *Linguistique historique et Linguistique générale* (Paris, 1958), pp. 175–98; W. Porzig, "Zur Aktionsart in der indo-germanischen Präsensbildungen," *Indo-germanische Forschungen* 45 (1927): 152–67, in which the difference between aspect and mode of action is introduced; G. Guillaume, *Temps et verbe* (Paris, 1929); J. Holt, "Etudes d'aspect," *Acta jutlandica* (Copenhagen, 1943), which has considerable information on the history of the problem of aspect and a copious bibliography; H. Reichenbach, *Elements of Symbolic Logic* (New York and London, 1947), chap. 7, sec. 51, an attempt to give a logical definition of the grammatical tenses; H. Yvon, "Aspects du verbe français et présentation du 'procès,'" *Le Français moderne* 19 (1951): 161–74; P. Naert, "Mode de présentation, aspect, mode d'action, détermination, et transitivité," *Studia linguistica* 14 (1960): 1–14; W. E. Bull, *Time, Tense and the Verb* (Berkeley, 1960); A. Klum, *Verbe et adverbe* (Upsala, 1961); B. Pottier, "Vers une sémantique moderne," *Travaux de linguistique et de littérature* 2, no. 1 (1964): 107–38, which presents a classification of aspects that is applicable to all parts of speech; H. Weinrich, *Tempus, besprochene und erzählte Welt* (Stuttgart, 1964); E. Benveniste, *Problems in General Linguistics*, trans. M. E. Meek (Coral Gables, 1971), chap. 19; idem, "Structure des relations d'auxiliarité," in *Problèmes de linguistique générale II* (Paris, 1974), chap. 13; R. Martin, *Temps et aspect: Essai sur l'emploi des temps narratifs en moyen français* (Paris, 1971); H. G. Klein, *Tempus, Aspekt, Aktionsart* (Tübingen, 1974); and H. G. Schogt, *Le Système verbal du français contemporain* (The Hague, 1968). On aspect within nouns, see E. Benveniste, *Noms d'agent et noms d'action en indo-européen* (Paris, 1948); and H. Quellet, *Les Dérivés latins en -or* (Paris, 1969).

Modality

Logicians and linguists have often judged it necessary to distinguish, in an act of enunciation, a representative content, sometimes called **dictum** (the relating of a predicate to its subject), and an attitude on the part of the speaking subject with regard to its content (the **modus,** or **modality**). Thus the utterances (1) "Peter will come," (2) "Let Peter come!" (3) "Peter may come," and (4) "Peter must come" seem to have the same dictum and to differ only through the modus. These examples show that the modus has varied means of expression (the grammatical mode in [2], the modal auxiliary in [1], [3], and [4]). In addition, in many cases there is no precise criterion for distinguishing what is connected to the predicate (and internal to the dictum) and what is an attitude with respect to the predication (belonging thus to the modus). Faced with this difficulty—one already encountered with regard to the chronological indications (cf. p. 306)—we propose to maintain in the category of modality only those indications that cannot be integrated into the predicate. Some examples follow.

Assertion

In conformity with the philosophy of Descartes, the *Port-Royal Grammar* distinguishes, in every act of judgment, two mental operations stemming from two different faculties: (*a*) the representation of the subject and the predicate (linked to the conceptual faculty, which Descartes calls understanding [*entendement*]) and (*b*) the attribution of the predicate to the subject, that is, the **assertion** (linked to the judgmental faculty, which Descartes relates to the will [*volonté*]). In "The earth is round," according to this view, the verb *to be* expresses the assertion; this is expressed as well, but in a form not subject to material isolation, in all verbs (see above, p. 4). The Port-Royal grammarians explicitly place assertion in the same category as desires, commands, and interrogation.

Although for different reasons, the logician Frege also reaches the conclusion that the assertion and the asserted proposition must be separated. For if we were to agree to the connection made by the *Port-Royal Grammar* between verb and assertion we would be obliged to find an assertion in the conditional subordinate clause of "If the clock is right, I am late"; this is scarcely acceptable. For Frege, what justifies the recognition of an assertive modality in the simple utterance "The clock is right" is precisely the comparison with the conditional. Assertion is what is found in the simple sentence, not in the conditional. More generally, Frege thinks that when a relationship is established between two propositions (a logical relationship, in any case), the modality of assertion detaches itself from the one and the other to attach itself to their junction. This distinction of the proposition (whether simple or composed of other propositions) and its assertion has proved indispensable to the logician. Let *p* and *q* designate two propositions, and ⊢ the sign of assertion; the logician must distinguish between the following utterances:

(1) ⊢ (*p* → *q*) (assertion that *p* implies *q*).
(2) If ⊢ *p*, then ⊢ *q* (affirmation, at another level, that the assertion of *p* implies that of *q*).

Negation. Take the utterance "Peter is not helpful." Should we (*a*) consider it as the assertion that a negative predicate (*not to be helpful*) is to be attributed to Peter or (*b*) see in it a modality of negation applied to a positive proposition? The two solutions can be schematized as follows:

	modality	predicate	subject
(*a*)	⊢	not to be helpful	Peter
(*b*)	Negative	to be helpful	Peter

In certain cases, solution (*a*) seems to impose itself—for example, for the utterance "I have not read certain works by *X*." It is clear in fact that we would be misconstruing the utterance if we described it as a modality of negation applied to the proposition "I have read certain works by *X*." Solution (*a*) allows us to understand, furthermore, why the introduction of the negative marker *not* often produces a meaning that is contrary, and not simply contradictory, to the meaning of the positive sentence (the utterance "He doesn't like cops" cannot be understood as the denial of the proposition "He likes cops"). It seems in fact that the negation is attached then to the predicate, which is transformed into its extreme opposite.

In other cases, however, the modal solution (*b*) is advantageous—for example, when the negation is represented by an expression such as "It is false that. . . . " If we replace *not* by *It is false that* in the preceding examples, we in fact change their meaning, in such a way that the modal presentation is appropriate (Bally says that the modality is then explicit; in the case of "It is false that . . . " [or in Latin, *Nego* . . .] medieval logicians spoke of the designation of negation, not simply of its exercise). Furthermore, this modal solution is very close to intuition when the negative utterance is interpreted, psychologically, as the rejection of a prior positive utterance (real or supposed). I only announce to someone that I did not go to Paris if I attribute to him the opinion that I might have gone there. We may describe this phenomenon by saying that the negative utterance takes as its object a positive proposition (the one affirmed in the positive utterance that is being opposed) and affects it with a modality of negation. It is understandable, then, that the same negative marker *n't* (*not*) that expresses the contrary in "He doesn't like cops" expresses the contradictory in "He doesn't like women." It is reasonable enough to say, in fact, that the second utterance includes a modal negation, that is, that it presents itself as the refusal of the pre-existing affirmation "He likes women," an affirmation that need not have been made explicit in the preceding dialogue, given that this taste is habitually recognized as normal. It is easy to verify, on the other hand, that the first utterance, which causes us to pass from an idea to its opposite, hardly presents itself, for its own part, as questioning a natural disposition of the mind.

Logical and Deontic Modalities

The attribution of a predicate to an object may be presented as a fact, as a possibility, or as a necessity. Logicians then speak, respectively, of categorical, hypothetical, and apodeictic judgments, and they often restrict the category of modality to this tripartite division. However, many languages seem to connect possibility and necessity to two notions that are analogous but relate to an appraisal in moral terms: the notions of right and obligation (logicians call these notions **deontic** and construct special systems to represent their formal properties). Thus the French verb *pouvoir* ("can," "to be able") expresses both possibility and right, and *devoir* ("to owe," "to have to," "must") expresses necessity and obligation. English and German possess distinct verbs, to be sure, for these four notions, but they link them nonetheless, to the extent that these verbs belong to a category that is particularized both morphologically and syntactically, that of the modal auxiliaries. (N.B. The parallelism between the two kinds of notions may be pursued: the impossible is the negation of the possible, just as the interdiction is the negation of the right; the contingent is the negation of the necessary, just as the optional is the negation of the obligatory.)

As we did in the case of negation, we may ask whether the notions enumerated above are true modalities, exterior to the subject-predicate division, or whether they may in fact be integrated to the predicate. At first glance, nothing seems to rule out representing the utterance "Peter must be nice" as possessing only the assertive modality. This analysis becomes difficult, however, when we examine utterances such as "Peter must be punished," where there is no attribution of duty to Peter, but the entire proposition "Peter must be punished" is inflected by the modality of obligation. It seems possible then to recognize authentic modalities in sentences including *must* or *can* or beginning with a true modal proposition such as "It is necessary that . . . " or "It is possible that . . . " (we shall not say as much for sentences including *have the possibility* or *have the right*, in which the modal nuance can always be brought back to the predicate).

The existence of an extra-predicative modality is even clearer for utterances such as (1) "Perhaps Peter will come." It is characteristic of such an utterance that it cannot be the object of a modal negation [343]: we may not say "It is false that perhaps Peter will come." For this reason, (1) can be connected with (2) "Unfortunately Peter will come," which is not a possible object of negation either. Utterance (2) does not affirm the undesirable character of Peter's coming; it enacts it: by saying *unfortunately*, the speaker behaves like someone who is not happy. Likewise, (1) does not affirm possibility, but enacts it: by saying "perhaps," we do more than present Peter's coming as envisageable; we envisage it, in fact. Thus, precisely in those cases in which modalities present the extra-predicative character most clearly, they tend to rejoin the broader category of speech acts [343]. It is perhaps in this framework that they will one day receive a somewhat more systematic linguistic treatment.

● On the philosophical problem of modality, see L. Brunschvicg, *La Modalité du jugement* (Paris, 1897). A presentation of modal logic is found in *Encyclopédie de la Pléïade* (Paris, 1955–), vol. 12, *Logique et connais-*

sance scientifique (1967), ed. J. Piaget, pp. 251–65. For a detailed exposé, see A. N. Prior, *Formal Logic* (Oxford, 1955), pt. 3, chap. 1; and especially, idem, *Time and Modality* (Oxford, 1957). On linguistic expression of modality, there are numerous observations in F. Brunot, *La Pensée et la langue*, 2d ed. (Paris, 1926), bk. 12; a more systematic treatment is found in C. Bally, *Linguistique générale et linguistique française*, 4th ed., rev. (Bern, 1965), secs. 27–54, and "Syntaxe de la modalité explicite," *Cahiers Ferdinand de Saussure* 2 (1942): 3–13. See also J. M. Zemb, "La Structure de la modalité dans le système verbal allemand contemporain," *Etudes germaniques* 24 (1969): 497–518; and G. Gougenheim, "Modalités et modes verbaux en français," *Journal de psychologie* 67 (1970): 5–18. On negation, the viewpoint of G. Frege, speaking as a logician and refusing to grant the status of modality to logical negation ("Die Verneinung," a 1918 text reprinted in Frege's *Kleine Schriften*, ed. I. Angelelli [Darmstadt and Hildesheim, 1967]), may be compared with linguistic studies like those of O. Jespersen (*Negation in English and Other Languages* [Copenhagen, 1917] or D. Gaatone (*Etude descriptive du système de la négation en français contemporain* [Geneva, 1971]). For the treatment of negation in generative grammar, see, for example, E. S. Klima, "Negation in English," in *The Structure of Language*, ed. J. A. Fodor and J. J. Katz (Englewood Cliffs, 1964); and S. D. Smith, *Meaning and Negation* (The Hague, 1975). The principal problems raised by negation are presented in *Logique et analyse*, vol. 15, nos. 57 and 58 (1972); most of the articles are in English.

The linguistic theory of A. Culioli (presented in A. Culioli, C. Fuchs, and M. Pécheux, *Considérations théoriques à propos du traitement formel du langage* [Paris, 1970]) defines a general framework in which a very precise place is marked out for an eventual theory of modality (Culioli's "lexis" is still more limited than the traditional "dictum").

DISCURSIVE TIME

The features marking time in the morphology of a language do not enter into a simple and direct relationship with what we call time on the existential plane (nor with the various philosophical conceptions of time); one proof of this (among others) is the presence, in English and other languages, of two distinct words for linguistic time and lived time: in English, *tense* and *time*; in German, *Tempus* and *Zeit*; and in French, the word *temps* has both meanings. This linguistic dichotomy stems from the fact that temporal distinctions may be marked by many means other than verb tense (adverbs and complements of time, dates); in certain languages like ancient Hebrew, an essential element of the notion of time—the chronological distinction of past, present, and future—is not even directly marked within the verb. In this article, as in the preceding one, we shall be dealing with phenomena that are equally distant from time and tense: more precisely, we shall examine the representation of time with respect to the instance of enunciation. This is what we shall call, in the broad sense, **discursive time.**

Discursive time is organized around the present, a purely linguistic notion that designates the moment at which one is speaking. The other verb tenses (in the Indo-European languages, at least) are subdivided into two major groups, according to the relationship that they maintain with the present and, more generally, with the enunciative act [323ff.]. Tenses in English, for example, are divided into the following series: (1) *he sings, he is singing, he sang, he has sung, he will sing,* and so on; and (2) *he sang, he was singing, he had sung, he would sing,* and so on. In the first group, dating is accomplished with reference to the enunciative situation; more precise chronological indications with respect to the present are provided by means of temporal deictics [252] (*yesterday, last year,* and so on); the action described thus enters into contact with the present moment of enunciation and thus with the speaker and the addressee. In the second group, on the other hand, a group that attempts to hide its own conditions of enunciation, the events are situated with respect to each other and with respect to an "objective" chronology; the action described is isolated from the present, not by temporal distance (hours, years, and so on), but by the coded intention of the speaker.

Thus it is appropriate to study separately the grammatical tenses that participate in one group or the other, not only because certain tenses are only utilized in the first (present and future) and others, only in the second (the imperfect, the French *passé simple*), but especially because those that are used in the two modes of relationship to the enunciative act have very different values in that act. For example, in the first group, the English preterite is opposed to the present and future, marks the past, and thus constitutes an element of dating; this does not hold true in the second group, in which the present and future tenses are unknown and the preterite is already situated with respect to a past. The fact that a verb is, grammatically, in a past tense, then, provides no information and does not even constitute a rough outline of dating.

I. Several descriptions and interpretations of this division have been proposed. The German psychologist K. Bühler promoted the idea of a division between the tenses related to the "I-here-now" system (deixis) and the others. E. Benveniste opposes discursive time (present, future, *passé composé*, pluperfect) and historical time (*passé simple*, or aorist; imperfect; conditional; pluperfect; prospective). W. E. Bull regroups the tenses that refer to the present moment (the primary tenses) and those organized around a point situated in the past (retrospective tenses). K. Heger, whose work is based on Bühler's division, proposes as fundamental categories "now" and "other than now." H. Weinrich divides the tenses into **discursive** and **narrative** categories, according to whether the interlocutors consider themselves directly concerned by the action described or not.

Narrative literature, and even more generally, all narrative, uses preferentially the tenses of the second group (historical, nondeictic, narrative, and so on). We must not conclude from this that the events evoked are necessarily situated in the past: anticipatory novels use the same tenses, and, conversely, we may use the tenses of the first group for past actions that are not situated at the level of narrative. The tenses used for narration signify, in effect, the rupture existing between the moment of narration and the narrative evoked; for this reason, they have sometimes been taken as an index of fiction (K. Hamburger).

● See K. Bühler, *Sprachtheorie* (Jena, 1934); E. Benveniste, *Problems in General Linguistics*, trans. M. E. Meek (Coral Gables, 1971), pp. 205–15; W. E. Bull, *Time, Tense, and the Verb* (Berkeley, 1960); K. Heger, "La Conjugaison objective en français et en espagnol," *Langages* 3 (1966): 18–39; H. Weinrich, *Tempus, besprochene und erzählte Welt* (Stuttgart, 1964); K. Hamburger, *The Logic of Literature*, trans. M. J. Rose, 2d ed., rev. (Bloomington, 1973); and E. Benveniste, "Le Langage et l'expérience humaine," in *Problèmes de linguistique générale II* (Paris, 1974), pp. 67–78.

II. The problems of temporality that arise within an organized discourse are relatively independent of the grammatical tenses, as we have just seen. They become particularly complex in the case of fiction, that is, of a representative discourse within which must first be distinguished: **story time** (fiction time, narrated or represented time), the temporality appropriate to the universe evoked; **writing time** (narration time, recounting time), time linked to the process of enunciation, present as well within the text; and, although less clearly represented, **reading time,** the time necessary for the text to be read. These three temporalities are inscribed *within* the text. But alongside these **internal times** there exist also **external times,** with which the text enters into relationship: **writer's**

time, reader's time, and finally **historical time** (that is, the time that is the object of the science of history). The relationships maintained by all these categories define the temporal problematics of a narrative.

Before confronting this problematics in detail, let us point out another possibility for the study of textual time: while remaining within the time of the story alone, it is possible to discern the conception of time that is manifested there (and then to look upon the writer as a philosopher who would treat time as form, intuition, or concept). Numerous studies of a philosophical nature have found their starting point in this approach.

- D. S. Likhachev, *Poetika drevnerusskoi literatury* (Leningrad, 1967), pp. 212–352; E. Staiger, *Die Zeit als Einbildungskraft des Dichters* (Zurich, 1939); G. Poulet, *Studies in Human Time,* trans. E. Coleman (Baltimore, 1956); G. Müller, *Die Debeutung der Zeit in der Erzählkunst* (Bonn, 1947); idem, "Aufbauformen des Romans," *Neophilologus* 37 (1953): 1–14; and H. Meyerhoff, *Time in Literature* (Berkeley, 1955).

III. Among the relationships maintained by the internal times, particular efforts have been made to describe the one that unites story time with writing time. This latter is always present because of the order in which the parts of the text are to be read (in the simplest case, writing time and story time coincide); sometimes this temporality of writing is in turn represented: the book relates not only a story but the story of the book itself. These two temporalities maintain a relationship from several different perspectives.

1. Each temporal system has its own direction. In the simplest case, the two times move in the same direction, on a perfectly parallel course. Events succeed one another in the universe evoked in a manner analogous to the sequence of sentences that relates them in the text. This ideal parallelism is extremely rare, for, on the one hand, the universe evoked is organized along several temporal lines (for example, several characters), and on the other hand, the narrative has its own requirements, which are not those of the so-called reality. The parallelism will then be broken, and in two ways:

a) By **inversions:** some events are reported earlier than others that are nonetheless chronologically anterior. A classic case is the introductory cadaver of detective stories in which we learn only later on what led to the death. The Russian formalists were particularly interested by this type of "deformation" of the represented reality; they saw in it the essential difference between subject and fable.

b) By **embedded stories:** the order in the main story is not inverted, but interrupted in order to begin a second, then a third, and so on (the best-known example is *The Arabian Nights' Entertainments*). Here again, we follow temporal order in the usual fashion; but, firstly, we are no longer dealing with just one temporal chain, and secondly, the embedded story may just as well be a projection into the future.

These ruptures in the temporal parallelism between story and writing are often used to create the effect of **suspense,** a term that designates the experience of the reader who is waiting impatiently to see what happens next. Such an effect is created by different ways of playing with temporality: enigmatic events are exposed in such a way that a return to the past is necessary in order to explain them (relationship between past and present); or an audacious project is reported, and then its realization is announced (relationship between future and present); or, finally, the characters are simply placed in a particularly dangerous situation, in which case the dominant factor is the possibility of forgetting about the writing time, as the reader identifies with the characters.

2. The distance between two temporal systems is variable. First, let us consider two extreme cases: the one in which no relationship can exist between the two temporalities (legends, myth, and so on) and the one in which the two coincide totally, in which case the narrative is the "dictated" monologue of the protagonist (if the protagonist were killed, his monologue would be interrupted). Between these extremes, we can distinguish an unlimited number of intermediate cases: for example, one in which the narrator records in the evening what has taken place during the day; or one in which the narrator begins to relate an event several months after it happened, but the story has not yet come to an end. This type of relationship is particularly clear in first-person narrative.

3. There are quantitative differences between units of story time and units of writing time.

a) If to one unit of story time there corresponds no unit of writing time, we shall speak of *ellipsis*, an example would be entire years of a character's life going unmentioned.

b) If to one unit of story time there corresponds a lesser unit of writing time, we shall speak of *résumé*: in one page a long period of the character's life might be summarized.

c) If to one unit of story time there corresponds an identical unit of writing time, we have *direct style*: the conversation of the characters is reproduced verbatim in the text.

d) If to one unit of story time there corresponds a larger unit of writing time, we have *analysis*: the time of the story continues, but it is slowed down, since each fact may be a pretext for extended analysis (as in Proust).

e) If no unit of story time corresponds to a given unit of writing time, we have *digression*, or suspension of time. The digression may be in the form of a **description** (of place, person), of a philosophical **reflection**, and so on.

The same relationship between the two times may be marked by typographical blanks (divisions into paragraphs, chapters) that may or may not correspond to ruptures in the story time.

4. The quantity of events is a determining factor for the appreciation of rhythm or density; but the question here is one of absolute value, not relative values. On the level of temporality, "dense" pages do not relate many years, but many events (the two may coincide). The absolute density of events may vary in the course of a book, following a rigorous pattern or not. In the classical novel, for example, the exposition unfolds to a slow rhythm (few events), and the rhythm accelerates toward the end.

5. Finally, the projection of story time onto writing time varies in nature according to whether it is simple, as in all the cases evoked until now, or double, or triple, and so on. The double projection takes several forms:

a) **Simultaneity,** which is a spatial redoubling within the story line, a redoubling that the writing time projects in its linear development;

b) Stereoscopic vision, according to which a single scene on the level of story time will be narrated several times, by one or several characters; and

c) Repetition of part of the text, which corresponds to another doubling of an event in the writing time.

We find similar distinctions in the narrative field of vision [328ff.], since the categories of time and person are closely connected. The existence of a (narrator's) viewpoint—the narrator can never be totally absent—signifies the simultaneous existence of a temporality of writing. Conversely, it is through the organization that he imposes on the story time that the narrator often makes his presence felt.

The reading time, in its relationships with the other internal times, has received much less attention, in part because narrator and reader must very often be identified. However, the role of the reader may be explicitly designated (the circumstances in which we are reading the story are represented). Execution time, which characterizes the folkloric genres, seem to be modeled on reading time.

● See D. S. Likhachev, *Poetika drevnerusskoi literatury* (Leningrad, 1967); L. S. Vygotskii, *The Psychology of Art,* trans. Scripta Technica (Cambridge, Mass., 1971); J. Pouillon, *Temps et Roman* (Paris, 1946); G. Müller, *Die Bedeutung der Zeit in der Erzählkunst* (Bonn, 1947); A. A. Mendilow, *Time and the Novel* (London, 1952); E. Lämmert, *Bauformen des Erzählens* (Stuttgart, 1955); J. Ricardou, *Problèmes du nouveau roman* (Paris, 1967), pp. 161–71; and G. Genette, "Le Discours du récit," in *Figures III* (Paris, 1972), pp. 67–282.

IV. The relationships between internal and external times have been studied chiefly from the sociological and historical perspectives. A text establishes relationships of differing intensity with the real (historical) time in which the events represented are supposed to have taken place. The historical novel is at one extreme here: it pretends to be true, in the description of the story. At the other extreme we find the fairy tale, whose action unfolds in a universe that has no relationship of continuity with the historical universe; it describes a closed universe. Usually, even when a novel does not intend to be historical at all, it is easy to recognize the period in which the action is situated.

Writing time plays a role, of course: willingly or not, writers participate in a cultural period, in its systems of representation, and so on. Finally, the reader's time is responsible for the new reinterpretations that each century (each cultural synchrony) gives to the works of the past.

• See A. A. Mendilow, *Time and the Novel* (London, 1952).

ENUNCIATION

Linguistic production may be regarded either as a sequence of sentences, identified without reference to any specific circumstances of occurrence (the sentences may be pronounced, transcribed by means of various writing systems, printed) or as an act in the course of which these sentences are actualized, assumed by a particular speaker in specific spatial and temporal circumstances. From this alternative stems the opposition between the **utterance** (in French, *énoncé*) and the speech situation, sometimes called the enunciation (*énonciation*). However, when the term **enunciation** is used in linguistics, it is taken in a narrower sense: it refers neither to the physical phenomena of speech production or reception, which fall within the province of psycholinguistics or one of its subdivisions [71], nor to the modifications introduced into the global meanings of the utterance by the speech situation [333ff.]; it refers rather to elements that belong to the language code and whose meaning depends, nevertheless, on factors that vary from one speech act to another—for example *I, you, here, now*. In other words, what this linguistic approach focuses on is the imprint of the process of enunciation in the utterance.

The linguistic aspects of enunciation have never been of central concern to linguists; this explains a certain terminological inconsistency in the studies devoted to them. The category is certainly present even in the Greek and Latin grammars; but the American semiotician C. S. Peirce was the first to describe its ambiguous nature. It is a question at one and the same time of symbols, that is, of signs belonging to the language code (*I* is a word in the English lexicon), and of indexes, that is, of signs containing an element of the speech situation (*I* designates the person who is speaking at this moment, in this place) [86].

Linguists have most often used the term "deixis" in referring to enunciation. However, this word masks an important opposition (as K. Bühler pointed out): one group of deictic forms refers to previous elements in the utterance itself (for example, the pronouns *he, she, it*), whereas another group refers to elements of the speech act (*I, you*); in other words, anaphoric deixis is confused with indexical deixis [281ff.]. More recently, the work of linguists like Jespersen, Jakobson, and especially Benveniste has made it possible to begin a precise and systematic study of these facts.

The primary elements constituting a process of enunciation are the **speaker,** who produces the utterance, and the **hearer** (or **addressee**), to whom the utterance is addressed (both are called **interlocutors**). From this point on, the organization of the indexical linguistic forms may be envisaged in two ways, according to whether grammatical or semantic categories are in question.

In the case of grammatical categories, the following elements may be identified: the personal pronouns of the first and second persons; the demonstrative pronouns; the adverbs and adjectives that Bally called relatives (*here, now, yesterday, today*, and so on); and the verb tenses, always organized around the present, that is, the time of enunciation. We shall add certain verbs taken in the first person singular (*I believe that . . . , I conclude that . . .*); and the *performative* verbs [342ff.], that is, those that in the first person singular of the present tense accomplish in and of themselves the action that they designate (for example, *I promise . . . , I swear . . .*). This second group differs from the first, in which the object of reference varies with the context; yet, both groups provide information on the process of enunciation. Information is similarly provided by certain strata of the lexicon in which there appear **evaluative** and **emotive terms** (terms containing semantic features that imply a judgment or a particular attitude on the part of the speaker).

Modalizing terms such as *perhaps, certainly,* and *doubtless* place the speaker's assertion in suspension, and in so doing they too are related to the enunciative process. Finally, the syntactic functions (subject and predicate) relate to the enunciation according to diverse modalities: the elements that express the attitude of the speaker toward what he is talking about are tied to the predicate, never to the subject. If evaluative terms occur within the subject of the sentence, they are interpreted as quotations, as names proposed for the corresponding expressions.

The same problems are encountered if we begin with semantic categories, which are of four types: identity of the interlocutors, time, place, and modalities of the enunciative act (or the relationship between the interlocutors and the utterance). The English pronouns *I* and *you* allow us only to identify the protagonists of the enunciative process, whereas in certain East Asian languages, indications as to the social status or the mutual relationships of the interlocutors are added. Indications of time and place are always organized from the starting point of the act of enunciation itself, that is, on the basis of the adverbs *here* and *now*; however, many other lexical items refer to time and place as well—for example, verbs such as *to come.*

The problem of reference [247ff.] is closely connected to the enunciative process; as Peirce observed, in order for a sign to denote, it has to pass through the intermediary of an "index." The question of truth, subordinated to that of referentiality, is equally inconceivable outside of the enunciative process: in itself, an utterance is neither true nor false; it becomes true or false only in the course of a particular act of enunciation.

- See E. Benveniste, *Problems in General Linguistics,* trans. M. E. Meek (Coral Gables, 1971), pp. 195–246; C. Bally, "Les Notions grammaticales d'absolu et de relatif," in *Essais sur le langage* (Paris, 1969), pp. 189–204; R. Jakobson, "Shifters, Verbal Categories and the Russian Verb," in *Selected Writings II* (The Hague, 1971), pp. 130–47; A. W. Burks, "Icon, Index, Symbol," *Philosophy and Phenomenological Research* 9 (1949): 673–89; C. J. Fillmore, "Deictic Categories in the Semantics of 'Come,'" *Foundations of Language* 2 (1966): 219–27; J. R. Searle, *Speech Acts* (London, 1969); and *Langages* 17 (1970): *L'Enonciation,* ed. T. Todorov.

The study of the enunciative process has repercussions in two neighboring areas, sociolinguistics [61ff.] and stylistics [75ff.].

As an individual act, enunciation falls within the sphere of a total study of social behavior and, more particularly, within the province of linguistic anthropology [64ff.]. The latter borrows from the concept of enunciation several of its fundamental categories. An example of such borrowing is the opposition introduced by Austin between illocutionary and perlocutionary forces [343ff.]: the internal structure of an action is opposed to the particular results that it achieves. The illocutionary force of an imperative sentence, for example, consists in the fact that an order is given to someone; its perlocutionary force, in the fact that the imperative is followed by an effect. A strictly linguistic anthropology would include only illocutionary force in its field of study.

Another relationship is possible between the model of the enunciative process elaborated on the basis of a linguistic analysis and the description of speech acts provided at the anthropological level. Here we may quote the linguistic analysis undertaken by the American logician J. R. Searle: "First and most important, there is the point or purpose of the act (the difference, for example, between a statement and a question); second, the relative positions of S [speaker] and H [hearer] (the difference between a request and an order); third, the degree of commitment undertaken (the difference between a mere expression of intention and a promise); fourth, the difference in propositional content (the difference between predictions and reports); fifth, the difference in the way the proposition relates to the interest of S and H (the difference between boasts and laments, between warnings and predictions); sixth, the difference between a promise, which is an expression of intention, and a statement, which is an expression of belief); seventh, the different ways in which an utterance relates to the rest of the conversation (the difference between simply replying to what someone has said and objecting to what he has said)" (*Speech Acts*, p. 70). The oppositions disclosed above obviously make it possible to establish a categorization of what constitutes the object of linguistic anthropology.

● See J. L. Austin, *How to Do Things With Words* (Cambridge, Mass., 1962); and J. R. Searle, *Speech Acts* (London, 1969).

The enunciative process is always present, in one way or another, within the utterance; the different forms of its presence, as well as the degrees of its intensity, provide a basis for establishing a typology of discourse. Several oppositions, established through diverse stylistic analyses and based on categories arising from the enunciative process, will be pointed out here.

1. The opposition of a discourse centered on the speaker to a discourse organized around the addressee. Common sense allows us to distinguish an orator who does not know his public (the addressee implicit in the discourse is modeled in the likeness of the speaker himself) from one who adapts his speech to the listeners present before him (the implicit addressee is independent of the speaker). This commonplace intuition may be made explicit and precise. L. Irigaray has proposed a similar typology of discourse that coincides with a psychoanalytic typology of speakers: obsessional and hysterical.

2. The opposition of the explicit (or autonomous) discourse to the implicit, situational discourse. This distinction is encountered in the theses of the Linguistic Circle of Prague: "Two directions of gravitation: in the one, the language is situational, i.e., depends on complementary extra-linguistic elements (*practical language*); in the other, the language tends to constitute a whole which is as closed as possible, tends to become complete and precise, and to use term-words and judgment-phrases (*theoretical* or *formulative* language)" (translated from "Thèses présentées au Premier Congrès des philologues slaves," in *A Prague School Reader in Linguistics*, ed. J. Vachek [Bloomington, 1964], p. 42). This opposition may be maintained without a concomitant identification of the two tendencies described with conversation on the one hand, the scientific text on the other. More recently, B. Uspenskii has used a similar opposition in order to establish his own psychological typology.

3. The opposition of a discourse with few indications concerning the enunciative process to one that continually refers to it. Freud distinguished these two types of utterances in analytic work. Benveniste studied them under the respective labels of "history" and "discourse." This opposition, like the preceding ones, does not compare pure qualities, but rather quantitative predominances.

4. V. Voloshinov, a Soviet linguist and literary critic writing in the twenties, in studying the **quotation,** that is, an utterance whose enunciative process is reproduced, showed how yet another discursive opposition functions within literary texts. The quoted utterance and the quoting utterance may or may not be in a relationship of continuity: the language of the narrator and that of the characters may be similar or different. One utterance or the other may undergo transformations: the narrator's discourse is assimilated, in Dostoevsky's work, to the words of the characters he is presenting; in indirect style, on the contrary, there is a tendency to make the quoted utterance resemble the quoting one. In a third case, no interpenetration can be observed between quoting and quoted utterances.

All of these oppositions remain to be integrated into a general theory of styles [300ff.].

Another application of the categories pertaining to the enunciative process in rhetorical and literary analysis touches on the problem of point of view [328ff.]. The narrator of a text is in effect nothing other than an imaginary speaker, reconstituted on the basis of the verbal elements that refer to him.

● See L. Irigaray, "Approche d'une grammaire d'énonciation de l'hystérique et de l'obsessionnel," *Langages* 5 (1967): 99–109; B. A. Uspenskii, "Personologicheskie problemy v lingvisticheskom aspekte," in *Tezisy dokla-*

dov vo vtoroi letnei shkole po vtorichnym modeliruiushchim sistemam (Tartu, 1966), pp. 6–12; T. Todorov, "Freud sur l'énonciation," *Langages* 17 (1970): *L'Enonciation*, ed. T. Todorov, pp. 34–41; V. Voloshinov, *Marxism and the Philosophy of Language*, trans. L. Matejka and I. R. Titunik (New York, 1973), pp. 109–59; and M. Bakhtin, *Problems of Dostoevsky's Poetics*, trans. R. W. Rotsel (Ann Arbor, 1973).

POINT OF VIEW IN FICTION

Historical Background

Point of view refers to the relationship between narrator and represented universe. The category is thus tied to the representational arts (fiction, figurative painting, cinema; to a lesser degree, theater, sculpture, architecture); it is a category that is concerned with the very act of representing in its modalities, namely, in the case of representative discourse, the act of enunciation in its relationship with the utterance. Although (narrative) point of view is inherent in all representational discourse, the theory of point of view has been developed only recently, at the end of the nineteenth century (notwithstanding isolated insights that can be found in earlier periods). This new awareness coincided with a feverish exploitation, by writers, of the different writing techniques appropriate to each point of view. Today we are witnessing, on the contrary, a double retreat: at least a part of modern literature tends to refuse representation; thus the category of point of view is becoming less important. On the other hand, literary criticism, which once saw in point of view the secret of the literary art, is discovering that the category includes a series of distinct features, that it has after all only descriptive value, and that it cannot serve as a criterion for success.

Efforts have long been made to find a single opposition around which to organize all the features connected with the relationship between the narrator and the represented universe. From these efforts, syncretic terms have arisen to group several categories in one or to postulate their solidarity. Thus O. Ludwig distinguished between the narrative proper and the scenic narrative (in which events are presented to be "seen"—in the theater, for example); P. Lubbock distinguished between panoramic vision (in which the narrator embraces whole years at a glance and "witnesses" an event simultaneously from several vantage points) and scenic vision (in which events unfold, as they happen, before our eyes). In the same period B. Tomashevskii writes: "Either the tale is told objectively by the author as a simple report, without an explanation of how the events became known (the objective tale), or else it is told by a designated narrator who functions as a relatively specific character. . . . Thus two basic types of narration exist" ("Thematics," p. 75)— the objective and the subjective. More recently, Uspenskii has proposed reducing everything to the opposition between internal and external points of view (with regard to the represented universe). The difficulty is evident: each of the foregoing oppositions covers several independent categories.

● See O. Ludwig, *Studien* (Leipzig, 1891); H. James, *The Art of the Novel* (New York, 1934); P. Lubbock, *The Craft of Fiction* (New York, 1921); B. Tomashevskii, "Thematics," in *Russian Formalist Criticism: Four Essays*, ed. L. T. Lemon and M. J. Reis (Lincoln, 1965), pp. 61–95; C.-E. Magny, *The Age of the American Novel*, trans. E. Hochman (New York, 1972); B A. Uspenskii, *A Poetics of Composition*, trans. V. Zavarin and S. Wittig (Berkeley, 1973); N. Friedmann, *Form and Meaning in Fiction* (Athens, Ga., 1975), pp. 134–66, which includes an historical overview and an abundant bibliography; and F. Van Rossum-Guyon, "Point de vue ou perspective narrative," *Poétique* 4 (1970): 476–96.

Analysis

At the linguistic level, the category of point of view is tied to that of person, in the sense that the latter brings into play the relationships established between the protagonists of the discursive act (*I* and *you*) and those of the utterance itself (*he* or *she*): the concept of point of view thus implies those of utterance and enunciation [323].

The narrative process includes at least three protagonists: the character (*he* or *she*), the **narrator** (*I*), and the **reader** (*you*)—in other words, the one who is spoken about, the one who speaks, and the one who is spoken to.

Very often the image of the narrator is a double one: it is sufficient for the subject of the enunciation to appear itself in the utterance for there to arise, behind it, a new subject. In other words, as soon as the narrator is represented in the text, it becomes necessary to postulate the existence of an **implied author,** the one who is writing and who must in no case be confused with the person of the author in flesh and blood:

only the former is present in the book itself. The implied author is the one who organizes the text, who is responsible for the presence or absence of a certain part of the story; it is this author whose existence is obliterated by psychological criticism, since such criticism identifies him with the person of the writer. If no person is interposed between this inevitable author and the represented universe, it is because the implied author and the narrator have been fused. But most of the time the narrator has his own, unmistakable role. This role varies from one text to another: the narrator may be one of the major characters (in a first-person narrative), or he may simply make a value judgment (with respect to which, at another point in the text, the author may register his disagreement) and thus accede to existence.

The reader must not be confused with real readers either: here again we are dealing with a role inscribed in the text (just as there are inscribed in every discourse bits of information concerning the addressee). The real reader accepts or rejects this role; he does or does not read the book in the order that has been proposed to him; he does or does not associate himself with the book's implicit value judgments (judgments directed at the characters, incidents, and so on). Sometimes the image of the narrator and that of the reader coincide; at other times the narrator is situated among the characters.

The relationships between implied author, narrator, characters, and implied reader define, in their diversity, the problematics of point of view. Several variables capable of combination may be identified here.

1. *The enunciative context.* The narrative may be presented as self-evident, as natural and transparent; or, on the contrary, the act of enunciation may find itself represented in the text. In this latter case, the texts in which the interlocutor is also present (the narrator is seated at the hearth on a winter night and is addressing a young person of his acquaintance) are to be distinguished from texts in which the interlocutor is absent and which may either (*a*) confront the reader directly with the narrator's discourse (the reader is the one to whom the narrator is addressing himself) or (*b*) represent the very act of writing itself, in which case it is then explicitly stated that what we are reading is a book, and the process of its creation is described. Many of Maupassant's short stories illustrate the case in which the interlocutor is present; the majority of first-person novels illustrate that of the absent interlocutor; and books such as Sterne's *Tristram Shandy* or Diderot's *Jacques le Fataliste* are examples of the third case.

2. *The identity of the narrator.* There may be one or several narrators; in the latter case, the narrators may be situated either at the same level or at different levels. These narrative levels depend upon the type of

relationship existing between sequences within a single narrative (embedding or linking) [298]: in the epistolary novel, for example, the authors of the letters are situated, *a priori*, on the same level; this is true for the ten narrators of Boccaccio's *Decameron* (their narratives are linked among themselves). On the other hand, the overall framework of the *Decameron* has its own narrator, who is not situated at the same level as the others: he can report the enunciative acts of the others, whereas the converse is not true.

3. *Narratorial presence.* In discussing narrational presence, it is possible to make clear distinctions of level.

a) The narrator is present at the level of the universe evoked or at the level of the narrative. In the first case, there is contiguity between characters and narrator; in the second (as in *Jacques le Fataliste*), the narrator does not intervene in the represented universe but describes himself explicitly as in the process of writing the book. The two solutions may be combined: *Tristram Shandy* describes himself both as character and as author. In the similar case of memoirs, the two contexts still remain disconnected; but in a journal, or an epistolary novel, the act of writing intervenes ultimately in the very account of the action itself (as in Butor's *L'Emploi du temps* or in Laclos's *Les Liaisons dangereuses*).

b) When the narrator is represented at the level of the characters, he may be either "agent" or **witness;** these two terms in effect designate the two extreme limits between which an endless number of particular cases can be situated: the narrator is sometimes the main character, sometimes an anonymous being of whom we know practically nothing beyond his mere existence (as in Dostoevsky's *The Brothers Karamazov*).

4. *Narratorial distances.* In discussing narrated distances, it is necessary to introduce the plural, for the distances in question may reach from implied author to narrator, from narrator to characters, from narrator to implied reader, from implied author to implied reader, from implied author to characters, and so on (each of these cases could be illustrated by countless examples). Furthermore, the very nature of the distance may vary: it may be moral and affective in nature (the difference is in the value judgments made), intellectual (the difference is in the degree of comprehension of events), temporal and spatial (relative distancing of the opposed terms noted above). These different modalities of distance may vary even within the same work. Each of the distances may also be reduced to zero; such reductions create complex narrative roles. Finally, the distances may be more or less explicit, established in a more or less systematic fashion, and so on.

5. *Narratorial "knowledge."* The omniscient narrator is frequently opposed to the one whose knowledge is limited; once again, these are two isolated cases in a continuous series. The following distinctions may be made in this context:

a) We may distinguish internal and external viewpoints: the narrator describes the mental universe of the character from without or from within. Where he introduces himself into the mind of a character, the technique may be applied to a single hero or to several; and in this latter case, the passage from one consciousness to another may or may not follow a rigorous pattern. It is when the effort to justify the narrator's knowledge is reduced to a minimum that we speak of an omniscient author (or narrator).

b) We may also distinguish degrees of depth, uneven penetration by the narrator (or his **angle of vision**): he may describe only behavior and be content with observing; he may report a character's thoughts (which only the character himself is supposed to know); or he may provide information about proceedings about which the character himself knows nothing (this ambition is often based, in the twentieth century, on the workings of the unconscious). We may also make a distinction between the types of knowledge implied: psychological knowledge, knowledge of events, and so on.

c) We must add the phenomenon evoked in Aristotle's *Poetics* by the term **recognition.** The term obviously implies an earlier moment at which, in place of correct knowledge, ignorance and error were to be found; in other words, a defective point of view from the standpoint of truth.

6. Finally, these categories of point of view must be distinguished from the linguistic means that assure their expression. It is impossible to identify a point of view with verbal devices that may have a number of very different expressive functions. For example, whether the narrative is related in the first or the third person (or in the second) is very important, but this in no way represents a prejudgment of the presence, the knowledge, or the distances of the narrator; the third-person narrative, for example, precludes neither a strong narratorial presence nor the reduction of distance between narrator and characters, nor the limited character of the narrator's knowledge of the protagonist's motivations. Similarly, the use of the **summary** and of the **scene,** on which H. James and P. Lubbock focused attention, does not entail any assumptions about the type of point of view adopted. At best we may speak of an affinity between the categories of point of view and of style [300ff.], but not of equivalence nor of absolute solidarity.

● See K. Friedemann, *Die Rolle des Erzählers in der Epik* (Leipzig, 1910); P. Lubbock, *The Craft of Fiction* (New York, 1921); J. Pouillon, *Temps et Roman* (Paris, 1946); W. Kayser, "Qui raconte le roman?" *Poétique* 4 (1970): 498–510; F. Stanzel, *Typische Formen des Romans* (Vienna, 1955); W. Booth, *The Rhetoric of Fiction* (Chicago, 1961); B. Romberg, *Studies in the Narrative Technique of the First-Person Novel* (Stockholm, 1962); B. A. Uspenskii, *A Poetics of Composition*, trans. V. Zavarin and S. Wittig (Berkeley, 1973); G. Genette, "Le Discours du récit," in *Figures III* (Paris, 1972), pp. 67–282; and M. Bal, "Narration et focalisation," *Poétique* 29 (1977): 107–27.

SPEECH SITUATION

The set of circumstances surrounding the occurrence of an act of enunciation (whether written or oral) is known as the **speech situation.** By this we mean at once the physical and social setting in which the act takes place, the identity of the interlocutors, their image of the act of enunciation, their views of each other (including the idea each has of what the other thinks of him), the events that have preceded the act of enunciation (especially the previous relations between the interlocutors and in particular the verbal exchange in the course of which the enunciative act in question takes place). (N.B. These circumstances are sometimes called the **context.** But it is convenient to reserve this latter term to designate the strictly linguistic surroundings of an element [a word or phonic unit] within an utterance, that is, the series of elements that precede and follow it in the utterance, or in more technical terms, the syntagmas [106] to which these elements belong.)

It is a trivial observation that most—perhaps all—acts of enunciation are impossible to interpret if only the utterance used is known and nothing is known about the situation: not only will it be impossible to learn what motivated the utterance and what effects it may have had, but more importantly still—this is the only problem which will be considered here—it will be impossible to describe accurately the intrinsic value of the enunciative act or even the information that it communicates.

- On the *de facto* importance of the speech situation, see T. Slama-Cazacu, *Langage et contexte* (Copenhagen, 1961), esp. pt. 2, chaps. 2 and 3; and J. A. Fishman, "Who Speaks What Language to Whom and When," *La Linguistique* 1, no. 2 (1965): 67–88.

We may first ask of what this dependency consists. Knowledge of the speech situation may be necessary in the following circumstances:

a) In order to determine the referent of expressions used. This is obvious in the case of the deictics [252] (*I, you, this, here, now*), which designate objects only by situating them with respect to the interlocutors [324]. But it is also true for most proper names (*John* is that person in our surroundings, or about whom we have spoken, whose name is John) and even for many expressions introduced by a definite article (*the doorman* is the person who is the doorman in the building we are talking about).

b) In order to choose between different interpretations of an ambiguous utterance. We choose between the two meanings of "Jack rented a car this morning" according to whether Jack is known to have cars for rent or not.

c) In order to determine the nature of the speech act accomplished. (N.B. The nature of a speech act, or its illocutionary value [343ff.], is entirely different from its real or expected effect.) The utterance "You'll go to Paris tomorrow" is understood as a promise, as a piece of information, or as an order, depending on the relationships existing between the interlocutors and the value they attach to going to Paris (the role of intonation [179], while incontestable, seems insufficient to exempt us from recourse to the speech situation).

d) In order to determine whether an act of enunciation is of normal or abnormal character. A given utterance that is normal in certain situations is out of place in others and thus will take on a special value (it will have to be described, in these situations, as precious, emphatic, pedantic, familiar, crude).

For all these reasons, it would seem difficult to say that the speech situation does not interest the linguist, even if we grant that the linguist takes as his object utterances themselves, not individual enunciative acts. For in fact it is not easy to see how to describe an utterance without saying what becomes of it in the different types of situations in which it may be used. Even while considering an utterance outside of its situational context, we are very often obliged to characterize it with respect to possible speech situations.

Even when it is a matter of describing the content of words alone, B. Pottier finds it necessary to introduce certain features, called **virtuemes,** whose appearance requires a particular situation: thus the virtueme *danger* may be ascribed to *red.*

● See B. Pottier, *Présentation de la linguistique* (Paris, 1967), p. 27. For a general presentation of Pottier's linguistic theory, see his *Linguistique générale: Théorie et description* (Paris, 1973).

But once this *de facto* importance of the speech situation has been recognized, it remains necessary to decide how much importance can legitimately be attributed to it within a general theory of language. For most linguists, it is possible—and desirable—to exclude all situational considerations, even if the situational effects must be reintroduced subsequently, as an independent and supplementary factor. This amounts to saying that the situation concerns speech (*la parole*) and not language (*la langue* [118ff.]), or at least no more than a marginal region of language very close to its transformation into speech. The dependency of the utterance with respect to the situations in which it is used would thus be, if not an accidental phenomenon, in any case a secondary one that would respond more than anything to a desire for economy. Various supporting arguments may be offered:

a) One of the essential functions of language is to allow us to speak of things in their absence (and, by the same token, to act on them from a distance). Is this power of symbolic abstraction comprehensible if utterances cannot be described unless their use conditions are taken into account?

b) Suppose that an utterance *U* has the meanings *u'* and *u''*, according to whether or not the situation in which it is used includes the characteristic *C*. We can then always construct two utterances *U'* and *U''* that themselves possess, respectively, the values *u'* and *u''* independently of the characteristic *C*. Thus the three illocutionary values that the utterance "You'll go to Paris" is capable of assuming, according to the situation, may be obtained by using three utterances that do not require this same recourse to the situation (example: "I order you to go to Paris tomorrow"). Similarly, it is always possible to go to the extreme of designating oneself without referring to the speech situation and to the fact that one is the speaker, that is, without saying *I* (the author of an anonymous letter may mention himself by using a proper name). In a more general way, the natural languages possess the characteristic—which distinguishes them from the artificial languages—of being able to express everything that can be thought (Hjelmslev incorporates this feature into his definition of human language). Thus if the interpretation of an utterance borrows certain elements from the situation, it suffices to formulate these elements and to add this formulation to the initial utterance in order to liberate the latter from the speech situation. It seems reasonable, then, to present recourse to the situation as a sort of artifice, as a device that allows us to abridge discourse but is not essential to language, for language itself provides the means to avoid it.

- For an illustration of this thesis, see, for example, L. Prieto, *Messages et signaux* (Paris, 1966), pt. 2, chap. 2.

c) Finally, a practical argument may be advanced: the number of possible contexts for an utterance is infinite, and it is not even subject to categorial analysis. We would thus be setting ourselves an impossible task if we were to presume to describe all the nuances of meaning that an utterance can take on as the situation varies. Simple prudence warns us to describe the utterance first, independently of its uses, and to regard as a later refinement of this description the introduction of situational effects.

- Arguments of this sort are found in J. J. Katz and J. A. Fodor, "The Structure of a Semantic Theory," *Language* 39 (1963): 176–80; and in N. Ruwet, *An Introduction to Generative Grammar*, trans. N. S. H. Smith (Amsterdam, 1973), chap. 1, sec. 2.1.

To these various arguments the following responses may be proposed:

a') The possibility of symbolic action offered by language implies, to be sure, that we can speak of a thing or of a situation in its absence, but not that we can speak in the absence of any thing or situation. From the fact that language is endowed with a relative power of abstraction, we should not conclude that it may be exercised in total isolation.

b') Let us concede that when an act of enunciation borrows certain informing elements from the speech situation, these elements can always be incorporated into the utterance itself, lengthening and complicating it. But, even when the global information is preserved, the mode of presentation of this information, and consequently the value of the enunciative act, may well be entirely transformed. Thus there is a difference between the act of presenting information explicitly and that of alluding to it. In order for allusion to operate, (1) the listener must already possess the information in question and (2) the speaker must know this. Allusion supposes, therefore, and introduces, between the participants in a dialogue, a sort of complicity that lies outside the explicit formulation. Why should the allusive devices included in language have economy as their basic function and the function of facilitating a whole intersubjective strategy as only an accidental consequence? This is particularly difficult to accept insofar as the personal pronouns are concerned. The fact that a speaker designates himself, not by his name, but by *I* and the addressee by *you* has implications regarding the nature of the relations between the interlocutors, according to Benveniste. As a result of this designation, in fact, speaker and addressee are apprehended directly as interlocutors, and their relationships are subsequently marked by the reciprocity bound up in discursive relations (the *I* is a potential *you*, and vice versa). As a particular application of this thesis, we may observe that the replacement of *I* and *you* by the interlocutors' names transforms the illocutionary value—the value as act—of numerous utterances. To say to someone: "I order you to . . . " is not to inform him that he has received an order but actually to issue an order to him. If we replace *I* and *you* by the interlocutors' names, *X* and *Y*, we can no longer justify interpreting the resulting utterance ("*X* orders *Y* to . . . ") as the accomplishment of the act of ordering. (The act of ordering requires that the one who formulates the order be recognized at the same time as the one who issues it—or as his spokesman.) In other words, if we define the signification of an utterance not only through its informative content but also through the type of relations its use introduces among the interlocutors, it is difficult to regard the allusions of an utterance to the speech situation as simple economy measures.

● For an interpretation of the pronouns that goes beyond the notion of economy, see E. Benveniste, *Problems in General Linguistics*, trans. M. E. Meek (Coral Gables, 1971). A comparison between Benveniste and Prieto can be found in O. Ducrot, "Chronique linguistique," *L'Homme* 7 (1967): 109–22. A general reflection on deixis is found in C. J. Fillmore, *Santa Cruz Lectures on Deixis*, Indiana Linguistic Club, 1975.

c') It is not absolutely self-evident that the linguist is undertaking an impossible task if he proposes to indicate the effect of the speech situation on the meaning of utterances. Three clarifications may be useful here:

1) It is not a question of indicating all the nuances that the situation is capable of adding to the meaning. It is a question, first of all, of not ruling out the description of expression, turns of phrase, utterances whose meaning is inseparable from the value they take on in a given type of speech situation, utterances whose meaning includes as an integral component an allusion to their use conditions (compare, for example, the idea of constitutive rules for usage, p. 343).

2) Two different speech situations (and even an infinite number) may have an identical effect on the interpretation of a given utterance. Each utterance then induces a sort of classification in the set of possible speech situations, leading us to group in a single class those situations that orient the utterance in the same direction. Thus we are able to define, using a procedure familiar to phonologists [171], certain **situational distinctive features,** each one being common to situations of a given class. Such features are the ones that should intervene in the description of speech situations.

3) Even if we wish to surpass the preliminary objective established in (1), it is possible to define a certain number of general laws, similar

to the laws of rhetoric, that govern in a given speech community the relationship of an utterance—any utterance at all—and its use conditions. To take an elementary example: when the content of an utterance is in contradiction with certain beliefs of which evidence is given in the speech situation, the utterance has to be interpreted as the statement, in the ironic mode, of the inverse of what it explicitly affirms (this is the rhetorical figure known as **antiphrasis**)—for example, "What glorious weather!" (in the face of a driving rain); "How generous they are at the Internal Revenue Service!"

LANGUAGE AND ACTION

There are scarcely any human activities that do not include the use of language as an integral feature. In describing a particular language, to what extent must we consider the use that speaking subjects may make of it?

Saussure suggests a negative response. Opposing language (*langue*) to speech (*parole*), he attributes to speech all that is involved in putting language to work, to use [118] (speech "executes" language, in the sense in which a musician executes a score). Since knowledge of language is supposed to be independent of knowledge of speech, the study of linguistic activity should be deferred, in the investigation of a language, until a purely static description of the code itself has been provided: we have to know what words mean before we can understand their use. The neopositivist logicians reach a similar conclusion in distinguishing three possible points of view on languages (natural or artificial). From the logical point of view, **syntax** determines the rules that make possible the construction of sentences, or formulae, by combining elementary symbols. **Semantics,** in mathematical logic, for its part seeks to provide the means for interpreting these formulae, for setting them into correspondence with something else; this "something else" may be reality or other formulae (of the same language or of another). Finally, **pragmatics** describes the use that can be made of the formulae by interlocutors seeking to act on each other. Semantics and syntax, which study the very core of the language, must be elaborated without regard to any pragmatic considerations.

- On this aspect of neopositivism, see C. W. Morris, *Foundations of the Theory of Signs* (Chicago, 1938), chaps. 3–5. See also R. Carnap, *Foundations of Logic and Mathematics* (Chicago, 1939), chap. 1.

Such asceticism in the consideration of language has something paradoxical about it, however; throughout the history of linguistics we find the inverse thesis, which subordinates structure to function and affirms the necessity of knowing *why* the language is, in order to know *how* it is. The concepts that may be suitable for its description can only be drawn from a reflection on its function. Once we have reached this point, however, we find ourselves obliged to establish a hierarchy among language functions; without this we shall fail to avoid the so-called naive finalism associated with the name of Bernardin de Saint-Pierre, which consists in accounting for the contexture of a thing by the multiple uses (often contradictory) that are made of it. In other words, we must try to distinguish the function for which language is made and what, above and beyond this, can be done with language. This need to distinguish what is inherent and what is extrinsic in linguistic activity has led the comparatists [9] to discuss the "basic" function of language; moreover, it has led K. Bühler to distinguish linguistic act and action, and it is this need, finally, that is at the origin of the notion of illocutionary act as elaborated by J. L. Austin.

What is the "basic" function of language? According to the *Port-Royal Grammar*, language was invented to allow men to communicate their thoughts to each other (A. Arnauld and C. Lancelot, *Grammaire générale et raisonnée* [1660; reprint ed., Paris, 1969]). But Arnauld and Lancelot add immediately that speech, in order to permit this communication, has to constitute an image, a picture of thought; consequently, grammatical structures must be a sort of copy of intellectual structures. This reconciliation between the communicative and the representational functions, the latter being a means toward the former, has been questioned by the comparatists. The study of language evolution seems to show in fact that the concern for economy in communication brings about a constant phonetic erosion that in turn disfigures the grammatical structures to the point of rendering them unrecognizable (see above, p. 11). It follows that the "advanced" languages, while continuing to satisfy—better and better—the needs of communication, can no longer pretend to any adequacy with respect to the structures of thought: they have lost their representational function.

Maintaining the comparatist dissociation of communication and representation, W. von Humboldt argued nevertheless that the latter has always been the fundamental function of language in the history of humanity: "Language is not simply a means of communication (*Verständigungsmittel*) but the expression of the mind and world-view of those who use it: social life is the indispensable auxiliary of its development, but by no means the goal toward which it tends" (translated from *Über den Dualis* (1827), in *Gesammelte Schriften*, 17 vols. [Berlin, 1903–36], vol. 6 [1907], p. 23). In constructing language, the human mind tends first to set up a mirror image of itself, thus taking possession of itself in a reflection that has become not only possible but necessary. Only the "primitive" languages have not yet reached this stage of development in which speech reflects thought. The Indo-European languages have long since reached this point, and the phonetic deterioration they have undergone in the course of time can no longer affect this achievement. To prove it, Humboldt tries to show, through detailed analyses, the representational function of apparently aberrant phenomena such as grammatical agreement, irregularities in conjugations and declensions, or the fusion of the root [10] and the inflections [200] in words. These phenomena would tend to manifest, in the strongest sense—that of making perceptible—the unifying effort of the mind introducing unity into the multiplicity of the empirical data. The very essence of language is thus an **act** (ἐνέργεια) of representation of thought.

● See in particular Humboldt's "Über das Entstehen der grammatischen Formen und ihren Einfluss auf die Ideentwicklung" (1821), in *Gesammelte Schriften*, 17 vols. (Berlin, 1903–36), vol. 4 (1905), pp. 285–313; it is also available in a recently reprinted French translation entitled *De l'origine des formes grammaticales* (Bordeaux, 1969).

There is much to separate K. Bühler from Humboldt, since the former's philosophy is based on the results of phonology [171], which bases its entire analysis on the function of language in communication. And yet Bühler supports the Humboldtian view that what is essential in a language is a certain mode of activity of the human mind. More precisely, he attempts to reconcile this idea with the Saussurian dogma that a study of language must precede a study of speech. To do so, Bühler makes a distinction between **act** and **action** (*Sprechakt* and *Sprechhandlung*) in language activity. Linguistic action is the action of using the language, of making a means of it: we speak to someone else *in order to* help him, deceive him, make him act in a certain way. This insertion of language into human practice is assimilated by Bühler to speech, in the Saussurian sense. This is not the case for the linguistic act, which Bühler associates with the act of signifying (*Zeichensetzen*), whose various modes were studied by medieval linguists, nor for the act that imparts meaning (*sinnverleihend*), isolated by Husserl. The linguistic act is thus inherent to the act of speaking and independent of the projects in which speech is involved. The study of this act thus constitutes an integral part of the study of language; it is even its central core.

Of what does this original linguistic activity, this pure signifying activity, consist? Although nothing in Bühler's text explicitly authorizes such a connection, it is perhaps legitimate to regard as an answer to this question Bühler's analysis of the act of communication. The latter is presented as a drama with three characters (the world, that is, the objective content spoken about; the speaker, and the addressee: someone is speaking to someone about something). Consequently, every linguistic utterance is always, essentially, a triple sign, and the act of signifying is always oriented in three directions. It refers (1) to the content communicated (in this sense it is *Darstellung*, "representation," or **representative function** [N.B. this word is not to be taken in Humboldt's sense or in the sense of the Port-Royal grammarians, which imply an idea of imitation]); (2) to the addressee, whom it presents as concerned by this content (this is the **appelative function** [*Appell*]); and (3) to the speaker, whose psychological or moral attitude it manifests (this is the **expressive function** [*Ausdruck*]). Bühler's originality lies in his assignment of an independent and properly linguistic character to these three functions. Take, for example, the expressive function, which may be realized by intonations (amusement, anger, surprise) or by certain modalizers (*"Let's hope* that we'll have good weather," *"Unfortunately* he is going to come"). It is linguistic in the sense that the modalizers and intonations are not mechanical consequences of psychological states, but a certain way of signaling them. And it is independent in the sense that it constitutes a very particular mode of signification: we do not produce the same signification of a psychological state when we express it ("Unfortunately he is going to come") as we do when we represent it ("It bothers me that he is going to come").

Bühler's schema has been completed by Jakobson, but its original intent has not been modified: it is still a question of determining which acts are inherent in the act of communication itself, independently of any of the speaker's other intentions and projects. Beyond the world (context), the **sender** (speaker, encoder [in French, *destinateur*]), and the **receiver** (hearer, decoder [in French, *destinataire*]), Jakobson brings into play, in order to describe the act of communication, the linguistic code used, the message composed, and, finally, the psychophysiological connection, the contact established between the interlocutors. Thus he adds to Bühler's three functions (rechristened **referential, expressive,** and **conative**) three others: **metalinguistic** (most utterances include, implicitly or explicitly, a reference to their own code), **poetic** (the utterance, in its material structure, is regarded as having an intrinsic value, as being an end in itself), and **phatic** (there is no communication without an effort to establish and maintain contact with the interlocutor; hence expressions such as "Well," "You know," and so on, and the fact that speech is experienced as if it constituted, by its very existence, a social or affective link).

- K. Bühler, *Sprachtheorie* (Jena, 1934), chap. 2: on the three functions of communication, sec 2; on the distinction between act and action, sec. 4. R. Jakobson's theory is presented in "Linguistics and Poetics," in *Style in Language*, ed. T. A. Sebeok (New York, 1960), pp. 350–77.

Independently of this reflection on the part of linguists, the philosophers of the Oxford school [95] have reached conclusions that lead in the same direction and perhaps even further: in the same direction, in that they too are attempting to determine what is accomplished in the very act of speaking (and not what one may accomplish by using speech); further, in that they integrate to this action inherent in speech a much more extensive area of human activity. The starting point of their research is the discovery, by J. L. Austin, of the opposition between **performative** and **constative** utterances. An expression is called constative if it tends only to describe an event. It is called performative if (1) it describes a certain action accomplished by its speaker and (2) producing this expression amounts to accomplishing that action. A sentence beginning "I promise you that . . . " is said to be performative, since by using it, we accomplish the act of promising; not only do we say that we are promising but, by so doing, we are promising. What is more, we would have to consider false a semantic representation of such sentences that failed to indicate this fact, that characterized them as simple descriptions of actions (on the same basis as "I am going for a walk"). The performatives thus have as a property that their intrinsic meaning cannot be grasped independently of a certain action that they allow us to accomplish. To use Morris's terms [338], we cannot establish the semantics of these expressions without including in them at least a part of their pragmatics.

But once this property has been discerned in the particular (and particularly spectacular) case of the performatives, we can see that it belongs to nonperformative expressions. This is the case for the imperative and interrogative forms. In order to describe the meaning of an interrogative expression, we have to specify not only that the speaker is expressing his uncertainty and his desire for knowledge but especially that he is accomplishing a particular act, that of interrogating. Or, by saying "You should do this," a speaker not only expresses his opinion as to what is best for his interlocutor but also accomplishes the act of advising. It was in order to formulate this generalization that Austin established his classification of the **speech acts.** In producing any sentence at all, we are accomplishing three simultaneous acts:

1. A **locutionary act,** to the extent that we articulate and combine sounds and evoke and link syntactically the notions represented by the words.

2. An **illocutionary act,** to the extent that the production of the sentence constitutes in itself a certain act (a certain transformation of the relationship between the interlocutors). The speaker accomplishes the act of promising by saying "I promise . . . ," that of interrogating by saying something like "Is it true that . . . ?" Austin gives three criteria for locating the illocutionary act: (1) It is an act accomplished *within* speech itself; it is not a consequence (willed or not) of speech. For this reason, (2) it can always be paraphrased and made explicit by a performative formula ("I am asking you whether . . . ," "I order you to . . . ," "I advise you to . . . "). Finally, (3) the illocutionary act is always conventional. This must not be taken to mean only that the phonic material utilized for its realization is arbitrary (which is the case for all linguistic expression). Austin means primarily that the illocutionary act is not the logical or psychological consequence of the intellectual content expressed in the sentence pronounced and that it is only actualized through the existence of a sort of social ceremonial, which attributes a particular value to a given formula used by a certain person in specific circumstances.

3. A **perlocutionary act,** to the extent that the act of enunciation serves more distant ends that the interlocutor may very well not understand even though he has mastered the language perfectly. Thus, by questioning someone, we may have as a goal doing him a favor, embarrassing him, making him believe that we respect his opinion.

Although Austin's examples have gone largely unchallenged, his general definition of the illocutionary act has often seemed inadequate, and there have been numerous attempts to make it explicit. Thus, in attempting to pin down more precisely the notion of the illocutionary, the American philosopher J. R. Searle began by defining the idea of a **constitutive rule.** A rule is constitutive with respect to a certain form of activity if failure to observe it takes away from the activity its distinctive character: the rules of bridge are constitutive with respect to bridge, since we cease to play bridge as soon as we disregard them. But the technical rules to which good players conform are not constitutive, only **normative** (for nothing prevents us from playing bridge and playing badly). It follows from this definition that the rules establishing the illocutionary value of utterances are constitutive with respect to the use of these utterances. For, if a sentence beginning with "Is it true that . . ." and uttered interrogatively were not used to accomplish the illocutionary act of questioning, i.e., of trying to elicit an answer, it would no longer be itself, that is, it would no longer be used as an English sentence. And by the same token, even though we may fail to keep our promises, we could not (except in a game) use a promise formula without actually taking on the obligation to accomplish what we have promised. To use this formula —giving it the full value that the English language attributes to it—is to accept this obligation for oneself. To be sure, that one must do what one has promised is only a normative rule, but it is a constitutive rule that in promising, one makes a commitment.

Going further in Searle's direction, we might say that an utterance is an illocutionary act if it has as its first and immediate function the modification of the interlocutor's situation. By promising, I give myself a new obligation, and this is not a secondary (perlocutionary) consequence of my words, since one cannot attribute meaning to them prior to this creation of obligation. And similarly, when I interrogate my interlocutor, I create a new situation for him, namely, the alternative of responding (and not just anything can pass for a response) or of being impolite. The alternative created by an order is that of obedience or disobedience. And advice (an act whose existence has, if we reflect on it, no necessity whatsoever but which corresponds to a convention of our social life) consists in partially withdrawing from the other, and taking upon oneself, the responsibility for the suggested act (this is why the refusal to give advice may be entirely different from an admission of incompetence).

Thus we can see how the study of illocutionary acts is related to Bühler's research and to Jakobson's: the distinction between the illocutionary and the perlocutionary corresponds to that between the act and the action, between what is intrinsic and what is supplementary in linguistic activity. In both cases, we recognize in the act of using the language something that is essential to language. But Austin's analysis allows us to go further: much more than the Jakobsonian functions, the illocutionary puts into play the most basic interpersonal relationships.

- On performatives and illocutionary acts, see J. L. Austin, *How to Do Things With Words* (Cambridge, Mass., 1962). The distinction between the illocutionary and the perlocutionary is discussed in particular by T. Cohen, in "Illocutions and Perlocutions," *Foundations of Language* 9 (1972–73): 492–503. Two attempts at redefining the illocutionary are in P. F. Strawson, "Intention and Convention in Speech-Acts," *The Philosophical Review* 73 (1964): 439–60; and J. R. Searle, *Speech Acts* (London, 1969). The first linguist to examine these questions is E. Benveniste, who accepts the idea of the performative (he even presented it, without using the term, in "De la subjectivité dans le langage," in *Journal de psychologie* 55 (1958): 257–65, which is reprinted as chap. 21 of his

Problems in General Linguistics, trans. M. E. Meek [Coral Gables, 1971])
but rejects the notion of the illocutionary act (in ibid., chaps. 22–23). A
history of the question appears above, on pp. 6ff. of this volume. The
major linguistic and philosophical problems linked to speech acts are
presented in P. Cole and J. L. Morgan, eds., *Syntax and Semantics* (Los
Angeles, 1975), vol. 3, *Speech Acts*.

APPENDIX: TOWARD A CRITIQUE OF THE SIGN

A series of discussions has developed in the last several years, in particular in France, over certain of the fundamental concepts of linguistics and especially of semiotics; these discussions have quickly led to radical questioning. It would have been unthinkable not to make room for them in this encyclopedia. It would have been somewhat incoherent to present them in the same framework as the body of concepts on which the sciences of language rest today—precisely the concepts that these discussions call into question. We have thus opted for this appendix—not creating, factitiously, the unity of a school but grouping, on the basis of certain of the preceding articles, the most important contributions of a research about which we can say at least that its focal point lies in a critique of the sign.

WRITING
[193]

Grammatology and Linguistics

During the last ten years, the study of writing—**grammatology**—has undergone a fundamental renewal and a change of level in the work of J. Derrida. On the one hand, one must observe (and with some astonishment) that almost everywhere (that is, everywhere in the West, where phonetic writing is dominant), spoken language has occupied a privileged position; it is taken to constitute language *par excellence,* of which written language is only an extended image, an auxiliary reproduction, or a convenient instrument—the signifier of a signifier. From this standpoint the spoken word is the truth, the "nature" and origin of language, whereas writing is only its bastard offspring, an artificial supplement, an unnecessary derivative in the last analysis. There is a value judgment here and an implicit structuring, whose unfailing presence is discernible throughout our Western tradition—a tradition qualified, for this very reason, as **phonocentric**—from a pre-Platonic period through Saussure (*Course in General Linguistics,* trans. W. Baskin [New York, 1959], chap. 6 of intro.).

On the other hand, this privilege of the phonic signifier over the graphic signifier can be legitimized only on the basis of the distinction between what would be an *inside* (where thought resides) and what would be an *outside* (where writing falls). Speech is the expression "closest" to "consciousness"—even if the voice is not conceived as a quasi-effacement of the signifier. Now, no allowance is made for such a scheme of things. From this scheme—thus from the depreciation of writing—is derived, in turn, the organization of our concept of the sign [100], with its chain of dissymmetrical differences: signified / signifier, concept / percept, content / expression. And it is again this scheme that governs our concept of truth, "inseparable from the claims of a *reason* conceived in the descendance of the *logos*," in which, therefore, "the ordinary and essential link with the *phonè* has never been broken." In short, there is a metaphysics of phonocentric writing, denotable as **logocentrism,** which, at its core, is metaphysics itself; and hence we under-

349

stand why logocentrism holds entrapped within its structure our thought in its totality, including even a model of scientific knowledge born at a certain moment in the history of writing, on the basis of a certain relationship between writing, signifier, and *phonè*.

Phonetic writing does not, however, exhaust the resources of writing. By no means is the latter always derivative; indeed, it can be shown that *the general possibility of writing grounds the possibility of language itself*: (1) There is an initial inconsistency, at the heart of Saussurian linguistics, between the general thesis of the arbitrariness [130] of the sign and the particular idea of a natural dependency of writing. (2) Unmotivated, every sign would be unthinkable without a durable institution, that is, without the installation of the **trace,** an "imprint" that is conserved in a "space of inscription," "retains" in the here and now the preinstituted differences, and through a structure of back-reference occasions the appearance of difference "*as such.*" (As can be seen, the nonmotivation of the sign, by necessitating the trace—that is, already, writing—implies *at the same time* spacing, temporalization, and the relationship with the other.) (3) If, as Saussure writes—but this time with regard to the value [16] of the sign—"a segment of language can never in the final analysis be based on anything except its noncoincidence with the rest" (*Course*, p. 118), if there are in language "only differences," then the structure of the language in its totality can only be that of a play of generation through reference, in which each "term" has no presence other than the trace, to which it is reduced, of all the others from which it remains absent ("writing is the play in language"). This is to say that the trace (and writing) is originary: *as a synthesis* in and through which the operation of difference gives form to each element; and since this form is an imprint, we are saying that writing inflicts language, even in its origin, with passivity. (Clearly, the differential character of the sign, by bringing grammatology to the fundamental principle of linguistics, implies that "the concept of writing must be reformed"; it implies an **archiwriting** (or "gram" or "difference"), which is logically prior to all the oppositions—including time / space and signified / signifier—on which the depreciation of the graphic was based, a writing that makes it impossible for any element of language (1) to be constituted except "on the basis of the trace in it of the others," (2) to have any origin for its production other than the trace, that is, "a non-origin," (3) to have any resource for its articulation other than the exteriority by which, as trace tissue, it has always been penetrated.)

This "general grammatology of which phonological linguistics would only be a dependent and circumscribed region" cannot become a field of positive knowledge, just as writing, taken to be "the most general concept of semiology," cannot be made a "scientific" concept. This does not result from a lack of argumentative rigor. Rather, it is because the "objectivity" of the object, like the "truth" of what I know about it— these notions are the (logocentric) conditions for the existence of science—belongs (with being, identity, origin, simplicity, consciousness) to those forms of presence that the trace necessarily unsettles. The thought of the trace cannot flow into that of the logos as soon as the latter is instituted as the repression, and eviction to the outside, of writing. This is why grammatology perceives a mandate to deconstruct— not by abolition, to be sure, but by going back to their roots—all the presuppositions of a linguistics that is subject to such a deconstruction only because of the progress it has achieved.

• See J. Derrida, *Of Grammatology*, trans. G. C. Spivak (Baltimore and London, 1976); for a summary, see idem, "Sémiologie et grammatologie: Entretien avec Julia Kristeva," in *Positions* (Paris, 1972), pp. 25–30.

SIGN
[99]

The Primacy of the Signifier

A turning point has been reached in the history of the concept of the sign, a turning point that the definition proposed earlier tried to take into account: all the classic definitions of the sign (Saussure's more than any other) rested on an equilibrium, if not a symmetry, between its two faces; today, in the wake of a series of critical reflections, the discourse on the sign is tilting toward the signifier, whose **primacy** is thus being underscored.

The discussion has developed on two levels, first on that of the sign itself. According to J. Derrida, the maintenance of a distinction of an essential nature between signified and signifier, content and expression, overlaps necessarily with the maintenance of the concept-percept distinction and its background—the distinction between what is transparent

to consciousness and what is external to consciousness—which historically is part of the same system as the privilege of the spoken word (the
voice) over writing [347] and which furnishes its armature to the
logocentric-idealist discourse [347] of metaphysics. Now, such a maintenance is logically unacceptable and can only institute an inconsistency
at the heart of semiotics. Because in opposition to all the formulae that
take the tack of semiotics and would have signifier and signified be
"the two faces of one and the same production," it implies that at least
in theory the signified would be (as a unit of pure intelligibility) thinkable in itself, independent of that which expresses it, immediate and
transcendental (in other words, according to the traditional schema of
the concept, it "would not refer back, in itself, in its essence, to any signifier" and "would emerge outside the chain of the signs"). Even more
radically, taking recourse to a distinction of the type inside / outside in
order to ground the sign is a move that is outflanked by semiotics once
the latter postulates as its fundamental law that "every process of signification is a formal play of differences," for in order for such a play to
be instituted, it is absolutely necessary that a "systematic production of
differences, the production of a system of differences," a difference
that is, finally, a trace [350]—constituting each element of the durable
inscription of its relation to the others—precede (ahead of any im-
mediacy) the signifier as well as the signified. In other terms, *"the signified is always already in the position of a signifier."* Or, to sum up
this discussion: the "symmetry" was tilting the balance surreptitiously
toward the signified, pushing semiotics off into the position of an auxiliary
technique, bondsman of a metaphysical foreknowledge; semiotics, as
soon as it is allowed to assume its role, puts the signifier in the position
of generator.

It is essential to see that the signifier-signified distinction remains, at
the level of the sign, indispensable, and J. Derrida stresses that if the
"primacy of the signifier" meant that there were no place for a difference between the signified and the signifier, the word *signifier* would
itself have no signified. What he indicates, on the other hand, is that
something functions as a signifier even within the signified: such is the
role of the trace. In short, the sign in its perfect symmetry is a "structural decoy": we cannot see how we could proceed without invoking the
sign, yet its deconstruction is vital: That this deconstruction entails, finally, that of metaphysics and truth in the sense of these terms to which
scientific tradition is attached—this is what grammatology has still to
demonstrate.

● See J. Derrida, "Sémiologie et grammatologie: Entretien avec Julia Kristeva," in *Positions* (Paris, 1972), pp. 25–30; and F. Wahl, "La Structure,

le sujet, la trace," in O. Ducrot et al., *Qu'est-ce que le structuralisme?* (Paris, 1968).

It is no longer at the level of the sign, but at that of the **signifying chain,** that the debate animated by J. Lacan in the name of psychoanalytic experience is instituted: the discovery of the unconscious is the discovery of a subject whose place, excentric from the standpoint of consciousness, can be determined only when certain returns of the signifier are encountered and through knowledge of the laws governing the displacement of the signifier. This amounts to registering both the exteriority of the signifying order with respect to the subjects of conscious utterances that we imagine ourselves to be, and its *autonomy;* that exteriority and autonomy are determining factors in the real significacation of that which enunciates itself in us.

In regard to a definition of the sign, three points are to be retained from this approach:

1. J. Lacan proposes to take literally the horizontal line [*barre*] in the algorithm $\frac{\text{signifier}}{\text{signified}}$, that is, to understand it as a "barrier resistant to signification" that marks, not a movement from signifier to signified, but the very operation (the formal play) of the signifier, an operation that is reducible to combinatory laws (that is, the arrangement of differential elements according to the rules of a closed order), irreducible to laws of content or of meaning.

Inversely, these laws, which are meaningless in themselves, govern the order of meaning: the signifier is, in its segmentations and combinations, the determining factor in the genesis of the signified. Or "the notion of the signifier is opposed to that of the signified"; and "the signifier has an active function in the determination of effects whereby the signifiable appears as the bearer of the signifier's mark and, by this same passion, becomes the signified."

2. This elaboration upon the signifier's function produces much more than a simple tilting within the sign, since as soon as the question is one of signification, the relevant unit is no longer the sign itself (for example, the word in the dictionary), but the signifying chain, which generates a meaning effect at the moment when it turns back upon itself, its end allowing the retroactive interpretation of its beginning: "the signified slides under the signifier" without there being a valid means for establishing a correspondence at each moment, and signification appears only at moments of punctuation in the chain. In this regard, J. Lacan notes that if the signifier forms the (synchronic) material of language the assemblage of which is to be conceived as a place, the signified is thought (diachronically) as the set of discourses pronounced

(written) and always occurs as a moment. This does not imply that "chain" must be understood in the limiting sense of linearity appropriate to speech.

3. As soon as the debate over signification has thus shifted from the sign to the chain, the definition of the signifier (and this is doubtless the most important point) will necessarily be articulated into a system that is governed by three terms in their interrelationship: subject, object, and vacillation.

Vacillation, owing to the fact that the signifier only fulfills its function—that of generating signification—by eclipsing itself so as to make way for another signifier, with which it will form a chain. To assume the role of the signifier is to acquire the status of an oscillating, or beating, "feature" (differential and combinable) that will be shunted backward by another feature *that adds itself to it*. Such is the law of a "process which in its principle is alternating, which requires (of the signifier) that it leave its place, if only to return there circuitously." On the basis of this process, the signifier will be designated, not by one, but by at least two symbols: S_2, the chain of signifiers formed up to that point; and S_1, the additional signifier, which carries the chain forward.

Subject, since the autonomy and the primacy of the signifier are demonstrated by the observance, in its register, of an unconscious discourse the subject of which is positioned as a subject of enunciation (out of phase in relation to the subject that, in the guise of the conscious ego, pretended to be speaking in the utterance). This subject is nowhere before the signifier nor outside of it, receives its place from the signifier, yet cannot have a place anywhere within it, except in its function as a *lack* whose place is held by a signifier, namely, at each "moment" of the process of enunciation the additional signifier that supports the enunciation in its forward movement. Hence the characteristic formula: "The institution of the register of the signifier derives from the fact that a signifier represents a subject for another signifier." For this subject— askew with respect to the utterance, and represented-lacking in the signifier—the symbol $\mathcal{S}$, which shows it to be divided, will be appropriate.

Object, by which we mean the one toward which writing or discourse is headed, without which there would be no chain to move along. This object is also out of phase in relation to the one that the utterance designates (let us say the object of demand or of need) and is also always lacking, always *lost*, since the subject has never finished with the work of signification (with desire). This object, if the subject happens to "fall under the chain," falls itself, seemingly into the middle of the chain, since the chain will pursue it (the object) all along its trajectory and in an incessant working in reverse. Its insurmountable alterity will be represented by the symbol *a*.

With S_1, S_2, $\mathcal{S}$, and a, we have the minimum set of terms absolutely necessary for the description of a structure of the signifier. Here we can only point to the reform that that structure commands in a tradition of knowledge governed by another structure, namely, that of the sign.

By setting forth the primacy of the signifier and at the same time releasing language from the model of the sign, we release it as well from the model (always subjacent for semioticians, since the Stoics at least) of communication. This is what emerges from the clash between the following two formulae: "the sign is what represents something for someone" and "the signifier is what represents a subject for another signifier." Over against a science that had been constituted (since Descartes at least) by "suturing" the place of the subject and by positing the exteriority of the object, there will appear the necessity, for everything that has to do with signification, of reintroducing the double lack of the subject and the object. We shall simply observe, in conclusion, that this subject, $\mathcal{S}$, *divided* by the intervention of the signifier, can only be located within the structure sketched above, where, moreover, this division of the subject is perceived as leaving a *remainder* (*reste*), which is precisely the object, a.

Remark. It is in the dimensions of the signifying chain that we must link a passage from one of Jakobson's formulae—metaphor and metonymy (selection and combination) [111] are the two axes of language—to two formulae of Lacan: (1) *condensation is a metaphor* in which the repressed meaning of the subject's desire is stated; and (2) *displacement* is a metonymy that marks the nature of desire, namely, desire of something else that is always lacking. For these two formulae are governed by the fact that it does not suffice, in order to make a trope, to put one word in the place of another on the basis of their respective signifieds. The metaphor, much more precisely, is the emergence in a given signifying chain of a signifier coming from another chain; this signifier crosses the ("resistant") bar of the algorithm so as to disturb, by its disruption, the signified of the first chain, where it produces an effect of nonsense—showing that the emergence of meaning occurs prior to the subject. As for metonymy, it serves much less to refer back from one term to another contiguous one than to mark the essential function of the lack within the signifying chain: the connection of the signifiers allows the operation of the "turnaround" [*virement*] in a discourse of that which, however, never ceases to be lacking in it, namely, in the last analysis, pleasure [*jouissance*].

● See J. Lacan, *Ecrits* (Paris, 1966), particularly "Le Séminaire sur la lettre volée," "La Chose freudienne," "L'Instance de la lettre," "La Signification du phallus," and "Subversion du sujet"; idem, "Radiophonie," *Scilicet*

2–3 (1970); and F. Wahl, "La Structure, le sujet, la trace," in O. Ducrot
et al., *Qu'est-ce que le structuralisme?* (Paris, 1968). On the remark, see
Lacan, *Ecrits* ("L'Instance de la lettre," and "La Métaphore du sujet");
idem, "Radiophonie, III," *Scilicet* 2–3 (1970); and "Condensation et
déplacement," *Scilicet* 2–3 (1970).

TEXT
[294]

The Text as Productivity

As we noted earlier, the **text**—inasmuch as it is a certain mode of
linguistic operation—has been the focal point of a conceptual elaboration in France during recent years, centered around the journal *Tel
Quel* (notably the contributions of R. Barthes, J. Derrida, P. Sollers,
and especially J. Kristeva). In opposition to any communication and
representational (thus reproductive) use of language, the text is defined
here essentially as *productivity.*

This amounts to saying—to approach this definition little by little,
as if from the outside, through the normative aspects that it envelops—
that in practice, a textual writing supposes that the descriptive orientation of language has been tactically thwarted and replaced by a procedure that, on the contrary, gives full play to its generative power. This
procedure will be, for example, at the level of the signifier, the systematic
recourse to analyses and combinations of the anagrammatic type. At
the semantic level, it will be the recourse to polysemy (to the point
where, as in Bakhtin's dialogism [302], a single "word" proves to be
conveyed by several "voices," to be located at the crossroads of several
cultures), but it will also be a "blank" writing that escapes all the
"depths" of worlds by systematically dispelling connotations and by
restoring the apparatus of semic distinction to its arbitrariness. At the
grammatical level, it will be the appeal to a grid or matrix that controls
the variations of person or tense, no longer according to the canonical
structures that convey verisimilitude [261ff.], but according to an organized exhaustion of the possibilities of permutation. It will also be—

and to a certain extent at each of the levels we have just evoked—the putting into play within writing itself of the relation addresser-addressee, writing-reading, as the relation of two productivities that intersect and create space by intersecting.

Defining the text as productivity amounts to saying—to bring ourselves now, and symmetrically, to the ultimate *theoretical* implications of such a definition—that the text has always functioned as a *transgressive* field with regard to the system according to which our perception, our grammar, our metaphysics, and even our scientific knowledge are organized, a system according to which a subject, situated in the center of a world that provides it with something like a horizon, learns to decipher the *supposedly prior meaning* of this world, a meaning that is indeed understood to be originary with regard to the subject's experience of the world, a system that can only be, indissolubly, that of the *sign* [99].

To the idealism of a meaning anterior to that which "expresses" it, the text would then oppose the materialism of a play of signifiers that produces meaning effects. To the staticity of a discourse limited by what it has sought to copy, the text would oppose an *infinite play* ("premeaning"), divided into readings (or "lexias") according to the endless paths on which the combination and intersection of signifiers take place. To the unity of a substantial subjectivity that is supposed to uphold discourse in its totality, the text would oppose the mobility of an *empty enunciation*, varying in accord with the reorganizations (perceived or unnoticed) of the utterance. To the intimate model of the voice, which is simultaneously in close proximity to the soul and to meaning (to phonologocentrism) [347], the text—with its play of signifiers lacking any starting point or end point or interiority—would necessarily oppose the substitution (*relève*) to be achieved by a reflection on writing, or grammatology [350]). To the aestheticizing ideology of the art object as a work that is situated within history or in literature as the object of a history of the ornamental, the text would oppose the reinsertion of its signifying practice—situated as a specific practice—within the *articulated whole of the social process* (of transformative practices) in which it participates [364]. We can already see why, as soon as it is constructed, this concept of the text is found to have operative value, not only on the level of "literary" practice but also, and with equal import, on the level of an unsettling of the philosophical tradition and on that of a theory of revolution.

But we shall grasp what this definition of the text covers only by returning—with J. Kristeva—to the crucial term of **productivity,** by which we are to understand that the text "makes work of language" by *going* *back to what precedes it*; or better, that it opens a gap between, on the one hand, the "natural" language of everyday usage, destined for representation and comprehension, a structured surface that we expect to reflect the structures of an outside and to express a subjectivity (individual or collective), and, on the other hand, the underlying volume of signifying practices, "where the meaning and its subject sprout" at every moment, where significations germinate "from within the language and in its very materiality," according to models and in a play of combinations (those of a practice within the signifier) that are radically "foreign" to the language of communication. To "work the language" is thus to explore how it works, but on the condition that the models for what speaks meaning on the surface and what effectuates it in depth are not specified as the same. "We shall designate by the term **signifiance** this *work* of differentiation, stratification and confrontation which is practiced in language, and which deposits on the line of the speaking subject a signifying chain which is communicative and grammatically structured."

"Not subject to the regulatory center of a meaning," the generation process of the signifying system cannot be unitary. It is plural and infinitely differentiated; it is mobile work, an assembly of seeds in a nonclosed space of production and self-destruction. It is—at the levels of what will be the signifier and signified, the material of language and its grammatical forms, the sentence and the organization of discourse (with its positioning of a subject)—the play, without limits or center, of possibilities for articulation that are generative of meaning. Nothing specifies signifiance better than this "differentiated *infinity*, whose unlimited combinatorial never finds a frontier." Signifiance is, in sum, the endlessness of the possible operations in a given field of language. And it is no more one of the combinations that may form a given discourse than it is any of the others.

It is this dynamic infinity that accounts, at all levels, for the properties through which the text—henceforth redefined as a writing in which signifiance deposits itself—differentiates itself from the common sentence and "doubles" it with an operation that is other to such an extent that it will have to be called *translinguistic*. This occurs with the categories of the language, which the text, in the rigor of its practice, redistributes—substituting for the sign unit a minimal signifying set, "which, in order to constitute itself, may dislocate the word or else not respect its confines, whether by encompassing two lexemes, or by breaking another into phonemes" (the important point is that, since it has destroyed the sign, this set no longer marks anything but a contingent distribution of infinite signifiance, destined to disassemble itself and to slide; the textual unit would be, on this basis, better designated as a "signifying differential"); or again, substituting for the sentence units signifying complexes that, far from being linked linearly, will, in order to form a text, apply themselves (in the logical sense of the term) plurally to each other and, in particular, far from "enunciating something about an object" (predicative proposition), will construct themselves on a matrix of nominal (rather than verbal) modification where nothing is actualized about anything, where signifiance, "in the germination, always reenacted, of its differences," by producing "an inexhaustible and stratified domain of uncouplings and combinations exhausting themselves in the infinity and the rigor of their marking," allows nothing to be seen other than the limitless genesis of signification itself: "scene of signification where what transpires cannot be said to be because it is always in the process of being." This shift into the translinguistic affects the laws of grammar, as well as those of syntax or semantics, which the text does more than rework; for it substitutes for the very idea of predetermining laws of language that of an order whose interdependent parts "get the upper hand successively in different conditions of use," of a network of multiple connections with variable hierarchies. The shift also affects discourse itself, which, far from being a closed unit, even in regard to its own work, is worked by the other texts ("every text is absorption and transformation of a multiplicity of other texts"), traversed by the supplement without reserve and the surmounted opposition of **intertextuality.**

At all these levels, what we encounter (and what makes reading possible) is "the expansion in the text of a function which organizes it"; hence the proposed generalization of the model of the Saussurian anagram [190] as a **paragram.** "We call paragrammatic network the *tabular* (not linear) *model* of elaboration" of textual language. "The term *network* replaces univocity (linearity) by encompassing it, and suggests that each set (sequence) is both end-point and beginning of a multivalent relationship." The term "paragram" indicates that each element functions "as a dynamic mark, *as a moving 'gram'* which *makes a meaning* rather than expressing it."

Finally, it is essential that there be a *textual logic* encompassing the logic of the sign (which is the very logic of Aristotle) if the text is to function as an "infinite ordered code" of which all codes (in particular, that of linear logic) are only subsets, a logic whose two most prominent features are (1) that only set theory could permit the formalization of an expanding operation like the one of paragrams and (2) that transgressing the classical prohibitions without suppressing them, the logic of the text engulfs them in a nonsynthetic assemblage, through a negation without disjunction: "coexistence of *monologic* discourse (synthetic, historical, descriptive) and of a discourse destroying this monologism"— *dialogism*, in the ultimate meaning of this Bakhtinian word.

This series of gaps leads to the displacement of the primary opposition between language of communication and signifiance onto a second opposition, in the text itself, insofar as the text is a writing on a dual basis that opens the "inside" of the sign to the "outside" of signifiance: an opposition between the **pheno-text**—where, in one sense, the signifying activity is phenomenalized, spread out flat in a structured signification that functions as a dissimulatory screen, but where, in another sense, communicative language itself serves, through the play of its transgression, to mark and to manifest signifying productivity (even in the position of the structure, the thickness at work in its "engenderment" is inscribed, "exposed" or "deposited")—and the **geno-text,** which is that engenderment, therefore signifiance itself, as the "operation of the generation of the pheno-text" in the fabric and the categories of language, an operation that extends to the installing (by the "nonsubject" [*hors sujet*] of language [*langue*]) of a subject for discourse. "Textual specificity resides in the fact that it is a translation of the geno-text into the pheno-text, discernible in reading by the opening of the pheno-text to the geno-text."

It will be remarked that if the two terms are not definable independently of each other, their relations are not those of Chomsky's deep and surface structures [235], since it would be useless to seek in the geno-text a structure that would reflect in an archetypal form the structures of the communicative sentence (S-P). The geno-text is made up of the signifiers in their infinite differentiation, of which "the signifier of the present-formula-of-the-stated-subject is only a frontier." The pheno-text is situated in the geno-text, which exceeds it on all sides and for which it is not an end but a cut-off point or a limit, traced within the arrangement that is possible in language at a given moment, a generative process that also allows us to say of the pheno-text, but perhaps more metaphorically, that it is a "remainder."

It may be worthwhile to note, finally, a radical methodological divergence between the work of the signifier as it is implied in this definition of the text and the signifying chain as J. Lacan has defined it [353]. Confusion could arise from the fact that both go beyond the linguistics of the sign and of communication by an appeal to what, in the signifier, detaches itself from them. For Lacan, it is a question, starting with a substitution of one discourse for another, of rearticulating the subject and the object (of enunciation) as a lack within the larger unit of the signifying chain. For Kristeva, it is a matter of "pulverizing" the subject, and no intention toward the object is involved; this is because the pertinent dimension for the study of the signifier is no longer found in a unit of signification, but in a dynamic whereby the units that generate meaning make themselves, envelop each other, and decompose themselves endlessly. The work here is accomplished without fixed articulation, from the vanishing term of the signifying differential to the infinity of combinations to which, prior to any categorial laws, then throughout the development of these laws, the signifier lends itself in the process of its formation. There is a difference in purpose, moreover, well marked in the two crucial figures of a structure of the speaking subject and of a germination of the text.

● See J. Kristeva, *Semeiotekè* (Paris, 1969). See also R. Barthes, *Critique et vérité* (Paris, 1966); idem, *S/Z*, trans. R. Miller (New York, 1974); and P. Sollers, *Logiques* (Paris, 1968).

SEMIOTICS
[84]

Semiotics against the Sign

The discussion bearing on the concept of the sign and on its entrenchment in the idealist-logocentric tradition, as well as in a pre-critical philosophy of communication [351], could not, by definition, fail to have consequences for semiotics. J. Kristeva has initiated a reorganization of the discipline through a critical examination of the matrix of the sign, adopting as the axis of her proposition—and "center of its interest" —the concept of the text as productivity [356], as she has elaborated it.

The contribution of the concept of text consists in opening semiotics, the science of signification, to signifiance [358] as specific work in and of language, prior to any structured enunciation, at a level of alterity with respect to any usable language, and in providing at the same time, in the concept of signifying practice [358], an instrument that can be applied to all modalities of the production of meaning. With textual practice and in its field, we are thus already in an "other" semiotics, for which J. Kristeva proposes the term **semanalysis.**

Starting with the text (as "juncture") and over and beyond "communicative language" (which remains on the surface), to explore (in volume) language as production and transformation of signification—such is the initial program of semanalysis. In practical terms, semanalysis is a "reflection on the *signifier producing itself as text.*" And to practice it would mean being able on every occasion to show how the "generation process of the signifying system" (the *geno-text* [360]) is "manifested" in a given text (in the *pheno-text* [360]) precisely insofar as it merits the name of text. Figuratively speaking, semanalysis will have to traverse the utterance—its organization, its grammar, and its science—in order finally to "attain that zone where the *seeds* of what will signify in the actualization of language are gathered." In theoretical terms, semanalysis introduces an opening in the classical concepts of sign and structure so as to move into the "other" space of the signifying infinity, which is given over to permutation, suited for all the categorial divisions, and not subject to monopoly by any subject, since the subject will itself be a product of this engenderment. Hence arises this term—"signifiance" —forged on the model of psychoanalysis; signifiance constitutes, in its mechanisms and its dynamized objects, something like a series of other stages with respect to which the structure of manifest discourse, articulated with the sign, is no longer anything but a *"falling out of phase,"* functioning as a screen. Thus this further connotation of semanalysis, that is, that it is toward a critical and deconstructive science of meaning that we are working when, starting from the discourse of a subject or of a story, we shift away and "move back through the production of signifiance," effecting an unraveling of signifying operations in their topographic specificity or their historical becoming, exploring their topology. The ultimate program would be to seeking to describe the very development of signification, in the diversity of its modes.

From this displacement of semiotics toward the production of signification before the sign, there obviously results a series of reinterpretations, of which we shall retain at least two because they allow us to show how, in recasting itself, semiotics has come to claim a dominant position within a global restructuring of knowledge.

First, a consequence with an epistemological cast. Although semiotics (like linguistics) has never stopped seeking to establish models of signifying systems and although—attempting to establish axioms on which it is grounded—it has given preference to models borrowed from the formal sciences, logic or algebra, it has been in the same way that one abstracts, in a representational operation, the form from the content.

Already in this early stage semiotics found itself, however, in a singular position: even while producing models of signifying practice, it could not fail to take these same models as an object (as signifying systems in their turn), that is, to make a theory of the modeling process. Semiotics was thereby already going beyond science, as representation in a model, into the theory describing the production of such a representation. As a result of this, all the sciences on which semiotics is modeled could be said at the same time to be subverted by semiotics. With signifiance we advance yet another step, since it makes us perceive the production of meaning as, by definition, *heterogeneous in relation to everything representable*. This will entail an important consequence for the relations of semiotics to the formal sciences: "The whole problem of contemporary semiotics seems to us to lie there: to continue to formalize the semiotic systems from the point of view of *communication* . . . or else to open . . . this other stage which is the production of meaning interior to meaning" and try to construct on the basis of a new type of object a new type of scientific problematics. A formalism isomorphic with signifiance thus could only find adequate models where there already exists an "infiltration of scientific thought within the nonrepresentable": in mathematics, essentially—on the one hand, negatively, because mathematics, too, "escapes the constraints of a language elaborated on the basis of the Indo-European subject-predicate sentence", because, more generally, "a number neither *represents* nor *signifies*"; on the other hand, positively, because if every signifying set [358], instead of representing a signified, "marks a *plural* and *contingent* distribution of the signifying infinity," its function could not be better described than as "numerical," participating in the same "movement of demarcation and ordination," in the same process of recasting a signifying fabric through accumulation and interruption, through combination and referral. "The textual signifier is a numbering [*nombrant*]." And here we have to understand the nature of the number itself, devoid of any contamination by the sign— that is, the number is an "object" produced by nothing exterior to the marking that institutes it: "infinity which shows itself by marking itself," number is a self-actualizing, differentiated signifiance.

Second, a properly theoretical consequence: an appeal to the concept of signifying practice for an articulation between semiotic work and dialectical materialism. "The materialism-idealism battle is being played out today in the following place: to recognize (materialist gesture) or not (idealist gesture) a signifiance (which is not the meaning of speech, but its germination) outside of subjectivity." Because the text is only thinkable in the materiality of language, because signifiance confronts our ordinary language and the logical-conceptual system of the signified that we have based on it with an outside that surrounds them with its reality and whose alterity, or exteriority, they could not pretend to reduce, it can be said that a materialist semiotics is being established. And it is a nonmechanist materialism, since this exteriority is not that of a process but that of a practice, of a productive work in the very matter of the product, prior to the production of any subject: "work which means nothing, production which is silent, which marks and transforms, anterior to circular speech, to communication, to exchange, to meaning." The opposition, operative on the economic level, of exchange and of work would recur here, subsumed by the opposition of communication and production of meaning. Additionally, because all social practice is semiotic practice, and because every infringement upon the (communicative) taboos of such a practice operates in the "vast process of material and historical movement," the text will be "doubly oriented: toward the signifying system in which it is produced and toward the social process in which it participates." We can say the same about everything that puts to work any signifying practice whatsoever: a *topology* of the signifying practices, formed "according to the particular models of production of meaning which establish them," will then be an essential task for history; and history, marked by this diversity of practices, will lose all linear character: "the text is the object which will make possible the reading of a *stratified history*, with a splintered temporality, a recursive, dialectical history which is irreducible to a single meaning but made up of types of signifying practices whose plural series remains without origin and without end." Finally, if all semiotics aims to be a scientific theory of signifying systems, then semanalysis, by moving toward the very production of these systems in language and toward their history in relation to that of social work, may project itself as the science of meaning (thus of knowledge) in its material conditions and developments, thus laying the foundations of a materialist gnoseology.

We should note that it is through the same movement that J. Kristeva, while aiming at a mathematical axiomatization of semiotics, follows mathematics itself in its ultimate movement beyond what is representable—in that sphere where the dynamic construction of plurality operates in its designation alone—and, by integrating textual practice to the set of signifying social practices, summons Marxism to conceptualize work prior to its representation in exchange. We shall venture here the hazardous hypothesis—but one that appears to have offered valuable insight into the semanalytical project—that the semiotics of the text tends to forge a passage from a restricted materialism (represented in an unaltered system of variables) toward a generalized materialism.

We shall note, finally, that on this path, in subsequent stages of her work, J. Kristeva has attempted to show the dialectical character of the logic that governs the signifying practices. In the face of formal logic—a logic of the homogeneous (as a logic of expression)—the "logic of the *production* of signifying systems" can only be a logic of contradiction. This must be understood, initially (in a still limited sense), on the basis of the fact that poetic language (or the text) is the one in which "contradiction goes so far as to represent itself as the law of (its) functioning"; hence the infinite opening (as we have seen) of such a language, caught up in work: "the text would be the return from concept to contradiction as infinity and/or ground." In short, "contradiction reveals itself as the basic matrix of all significance." Yet this must be understood, above all, through a passage to that which ultimately determines the signifying practices as a necessary linkage of meaning to that which is heterogeneous in relation to it; it is further understood that this heterogeneity, in the perspective in which meaning (and with it the subject and understanding) is grounded, is to be sought on the one hand in the body and in death (above and beyond the unconscious of psychoanalysis), on the other hand—and principally—in history (as it is governed by the class struggle); thus, in the last analysis, that a dialectic posits the laws of production of meaning, precisely insofar as meaning emerges from (and in) *matter.*

- See J. Kristeva, *Semeiotikè* (Paris, 1969), and idem, "Matière, sens, dialectique," *Tel Quel* 44 (1971): 17–34. For a field of application, see also J. L. Schefer, *Scénographie d'un tableau* (Paris, 1968).

INDEX OF TERMS DEFINED

A

Absolute arbitrariness, for Saussure. *See* Arbitrariness, absolute, for Saussure
Accent. *See* Stress
Accentual meter. *See* Meter, accentual
Acrophony, 196
Act, linguistic: and action, linguistic, for Bühler, 340; for Humboldt, 340
Act, speech. *See* Speech act
Actant: narrative, 224; for Tesnière, 213
Action, linguistic. *See* Act, linguistic, and action, linguistic, for Bühler
Addressee, 324
Adequacy: descriptive, 40; explanatory, 41; of a generative grammar, 39; of a linguistic theory, 40; observational, 39
Adjectival clause, 282
Adjective, 252
Affinities among languages, 60
Affirmation, 272
Affix, 200
Agglutinating languages, 12
Aggregates, logical, 195
Agrammatical aphasia, 162
Agraphia, 163
Agreement, 51
Aktionsart, 311. *See also* Aspect, objective
Alexia, 164; literal, 164; verbal, 164
Allegory, 258
Alliteration, 277
Allomorph, 201
Allophone, 172
Alphabet, 195
Alternating rhyme, 191
Alternation, 17
Amalgamation, of monemes, 202
Ambiguity, 236
Amnesic aphasia, 163
Amphibrach, 187
Anagram, 190
Analogy: and anomaly, in classical

linguistics, 131; and association of ideas, 13; and linguistic change, 125
Analysis: componential, 265; content (*see* Content analysis); discourse, 295; narrative, 295; propositional, 296; rhetorical, 295; semic, 265; structural, 83; thematic, 295
Analytic philosophy, 94
Analyzability, in generative linguistics, 231
Anapest, 187
Anaphor, 281
Anarthria, 161
Anarthric child, 157
Angle of vision, 332
Anomaly, semantic, 128. *See also* Analogy, and anomaly, in classical linguistics
Antanaclasis, 277
Antecedent, in the anaphor, 281
Anthropology, linguistic. *See* Linguistic anthropology
Antigrammatical rhyme, 191
Antiphrasis, 338
Antisemantic rhyme, 191
Antithesis, 277
Aphasia, 161. *See also names of individual aphasias*
Aphasic grammar. *See* Grammar, aphasic
Appearance, transformation of, 292
Appelative function, for Bühler, 341
Arbitrariness: absolute, for Saussure, 131; linguistic, 130; relative, for Saussure, 131
Archimorpheme, 112
Archiphoneme, 112
Archiwriting, 350
Argument. *See* Predicate and arguments
Aspect, 307; completed, 309; continuative, 311, imperfective, 307; inchoative, 311; objective, 311 (*see also Aktionsart*); perfective, 307; semantic, 295; subjective, 311; syntactic, 295; terminative, 311;

D

Dactyl, 187
Dactylic rhyme, 191
Deep structure, 244
Deficiency, 113
Definite descriptions. *See* Descriptions, definite
Deictic, 252
Delimitation of units, 17
Delimitative function. *See* Demarcative function
Delivery instance, 188
Delivery model, 188
Demarcative function, 178
Dementia, 163
Demonstrative, 251
Denotative language, for Hjelmslev, 23
Deontic modality. *See* Modality, deontic
Dependency, syntactic, 212
Derivation: in diachrony, 13; in generative grammar, 228; in synchrony, 140
Description, 322; transformation of, 292
Descriptions, definite, 250
Descriptive adequacy. *See* Adequacy, descriptive
Descriptive level, 238
Descriptive linguistics, 137
Determinative complement. *See* Complement, determinative
Determiner, 253; semantic, 196
Diachronic phonology. *See* Phonology, diachronic
Diachrony, 137
Dialect, 58
Dialectology, 58
Dialogue, 303
Dictionary, 51
Dictum, 313. *See also* Modus
Direct style. *See* Style, direct
Discourse, reported, 302
Discourse analysis. *See* Analysis, discourse
Discovery procedure, in grammar, 34
Discursive tense. *See* Tense, discursive
Discursive time. *See* Time, discursive
Discursive transformation. *See* Transformation, discursive
Discursive universe, 247
Disorders: enunciation, 161; language, 161; performance, 165; speech, 161
Distich, 192
Distinctive feature, 173; binary nature of, 173; semantic, 265; situational, 337
Distinctiveness, phonological, 171

Distribution, 32; complementary, 172
Distributional class. *See* Class, distributional
Distributionalism, 31
Distributional structure, 34
Dominance, 150
Double articulation, 53
Dramatic genre, 153
Duration, of a sound, 177
Dysarthria, 161
Dysgraphia, 163
Dyslexia, 161
Dyslogia, 163
Dysphasia, 161

E

Ellipsis, 277
Embedding: in generative grammar (*see* Parentheses, embedded); of narrative sequences, 298
Emblem, 225
Embrayeur, 252
Emic point of view, 36
Emotive style. *See* Style, emotive
Emotive term, 324
Emphasis. *See* Stress, semantic
Encoding, 254
Endocentric construction. *See* Construction, endocentric
End rhyme, 190
Enjambment, 187
Enunciation, 323
Enunciation disorders. *See* Disorders, enunciation
Enveloping rhyme, 191
Environment, 32
Epic genre, 153
Equivocal rhyme, 191
Ethnolinguistics, 63
Ethnoscience, 62
Etic point of view, 36
Etymology: historical, 8; popular, 140; as research into the "truth" of words, 130
Evaluative style. *See* Style, evaluative
Evaluative term, 324
Evocation of milieu, 256
Exocentric construction. *See* Construction, exocentric
Expansion: in distributional linguistics, 32; for Martinet, 213
Explanatory adequacy. *See* Adequacy, explanatory
Explicit linguistic description, 37

O

Object, of linguistics, for Saussure, 118
Objective aspect. *See* Aspect, objective
Objective theories, 81
Obligatory transformation. *See*
  Transformation, obligatory
Oblique context, 249
Observational adequacy. *See* Adequacy,
  observational
Opaque context, 249
Opposition: principle of, 19; privative,
  112
Oppositional signification. *See*
  signification, oppositional
Opposition of meaning, 27
Optional transformation. *See*
  Transformation, optional
Order: logical, 296; spatial, 296;
  temporal, 296
Ordinary language, philosophy of, 95
Oriented category, 116
Oxford school, 95
Oxymoron, 278
Oxytonic rhyme, 191

P

Paradigm, 108
Paragram, 359
Paragraph, 294
Paralipsis, 278
Parallelism, 185
Paraphasia, 163
Paraphrase, 287
Parentheses: embedded, 229; labeled,
  229
Parody, 256
Parole, 118
Paronomasia, 278
Paronymy, 256
Paroxytonic rhyme, 191
Participation, principle of, 114
Parts of speech, 203
Patois. *See* Dialect
Pause: metric, 187; verbal, 187
Perfective aspect. *See* Aspect, perfective
Performance, 120
Performance disorders. *See* Disorders,
  performance
Performative utterance, 342
Period, in literary history, 151
Perlocutionary act, 343
Personal encoding. *See* Encoding
Phatic function, for Jakobson, 342

Pheno-text, 360
Philosophy of language. *See* Language,
  philosophy of
Phonation, 157
Phonematics, 176
Phoneme, 171
Phonemics, 171
Phonemic transcription. *See*
  Transcription, phonemic
Phonetic law, 8
Phonetics, 171; for Saussure, 170; for
  Trubetzkoy, 119
Phonetic symbolism. *See* Symbolism,
  phonetic
Phonetic transcription. *See*
  Transcription, phonetic
Phonic programming, aphasia of, 162
Phonocentrism, 349
Phonography, 195
Phonological component, in a
  generative grammar, 54
Phonological distinctiveness. *See*
  Distinctiveness, phonological
Phonological universals. *See*
  Universals, phonological
Phonology: diachronic, 141; generative,
  175; for Saussure, 170; for
  Trubetzkoy, 119
Phrase-structure rules, 227
Phrastic programming, aphasia of, 162
Pictography, 193
Pidgin, 59
Pitch, of a sound, 177
Plereme, 23
Plot, 298
Poetic function, for Jakobson, 341
Poetics, 79
Poetry, 153
Point of view, 328. *See also* Emic point
  of view; Etic point of view
Polyglot aphasics, 165
Polysemy, 236
Popular etymology. *See* Etymology,
  popular
Portemanteau morph. *See* Morph,
  portemanteau
Pragmatics, 338
Pragmatic theories, 81
Predicate: and arguments, 270;
  grammatical, 210; grammatical, for
  Martinet, 213; grammatical, for
  Tesnière, 212; logical, 269; narrative,
  217; psychological, 271
Prefix, 200
Presupposition: relationship of, for
  Hjelmslev, 109; semantic, 272
Primacy, of the signifier, 351

INDEX OF AUTHORS

378